A several movement towards
calamity — growing alarm
Pairs of poems. Are on opp
sides.

What Do all This The men on the Penobscot
written to Turnpike

The Supreme Court under
Morrison R. Waite, 1874–1888

CHIEF JUSTICESHIPS
OF THE UNITED STATES SUPREME COURT

Herbert A. Johnson, Series Editor

*The Chief Justiceship of
Melville W. Fuller, 1888–1910*
James W. Ely Jr.

*The Supreme Court in the Early Republic:
The Chief Justiceships of John Jay and Oliver Ellsworth*
William R. Casto

The Chief Justiceship of John Marshall, 1801–1835
Herbert A. Johnson

*Division and Discord:
The Supreme Court under Stone
and Vinson, 1941–1953*
Melvin I. Urofsky

*The Supreme Court under
Edward Douglass White, 1910–1921*
Walter F. Pratt Jr.

*The Chief Justiceship of
Warren Burger, 1969–1986*
Earl M. Maltz

*The Supreme Court under
Earl Warren, 1953–1969*
Michal R. Belknap

*The Chief Justiceship of
Charles Evans Hughes, 1930–1941*
William G. Ross

*The Supreme Court under
Morrison R. Waite, 1874–1888*
Paul Kens

The Supreme Court under Morrison R. Waite, 1874–1888

Paul Kens

The University of South Carolina Press

© 2010 University of South Carolina

Published by the University of South Carolina Press
Columbia, South Carolina 29208

www.sc.edu/uscpress

Manufactured in the United States of America

19 18 17 16 15 14 13 12 11 10   10 9 8 7 6 5 4 3 2 1

Library of Congress Cataloging-in-Publication Data

Kens, Paul.
   The Supreme Court under Morrison R. Waite, 1874–1888 / Paul Kens.
    p. cm.
   Includes bibliographical references and index.
   ISBN 978-1-57003-918-8 (cloth : alk. paper)
   1. United States. Supreme Court—History—19th century. 2. Constitutional history—
United States. 3. Waite, Morrison R. (Morrison Remick), 1816–1888. I. Title.
   KF8742.K46 2010
   347.73'26—dc22

                                                           2010006341

This book was printed on Glatfelter Natures, a recycled paper with 30 percent postconsumer waste content.

*For Carla—
and in memory of her parents,
Floyce Underhill and Kitty Underhill*

Contents

List of Illustrations ix
Series Editor's Preface xi
Acknowledgments xv

    Introduction: Traditional Court, Turbulent Times 1
1 Waite, Waite, Don't Tell Me 15
2 Freedom Detoured 32
3 After the Compromise 53
4 Romancing the Rails 62
5 The Last Gasp of the Rights of the Community 78
6 Too Big to Be Allowed to Fail 90
7 Sinking Fund 98
8 A Change Is Gonna Come 110
9 Interstate Commerce 126
10 The Big Country 135
11 Equal Rights: Tales of the Old West 151
    Conclusion: Legacy of the Waite Court 162

Notes 173
Index of Cases 207
Subject Index 211

Illustrations

Following page 52

Chief Justice Morrison R. Waite

The Waite Court

"The Electoral Commission, 1877"

The Louisiana Murders

"The Disputed Prize"

"Stanley Matthews—His Narrow Escape"

Series Editor's Preface

On the rare occasions when I am awake before sunrise, I have been aware of the dim glow in the sky that heralds the beginning of another day. At the same time it remains a matter of conjecture exactly where over the horizon the sun will actually appear. It is that combination of certainty and uncertainty that rivets attention and creates anticipation concerning what the new day will bring. Paul Kens's perceptive study of the U.S. Supreme Court under Chief Justice Morrison R. Waite similarly calls our attention to a critical but little understood period of the Court's history. It was a time when "tendencies" provided a key to the current work of the justices, but also pointed to future developments as yet but also little understood.

Historiographically, the Waite Court has always been considered to be "transitional," reacting but slowly to the revolutionary changes wrought by the post–Civil War amendments to the federal Constitution. However, the sleeping giant of substantive due process earlier disturbed by *Wynehamer v. The People* (1856)[1] and *Dred Scott v. Sanford* (1857)[2] had gained new birth with the Fourteenth Amendment; the result was a massive alteration in the dynamics of the federal system, which provided a powerful instrumental tool for reshaping American law after 1868. Kens is quite correct in rejecting characterization of the Waite Court as being "transitional." In the wake of a massive earthquake, a flood, or a forest fire, one does not make piecemeal or fine-tuned adjustments or "transitions"; survival demands intentional rebuilding and redesigning the landscape. No less strenuous exertion faced Waite, his Court, and their successors, as they struggled with the scope and varied implications of nationalized due process and equal protection clauses.

Not surprisingly the legal profession in general, and the Waite Court in particular, was cautious in accepting the full implications of the Fourteenth Amendment. Just a year before Waite became chief justice, the Chase Court upheld a Louisiana monopoly of New Orleans slaughterhouse operations in the face of a novel substantive due process challenge. That decision, in the *Slaughterhouse Cases*,[3] triggered a forceful dissent from Justice Stephen J. Field that would, over the course of the next quarter century, become ruling case law under Waite's successor, Chief Justice Melville W. Fuller. Early in the Waite chief justiceship, the Court affirmed state authority to regulate both grain elevators and railroads, citing the traditional view that businesses impressed with vital public interests were necessarily subject to legislative regulation.[4] Yet the Waite Court also adopted positions concerning public lands that tended to favor excessive continental railroad claims on the government's largesse and swept aside the ethical, equitable, and humanitarian entitlements of preemptors and other settlers. Suspicious of flamboyant railroad financing practices, the justices protected the federal government's subsidies through validating U.S. government sinking fund arrangements despite powerfully persuasive arguments that the law took property without due process of law.[5] This was thus a time when the Court moved hesitantly and inconsistently toward a new era of constitutional interpretation.

Chief Justice Waite's selection to preside over the Court raised eyebrows in both the political and the legal communities. Without exception, all of his predecessors had been selected from among former members of presidential cabinets. Measured by those standards, Waite represented a marked departure; his principal public office before his nomination to lead the Court was as a commissioner on the U.S. delegation that settled the Alabama claims against Great Britain. This diplomatic service, dealing with damages sustained by the United States through British outfitting Confederate privateers during the Civil War, would have given Waite some limited familiarity with international law. But it was scarcely helpful to a successful private lawyer facing de novo the complex constitutional issues then arising in the Supreme Court. Despite that modest résumé, the new chief justice brought with him more than average familiarity with the world of corporate finance and railroad operations. He also proved to be willing to undertake the authorship of major opinions that might trigger controversy, thus shielding his colleagues from public criticism and emphasizing collegial and institutional support for the Court's decisions. Fortunately for the Court, Chief Justice Waite grew into the stature and skills required by his new position, for the times were difficult for the Court, which was beset with a troubled postwar history as well as widening doctrinal divisions among the justices themselves.

Outside the windowless basement room of the U.S. Capitol that housed the Court until the New Deal era, changes were in embryo that would have a profound impact upon the Court and constitutional law until the present day. Antebellum respect for the dignity of the Constitution and the rule of law had always served as insulation against the heat of political discourse. That custom had been shattered first by the Taney Court's indiscretions in the *Dred Scott* case, and then by the Chase Court's blunder and penitence in the two legal tender cases.[6] Increasingly, the Waite Court was drawn into the political turmoil of the day. The 1881 confirmation of Justice Stanley Matthews, approved by a majority of one vote in the Senate, graphically illustrated for the first time the potential impact of organized private interest groups on the selection of Supreme Court justices. And the participation of five sitting Supreme Court justices on the commission that resolved the contested issues in the 1876 presidential election only blurred further the distinction between politics and the rule of law.

That tension, between political or practical necessity and traditional rule of law principles, has dominated American constitutionalism during and since the Waite era. Post–Civil War America desperately needed a transcontinental transportation system that was possible only with massive government financial assistance; it also needed strong legal and constitutional protections for private investment capital. These public policy concerns inevitably made an impression upon the Supreme Court and reshaped the justices' approaches to the post–Civil War amendments and to the newly reorganized federal system. That adaptive process began in the Waite era, even if very slowly and most reluctantly. Subsequently, in New Deal legislation after 1937, it would also give rise to strong federal restraints upon the excesses of free market economics. In both situations the innovations exposed severe differences of opinion among the Supreme Court justices. Thus this study lends additional insight into the coverage of three earlier volumes published in this series, dealing with the U.S. Supreme Court from 1888 to 1941.[7]

Readers will appreciate Kens's analytical skills and broad familiarity with the Court's case law during this time period. He has cast a steady and impartial gaze upon this troubled period of Supreme Court history, and has provided a critical, but not judgmental, presentation of the achievements, as well as the foibles, of Morrison R. Waite and his associates. Most important, he has demonstrated the need to think more objectively about these earliest years of what historians have tended to characterize—perhaps too facilely—either as a "Gilded Age" or as the much-maligned "Lochner Era."

Herbert A. Johnson

Acknowledgments

Every major research project is, for me, something of a journey. This one has taken me across the nation in search of information and into subjects of which I had little knowledge before I started. Now that I have finished, it is a pleasure to be able finally to thank the many people who have helped me along the way. My deepest thanks goes to my wife, Carla Underhill. Carla has truly been a full partner in this project, as she has been in my earlier books. In addition to providing encouragement and support, she has carefully read and critiqued every draft of the manuscript. Although she has developed a broad knowledge of legal history, Carla is a physician. By training and disposition she is particularly adept at identifying vagueness and inconsistency. She sees weaknesses and problems I have missed, and I rely on her to provide the critique I trust most.

Friends and colleagues have been very generous in sharing their ideas and time. I have spent hours exchanging ideas with my good friend Bartholomew "Bat" Sparrow. Bat carefully reviewed this entire manuscript and provided encouragement as well as much helpful criticism. James W. Ely Jr. also reviewed the entire manuscript. Over time Jim and I have often reviewed each other's writing projects. I have come to count on him to keep me honest and to help me avoid overstating my claims. In addition to commenting on my work, Pamela Brandwein was extremely generous to allow me to read and use her then-unpublished manuscript on the state action doctrine and civil rights. I look for her book to be published soon. I am also grateful to Robert Kaczorowski, who kindly took the time to review the manuscript and provide comments.

A special thanks goes to Herbert Johnson, who is the editor of the University of South Carolina Press series on the history of the Supreme Court. Herb asked me to take on this project and thus join the distinguished authors who have written other books in the series. I appreciate that, but, even more, I appreciate his style. Herb allowed me complete freedom to write this story. Yet, at the same time, he was fully involved at key stages of the project. He read more than one version of the manuscript, identified errors involving everything from facts to grammar, and consistently provided helpful comments.

While working on this project, I participated on several conference panels that seemed like detours at the time. As it turned out, each had an impact on this book. When Peter Hoffer organized a panel on revolutions in constitutional law, I was asked to explain why *Lochner v. New York* was revolutionary even though most of today's legal historians insist it was not. The result of my effort is reflected in chapters five, seven, and eight. Sanford Levinson and Bat Sparrow asked me to present a paper on expansion prior to the Civil War at a symposium on the Louisiana Purchase and American expansion that they had organized. It was then that I began to formulate ideas that appear in chapters ten and eleven. Later I presented a version of chapter five in a panel at the American Society for Legal History. There I reaped the benefit of Michael Les Benedict's comments and gathered new ideas from the other presenters, Christopher Waldrep and Pam Brandwein. Many thanks are owed to them and to Robert Cottrol, Mark Tushnet, H. W. Brands, and Elliot West, who, by participating in these panels, helped make this a better book.

I owe a debt of gratitude to people and institutions that helped me find the time to finish this project. First, it is important to note that my project received the support of a National Endowment for the Humanities Fellowship. This fellowship gave me a year of release from my teaching responsibilities and allowed me to complete the research and writing that became chapters five, seven, and eight.

My own university, Texas State University–San Marcos, also supported my work by granting me developmental leave for one semester and by awarding me a research enhancement grant to pay for some of the travel expenses related to my research. Slightly less dramatic, but no less important, is the support I have received from the chair of my department, Vicki Brittain, who has done whatever she could to help me achieve my goals. Other members of our department helped me with important details. Jenni Small frequently provided computer support. Using Photoshop, she also manipulated and made more legible the photographs I took of hundreds of written documents. Pam Tise undertook the difficult job of checking all my references. Because of their efficiency, Coleen Rankin, Jo Korthals, and Dodie Weidner have given me time I might have otherwise spent negotiating though the details of university business.

Most of my research was done at or connected through the Alkek Library at Texas State University–San Marcos and the Perry Castenedas Library and Tarlton Law Library at the University of Texas at Austin. Many thanks go to Bat Sparrow, Gary Freeman, and John Higley, who made the arrangements that allowed me to have full use of the facilities at the University of Texas. During the course of this project, I was fortunate to have the help of efficient and knowledgeable librarians at these libraries and at the Newberry Library, the National Archives, the Library of Congress Manuscript Division, and the Library of Congress Law Division. I am especially grateful to Nan Card, curator of manuscripts, Rutherford B. Hayes Presidential Center. When circumstances prevented me from making a planned visit to the library, Nan helped me identify the documents I needed and sent copies to me in the mail.

Many people helped make this book better than it otherwise would have been. My thanks go to all of them.

Introduction

Traditional Court, Turbulent Times

"THE PANIC: EXCITEMENT IN WALL STREET"—that was the headline greeting readers of the *New York Times* on the morning of September 19, 1873. The panic of the previous day, Thursday, September 18, had begun with a brief notice that Jay Cooke & Co. had suspended payments to its depositors. Although the company's announcement was brief, its impact was earth shattering. In an era known for its cutthroat, risk-taking financiers—like Jay Gould, Jim Fisk, and Collis Huntington—Jay Cooke was widely considered to be the preeminent financial wizard. Cooke had pioneered the practice of selling investments in small amounts of shares to individuals who had never before owned stocks and bonds and then used that technique to help the Union finance the Civil War.[1] He was a hero, honored by Lincoln for playing a part in saving the Union, and admired generally for his business acumen. The news of his company's failure shook investors and brokers to the core.

News reports described the reaction as a "mad terror." The *New York Times* observed that "the brokers stood perfectly thunderstruck for a moment, and then there was a general run to notify the different houses in Wall Street of the failure. The brokers surged out of the exchange tumbling pell-mell over each other in general confusion and reached their offices in race-horse time." News of the panic spread in every direction, the *Times* continued. Hundreds of people gathered outside the Cooke company's office "and peered curiously through the windows, as if some wonderful transformation was about to be witnessed." Only "energetic pushing and the use of strong language" allowed the police to prevent the crowd from storming the building. But a wonderful transformation did not take place. Instead, the panic "fed on itself and grew to a point that there was no one with enough nerve or money to arrest it."[2]

The impact of economic collapse—the loss of jobs, loss of investments, and fear of being unable to provide the basic necessities of life—is all too familiar to Americans living at the time this book was written in 2009. And economic depressions were not uncommon in the early years of our nation's history. But that "Black Thursday," as it came to be called, ushered in an economic depression the likes of which the nation had never before seen. One broker called it "the worst disaster since the Black

Death."[3] That may have been an exaggeration, but the resulting depression, which lasted until 1879, is generally thought to be second only to the Great Depression of 1929 in terms of the damage done to the economic and social fabric of the nation.[4]

On that Black Thursday Morrison R. Waite was in Columbus, Ohio, serving as president of the Ohio constitutional convention. In four months, however, the successful but unpretentious Toledo attorney would be presiding over an even more prestigious forum. On January 19, 1874, President Grant nominated Waite to be the seventh chief justice of the U.S. Supreme Court. Morrison R. Waite took the oath of office on March 4, 1874, and served as chief justice of the Supreme Court from that day until his death on March 23, 1888.[5]

Legal historians and constitutional scholars tend to portray these fourteen years as a relatively uneventful time in terms of evolution of constitutional doctrine. Indeed, Waite is one of the least well known chief justices, and few cases from the Waite Court era remain part of today's constitutional discourse. Even constitutional scholars and legal historians describe the years of Waite's tenure as chief justice as transitional. They are often treated simply as a prelude to the more eventful era that followed. Many of the cases we do remember are famous not for the majority opinions themselves, but for the opinions of the dissenting justices that set the stage for later changes.

The curious thing is that, although the era may seem uneventful to constitutional historians, economically and socially these years were anything but. The era began in the shadow of the Civil War. It ended with America on the verge of becoming an industrial economy and world power. The years between 1874 and 1888 experienced racial violence and continued sectional rivalries. The country went through a commercial revolution with the growth of powerful corporate businesses, which, in turn, produced agrarian discontent and labor strife. These years witnessed westward expansion, which offered great opportunities but as George Custer's defeat at Little Big Horn in 1876 illustrated, also produced violent turmoil. This was a time that tested what Americans meant when they talked about states' rights and federalism, liberty and equality, or democracy and the rights of the people.

This period actually was a pivotal time in the evolution of the American Constitution. The Waite Court played an important role in shaping that evolution but not necessarily the same role we are used to seeing from the Supreme Court in modern times. We are used to thinking of famous cases as ones where the Supreme Court initiates a change in the way a generation interprets the constitution. *Brown v. Board of Education* (1954) and *Roe v. Wade* (1973) provide the classic examples.

Rather than initiating a change, however, the Waite Court was more often reacting to changes that came from Congress, or to changes proposed in dissenting opinions or the theories of lawyers and legal scholars. It tended to see itself as the keeper of tradition. For this reason the significance of most of the decisions needs to be placed in context to be fully appreciated. The history of the Waite Court can best be told by submersing the cases and constitutional conflicts in the context of the political, social, and economic times.

Three factors tended to dominate those times: the legacy of the Civil War and slavery, an ongoing revolution in commerce, and the consolidation of westward expansion. Whether solely or in combination, each touch just about every issue Americans of the day faced. They strained Americans' thinking about the purpose, nature, and structure of government, and therefore ultimately about the meaning of the Constitution. Naturally the Waite Court played an important role in the attempt to sort this out.

To understand the Waite era a reader looking from the twenty-first century should keep in mind that many of the characteristics of the Constitution, the political system, and the Court that we take as a given today were different or did not exist in Waite's time. Presumptions modern Americans might make about these things were not valid then.

At the time Waite took office the federal government did not have as great an impact on peoples' daily lives as it does today. Rules and regulations governing such things as society, business, family, or crime were almost solely matters of state law. Justices of the Waite era came of age in a time when people might talk about "these united states" rather than "the United States," and a court decision might describe the role of "the several states." These might seem like nothing more than archaic turns of a phrase, yet they reflected a common attitude toward the Union that envisioned a greater role for the states rather than for the federal government. The nature of the Union was disputed, to be sure; that is part of what the Civil War was about. But even the most ardent nationalists of the post–Civil War era would be stopped in their tracks by what modern Americans accept with little question as the federal government's function. It is true that vestiges of concern about the expanding role of the federal government exist today. It can be seen in libertarian political campaigns. Even more significantly, the Supreme Court in 1995 and 2000 overruled federal laws creating gun-free school zones and a federal violence against women act.[6] But the modern reaction to federal power is relatively tepid compared to the concerns of mid-nineteenth-century Americans.

A related point that might bewilder modern Americans is that during the Waite era, standard constitutional doctrine held that the Bill of Rights did not apply to the states. This rule came from an 1833 case called *Barron v. Baltimore,* and it did not change until after the Waite era.[7] Today many cases involving free speech, the rights of people accused of committing a crime, or other civil liberties come from claims that a state law is unconstitutional. This kind of claim was not available under the rule of *Barron v. Baltimore,* and thus the Court's role as a guardian of civil liberties was quite different than it is today. But one opinion from late in the Waite era portended the change. It was Justice John Marshall Harlan's dissent in the 1884 case *Hurtado v. California,* which is discussed in the conclusion.[8]

Ideas about the proper role of the federal government and the states were in transition during Waite's time. The Civil War, the Reconstruction Amendments, and legislation of the time tended to promote the idea of increasing the authority of the federal government. Commercial revolution and westward expansion had this effect as well. Like everyone else, the justices of the Waite Court were struggling to set the boundaries.

Although the Civil War had ended almost a decade before Waite took office, it was the life-defining experience of almost every adult American of his generation. The war had crumbled the Union and shaken its foundation, and Americans in Waite's time were still trying to put it back together. The Thirteenth, Fourteenth, and Fifteenth amendments, which were ratified soon after the Civil War, were part of that effort. The meaning of these amendments, which are called the "Reconstruction Amendments," or "Civil War Amendments," will be discussed in detail in the chapters that follow.

Although their meaning remains a subject of dispute to this day, it is clear that they were at the very least intended to free the slaves, guarantee civil and political rights for blacks, and guarantee that the right to vote not be denied on account of race.

Whatever their goals or inspiration, the Reconstruction Amendments, especially the Fourteenth, were written in sweeping language that allowed them to reach into subjects other than protecting the civil and political rights of blacks. In fact, of the three Reconstruction Amendments, only the Fifteenth, which deals with the right to vote, mentions race at all. Vague and sweeping language not only left open questions about what practical protections the amendments offered to blacks but also about what else the amendments did. Consequently tentacles of these amendments are found in many of the constitutional debates of the Waite Court era.

It is impossible to describe the impact of the Reconstruction Amendments and history of the Waite Court without going back just a short time to consider a case called the *Slaughterhouse Cases* (1873). This case, which is the subject of chapter 1, was decided about a year before Waite took his seat. It presented the first opportunity for the Supreme Court to interpret the Reconstruction Amendments. And, as if to underscore the breadth of the Reconstruction Amendments, it had nothing to do with civil rights for blacks. Rather, the case involved a claim by white New Orleans butchers that a law requiring them to ply their trade at a central slaughterhouse violated their rights under the Thirteenth and Fourteenth amendments.

It is common for constitutional history to treat the *Slaughterhouse Cases* as a pathbreaking moment—path breaking in two directions. Taking a step down one path was Justice Samuel Miller's opinion for the majority. The butchers had argued in part that the central slaughterhouse law violated the Fourteenth Amendment's guarantee, "No State shall make or enforce any law which shall abridge the privileges or immunities of citizens of the United States." But Miller, using a very narrow or restricted definition of what rights come under "privileges or immunities of citizens of the United States," rejected their claim. According to standard narrative, Miller's interpretation of privileges and immunities had the long-term effect of limiting the reach of the Fourteenth Amendment as a means of protecting the rights of racial minorities.

Dissenting in the case, Justices Stephen Field, Joseph Bradley, and Noah Swayne set off on a completely different path. They introduced a theory that the Reconstruction

Amendments created new guarantees of economic liberties for everyone. Eventually, after the Waite era had ended, their idea would be honed into a doctrine that used the Fourteenth Amendment guarantee that "No state shall deny any person life, liberty, or property without due process of law" as a means of placing a constitutional limit on the power of states to regulate economic matters. As a result, it became a useful tool for protecting the interests of business elites.

There is an air of inevitability running through the conventional treatment of this story about the changes in constitutional doctrine during the late nineteenth century. With the advantage of hindsight, modern constitutional history texts and constitutional law casebooks tend to assume that the Waite Court was merely a stepping stone along the path of reduced protection for minorities, on the one hand, and the path of providing a tool for protecting the interests of business elites, on the other. However, the chapters that follow reveal that much of the history of the Waite Court involves the question of whether the Court of that era marched forcefully, tiptoed gingerly, or was dragged down these paths. Moreover looking more closely at the Waite era raises the question of whether the paths that constitutional doctrine eventually took were as inevitable as the conventional narrative suggests.

The first Supreme Court cases involving civil rights for blacks did not occur until 1876 when the Court decided *United States v. Cruikshank* and *United States v. Reese*. These cases, which are covered in chapter 2, involved the issue of to what extent the federal government could use its power to guarantee full equality for black citizens. It is surprising that it took so long for that question to first reach the Court because at the time Waite took office questions of race, equality, and civil rights permeated the political and social issues of the day.

With little more than a decade having passed since the end of the Civil War, appeals to loyalty—then referred to as "waving the bloody shirt"—still carried political weight. Republicans, who dominated Congress, successfully enacted legislation designed to use the federal government to protect the rights of the freedmen. Meanwhile, Southern extremists turned to violence and intimidation to discourage blacks from voting or holding office and as a means of maintaining social and economic control over the former slaves. *United States v. Cruikshank* arose from a particularly violent and disturbing incident, the Colfax massacre, in which a heavily armed gang of white men killed scores, perhaps hundreds, of black Louisianans at the Colfax Parish courthouse.

In *Cruikshank* leaders of the Colfax massacre were charged with violating a law that we might interpret today as the federal crime of conspiring to deprive a person of his or her civil rights. But the Court rejected the idea that the federal government had such jurisdiction. Instead, it viewed the Colfax massacre as a case of murder. It was the prosecution of the kind of criminal act that traditionally fell within the power of the states, not the federal government. The Court's ruling thus limited the reach of the federal government's jurisdiction and, in the process, revealed the Court's attachment to a model of federalism that existed before the Civil War. The decision thus frustrated the hopes of Republicans who believed that federal enforcement provided the only way to assure the rights of blacks living in the South.

Because Republicans depended upon the vote of black men in the South, the party's desire to assure civil and political rights for blacks was closely tied to its desire to stay in power. Another event in 1876 added urgency to their fear of losing control. That was the year of the disputed presidential election between Republican Rutherford B. Hayes and Democrat Samuel Tilden. Chapter 2 concludes with an account of the election of 1876 and the subsequent "Compromise of 1877." It is said that the compromise gave Hayes the presidency in exchange for, among other things, a promise to remove federal troops from the South and to allow the Southern states freedom to handle racial problems free of federal interference. A special electoral commission that included five justices of the Supreme Court ultimately played a key role in the outcome of the election.

The Compromise of 1877 did not put an end to disputes over civil rights. Chapter 3 returns to that subject, specifically considering cases after the compromise and after the new appointments to the Court in 1880–82. In an 1883 decision called the *Civil Rights Cases,* the Court overruled provisions of the Civil Rights Act of 1875 prohibiting racial discrimination in public transportation and public places such as taverns, theaters, and inns. Building on ideas established in *Cruikshank* and *Reese,* the Court ruled that the Fourteenth Amendment gave Congress the power to prohibit only discrimination that resulted from state action. Under this so-called state action doctrine, the Civil Rights Act was held to be unconstitutional because Congress had attempted to prohibit discrimination by private individuals, and therefore had stepped outside its authority.

Justice John Harlan was among those critics who viewed the majority's opinion as excessively narrow and contrary to the purpose of the Thirteenth and Fourteenth amendments. Although he was appointed in 1877 and certainly had an impact on all kinds of cases, Harlan's dissent in the *Civil Rights Cases* kindled his reputation as the Court's lone defender of civil rights for blacks. After the Waite era he shored up that reputation with an even more famous dissent in *Plessy v. Ferguson* (1896), where he coined the often-used phrase, "our constitution is color-blind."

Because of the cases like *Cruikshank, Reese,* and the *Civil Rights Cases,* as well as the state action doctrine, historians commonly describe the Supreme Court as having been complicit in the Compromise of 1877. It is said to have played a role in abandoning the destiny of blacks to the Southern states, and to have laid the foundation for the racial segregation that characterized the Jim Crow era from the 1890s to 1950s. Eric Foner, for example, charged the Court with "emasculating the postwar Amendments," and William Wiecek calls the Court a major contributor to "dismantling the structure of freedmen's rights."[9] It may be unfair to cherry pick phrases from these careful historical accounts, but the phrases suggest a particular attitude, one that is captured in the subtitle of Charles Lane's recent book, *The Day Freedom Died: The Betrayal of Reconstruction.*[10]

Isolating the Waite Court from developments that took place later casts a somewhat different hue. There is little doubt that the opinions of the Waite Court did reflect impatience with Reconstruction and a lack of concern for Southern blacks. But the Court did not betray Reconstruction so much as it struggled with it. In a recent biography of Justice Miller, for example, Michael Ross maintains that Miller's narrow interpretation of the privileges and immunities clause was motivated more by fear that the clause might be misused to protect business elites than it was by impatience with Reconstruction.[11] In another recent study, Pamela Brandwein has observed that the Court's adoption of the state action doctrine in the *Civil Rights Cases* did not entirely foreclose on Congress's power to prohibit private discrimination. Rather, it recognized a concept she calls state neglect and left room for the possibility of the federal government stepping in when a state failed to satisfy its duty to prevent private discrimination.[12]

As Michael Les Benedict and Pamela Brandwein have pointed out, understanding the Court's struggle with Reconstruction hinges on understanding the justices' frame of references regarding federalism.[13] Other modern legal histories also recognize the significance of federalism; some even emphasize it. But a subtext running through many studies is that the Court contrived an interpretation of federalism that served as an excuse for justifying racist and partisan opinions. After carefully explaining the issues of federalism, for example, Robert Kaczorowski concludes that the Court's failure to find solutions that would preserve the national government's authority to protect civil rights was partially due to the racism, economic self-interest, and partisanship that characterize the political order of the times.[14]

The justices who made up the Waite Court were weaned on a tradition of federalism that emphasized state authority and a limited role of the federal government in everyday life. They saw a strong federal government as the main threat to individual liberty and envisioned the states as the protectors of the rights of citizens. Although the Reconstruction Amendments were undoubtedly intended to change this formula, the question troubling the Waite Court was, how much? A close look at the Waite-era opinions, those concerning civil rights as well as opinions on other subjects, reveals that federalism was more than a mere ruse. It, once again, shows that the Waite Court was a keeper of tradition.

Westward expansion revealed something more about the Court's attitude toward civil rights and minority groups, however. Disputes coming from the western frontier brought into the picture other disfavored groups: Chinese in California, American Indians throughout the West, and Mormons in Utah. Many of these cases were either rooted in treaties or arose in territories rather than in states. Thus, unlike disputes involving Southern states, they were disputes in which there was no question that the federal government had authority to act. In these decisions, the impact of prewar ideals of federalism was stripped away, revealing that the justices of the Waite Court were also guided by an unabashed and unflinching certainty in the superiority of their own race, gender, and religion.

There can be no doubt that the racial attitudes of the justices influenced the civil rights cases of the era. But for many of the justices of the era, the influence was not a matter of hate, strategy, or following raw public opinion. It was a matter of sentiment—the subtle but also deeply held attitudes, feelings, and opinions that formed the core of their thinking. One might argue that this is a distinction without a difference: the outcome is the same. The difference, however, gives us a better understanding of the evolution of constitutional doctrine. It also provides some understanding of the factors at play in judicial decision making.

In 1877, the year of the compromise that gave Hayes the presidency, the country also witnessed its first nationwide labor strike. What began in West Virginia as a dispute between workers and the Baltimore and Ohio Railroad shocked the nation as it spread from coast to coast in a matter of weeks. The Great Strike of 1877 demonstrated how interconnected the country had become. America was undergoing a commercial revolution in the last half of the nineteenth century. It was moving from an economy that was primarily local to one that was national and interconnected.

The Great Strike of 1877 started as a railroad strike, and railroads are everywhere in this story. They provided the system of transportation that allowed the commercial revolution to take place. In that role they assumed a great deal of power over the economic system as a whole and the everyday lives of many Americans. They also came to symbolize the surging power of corporations in the American political, economic, social, and legal system. Railroads come into play in chapters 4, 5, and 6 in cases involving corporate charters, railroad bankruptcies, municipal and state aid to build railroad lines, and regulation of railroad rates and business practices. At first glance these may not appear to be exciting topics, but most of these disputes took place in the atmosphere of a frontier, either geographic or economic or both. They determined whether communities would rise or fall, whether fortunes would be made or lost, and whether dreams would be realized or dashed.

Some people also thought the outcome of these disputes would influence the direction of American democracy. This was evident in the Illinois constitutional convention of 1869–70, where delegates debated the authority and duty of the state to regulate railroads in particular and corporations in general. The claims in support of the state's authority to regulate emphasized two principles. First was the principle that businesses, especially railroads and corporations, held their property subject to common good, the right of the public, or the rights of the community. The second was that corporations, being a creation of the state, were subject to the control of the state.

Where advocates maintained that American traditions of popular sovereignty and democracy justified, or even required, regulation, railroad and other corporate interests argued that the concepts of liberty and limited government prohibited it. As a practical matter, however, tradition favored regulation. As Harry Scheiber and William Novak have shown, regulation of business was commonplace in nineteenth-century America and supported in common law. Furthermore, while the courts always recognized the importance of private property, the principle that the *use* of property is subject to the rights of the community was well established in constitutional law.[15]

The most famous expression of this precedent is found in the *Charles River Bridge* case of 1837, where Chief Justice Roger Taney wrote, "While the rights of private property are sacredly guarded, we must not forget that the community also have rights, and that the happiness and well being of every citizen depends on their faithful preservation."[16] The issue in this case was whether the state had violated the

Constitution's Article I, Section 10, prohibition that no state shall pass any law "impairing the obligation of contracts." Chapter 4 discusses contract clause doctrine leading up to a group of 1877 opinions often referred to as the Granger Cases. In these cases the Waite Court applied traditional contract clause precedent to uphold laws that regulated railroad rates and practices.

The most momentous of the Granger Cases was unique in that it involved neither railroads nor the contract clause. Constitutional change and evolution of the economic system converged in the case of *Munn v. Illinois* (1877), which is the subject of chapter 5. In *Munn* the owners of several immense grain elevators argued that an Illinois law setting maximum rates they could charge for the storage of grain deprived them of their property without due process of law.

Although the owners based their case on the Fourteenth Amendment, the due process guarantee is also found in the Fifth Amendment. Earlier court decisions did not treat due process as an absolute guarantee, but rather as a guarantee against the arbitrary taking of property. The most traditional and least controversial view of due process held that the state could not take a person's property except by properly enacted legislation or through correct judicial procedure. The elevator owners' theory in *Munn* was that due process meant more than a guarantee of correct procedure. They argued that the law setting maximum rates was so unjust that it deprived them of property without due process, even though it was legally enacted by a democratically elected legislature. This theory, which later came to be called "substantive due process," was not unique, but it was very unusual and would become extremely controversial.

The Court ruled in *Munn* that the Illinois law setting maximum rates for the storage of grain was constitutional. Chief Justice Waite, who wrote the majority opinion, reasoned that the states have the authority to protect the general welfare by regulating businesses involving public interest. At the heart of the decision was Waite's application of the standard burden of proof in contract clause cases: a presumption that properly enacted state economic regulations were valid. To that extent the case represented a victory for state economic regulation.

But Waite also offered a caveat that, under some circumstances, state regulation could constitute a deprivation of liberty and property without due process of law. In addition, Justice Stephen Field wrote a dissent in which he forcefully articulated a theory of economic liberty that used the Fourteenth Amendment to strictly limit state economic regulation. By the 1890s, after Waite had left the bench, the majority of the Court would seize on Waite's caveat and Field's dissent and adopt a constitutional doctrine of due process that held that an economic regulation would be considered invalid unless a state could demonstrate that the law fell within a certain set of governmental functions called the "police powers of the states." This shift in presumption was subtle but momentous.

Constitutional historians debate when the shift occurred, some pointing to *Chicago, Milwaukee, & St. Paul Railway v. Minnesota* (1890), others to *Smyth v. Ames* (1898) or even to *Lochner v. New York* (1905).[17] Until the 1970s, most historians described this shift as a virtual coup d'état in which the Supreme Court improperly attached laissez-faire economic theory to the Constitution through the open-ended language of the due process clause. However, following the lead of Charles McCurdy, the vast majority of modern constitutional historians now maintain that the use of the due process clause to overrule state economic regulations was not a break in constitutional tradition but rather a natural extension of antebellum American traditions that emphasized individual liberty and limited government. *Munn*'s role in either of these versions of constitutional history is one of setting the stage for change. As such, the case is usually thought of as a window to the future.[18]

But *Munn* also provides a window to the past. Taking advantage of that perspective, chapters 4 and 5 reveal that Chief Justice Waite's opinion reflected a very traditional view of the authority of the state to regulate business that balanced property rights against the rights of the community. Modern constitutional discourse overlooks this tradition. Emphasizing Waite's caveat and Field's dissent, it leaps forward to cases decided after the Waite era and concludes that the Court "quickly moved away" from the majority's position in *Munn*.

The modern narrative's leap forward has left a mistaken impression. For more than a decade the Waite Court actually resisted attempts on the part of attorneys for the business elite to reverse its holding in *Munn*. Chapters 5 and 8 describe how these attorneys experimented with various strategies to mold into the Constitution a protection against government regulation. Although the Waite majority conceded some of their points, it was only after Melville Weston Fuller replaced Waite as chief justice in 1888 that the doctrine of entrepreneurial liberty that business interests favored began to take hold.

The history of the Waite Court's response sheds light on two very disparate ideas that are prevalent in constitutional and political theory today. The first is a libertarian view that criticizes the *Munn* decision's presumption in favor of state regulation. Arguing that the proper presumption should be in favor of individual liberty, modern scholars like Randy Barnett emphasize that when the Supreme Court eventually rejected the *Munn* decision and adopted substantive due process, it was protecting fundamental liberties from excessive and arbitrary legislation.[19]

The second idea is a communitarian view exemplified by Mary Ann Glendon, who focuses on the negative impact of "rights talk" on modern American political dialogue. Glendon uses the term "rights talk" to describe the growing tendency to couch debates in terms of individual rights rather than public policy. Her view, one that is popular among today's political conservatives, holds that this misplaced obsession with rights grew out of the civil rights movements of the 1950s and legislation and court decisions of the 1960s.[20]

The history of the Waite Court demonstrates that there was, contrary to both of these theories, a long tradition in the United States of government regulation of business for the common welfare. The *Munn* decision recognized this and, while doing so, emphasized the role of democratically elected legislatures in determining the limits of regulation. Lawyers for the business elite who opposed the *Munn* decision deliberately sought to reverse this presumption. Their theory of substantive due process did not merely reflect a transition in constitutional doctrine. It was more akin to a revolution. Not only would it eventually insulate business from government regulation, it would also turn debates over economic regulation into matters of individual rights rather than public policy. It was, in other words, an earlier version of the "rights talk" that modern conservatives so disdain. Although its target may have been different, it had the same consequence of undermining political dialogue.

Another aspect of the nineteenth-century debate over the reach of government regulation was that the concept of individual liberty became mingled with the growing importance and power of corporations. The Crédit Mobilier scandal, which involved government subsidies for building the transcontinental railroad, brought this out more than any other event of the time.

The federal government provided two types of aid for building the railroad. In addition to land grants, which are part of the treatment of westward expansion in chapter 10, it gave the railroads financial aid in the form of bonds that were, in essence, a loan. By the mid-1870s railroad critics and some people in government were becoming concerned that companies would not be able to repay the loans when they became due. Their worries were intensified by the Crédit Mobilier scandal, which revealed that key directors of the Union Pacific were skimming profits from the railroad into their own separate corporation. In response, Congress passed a law that set aside certain railroad income into a trust fund, called a sinking fund, which was intended to assure the money would be available for repayment of the bonds.

Chapter 7 begins with a discussion of the *Sinking Fund Cases,* which reached the Supreme Court in 1879. When the railroad companies challenged the law as unconstitutional, the Court once again entered into an ongoing debate over the extent to which the people have the power to control corporations. Conversely it faced the question of whether corporations have the same constitutional rights as flesh-and-blood humans. Although the Court did not fully answer either of these questions, it ruled that Congress did have the power to create a sinking fund.

The Waite Court's early decisions regarding economic regulation were a great disappointment to railroads and the business elite. Beginning in 1880, however, they sensed an opportunity to mold the Court into an institution more sympathetic to their interests. In less than a year and a half, between December 1880 and April 1882, there were four new appointments to the Supreme Court. Chapter 8 discusses these appointments, especially the appointment of Stanley Matthews, a prominent railroad lawyer whose nomination faced stiff opposition.

Chapter 8 also discusses the impact of the new appointments with respect to economic regulation. It demonstrates that although lawyers for the business elite hoped the changes would provide an opportunity to reverse the precedent growing out of *Munn* and the *Sinking Fund Cases,* they continued to be frustrated during the remainder of the Waite era. One glaring exception, however, came in *Santa Clara County v. Southern Pacific Railroad,* an 1886 decision that to this day remains famous for establishing the rule that corporations are "persons" for purposes of the Fourteenth Amendment.

Everyone in the nineteenth century agreed that the Constitution allowed some regulation of business. The debate over substantive due process involved questions of what kind and how much. The revolution in commerce, especially the new system of transportation, also intensified another related issue: the question of whether the source of the regulation should be the states or the federal government.

Despite Article I, Section 8, of the Constitution, which gives Congress the power to regulate commerce among the states, the federal government rarely enacted economic regulation before the end of the nineteenth century. Most economic regulation came from the states. This system worked fairly well before the Civil War. When commerce clause questions did arise, the Court as a general rule tended to allow state regulations to stand if they did not impose a direct barrier to interstate commerce and if Congress had not previously enacted regulation.

As the economy became more interconnected, however, state regulation tended to become burdensome, complicated, and sometimes unworkable. By the 1870s calls for a federal system of regulation to supplant the maze of state laws came from reformers and the railroad industry alike. But Congress did not act until 1887, when it passed the Interstate Commerce Act. Chapter 9 describes the Court's attempts to deal with the problem of interstate commerce in the meantime.

The new interconnectedness was also brought to light by the prevalence and ramifications of railroad bankruptcies, which are discussed in chapter 6. In the new economy the failure of any single railroad had the potential to cripple interstate commerce. The subject of bankruptcy was also similar to interstate commerce in the sense that Article I, Section 8, of the Constitution also gives Congress the power to enact a uniform system for dealing with bankruptcy. Congress did not do so until 1898, however, and federal judges were forced to step into the void. They responded by developing some innovative bankruptcy doctrine, and one question running through chapter 6 is to what degree the federal courts, including the Supreme Court, thus became involved in initiating or guiding public policy.

Westward expansion, the last of the three factors dominating the Waite era, tends to blend into the others. It helped clarify the issues related to civil rights and intensified the impact of the revolution in commerce. One area in which it stands alone, however, is in disputes over the untapped wealth and enormous potential for profit that lay in the vast territory west of the Mississippi River.

These disputes were no doubt about profit and livelihood, but there was an undercurrent of political philosophy present as well. By the time Waite had become chief justice, Congress had enacted the Homestead Act of 1862. This law was the culmination of a long campaign for land reform that aimed at distributing the public domain in small parcels to individual owners who would cultivate their plots and live on the land. This homestead movement was rooted in the belief that having a large class of "yeoman farmers" was essential to a healthy democracy. For homestead reformers, settlement of the West offered a unique opportunity to increase the presence of this class of self-sufficient citizens and thereby counterbalance the political influence of a wealthy and connected elite. The homestead movement was a model that built government and society from the bottom up.

Given its enactment of the Homestead Act, it appeared that Congress was committed to this model. That was not necessarily true, however. Chapter 10 describes how holders of Mexican land grants, land speculators, and railroads were able to exploit inconsistencies in government land policy. It also examines how the Waite Court, like courts before and after, gradually developed rules that favored those claiming large blocks of land.

Past histories of the Waite Court have placed great stock in the impact of the Court's workload. There is little doubt that the Court was overworked. One reason for this was that until Congress reorganized the federal judiciary in the Circuit Court of Appeals Act of 1891, justices of the Supreme Court had the duty of "riding circuit." Each sat as the senior federal judge for a particular region of the country.

For some, like Stephen Field, riding circuit in the region they served required arduous travel. Field's circuit covered California and the West Coast. Before completion of the transcontinental railroad, he traveled by sea from the East Coast, crossed the Isthmus of Panama, then continued by steamship up the Pacific coast to San Francisco. Even after the completion of the railroad, Field's trip must have been taxing. Not all of the justices traveled so far, but riding circuit added to the workload even of those who covered regions closer to the nation's capital.

During some of the time Waite was chief justice, the Court faced an additional burden. There were times before the early 1880s appointments when up to four of the justices were incapacitated to a degree that they could not write opinions. This will be covered in more detail in chapter 8.

The jurisdiction of the federal courts also increased during the years after the Civil War. The Reconstruction Amendments created new rights that could be tested in federal courts. Federal statutes created more specific rights. Some statutes, called removal statutes, specifically provided moving cases from state courts to the federal courts. These were originally intended to allow blacks and Southern unionists to escape the jurisdiction of hostile state courts, but eventually railroads and other business interests used them for the same purpose.[21]

In addition, the Court did not have as much control over the number of cases it heard as does today's Court. Today the Court uses a procedure called writ of certiorari to choose which cases it wants to consider. In Waite's time the rules of procedure governing appeals to the Supreme Court left little room for discretion.

Donald Grier Stephenson Jr. describes the Waite Court as "the most burdened, the hardest working, and the most productive in Supreme Court History."[22] Emphasis on the Court's burden nevertheless tends to leave an impression that the Court resisted expanding its authority because it already suffered under a heavy workload. This may be true, but a closer look suggests that the Court's resistance to expanding its authority also came from a principled belief that the judiciary played an important but limited role in American democracy.

This belief emphasized popular sovereignty and found expression in a rule of interpretation holding that the acts of a legislature, being manifestations of popular sovereignty, should be presumed to be valid. It also rested on an understanding that popularly elected legislatures could be every bit as much a guardian of individual liberty and rights of the community as the courts.

This is important to keep in mind because modern Americans tend to be conditioned to the idea that the Supreme Court alone, or at least primarily, is the institution in our society designated to mold the Constitution. This is not true even today, but it is how we are inclined to think. Thus we tend to admire the Court, or criticize it, as an instrument for bringing about social change. One of the lessons learned from tracing the history of the Waite Court comes in the form of a reminder that the judiciary often functions not as an architect of change but rather as the keeper of tradition.

The Waite Court was traditional, not so much in the sense that it supported the establishment but in the sense that it tended to look backward for its cues and tended to follow the path that had already been laid. Of course following tradition in this way may be judged good or bad depending on the circumstances and one's point of view. Furthermore it is not always easy to tell whether a decision represents a keeping of tradition or is initiating change. Perhaps that is also part of the lesson learned from the history of the Waite Court that follows. And perhaps the Waite Court's tendency to act as keeper of tradition rather than architect of change explains why relatively few cases from the era have survived to be part of our constitutional discourse.

1

WAITE, WAITE, DON'T TELL ME

Morrison R. Waite was not President Grant's first choice to fill the seat that had become vacant when Chief Justice Salmon P. Chase died in May 1873. Quite to the contrary, the president's efforts to replace the deceased chief justice lasted eight months and was at times such a fiasco that one member of Congress sarcastically suggested a bill to abolish the chief justiceship "so as to spare the president the mortification of further appointments."[1] It did not help matters that three sitting justices, Samuel F. Miller, Noah H. Swayne, and Joseph Bradley, coveted the position. Each had supporters among powerful Republicans, and Miller and Swayne in particular lobbied hard for the appointment.[2] Grant, however, decided against appointing from inside the Court, and on November 8, 1873, he offered the job to Senator Roscoe Conkling of New York. Conkling, a powerful figure who was renowned for his arrogance, rejected the seat.

Surprised, and probably embarrassed, Grant reportedly offered the seat to two other senators, Timothy O. Howe and Oliver P. Morton, both of whom turned him down. Next, he offered it to Secretary of State Hamilton Fish, who also declined. Grant's next choice, Attorney General George H. Williams, accepted the nomination. However, charges of corruption derailed Williams's nomination. Among other things, he was said to have mingled Justice Department money with his personal accounts to purchase extravagances for his own use. On January 7, 1874, bowing to pressure from Senate Republicans, Williams withdrew his name.

Within a few days Grant selected Caleb Cushing for the post. Although the seventy-four-year-old Cushing was a respected lawyer, he was burdened by a proslavery past. In the 1850s, while serving as President Franklin Pierce's attorney general, Cushing had defended the *Dred Scott* decision. Although he belatedly converted to Republicanism, party purists still detected taint, and he was attacked vehemently in the press. The *New York Times,* for example, charged that "Jeff Davis himself could not have picked a man more pleasing to the Democrats."[3] And the *Nation* observed that in nominating Cushing, "the President has at last entered the small circle of eminent lawyers and then with great care chosen the worst man in it."[4] In the face of intense opposition from within the president's own party, on January 14 Cushing asked Grant to withdraw his name.

Perhaps the party faithful were relieved when, on January 19, Grant turned to the relatively unknown Morrison R. Waite to fill the post. The nomination did not receive universal acclaim. Critics maintained that Waite was not qualified for the job of chief justice. The *Chicago Times* conjured the ghosts of former chief justices to express its dissatisfaction: "Verily, the shades of Jay and Marshall, and Taney, and Chase may arise to protest against a profanation of this venerated seat by a man so utterly incapable of filling it acceptably."[5] Most of the objections took a milder tone, however. Describing Waite as a gentleman of only limited or local legal practice who had never argued a case before the nation's highest tribunal, the *New York Times* reported that "the judges of the Supreme Court regret that the selection has not been made from lawyers known and admitted by the entire country as in the first ranks of their profession."[6]

Indeed, Justices Field and Miller both expressed reservations about Waite, referring to him as "mediocre," "a man of fair but not great abilities," and of "limited legal acumen."[7] The *Nation* agreed that the president had, with remarkable skill, avoided choosing a first-rate man. Waite, it said, "stands at the front rank of second-rate lawyers."[8]

Even critics agreed, however, that Waite was "a man of the highest character and best possible standing at the bar of his own state."[9] Although he was relatively unknown in the national political scene, Waite was not necessarily unsuited for the job of chief justice. He was born on November 27, 1816, in Lyme, Connecticut, to a family that traced its roots to the American Revolution. Although he described his father as a country lawyer, the elder Waite served as chief justice of the Connecticut Supreme Court for about twenty years.

Morrison Waite received the best education available in his time. From a modest beginning in the Lyme schoolhouse, he attended a prestigious private school, Bacon Academy, and then went on to Yale College. While at Yale he became a close friend of William Evarts, who would go on to be one of the leading lawyers and political figures of his time. In those days the typical legal education consisted of "reading law" in the office of an established lawyer. In 1837, after graduating near the top of his Yale class, Waite returned to Lyme to read law with his father.[10]

Like many young New Englanders of his generation, Waite soon left his hometown in search of success in the western frontier. In 1838 he settled in Maumee City, a growing town in northwestern Ohio, where his uncle worked as a merchant. There he took a job with Samuel M. Young, a lawyer who had arrived in Maumee a few years earlier. Together, Young and Waite built a successful legal practice specializing in business and property issues. When Toledo became the county seat in 1850, Waite moved there to set up a branch office. Young left the firm in 1856 and went on to become a successful businessman.

The Toledo area was frontier at the time Waite arrived. Ohio was so sparsely populated that lawyers and judges "rode circuit," with a group of perhaps two or three lawyers and a judge riding horseback from town to town to hear cases. They sometimes shared rooms in pioneers' log cabins and held court wherever they could. Because there were no libraries and few books available, Waite honed his memory for the law. In these early years he polished his legal skills and developed a reputation for fairness and honesty. As the state grew Waite's legal practice in Toledo became more conventional and prospered. By the time Grant tapped him for the high court in 1874, he was considered to be one of the best lawyers in northeastern Ohio.

Although Waite was active in politics, he did not harbor any particular ambitions for high public office. He landed in Ohio as a "Henry Clay Whig"—attuned to the interests of business and government involvement in promoting economic prosperity.[11] According to his biographer C. Peter Magrath, however, life on the frontier also molded Waite's political ideals by adding a strong faith in self-government.[12]

In 1849 Ohio Whigs took a position against slavery. Waite ran on that platform to win a seat in the state's House of Representatives, where he served one term in 1850. In 1854 Waite left the Whig Party. Along with other Whigs, antislavery Democrats, and Free-Soilers, he helped develop the Ohio Republican Party. Throughout the Civil War and afterward he became a mainstay in state Republican politics and even ran a losing campaign for Congress in 1862 as a conservative Republican. But Waite never again held significant elected office and was not particularly active in the national party.

The event that thrust Waite into the national scene, garnered Grant's attention, and eventually resulted in his nomination to the Supreme Court involved a legal dispute with Great Britain. The United States claimed that Great Britain had violated the rules of neutrality during the Civil War by supplying and outfitting Confederate ships in British ports. The countries agreed that the claim should be submitted to an international board of arbitration, with each side being represented by an agent and three legal counsels.

President Grant chose Assistant Secretary of State J. C. Bancroft Davis to be the U.S. agent to the Geneva Tribunal. His first two selections for legal counsel, Caleb Cushing and Waite's college friend William Evarts, came from the highest ranks of the nation's legal profession. His third pick, at the suggestion of Secretary of Interior Columbus Delano, was Morrison R. Waite.

When the Geneva Tribunal convened in June 1872, Waite comported himself well. While the more famous and flamboyant Cushing and Evarts handled most of the oral argument, Waite did much of the painstaking work that was essential for America's case. Marshaling evidence from Great Britain's own naval records, he proved that the British had allowed Confederate vessels to use British ports as a base of operations. The result was a satisfying $15.5 million judgment and even more satisfaction in terms of national pride.

Waite's performance at the Geneva Tribunal hearings and support of friends like Evarts brought him to the president's attention. On January 18, 1874, Republican Party insiders reported, "It seems highly probable that he [the president] will name Mr. Waite of Ohio. We are convinced Mr. Waite has every requisite except repute."[13] The following morning President Grant sent Waite's nomination to the Senate where, considering the pandemonium resulting from his earlier nominations, lack of repute may have been a positive factor. It took the Senate only two days to confirm the nomination by a vote of sixty-three to zero.

The Civil War was less than a decade in the past when Waite took the office of chief justice in March 1874. The Court's docket still contained some cases that involved disputes growing directly out of the war. In one the Court upheld a ruling that a loan of Confederate currency, made in May 1862, could not be repaid in Confederate currency that had become worthless after the war.[14] Scattered cases of this sort, some involving confiscation of property by Union or Confederate troops, remained on the docket for another decade.[15] Although they are not important in terms of constitutional development, they serve as a reminder that the Civil War was not history to Americans of Waite's time. It was recent memory.

By far the most lasting legacy of the Civil War in terms of constitutional law was the ratification of the three postwar amendments to the Constitution. Two of these Reconstruction Amendments had relatively straightforward expressed purposes. The Thirteenth Amendment, ratified in 1865, prohibited slavery and involuntary servitude. The Fifteenth Amendment, ratified in 1870, guaranteed that the right to vote shall not be denied because of a citizen's race, color, or previous condition of servitude. The Fourteenth Amendment, ratified in 1868, is less explicit. Section 1 reads: "All persons born or naturalized in the United States, and subject to the jurisdiction thereof, are citizens of the United States and of the State wherein they reside. No State shall make or enforce any law which shall abridge the privileges or immunities of citizens of the United States; nor shall any State deprive any person of life, liberty, or property, without due process of law; nor deny to any person within its jurisdiction the equal protection of the laws." Although the meaning of this language has remained controversial to this day, it is fair to say that, like the other two Reconstruction Amendments, its most immediate purpose was to guarantee political and civil rights for the former slaves. But the language of the Fourteenth Amendment is both vague and sweeping. Ultimately its reach would be as well.

Many of the ideas contained in these amendments—abolition of slavery, the right to vote, U.S. citizenship, privileges and immunities of citizens, due process, and equal protection—would be first defined and explained during the Waite Court era. The first case to address them, however, was decided on April 14, 1873, about nine months before Waite took office. To understand these issues and the legacy of the Waite Court it is necessary to go back to that time.

The case, known as the *Slaughterhouse Cases,* involved a Louisiana statute designed to centralize and regulate the slaughtering industry in the city of New Orleans.[16] There was little question of the need to regulate the industry. New Orleans butchers traditionally dumped waste, called offal, into the Mississippi River. And because most slaughterhouses were located upstream of the city, their means of discarding garbage contaminated the city's water supply. A city health official graphically described the problem: "Barrels filled with entrails, liver, blood, urine, dung, and other refuse, portions in an advanced stage of decomposition, are constantly being thrown into the rivers but a short distance from the banks, poisoning the air with offensive smells and necessarily contaminating the water near the bank for miles."[17] As a result of these practices, New Orleans suffered repeated cholera epidemics and gained a reputation as one of the unhealthiest cities in the United States.[18]

To address the problem, the Louisiana legislature passed a law authorizing one centralized slaughterhouse downstream from the city. It granted to the Crescent City Live-Stock Landing and Slaughterhouse Company an exclusive twenty-five-year franchise to build and operate the facility. The statute also prohibited slaughtering for profit in any other location. One company would control the central slaughtering facility under this plan, but the statute did not create a monopoly on the business of slaughtering. To the contrary, it expressly prohibited the company from refusing to allow any butcher to slaughter animals in its facilities, and it strictly regulated the fees the company could receive for the use of the facilities.[19]

The Louisiana legislature's approach to reducing the health problems associated with slaughtering animals in urban environments was not the least bit unusual at that time. European nations had much earlier used a system of centralized slaughterhouses, and by 1869 many American cities had adopted the practice as well.[20] The idea was not unique to the slaughtering industry. Using a centralized public market as a means of regulating trade and assuring safe products was a common practice in nineteenth-century America, fully supported by legal precedent.[21] Even the technique of giving an exclusive franchise to a private company was entirely common and sanctioned in constitutional law. In short, the legislature's plan to control the industry fit neatly into the mid-nineteenth-century ideal of the well-ordered market as well as the current trends for regulating businesses that posed a danger to the public health. Yet the plan met vehement resistance. Opponents charged that the statute was a product of corruption. The result, they claimed, was the grant of exclusive privilege to a monopoly of outsiders with no experience in the slaughtering industry. Politics and race also factored into the opposition. Enacted in 1869, the slaughterhouse law was a product of a Reconstruction legislature in which blacks joined with white Republicans to form a plurality in both houses in Louisiana. Many New Orleans whites chafed at being governed by a legislature made up of blacks and "carpetbaggers" and were inclined to view any laws it enacted as illegitimate.[22] Opposition also came from the established butchers of New Orleans, who sought an injunction in the state courts to prevent the company from implementing the terms of the slaughterhouse statute. After a series of suits and countersuits lasting more than a year, the Louisiana Supreme Court upheld the statute.[23]

Before ratification of the Reconstruction Amendments, the decision of the state's highest court would have ended the dispute. Under the view of federalism prevalent at the time, the federal government was supreme in its sphere of activity. But the federal sphere of authority was relatively small. It included only those powers enumerated in or implied by the Constitution. The vast majority of governmental functions, which were left to the states, were called the "police power of the states."

The boundaries of the "police power of the states" were broad and only vaguely defined. Typically judges described the state's police power as the power to make rules governing health, safety, education, morals, peace and good order, and the general welfare of the state. Over time, the definition would become controversial. In the 1870s, however, the slaughterhouse law was generally thought to be the kind of regulation that fell within the "police power of the states." Most lawyers and judges of the time would have agreed that the determination of how to regulate the slaughterhouse industry, or whether to regulate it at all, was entirely up to the states. With a display of adroit legal skill and good imagination, the independent butchers' attorney, John Campbell, used the new amendments to the Constitution to give the case a new life in the federal courts. Campbell took full advantage of the fact that the Reconstruction Amendments had not yet been tested in the Supreme Court. Posturing the dispute as one of arbitrary government power versus individual liberty, he argued that the new amendments gave the federal courts the authority to secure individual liberty, individual property, and individual security and honor from unjust legislation of state governments. His argument tied together the Thirteenth Amendment's prohibition of slavery and indentured servitude and the Fourteenth Amendment's guarantee that no state shall deny the privileges or immunities of citizens of the United States. He maintained that these privileges and immunities included immunity from compulsory work at the will of or for the profit of another, and a guarantee that any man may engage in any lawful pursuit for which he may have the requisite capacity, skill, or capital. They also included a right to be entitled to the full fruits of one's labor and a right to be free from monopoly.

It was true, he admitted, that the white butchers of New Orleans were not handcuffed and taken away in chains, as had been African slaves. Nevertheless, Campbell argued, the guarantees of the amendments were not confined to any race or class. Their guarantee of free labor applied to the white butchers as well as former slaves. The butchers had been compelled to close up their shops and prohibited from engaging in their trade except on the property and for the profit of the corporation. Their rights had been taken away and become the sole and exclusive privilege of a single corporation.[24]

John Campbell was a former justice of the U.S. Supreme Court who had resigned when Louisiana joined the Confederacy. His legal skill was legendary. But it was not enough to convince a majority of the Supreme Court that the slaughterhouse act violated the Constitution. Writing for a five-to-four majority, Justice Samuel Miller ruled that under the American system of government, the states had the power to regulate businesses such as the slaughtering industry. A Lincoln appointee, Miller took a seat on the Court in 1862 and served until 1890, two years after Waite's death. Miller's background gave him a unique perspective of the conflict over the slaughterhouse legislation. Born and raised on a farm in rural Kentucky, the future Supreme Court justice stood six feet tall and weighed more than two hundred pounds by the time he was a young adult. He looked like a strapping farm boy, but his inclinations pointed elsewhere.

When he was fourteen, Miller left the farm and went to work in a local drugstore. Six years later he entered the Medical School at Transylvania University. A cholera epidemic that hit the United States just before he entered school peaked his interest in prevention of disease and epidemics. And although the treatments he learned—bloodletting and doses of calomel or turpentine to induce vomiting—eventually and happily went out of favor, the experience instilled in him an interest in the prevention of disease and epidemics.

In 1836 Miller opened a medical practice in Barbourville, Kentucky, a stopping point for people traveling across the Cumberland Gap along the Old Wilderness Road. He saw the town plagued by repeated outbreaks of cholera, and although not yet aware of germ theory, he began to suspect that the disease was linked to the water. He also started to become disenchanted with the practice of medicine. In 1842 he married Lucy Ballinger, whose father, uncle, and brother were all lawyers. Perhaps inspired by his wife's family, he began to study law. In 1846 he was admitted to the bar and began practice in Barbourville. With an economy heavily dependent on the traffic of immigrants across the Cumberland Gap, Barbourville was entering upon hard times. By the late 1840s new routes along the Ohio River, along with the development of steamboats and railroads, began to cut into the town's trade. In 1850 the Miller family moved west to the Mississippi River town of Keokuk, Iowa. Barbourville's economic decline was not the only motivation for Miller's move, however. During his years there Miller had become an ardent and vocal opponent of slavery. When, in 1849, Kentucky voters ratified a new proslavery constitution, he decided it was time to leave the dying town and slave state.[25]

At the time, Keokuk was on the verge of an economic boom as a hub for the transportation of farm goods and steamboat traffic. Soon after arriving Miller joined the practice of one of the town's most successful lawyers. Both Keokuk and Miller prospered. But the town's prosperity was not assured. Although it billed itself as "the gate city to the west," it was actually engaged in a fierce competition with Burlington, Iowa, for the right to claim that title. When, in 1856, the main route of the Chicago, Burlington, and Quincy Railroad skipped Keokuk and went to Quincy, Illinois, instead, Keokuk's fortunes began to decline. The town tried to compete by issuing municipal bonds to draw railroads. But its efforts were to no avail. By 1859 Keokuk had only the debt incurred by its bonds, and its only remaining major industry was, ironically, hog slaughtering.[26]

In 1856 Miller participated in Iowa's first Republican Party Convention. Convention delegates chose him as their president and, that same year, nominated him to run for the state senate. Although Miller lost his election, Republicans did well in the state, and John Frémont, the Republican candidate for president, won Iowa. During the next presidential campaign in 1860, Miller vigorously campaigned for Lincoln throughout Iowa and southern Illinois.

In 1862, when Congress passed legislation reorganizing the federal judiciary, Iowa, Minnesota, Kansas, and Missouri were placed into a new Ninth Circuit. Political allies in Iowa had already been pressing for Miller's appointment to a vacant seat on the Supreme Court. Now, with that vacant seat targeted for a justice from a state in the new Ninth Circuit, they got their wish. On July 16, 1862, just one day after enactment of the judicial reorganization law, Lincoln nominated Miller to be an associate justice. Three days later the Senate confirmed the appointment.[27] In Miller, Lincoln undoubtedly appointed a staunch Republican. But as historian Michael A. Ross observes, Miller's political and judicial philosophy was shaped not only by his opposition to slavery but also by the experience of sharing in the dashed dreams of Barbourville and Keokuk. Describing Miller as belonging to the western wing of the

Republican Party, Ross explains that while all Republicans championed the benefits of free rather than slave labor, the western party members eventually came to believe that northeastern capitalists harmed their region in much the same way that slaveholders poisoned the South.[28] Something of this philosophy—its distrust of speculators, financiers, and creditors; its faith in the common farmer and worker; and its belief in the right of voters to address economic problems—was evident in Miller's early decisions.[29] It certainly helps explain his majority opinion in the *Slaughterhouse Cases*. Although the butchers' attorney, John Campbell, complained that the slaughterhouse law created an illegal monopoly, Miller viewed the statute as a normal exercise of the "police power of the states." Moreover he rejected Campbell's portrayal of the nature of that power. Where Campbell portrayed the dispute as a conflict between individual liberty and government power, Miller viewed the police power as a balancing between individual liberty and community interests. The police power, he said, was based not only upon the principle that all people ought to use their property so as not to injure their neighbors, but also upon the principle "that private interests must be made subservient to the general interests of the community."[30]

Miller also rejected Campbell's idea of the degree to which the Reconstruction Amendments had given the federal courts a new tool for overseeing state laws. Under the standard legal doctrine of the time, the Constitution's limitations on the states' use of the police power were very few. Federal courts did overrule acts of state legislatures, but their authority to do so was limited. For example, state laws that interfered with Congress's power to regulate interstate commerce were subject to the scrutiny of the federal courts. In addition, Article I, Section 10, of the Constitution contained a few specific limitations on state authority, most important the provision that no state shall pass any law "impairing the obligation of contracts." Otherwise, the Constitution did not interfere with the "police power of the states." Not even the federal Bill of Rights applied to state legislation.[31]

Campbell had argued that the Reconstruction Amendments changed both the nature of the state's police power and the character of American federalism. The amendments, he argued, placed a new limit on the states by allowing the federal courts greater latitude in protecting individual rights, including some not enumerated in the Constitution, against state legislation. Justice Miller agreed that the Reconstruction Amendments changed the federal system in some ways. That much was obvious. But he was unwilling to agree that the amendments' framers intended to reshape American federalism or create new rights. He believed the amendments had a much more limited purpose.

Although Miller did not try to precisely define that purpose, he did provide some parameters. "No one can fail to be impressed with the one pervading purpose found in [the Reconstruction Amendments], lying at the foundation of each, and without none of them would have been even suggested; we mean the freedom of the slave race, the security and firm establishment of that freedom, and the protection of the newly-made freeman and citizen from the oppressions of those who had formerly exercised dominion over him."[32] Miller made it clear that he was not saying only former slaves or African Americans could share in the amendments' protections.

Rather, he said, this pervading purpose should be used as a guideline. In construing the amendments the Court should look at their pervading spirit and the evil they were designed to remedy.[33]

Miller's opinion for the majority also rejected Campbell's claim that the slaughterhouse law violated his clients' constitutionally guaranteed rights to freely engage in their business or profession. In doing so Miller focused on the Fourteenth Amendment's guarantee: "No State shall make or enforce any law which shall abridge the privileges or immunities of citizens of the United States." Miller began by explaining that under the American system of federalism, certain rights were derived from being a citizen of the United States, and other rights were derived from being a citizen of a state. The privileges and immunities clause, he ruled, protects only the former. He provided some examples of what he considered to be the privileges and immunities of citizens of the United States, mentioning the right of habeas corpus, the right to petition Congress, and some others. But Miller did not intend his list to be exhaustive. It was unnecessary to go any further he said, because the rights the butchers claimed, if they existed at all, certainly did not fall into the category of privileges and immunities of citizens of the United States.[34] Although Miller's interpretation of the privileges and immunities clause was vague, he was clear about two things: the privileges and immunities clause protected some finite set of rights that were based directly on the language of the Constitution, and it did not create any new rights. Four justices dissented from the Court's decision, and three of them wrote separate opinions. The first written dissent came from Justice Stephen Field, who was one of the most flamboyant personalities ever to sit on the nation's high court. The preacher's son was raised in the Berkshire Hills of western Massachusetts and educated at Williams College. He began his career in an unremarkable fashion when he studied law and joined the practice of his brother David Dudley Field.[35]

In 1849, however, Stephen Field, like many other Americans, caught gold fever. Leaving his brother's New York practice, he traveled by boat to Panama, crossed the isthmus, and made his way up the Pacific Coast to California. He landed in San Francisco in the heat of the Gold Rush and quickly headed to Marysville, a budding supply center for the gold fields. The story of Field's experiences is the stuff of western novels. His memoir of the time tells of staring down William R. Turner, a local judge who threatened to "cut off his ear and shoot him on the spot." Field brings order to a courtroom by pulling out a pistol and threatening to shoot rowdy spectators. He challenges a fellow legislator to a duel, is saved from attack in a saloon, and is bushwhacked on the street while unarmed. Describing his experience as a pioneer, he recalled, "There was a smack of adventure to it. The going to a country comparatively unknown and taking part of the fashioning of its institutions, was an attractive subject of contemplation."[36]

Indeed, Field did take part in fashioning the institutions of California. Citizens of Marysville elected him as their first alcalde, the town's chief administrative and judicial officer. Active in the Democratic Party, he served one term in the state assembly in 1851. In 1857 he won election to the California Supreme Court and later became chief justice. Field was serving in that capacity in 1863 when Congress expanded the size of the U.S. Supreme Court during the Civil War, and Lincoln appointed him as the tenth justice. Like Miller, Field sat on the Court throughout the Waite era and beyond. When he retired in 1897 he had been on the Court for more than thirty-four years, setting a new record for longevity.

Throughout the Civil War and after, Field remained loyal to the Union and to the Democratic Party. In part, he owed his appointment to the Court to circumstances. Lincoln wanted a Californian on the Court, and Field held the highest judicial office in the state. He also had the support of many of the state's most important politicians. Ultimately, though, he owed much to the influence of his brother David Dudley, who had become a leader in the antislavery movement, joined the Republican Party, and been an early supporter of Lincoln.

Field possessed admirable intellect, a strong will, and an irascible personality that made him a lightning rod for controversy. As a state assemblyman and state judge Field was involved in shaping both the personal fortunes of Californians and the ideological backdrop of California. He continued to influence California politics after he took a seat on the bench. This was in part because U.S. Supreme Court justices were each assigned as the chief federal judge for a particular circuit. Until 1891, when Congress reorganized the judiciary creating the circuit courts of appeals, justices traveled to their circuit to hold court. As the U.S. Supreme Court justice who was responsible for riding the circuit covering California, Field returned to his home state just about every year. He was essentially the highest federal judicial authority in California.

This had the effect of making him even more influential in shaping the fortunes of the state, and even more controversial. Admirers say he brought order to the law in the new state. That may be true, but it was a certain brand of order, one that often favored the interests of large landowners and the Southern Pacific Railroad. At least that is the way it was perceived by homesteaders, independent miners, and the antimonopoly movement, who counted Field among their worst of enemies.[37]

Field's dissent in the *Slaughterhouse Cases* contained the embryo of a constitutional theory for which he is most remembered. The theory was founded upon two principles that grew out of the Fourteenth Amendment's guarantee that no state shall deprive any person of life, liberty, or property without due process of law. One of the principles later became known as "substantive due process." The most conventional meaning of due process was that it guaranteed that a person could not be deprived of property or liberty without proper judicial procedure. The theory of substantive due process went farther. It held that due process did not only mean that the proper procedures must be followed. It also required that the substance of any legislation that had the effect of depriving a person of liberty or property must be fair and just. The other principle, "liberty of contract," was founded upon the theory that the Fourteenth Amendment's protection of liberty and property included a right to enter into contracts free from government interference.[38]

These ideas would be debated in many cases during the Waite era but never fully accepted. After the Waite era, however, they would be molded into a doctrine of entrepreneurial liberty that allowed the Court to use the Fourteenth Amendment as a limit on state governments' power to regulate the economy. That doctrine, which is sometimes referred to as laissez-faire constitutionalism, would last from the end of the nineteenth century until 1937.

Field argued in his *Slaughterhouse* dissent that the Reconstruction Amendments had changed the relative powers of the state and national governments in very significant ways.[39] If Miller's narrow reading was correct, he warned, the amendments were "vain and idle enactment[s] which accomplished nothing."[40] Field disagreed not only with Miller's definition of federalism but also with his conclusion that the Reconstruction Amendments did not create new rights. In this early version of his thinking Field's attention focused on the privileges and immunities clause. "The privileges and immunities designated are those which of [natural and inalienable] right belong to the citizens of all free governments," he noted. "Clearly among these must be placed the right to pursue lawful employment in a lawful manner without other restraint than such as equally affects all persons."[41]

Justice Joseph Bradley wrote a separate dissent that took Field's general complaint in a different direction. Bradley agreed with Field that the Reconstruction Amendments were not limited to race but also guaranteed to all citizens of the United States rights common to citizens of all free states. He also agreed that among these rights was the right to pursue a lawful calling and that the slaughterhouse law violated this right. However, Bradley's opinion added one very important element to Field's formula. Where Field hinged his right to pursue a lawful calling on the Fourteenth Amendment as a whole, emphasizing the privileges and immunities clause, Bradley specifically stated that prohibiting people from entering into lawful employment "deprive[s] them of their liberty as well as property, *without due process of law.*"[42] While Bradley may not have realized it at the time, this addition was extremely significant because by the turn of the century the due process clause would become a powerful and controversial tool that the Supreme Court used to expand its oversight of state legislation.[43]

In his arguments Campbell had emphasized the evil of monopoly.[44] Field and Bradley picked up on that theme. Field emphasized the state's misuse of power. The act of Louisiana, he said, was a naked case of the state taking away the right to pursue a lawful and necessary calling and vesting it exclusively for twenty-five years in a single corporation.[45] Bradley focused on state action as well, but he also appeared to leave open the possibility that monopoly posed a danger regardless of whether it was state imposed.

The difference between Field's and Bradley's views of monopoly in their *Slaughterhouse* dissents seemed merely one of emphasis. A few years later, however, the two would split in the case of *Munn v. Illinois,* another case involving charges of monopoly.[46] Then their opinions would reflect more substantial differences in their views about the powers of government, the rights of the community, and monopoly as the source of privilege and a threat to liberty.

With the benefit of that hindsight, it is possible to detect a different tone in the opinions of the two men. Field's total emphasis was on state interference with individual rights. Quoting from Adam Smith and Sir William Blackstone, he emphasized that free government, in the American sense of the term, is one "under which the inalienable right of every citizen to pursue his happiness is unrestrained, except by just, equal, and impartial laws."[47] Bradley noted that the statute was dangerous for reasons other than its interference with pure individual rights. Exclusive privileges like the slaughterhouse law, he wrote, "are getting to be more and more regarded as wrong in principle, and as inimical to the just right and greatest good of the people."[48] For him, the state had the duty not only to avoid passing laws that interfered with individual rights but also to protect the good of the people. He went a step further. "This right to choose one's calling is an essential part of that liberty *which it is the object of government to protect;* and a calling, when chosen, is a man's property right. Liberty and property are not protected where these rights are arbitrarily assailed."[49] He did not specify who or what posed the threat.

Given his background, Bradley's distaste for monopoly must have surprised contemporary observers. In contrast to the western frontiersmen Waite, Miller, and Field, Bradley stepped onto the Court from the highest levels of the eastern establishment. He was not born into privilege but rather attained influence and power through discipline, diligence, and perseverance.

Born in Berne, a small town in upstate New York, Bradley was the first of twelve children. From an early age he displayed a strong desire for learning. Formal education in Berne took place only in the winter, when children were not otherwise occupied with chores. Although his parents were farmers, they prided themselves in learning and maintained a general library in the family home. After Bradley had devoured its contents, along with the contents of his uncle's library, he decided that he needed a more formal education.

A local teacher and Dutch Reform minister took him under his wing and helped to prepare Bradley for admission to Rutgers College—which was then affiliated with the Dutch Reform church. Bradley, who was one of the college's brightest students, graduated from Rutgers in three years. While there he made several influential friends. Perhaps the most influential of them was Frederick Frelinghuysen, the son of a prominent New Jersey family who would become a noted Republican senator and President Chester Arthur's secretary of state.[50]

After graduation from Rutgers, Bradley studied law and was admitted to the New Jersey bar in 1839. He soon joined the office of John P. Jackson, a successful attorney whose clients included the New Jersey Railroad and Transportation Company. This company was one of the myriad of holdings connected to the Joint Companies, a corporation so powerful in the New Jersey transportation industry and in New Jersey politics that it was simply called "the Monopoly." His association with Jackson thus opened the door for Bradley to become one of the most important railroad lawyers in New Jersey. By the time he was appointed to the Supreme Court, Bradley was chief counsel for the Joint Companies and one of its key lobbyists in both Newark and Washington. He also served as a director of the company and several of its subsidiaries.[51] Payment for his services often included company stock, which, in a display of ethics not very common in his time, he sold before taking his seat on the high court.[52]

Although business interests required Bradley to be deeply involved with politics, he did not seem particularly interested in elected office. Bradley began political life as a Whig in a strongly Democratic state. When the Whig Party collapsed in the late 1850s, he joined a coalition called the Opposition, which successfully elected the governor and several other state officials. As the Civil War approached, Bradley remained a strong advocate for preservation of the Union. Although he did not immediately link himself to the Republican Party, in 1860 he joined his friend Frelinghuysen and other Opposition members in supporting Lincoln.

By 1862 Bradley identified himself as a Union Republican. In an unsuccessful run for Congress on that ticket, he campaigned on a platform of preserving the Union. In these years Bradley did not appear to be motivated by a desire to abolish the institution of slavery. By the war's end, however, he came to believe that the preservation of the Union and the end of slavery were intertwined. He had also by that time become a full-fledged Republican.[53]

Although Bradley's political credentials did not make him an obvious choice for the Supreme Court, he was a prominent lawyer, having appeared before the Court six times in his career.[54] In addition, his connection to railroad interests made him a powerful insider who had influential friends. On February 7, 1870, when President Grant had the opportunity to make two appointments to the Supreme Court, one went to William Strong, who sat on the bench until 1880. The other went to Bradley, who was confirmed on March 22, 1870.[55] Bradley, like Miller and Field, also outlasted the Waite era. He was still serving on the Court when he died on January 22, 1892.

By all accounts Bradley was an eccentric man with a less than cheery personality. Cortlant Parker, his friend from Rutgers, described Bradley as "amusingly petulant" and "naturally eccentric."[56] Near the end of Bradley's career a less friendly observer of the Court described him as follows: "Bradley is a little dried-up anatomy of a man. . . . He has a big nose, sharp bright little eyes, iron grey hair and a pair of tightly closed lips. His skin hangs in wrinkles and all of his fat has long since gone to figures and judicial decisions. He is seventy-seven years old, but there is a chance he will live at least twenty-three years longer. There is not much of him to die, and when his soul is disembodied it will not be much freer than it is now."[57]

Given such unflattering descriptions of his personality, one might wonder how Bradley was ever successful as a lawyer and lobbyist. Perhaps it was because his contemporaries also agreed that he was highly intelligent and fair-minded. Historian Charles Fairman, an admirer of Bradley, noted that he possessed many of the characteristics of a great justice. In one respect in particular Fairman ranked Bradley as "No. 1 in the long list of justices." It was in his ability to pursue inquiry back to the crucial fact.[58]

In his *Slaughterhouse* dissent that "crucial fact" appears to be the existence of the monopoly. But given the fact that central slaughterhouses similar to the one in New Orleans were a common method of assuring sanitary conditions in urban slaughterhouses, it is hard to understand why Field and Bradley so fully bought into Campbell's attack on the monopoly. The explanation, for Bradley, at least, may be tied to a belief in the supremacy of the Union that he had displayed in the Civil War years and a view of the South that he had developed since then. His depiction of the slaughterhouse law as "one of those arbitrary and unjust laws made in the interest of a few scheming individuals, by which some of the Southern States have, within the past few years, been so deplorably oppressed and impoverished" clearly reflected a disenchantment with Reconstruction governments in the South.[59]

But Bradley's account of the purpose of the Reconstruction Amendments reveals an even more fundamental prejudice about the Southern states. "The mischief to be remedied was not merely slavery and its incidents and consequences," he wrote, "but that spirit of insubordination and disloyalty to the National government which had troubled the country for so many years in some of the States, and that intolerance of free speech and free discussion which often rendered life and property insecure, and led to much unequal legislation." Bradley concluded the Reconstruction Amendments represented "an attempt to give voice to the strong National yearning" for a condition in which American citizenship guaranteed the full enjoyment of every right and every privilege belonging to every freeman.[60] Although he wrote confidently here about a strong yearning to guarantee the rights of national citizenship, as we shall see in the coming chapters, Bradley was soon less confident about just what those rights were and what was the power of the national government to protect them.

The last of the dissenters, Justice Noah Swayne, could trace his American heritage to ancestors who had settled in William Penn's Quaker colony in 1710. Swayne, whose family moved to northern Virginia, was the youngest of nine children. His father died when Noah was four years old, leaving his widowed mother to support the family. Nevertheless Swayne received a good education for the times. He attended local schools until he was thirteen, then studied at a respected Quaker academy.

Like Miller, Swayne began his professional career studying medicine. He soon changed to law, however. After reading law in the office of a prominent attorney, he was admitted to the Virginia bar in 1823 at nineteen years of age. He then moved to Ohio to start his legal career.

Swayne began his political career as a Jacksonian Democrat. He was twice elected to the Ohio legislature and was appointed by Andrew Jackson to serve as the U.S. attorney for the District of Ohio. But Swayne was an ardent opponent of slavery and eventually grew uncomfortable with the Democratic Party's proslavery stance. He switched to the Republican Party in the 1850s and worked for its first presidential candidate, John Frémont, in 1856. Then, in 1860, he campaigned for Abraham Lincoln, who won both the Republican nomination and the presidency. Swayne, who also played an active part in securing the ratification of the Fifteenth Amendment, was committed to the Republican plan for Reconstruction.

Swayne had no judicial experience before his appointment to the Supreme Court, but he did have the support of the governor of Ohio and the state's entire congressional delegation. More significant, Justice John McLean, who was about to retire, made it known to the president that he wanted Swayne to succeed him. Thus, on January 21, 1862, President Lincoln nominated Swayne as his first appointment to the Supreme Court.[61]

In his first years on the high court Swayne proved to be an ardent supporter of national power, so his dissent in the *Slaughterhouse Cases* came as no surprise. He was not very certain about why the slaughterhouse law denied New Orleans butchers of their constitutional rights. To some extent, he deferred to Field and Bradley on that score. But Swayne, a staunch Republican, was very explicit about the reach of the Fourteenth Amendment. He vehemently attacked Miller's idea that the Court should be guided by the framer's intent to protect the rights of former slaves. The amendment makes no distinction on account of race or color, Swayne observed. "This court has no authority to interpolate a limitation that is neither expressed nor implied." Conveniently ignoring that he and his fellow dissenters proposed to mold into the Constitution a new right—the right to pursue a lawful occupation—he then concluded that the Court's duty "is to execute the law, not to make it."[62] Swayne was equally clear in his opinion about the impact of the Reconstruction Amendments on federalism. "By the Constitution, as it stood before the war, ample protection was given against oppression by the Union, but little was given against wrongs and oppression by the States. That want was intended to be supplied by this [the Fourteenth] amendment."[63]

Some of today's critics of the *Slaughterhouse* majority opinion maintain that Miller's very limited definition of the privileges and immunities that are derived from being a citizen of the United States virtually scratched the privileges and immunities clause from the Constitution. His narrow reading, they say, thus severely weakened the Fourteenth Amendment's protection for African Americans.[64] That was not Miller's intent, however. Rather, he was driven by the fear of expanding the amendment's protections beyond race.[65] Responding to the *Slaughterhouse* dissenters, Miller worried that an interpretation of the new amendments that would create new rights and radically change the federal system "would constitute this court as a perpetual censor upon all legislation of the States."[66]

Even the dissenters would have to agree that their right to pursue a lawful calling could not be absolute. That would leave the courts with the extremely subjective task of determining what legislation was legitimate and what legislation was oppressive. This was made obvious in another case decided on the same day as the *Slaughterhouse Cases.*

Bradwell v. Illinois raised the question of whether a state's refusal to allow a woman to practice law violated her constitutional rights. In 1869 Myra Bradwell petitioned the Illinois Supreme Court for a license to practice law. Bradwell had studied law in her husband's office and passed the Illinois bar exam with high honors. Later she would create the *Chicago Legal News* and mold it into one of the most important legal publications in the nation. She undoubtedly possessed the skills necessary to practice law. Yet the Illinois high court denied her petition, ruling that she was not of the class of persons the legislature had intended to be admitted to the practice of law.[67]

Like the New Orleans butchers, Bradwell argued that the state's refusal to grant her a law license violated her right to choose a profession or trade. The right to choose a profession or trade was recognized as a privilege and immunity of every white citizen, she argued. The Fourteenth Amendment clearly made it a privilege and immunity of every black citizen and, by implication, a privilege and immunity of female citizens as well.⁶⁸

Since they did not agree that the right to choose a profession was one of the privileges and immunities of citizens of the United States, Miller and the *Slaughterhouse* majority had no difficulty in rejecting Bradwell's claim. However Justices Bradley, Field, and Swayne, who had been champions of the butchers' right to pursue a lawful trade, now agreed with Miller. In their opinion the privileges and immunities of women as citizens do not guarantee a right to engage in any and every profession or occupation. "The natural and proper timidity and delicacy which belongs to the female sex evidently unfits it for many occupations of civil life," Bradley observed. "The paramount destiny and mission of a woman are to fulfill the noble and benign offices of wife and mother. This is the law of the Creator."⁶⁹ In *Bartemeyer v. Iowa*, still another case argued at the same time as the *Slaughterhouse Cases*, a saloon keeper maintained that a state law prohibiting the sale of liquor deprived him of his right to choose a trade or calling and deprived him of his property without due process of law.⁷⁰ It should come as no surprise that Miller and the *Slaughterhouse* majority rejected his argument. That was fully consistent with their position that the Reconstruction Amendments had not created new rights. What is more interesting is that Field, Bradley, and Swayne agreed with the outcome, which also seems at odds with their dissents in the *Slaughterhouse Cases*.

The fact that *Bartemeyer* did not involve a state-granted monopoly might have had something to do with their change of heart. But Field, in a concurring opinion, revealed that the difference had more to do with the reach of the right to pursue a lawful calling and the nature of the state's police power. "No one has ever pretended . . . that the Fourteenth Amendment interferes in any respect with the police power of the State," he wrote. "That power embrace[s] all regulations affecting the health, good order, morals, peace, and safety of society."⁷¹ Apparently, for the *Slaughterhouse* dissenters, Louisiana's plan to save downstream citizens from the ravages of disease was not a regulation affecting health, safety, or morals. Iowa's plan to save its citizens from the ravages of drink was.

All of these cases involved the question of what rights the new amendments to the Constitution protected, and to what degree they remolded the antebellum meaning of federalism by increasing the national government's power over the states. *Bradwell* and *Bartemeyer* showed that these matters were complex and that even the most nationalistic of the justices realized that there were limits to the Court's oversight of state legislation. Nevertheless, on the eve of Waite's appointment as chief justice, the Court seemed to be aligned five to four with regard to the meaning of the Reconstruction Amendments. Justices Clifford, Davis, Strong, and Hunt agreed with Miller's opinion that the amendments should have a very limited impact. Justices Field, Bradley, and Swayne, along with Chief Justice Chase, believed that the amendments protected a wide range of rights and substantially changed the federal system.

Chief Justice Chase, who was ill at the time the Court decided the *Slaughterhouse Cases,* would die within the month.[72]

As the new chief justice, Waite seemed to be walking into a hornets' nest occupied by men of big egos debating even bigger issues. Some thought he was not up to the task. Later Waite's biographer C. Peter Magrath wrote: "As an individual Morrison Waite was not spectacular. He lacked the intellectual brilliance of a Bradley, the boldness of a Field, the wit of a Harlan, and the aggressiveness of a Miller."[73] Although Waite was not well received at first, members of the Court warmed to him. His colleagues and later commentators agreed that he was a congenial, honest, and fair man who successfully managed the business of the Court and the often difficult relations among its members. This modest endorsement is usually all Waite receives, but a deeper look will show that he did more. The new chief justice had ideas of his own to add to the mix.

2

Freedom Detoured

Although Justice Miller had emphasized that the pervading purpose of the post–Civil War amendments was "freedom of the slave race" and "the protection of the newly made freeman and citizens from oppression," neither the *Slaughterhouse Cases* nor *Bartemeyer* nor *Bradwell* involved protecting the rights of African Americans. This changed in 1876 with two cases that tested the federal government's power to guarantee equal rights for blacks.

The source of Congress's power came from the Thirteenth, Fourteenth, and Fifteenth amendments themselves. All three include an enforcement provision. Section 5 of the Fourteenth Amendment is typical, "The Congress shall have power to enforce, by appropriate legislation, the provisions of this article." Just what this meant in practice was not as self-evident as it might seem and is still debated today.[1]

Republicans in Congress did not believe they could depend on the states, especially the former Confederate states, to assure equal rights for blacks. They feared that state action in the form of discriminatory policies, or state indifference, would thwart the amendments' promise of equal rights and protection from oppression. And they believed the amendments gave Congress broad and sweeping powers to step in and guarantee rights for blacks when it determined the states would not. With Republicans in control during Reconstruction, Congress enacted a number of laws designed to do just that. Most of these laws were challenged in the courts, and, although they raised a variety of issues, the underlying constitutional question in each of the cases asked to what degree the enforcement sections of the Thirteenth, Fourteenth, and Fifteenth amendments allowed Congress to enact laws that encroached on the sphere of authority that had traditionally been reserved to the states.

United States v. Cruikshank (1876) and *United States v. Reese* (1876) presented the Waite Court with the first opportunities to define the parameters of Congress's power. Both of these cases tested federal legislation called the Enforcement Act of May 31, 1870. Section 6 of this law made it a federal crime for two or more persons to conspire to injure, oppress, threaten, or intimidate any citizen in the free exercise or enjoyment of any right or privilege secured to citizens by the Constitution or laws of the United States or because of that citizen having exercised those rights or privileges. It also made it a crime to go in disguise with the intent of hindering another in the exercise of those rights and privileges.[2]

The trail of events leading to the first of these cases, *Cruikshank,* had nothing to do with abstract notions of Congress's power or the traditional sphere of state authority. It began on April 13, 1873, the day before the Supreme Court announced its decision in the *Slaughterhouse Cases.* On that Easter Sunday a group of heavily armed whites surrounded blacks who had gathered in the Colfax, Louisiana, courthouse. At the end of the day somewhere between 60 and 105 blacks were dead.[3] The count of the dead is disputed. That, by any standard, many were murdered in cold blood is not.

The Colfax massacre was possibly the worst instance of racial violence in Louisiana since the end of the Civil War, but it was not an isolated incident. Violence in Louisiana, as in other Southern states during the Reconstruction era, had political as well as racial undercurrents. Republicans controlled state governments during Reconstruction, but the grip of this coalition of Northerners who had settled in the South before the war, Northern carpetbaggers who had arrived after the war, and recently freed blacks was tenuous. It depended to some degree on the requirement that former Confederates take oaths swearing loyalty to the Union. Those unable or unwilling to do so were disqualified from voting. Even more, it depended on the reliable support of black men who had just obtained the right to vote. In the years right after the war the presence of the federal army helped guarantee that blacks would actually be allowed to vote.

Conservative whites "rejected the legitimacy of Republican government based on Negro suffrage."[4] Some organized into societies and clubs such as the Knights of the White Camellia, Swamp Fox Rangers, and Ku Klux Klan, and sought to restore white rule by violence and intimidation.

The Louisiana elections of April 1868 passed without incident, and Republican Henry Clay Warmoth became governor in July. The presidential election in the fall of that same year was another matter, however. Beginning in May armed gangs of whites began a campaign of murder and terror across the state. Commonly they singled out black leaders such as William R. Meadows, a state representative from Claiborne Parish. Other times they engaged in violence against Republican meetings and parades. State officials reported that the campaign of violence resulted in 784 people killed and 450 wounded. A later federal investigation placed the figures even higher.[5] The violence seemed to have had its intended effect. In the November 1868 presidential election President Grant, a Republican incumbent, received only about half the number of votes that had been cast earlier that year for Warmoth, the victorious Republican candidate for governor.[6]

Governor Warmoth's two-pronged response to the crisis set the scene for the showdown in Colfax. On the one hand, the governor sought to encourage peace by allowing conservative whites and Democrats to share in government patronage. On the other hand, he planned to maintain a grip on political power by controlling a "State Returning Board" with the power to canvass elections, discard polls where irregularities occurred, and declare the winners. To assure that his allies would be able to control the board, the governor, lieutenant governor, and secretary of state were made ex officio members.

Warmoth's strategy seemed to be working when Republicans won significant victories in the elections of 1870. However, while appeasement in the form of sharing patronage with Democrats may have satisfied some Democrats and conservative whites, the governor was fast losing support within his own party. Liberal Republicans viewed the appeasement strategy as a sign of weakness and desertion of the Republican cause. Consequently, by the time of the 1872 gubernatorial election the party became hopelessly split. Warmoth threw his support to a Fusion Party made up of conservative Republicans and Democrats. Liberal Republicans ran a separate ticket with William Pitt Kellogg their candidate for governor. One historian has described the election that followed as "some bizarre political theater of the absurd."[7]

The collapse of Republican dominance meant that the State Returning Board could not guarantee the party's victory. Instead, the board split into two panels: one declaring Kellogg the winner, the other awarding victory to the Fusion Party candidate John D. McEnery. Each took the oath of office on January 14, 1873. With two rival sets of governors, legislatures, and lower officials each claiming rightful authority, anarchy reigned in Louisiana. The dispute was not resolved until five months later when President Grant recognized the Kellogg government. In the interim, however, politically and racially motivated violence increased throughout the state.

This political turmoil provided the final ingredient for violence in Colfax, a small village that was the seat of government for Grant Parish. This new parish, named after the president, had been carved out of what had been a Democratic stronghold in the northern part of the state.[8] With a large majority of black citizens, it was intended to create a safe district for Republicans.

As in much of the rest of the state in 1873, both sides claimed victory in Grant County. In the confusion, three Republicans slipped through a window and occupied the courthouse. One of them was William Ward, a black Union army veteran and the leader of an all-black company of local militia. The others were R. C. Register, a black man who was the Republican candidate for sheriff, and Daniel Shaw, a white man who was the party's choice for judge.[9]

As news of their occupation and fear of impending violence spread, black residents and some white Republicans flocked to the courthouse in Colfax for protection. The defenders, only a few of whom were armed, constructed a crude barrier around the courthouse and built two cannons out of pipe. A few days later an army of whites arrived on the scene. This heavily armed group, under the leadership of the deposed sheriff Columbus C. Nash, was intent on taking back control of the courthouse and public offices.

After first demanding that the defenders surrender and then allowing women and children to leave, they began an attack. It took only a few skirmishes for the attackers to break through the blacks' outer ring of defense. With the outer ring breached, some of the defenders ran to the woods. Many of the fleeing men were shot and killed. The remaining defenders retreated to what they hoped would be the safety of the courthouse. But the attackers then set fire to the roof of the building. With the building in flames, most of the blacks saw no choice but to raise a white flag to surrender. A few, fearing the worst, hid under the floor and eventually died from asphyxiation.

As the surrendering blacks filed out of the courthouse someone fired shots, hitting two of the white attackers. Although no one was sure where they came from, the shots set off a wholesale slaughter of the surrendering blacks. That night, having been told that they were being taken to a jail, about fifty blacks who had survived were separated into pairs and executed. One of them, Benjamin Brimm, an elderly black man who was shot through the head and in the back, lived to tell of the executions.[10]

When federal troops arrived the next day between 60 and 105 black men and three white men were dead. Because the attackers threw some bodies into the Red River and mourning families carried off others, the precise number will never be known. Some of the white attackers fled to Texas and to other parts of Louisiana. Federal authorities arrested others and took them to New Orleans to stand trial.

Obviously, the most serious charge that could be made against these men was murder. Since both sides of the conflict had been armed, however, charges of murder or other criminal charges might be difficult to sustain. More significant, murder and most such criminal acts were state crimes, and federal authorities did not trust that a Louisiana court or a Louisiana jury would find them guilty. Before the Civil War the only charges these men would have faced would have been state prosecutions for homicide or related crimes. There would have been no possibility of federal jurisdiction. But the Reconstruction Amendments and the Enforcement Act offered a way to make this a federal case.

U.S. Attorney James Roswell Beckwith decided to bring federal charges against some of the white attackers for violating the civil rights of two black men who had been victims of the Colfax massacre: Levi Nelson, who had been killed, and Alexander Tillman, who had survived.

The original indictment, which ran 164 pages, charged that the defendants had violated Section 6 of the Enforcement Act of 1870 by banding together or conspiring to prevent or hinder citizens of the United States from exercising a wide range of rights and privileges guaranteed by the Constitution and laws of the United States. These included specific rights such as the right to peaceable assembly, to keep and bear arms, to their lives and liberty of person, to the equal benefits of laws and property enjoyed by white persons, to vote, and to not be put in danger of bodily harm because of exercising the right to vote.

To these relatively specific charges the prosecutors made a sweeping claim that the conspirators had denied Nelson and Tillman of "rights, privileges, immunities and protections secured to them as citizens of the United States, by reasons of their race or color." They added an even more sweeping claim that the defendants had conspired to deny Nelson and Tillman of the free exercise and enjoyment of "every, each, all, and singular the several rights and privileges secured under the Constitution and laws of the United States." Finally, hoping to stretch the federal reach, the prosecutors formulated a charge of "willful murder while so conspiring."[11]

The trial of the Colfax attackers began on February 23, 1874, in federal court in New Orleans. Presiding was Circuit Court Judge William Woods, an Ohio native and

Yale graduate who had served as a Union general in the Civil War. Woods was a highly regarded jurist and future justice of the U.S. Supreme Court who was appointed by President Hayes in 1880. At the time of the trial, however, he was the federal circuit court judge for the Fifth Circuit, which covered Georgia, Florida, Mississippi, Alabama, Louisiana, and Texas. The Colfax trial kept him in New Orleans for almost two months. But when a jury composed of nine whites and two blacks could not agree on a verdict, Judge Woods declared a mistrial.

A second trial of the Colfax attackers began on May 18, 1874. This time Supreme Court Justice Joseph Bradley, who was riding circuit, joined Judge Woods for part of the proceedings. On June 10, after a trial that lasted almost a month, three of the men, William Cruikshank, John P. Hadnot, and William B. Irwin, were found guilty on the conspiracy charges but not guilty of the charge of murder while conspiring.

Upon hearing the verdict, R. H. Marr, one of the attorneys for the defendants, made a motion for "arrest of judgment." This motion had the effect of asking the court to set aside the guilty verdict. The reason, Marr said, was that the charges brought against his clients were not within the jurisdiction of the federal courts. He claimed, in other words, that parts of the Enforcement Act were unconstitutional. Under the Constitution, he argued, the acts with which the defendants were charged concerned matters reserved to the states.[12]

Marr's motion produced a split opinion in the circuit court. Justice Bradley, agreeing with the defendants' position, was of the opinion that the indictments under which the defendants had been charged were defective and that the defendants should go free. Judge Woods, however, disagreed. He was of the opinion that the indictment had been valid and the convictions should stand. Under the rules of the time, the disagreement between the two judges and the resulting split decision allowed the case to be appealed to the U.S. Supreme Court under a procedure called "certificate of division."[13]

Bradley undoubtedly understood the importance of the issues raised in *Cruikshank*. Some scholars have implied that he split with Woods in order to assure the case would reach the Supreme Court. A clearer indication of the case's importance to Bradley, however, is that he wrote a careful and meticulous opinion for the circuit court.[14]

Democrats, who hoped *Cruikshank* would provide an opportunity to overrule the Enforcement Act and limit the reach of federal power to enforce the Fourteenth and Fifteenth amendments, lined up an impressive array of legal talent to appeal the defendants' cause to the Supreme Court. Reverdy Johnson, a former Democratic senator from Maryland, had been a member of the Joint Committee on Reconstruction—the congressional committee that wrote the Fourteenth Amendment. Philip Phillips was a former congressman who often appeared before the Supreme Court. R. H. Marr was a leading Louisiana lawyer who had handled the defendants' case in the circuit court. To this group was added John A. Campbell, the former U.S. Supreme Court justice who had represented the New Orleans butchers in the *Slaughterhouse Cases,* and David Dudley Field, the brother of sitting Supreme Court Justice Stephen Field.

On appeal, the defense attorneys first argued that the indictments under which their clients were convicted were unconstitutionally vague. But they also wanted to challenge the validity of the Enforcement Act itself, and the Court's decision in the *Slaughterhouse Cases* put them in a good position to do so. Of course they downplayed the part of Justice Miller's opinion that said the one pervading purpose of the Reconstruction Amendments was the freedom of the slaves and the protection of the newly made freemen and citizens from oppression. Otherwise they followed the general tenor of the *Slaughterhouse Cases,* arguing that the Reconstruction Amendments changed little in the American constitutional and legal system, had created no new rights, and did not significantly alter the structure of American federalism. Congress's authority to enforce the Reconstruction Amendments was limited to nullifying any infringement of rights by a state itself, argued David Dudley Field.[15] To define these amendments as giving Congress the power to regulate acts of individuals would result in a comprehensive federal code defining rights, superseding state legislation and reducing the states to mere appendages of the federal government.

This was an especially ironic position for Campbell, who, as attorney for the independent butchers, had vigorously argued that the amendments had given the federal government sweeping new powers to protect the individual's rights, including some rights not expressly written in the Constitution. Likewise, it was an ironic position for David Dudley Field, whose brother had vigorously dissented in the *Slaughterhouse Cases,* arguing that the amendments created a new right—the right to pursue a lawful calling.[16] Ironic though it may have been, this approach proved to be a good tactic.

On March 27, 1876, the Supreme Court overruled the convictions of Cruikshank, Hadnot, and Irwin. Chief Justice Waite wrote the opinion for the majority. Historians have suggested that the outcome may have been in part the result of the government's tactics in the case. Matched against the array of legal talent for the defense were U.S. Attorney General George H. Williams and Solicitor General Samuel Field Phillips, whose arguments were, at best, uninspired.[17] On appeal the government's lawyers decided to focus on just two counts of the original indictment, both of which dealt with conspiracy. One charged that the defendants had conspired to deprive Nelson and Tillman, who were "citizens of the United States of African descent," of their right to vote.[18] The second count charged that the defendants violated Section 6 of the Enforcement Act by conspiring to prevent Nelson and Tillman "from exercising every right granted or secured to them by the Constitution and laws of the United States."[19] The Court ultimately rejected both.

The advantage of the count that charged the defendants with conspiracy to interfere with the two men's right to vote was that it was not vague. The Enforcement Act expressly prohibited conspiracy to interfere with the right to vote. One problem with this charge, however, was that the Colfax massacre did not directly involve denying blacks the right to vote. Although prosecutors might theorize that the massacre represented an effort to intimidate blacks and discourage them from voting, or that it denied blacks the fruit of their electoral victory, the link to voting was tenuous. Everyone knew that the men who defended the Colfax courthouse had been killed because they were black men who had exercised the right to vote and then attempted to claim the political offices they believed they had won.[20] Yet despite these realities, the majority of the Court ruled that this count of the indictment was defective.

Chief Justice Waite's opinion revealed another problem with the charge of conspiracy to deny Nelson and Tillman the right to vote. Waite pointed to *Minor v. Happersett*, a case the Court had decided just a month earlier.[21] There the Court rejected a claim that the privilege and immunities clause of the Fourteenth Amendment required that women be given the right to vote. The *Minor v. Happersett* decision emphasized that qualifications for voting had been left to the states under the original Constitution, and the Fourteenth Amendment did not change that. The right to vote, the Court concluded, was not among the privileges and immunities of citizens of the United States.

Turning back to the indictment in *Cruikshank*, the chief justice had no choice but to recognize that the Fifteenth Amendment did create a new right with respect to voting. It provides that the right to vote shall not be denied on account of race, color, or previous condition of servitude. But Waite took a narrow view of this new right. The Fifteenth Amendment did not give blacks the right to vote, he said. Rather it gave them the right to be free from discrimination on account of race in the exercise of the right to vote.[22]

Therefore, in order to claim that the defendants had conspired to deny Nelson and Tillman of a right guaranteed by the Constitution or laws of the United States, the government would need to claim not that Nelson and Tillman were blacks who had been prevented or discouraged from voting, but that they were prevented or discouraged from voting because they were black. Waite concluded that the government had failed to meet that burden. "We may suspect that race was the cause of the hostility; but it is not so averred," Waite wrote. For him, the failure to expressly state this claim was a fatal flaw in the indictment. Because it was an essential part of the crime, he ruled that the Court would not supply it by implication.[23]

The point of the government's appeal, that the defendants conspired to prevent Nelson and Tillman "from exercising every right granted or secured to them by the Constitution and laws of the United States," posed a different problem for the government attorneys. They might easily demonstrate that the defendants had conspired to deny Nelson and Tillman of some kind of rights. But they would also need to demonstrate that the rights denied were rights that grew from the victims' status as U.S. citizens rather than rights that belonged to citizens of the state. To win, in other words, Williams and Phillips needed to convince the Court to interpret the Fourteenth and Fifteenth amendments in a way that might change both the definition of rights and the structure of federalism. This was an unenviable task given the precedent of the *Slaughterhouse Cases*. Yet with a new court, a new chief justice, and a case involving extending the rights of citizenship to the recently freed blacks—exactly the kind of conflict that Justice Miller had emphasized as the underlying purpose of the amendments—the government may have stood a chance of winning.

FREEDOM DETOURED

The government's attorneys offered several theories of why the defendants had conspired to deny Nelson and Tillman of their rights as citizens of the United States. One theory focused on specific rights by claiming that the defendants had conspired to deprive Nelson and Tillman of their right to peacefully assemble and their right to keep and bear arms.[24] These two rights, being part of the Bill of Rights, are undoubtedly rights of citizens of the United States. Nevertheless Waite rejected the proposition that they were the kind of rights protected by the Fourteenth Amendment or the Enforcement Act.

His rejection of this proposition was based on the 1833 case *Barron v. Baltimore*, where the Supreme Court had ruled that the Bill of Rights did not apply to the states. The right to peacefully assemble and the right to bear arms are written as limitations on Congress, he reasoned. They were guarantees only against interference by the federal government. If, beyond that, individuals possessed a right to assemble or bear arms it was not because they were citizens of the United States but rather because of some kind of natural right or right of citizens of any free society. It thus would be up to the states to choose whether to protect such rights. A claim that the defendants had conspired to deny Nelson and Tillman of their right to petition Congress may have fallen within the statute, he speculated. However, the Colfax massacre did not involve petitioning Congress, and the Enforcement Act did not prohibit conspiracies to prevent a meeting for any lawful purpose whatever.[25]

Waite's reasoning on this point is difficult for the modern mind to understand because, over time, the Supreme Court has ruled that most of the guarantees of the Bill of Rights protect persons against misdeeds of the states as well as the federal government. Americans have consequently come to think of the guarantees of the Bill of Rights as existing by virtue of their status as citizens of the United States. That was not the common understanding in antebellum America, however. The government's theory that the defendants had denied Nelson's and Tillman's right to assemble and right to bear arms was an awkward forerunner to what today has become known as the "incorporation doctrine." This theory expressed the belief that the Fourteenth Amendment changed the rule of *Barron v. Baltimore* and applied the Bill of Rights to the states. It thus required the Court to presume that the Reconstruction Amendments had fundamentally changed the structure of American federalism. In 1876 Chief Justice Waite and the majority were not ready to take that leap.

Federal prosecutors also took a sweeping approach to explain how the defendants had conspired to deprive Nelson and Tillman of their rights as citizens of the United States. The defendants' acts, they argued, represented a conspiracy to deprive the victims of life, liberty, and property without due process of law and to deny them equal protection of the law. This approach rested upon the idea that the guarantees of due process and equal protection, which are found in Section 1 of the Fourteenth Amendment, were themselves rights belonging to citizens of the United States. In essence, the prosecution's theory was that the Fourteenth Amendment prohibited one group of individuals from depriving another group of individuals of due process of law or equal protection of the laws.

Waite rejected that idea. The amendment prohibits a state from depriving a person of life, liberty, or property without due process of law, he reasoned, but adds nothing to the rights of one citizen against another. Likewise, it prohibits a state from denying any person equal protection of the law but does not add anything to the rights of one citizen against another.[26] This reasoning represented an early version of what would later become known as the "state action doctrine."

Perhaps it was because the attorney general and solicitor general suspected their arguments were weak that their second claim also took full advantage of the sweeping language of Section 6 of the Enforcement Act. They argued that the defendants had conspired to hinder Nelson and Tillman in the exercise of "every, each, all, and, singular" rights granted to them by the Constitution and laws of the United States.[27]

The strength of this argument—that it did not specify a particular right but was broad enough to cover all—was also its weakness. It suffered from a defect that in today's legal parlance would be characterized as being "void for vagueness." In criminal cases, the accused has a right to be informed of the nature and cause of the accusation, Waite wrote. Concluding that these charges were too vague and general, the majority ruled that they were "so defective that no judgment of conviction could be pronounced upon them."[28]

Justice Nathan Clifford wrote a separate opinion in which he emphasized that the indictments should be overruled simply because they were vague and indefinite.[29] But Clifford agreed with the majority with respect to the outcome of *Cruikshank*. A unanimous court, having concluded that the indictments were fatally flawed, overturned the verdict and set the defendants free.[30]

Another case decided the same day, *United States v. Reese*, actually addressed the question of whether provisions of the Enforcement Act were constitutional.[31] The case involved an 1873 election in Lexington, Kentucky, where state law required that citizens pay a capitation tax before they could vote. The capitation tax represented one common and effective technique for denying blacks the right to vote. It rested on the belief that a disproportionate number of blacks would not be able to afford to pay the tax. However, when a black man named William Garner tried to pay the capitation tax in Lexington, the city tax collector refused to accept his payment. Later, at the time of the election, Garner appeared at a polling place and presented an affidavit stating that he had offered to pay the tax but was refused. The affidavit did not impress voting inspectors Hiram Reese and Matthew Fouchee, who refused to let him vote.[32]

The U.S. District Attorney charged Reese and Fouchee with violating two sections of the Enforcement Act of May 31, 1870. Section 3 made it a crime for any election officer to wrongly refuse to receive or count the vote of a qualified citizen. Section 4 made it a federal crime to hinder, delay, or obstruct any citizen from doing an act that was required in order to qualify him to vote.[33] The issue in *Reese* was whether in passing these provisions Congress had exceeded the authority granted to it by the Fifteenth Amendment. Concluding that it had, the Supreme Court ruled that these two sections of the act were unconstitutional.

Chief Justice Waite first assigned the case to Justice Clifford. Clifford was of the opinion that the two sections of the Enforcement Act were constitutional, but would have overruled the convictions on the basis of the indictments being defective. Had he written the opinion, the impact of the decision would have been similar to that of *Cruikshank* in this respect. When it became evident that a majority of justices believed that the two sections of the act were unconstitutional, however, the chief justice assumed for himself the responsibility of writing the opinion.[34]

Waite once again began from the presumption that the Fifteenth Amendment does not confer a right to vote but only the right to be free from discrimination in voting on the basis of race, color, or previous condition of servitude. It followed that Congress's power under the amendment was limited to enforcing the right to be free from discrimination on account of race.

Section 1 of the Enforcement Act did refer to race, stating, "Citizens otherwise qualified to vote in the United States shall be entitled to vote without distinction of race, etc." But Waite did not see this section as being relevant. It merely declared a right. And the sections under which the defendants were actually charged were not confined to race. Thus the Supreme Court declared that Sections 3 and 4 of the Enforcement Act were unconstitutional because, read literally, they prohibited any unlawful interference with the right to vote, regardless of whether it was motivated by racial discrimination.

Undoubtedly the chief justice knew that Reese and Fouchee had refused to allow Garner to vote because he was black. But Waite was not willing to consider the obvious. Neither the actual facts of the case nor the intent of Congress mattered to him. The only thing that was important was the express language of the statute. "It might be possible for a court to imply the limitation of race into the relevant sections of the Act," he admitted. "But that would not be proper or prudent." Rather Waite warned that it would be dangerous to allow the legislature to cast a net large enough to catch all possible offenders and leave it to the courts to sort out who should be rightfully convicted and who should be set free. "To limit the statute in the manner now asked for would be to make new law, not to enforce an old one," he concluded. "This is not part of our duty."[35]

The chief justice's notion of judicial duty in this case did possess an admirable lawyerlike quality. It demanded that the indictment be carefully drafted. It also demanded that Congress write each section of the criminal law clearly enough to give notice of what acts would violate the law. But the opinion also suffered from excessive formalism and a refusal to recognize the obvious.

Justice Ward Hunt, who was the only justice to disagree with the outcome in *Reese*, had a distinctly different idea of what constituted judicial duty. Hunt believed that the convictions could be upheld even if one accepted the proposition that Congress's power was limited to enforcing the right to be free from discrimination on account of race. The language of section 1 made it clear that Congress intended the act to apply to race, Hunt observed. Even if Sections 3 and 4 were written as general prohibitions, he thought it was quite plain that Congress intended them as punishment for racial discrimination.[36] Rather than narrowly construe the language section by section, Hunt believed that the appropriate rule for interpreting the statute was to examine the circumstances surrounding enactment of the statute and consider the evil that it was intended to prevent.[37]

Hunt's career as a justice of the U.S. Supreme Court was short and not particularly noteworthy. He had been on the New York Court of Appeals, New York's highest appellate court, when President Grant appointed him to the U.S. Supreme Court in January 1873. By 1877 health problems caused Hunt to miss several of the Court's sessions, and, although he stayed on the bench until January 1882, a stroke in 1879 effectively ended his career.[38] Hunt's dissent in *Reese* was probably his most lasting legacy because it graphically explained the disturbing aspect of the majority's reasoning. In Waite's formalistic formula for interpreting congressional legislation lay the danger of making new law by failing to enforce the old one.

Shortly after delivering his opinions in *Cruikshank* and *Reese* Waite wrote to his cousin, "The two opinions I read last Monday, and which have been somewhat commented upon during the week cost me a heap of hard work, to say nothing of the anxiety."[39] His anxiety was understandable. As a practical matter the opinions were narrow. They merely overturned indictments and invalidated two sections of the Enforcement Acts because they were poorly drafted. Symbolically, however, the *Cruikshank* and *Reese* opinions represented a defeat for the plan for Reconstruction that the Radical Republicans in Congress favored and, perhaps, a setback for Republican ideals in general.

Waite's anxiety proved to be unfounded. The reaction to the cases, at least the reaction reflected in the popular press, was generally favorable. Southern and Democratic papers were predictably elated, describing the opinions together as "an exquisite piece of legal acumen" and comparing Waite to the great Chief Justices Jay, Marshall, and Taney.[40] More surprising and comforting to Waite was that the Northern press agreed. Ignoring the "fiendish deed" in Colfax, Louisiana, that had produced *Cruikshank*, Republican papers like the *New York Times* and *Chicago Tribune* praised the decisions.[41]

The *Times* admired Waite's statements about the limits of judicial power. "When courts can, as the court says, 'make a new law,' under the pretext of enforcing an old one, one of the most valuable safeguards of the Constitution is undermined. It is certainly a good sign when the Supreme Court is found in the same act holding Congress to strict limitations, and refusing to extend its own powers, even on the argument of the Government's lawyers."[42] Interestingly, it also admired Waite's opinion about the limits of congressional power. The *Reese* opinion, it wrote, served as a respectful but vigorous warning to Congress against the passage of hastily and loosely worded laws.

The *Times* admitted that the decision might seem, at first blush, a restriction rather than protection of the rights of citizens. Nevertheless it concluded that "although the Court may have rejected a claim by certain individuals that their rights had been denied," its interpretation displayed "utmost fidelity to the highest interests of the whole people." The *Cruikshank* opinion, it said, was less important but served as an admonition to federal prosecutors "that indictments must be drawn with the utmost regard for the rights of all concerned."[43] Although reaction to the decisions was less favorable in Congress, even there the comments were polite and deferential.[44]

More than one hundred years later, in the wake of the civil rights movement of the 1950s and 1960s, many critics have not been so kind. Regarding *Cruikshank*, one wrote, "This racist and morally opaque decision reduced the Fourteenth Amendment to meaningless verbiage as far as the civil rights of Negroes were concerned."[45] When viewing the opinions from the twenty-first century, it is certainly not unreasonable to describe *Cruikshank* and *Reese* as racist and morally opaque.[46] And given our knowledge that the century that followed produced state-imposed racial segregation in the South, it is understandable to characterize them as the beginning of the end of the federal government's role in guaranteeing to all races equal rights and privileges of citizenship. But other modern scholars have pointed out that the motivations driving the decisions were not so clear-cut, and that the impact of the decisions was not so great, as is sometimes claimed.[47]

It is important for the modern observer to recognize the role that federalism played in the decisions. Justices like Waite, Bradley, and Miller were among Republicans who fought the Civil War not only to secure freedom for the slaves but, even more, to preserve the Union. For many Republicans and Northerners, this ideal of preserving the Union meant maintaining the relationship between the states and the nation as close as possible to what it was before the war.[48]

Under the antebellum concept of federalism—the beliefs upon which all of the justices sitting on the Supreme Court were weaned—concentration of power in the federal government posed the greatest threat to individual liberty. With a few notable exceptions, the constitutional structure before the Civil War left to the states the duty of protecting civil and political rights.[49] Of course the Reconstruction Amendments undoubtedly changed this balance between the nation and states to some degree. The question was, to what degree?

Complicating the search for an answer was the fact that the Republican plan for Reconstruction of the South, especially with respect to ensuring the rights of blacks, completely flipped the ideals and presumptions that had been the underpinnings of federalism before the Civil War. Instead of seeing the national government as a threat to liberty, it viewed the national government as the guarantor of liberty.[50]

Radical Republican leaders like Charles Sumner and Thaddeus Stephens had no misgivings about the expansion of federal power. For others, however, the conflict in *Cruikshank* and *Reese* brought to a head the tension between their long-held ideal of federalism and the Republican desire to secure freedom for blacks—even if it meant imposing federal power on the states. It is possible that, rather than only being morally opaque, justices of the era were truly conflicted, perhaps even confused.

That appeared to be true for Justice Joseph Bradley, who heard the *Cruikshank* case while riding circuit in New Orleans and wrote an opinion for the circuit court. Although in some ways similar to the Supreme Court's opinion, Bradley's opinion in *Cruikshank* was more passionate: a surprising development given his reputation as the most analytical and circumspect member of the Court. Perhaps the reason was that Bradley's circuit court opinion was more than a response to the *Cruikshank* case. It represented his attempt to formulate a systematic doctrine governing the reach of Congress's power in light of the Reconstruction Amendments. And he agonized over the dilemma the case and the Reconstruction Amendments created.[51]

Given that Bradley had vigorously championed an expansive view of federal power in the *Slaughterhouse Cases,* one might have expected him to take a similarly expansive view of Congress's power with regard to the Enforcement Act. But this case was different. The *Slaughterhouse Cases* involved a lawsuit against the state for violations of federal rights. It was a legal dispute that required judicial determination. *Cruikshank* and *Reese* raised the question of the extent to which Congress could be proactive—that is, to what extent could it pass laws to enforce rights within the states. He explained the problem by looking at the extremes, neither of which was acceptable: "Either that congress can never interfere where the state laws are unobjectionable, however remiss the state authorities may be in executing them, and however much a proscribed race may be oppressed; or that congress may pass an entire body of municipal law for the protection of person and property within the states, to operate concurrently with the state laws, for the protection and benefit of a particular class of the community."[52]

Bradley reasoned that the key to solving the problem was to consider the nature and origin of the particular rights involved. The protection of rights derived from common law or natural law was traditionally the province of the states, he observed. The states had not only the power but also the duty to enforce those guarantees by enacting legislation and providing judicial remedies where appropriate. It was true that the U.S. Constitution also secured some of these rights, he admitted. But he went on to say that where rights are secured only by a declaration that the state or the United States shall not violate them, the federal power is limited to judicial oversight.[53]

The Fourteenth Amendment's guarantee that no state shall deny any citizen the privileges or immunities of citizens of the United States, which was of particular concern in *Cruikshank,* fell into this category. It did not create specific new rights, but rather applied to rights that otherwise existed. Whether Congress could enact legislation depended on the nature of the previously existing right. The rights claimed in the *Cruikshank* indictments fell into two categories. One group—the right to peaceable assembly and the right to bear arms—were not appropriate subjects of legislation because they were direct prohibitions on the federal government.

The other group of rights was connected to murder and intimidation and the right to vote. Traditionally it was the states' job to protect these rights either through specific legislation or by creating a legal and social order in which they could exist. Bradley saw the privileges and immunities clause as essentially an assurance the state did its job. It was intended to guard against tyranny of the state governments by providing citizens with a remedy in federal courts. To say that it also gave Congress the power to enact affirmative legislation to protect such rights would produce a greater change in the system of federalism than Bradley was willing to make. "This would be to clothe congress with power to pass laws for the general preservation of social order in every state."54

The Thirteenth and Fifteenth amendments were other matters altogether. Bradley reasoned that because they involved rights derived directly from the U.S. Constitution, Congress had the power to enforce them by passing affirmative legislation. The Thirteenth Amendment—which declares that neither slavery nor involuntary servitude shall exist in the United States—is written in the language of a prohibition. Yet Bradley reasoned that it was not merely a prohibition against passage of a law creating slavery but a declaration that slavery shall not exist. The amendment, he said, had an affirmative operation from the moment it was adopted. Because it enfranchised millions of former slaves—in essence creating a right to be free from slavery—Congress "acquired the power not only to legislate for the eradication of slavery, but the power to give full effect to the bestowment of liberty upon these millions of people."55

The Fifteenth Amendment is, likewise, written as a prohibition. It reads "the rights of citizens of the United States to vote shall not be denied or abridged by the United States or by any state on account of race, color, or previous condition of servitude." Yet Bradley found in this language a positive right that did not exist before. That right, which Chief Justice Waite borrowed for his Supreme Court opinion, was not the right to vote but rather the right to be free from discrimination with respect to the right to vote.56

At least one biographer has observed that slavery was not a major concern to Bradley before the Civil War, and that, at most, he considered it an abstract moral evil and worried that full emancipation would be disruptive to the nation's then existing economic and social arrangements.57 If this is true, Bradley's thinking certainly changed by the time he heard *Cruikshank* on the circuit court. His summary of the federal government's role in enforcing the Thirteenth and Fifteenth amendments bears this out. "The war of race, whether it assumes the dimensions of civil strife or domestic violence, whether carried out in a guerilla war of predatory form, or by private combinations, or even by private outrage or intimidation, is subject to the jurisdiction of the government of the United States," he wrote, "and when any atrocity is committed which may be assigned to this cause it may be punished by the laws and in the courts of the United States."58

Bradley's reasoning in *Cruikshank* reveals a man struggling to apply sometimes conflicting principles. For him, and other justices as well, securing the rights of recently freed African Americans was only one of those principles and, perhaps, not the most important. There is no doubt that the formula that emerged from the *Slaughterhouse Cases, Cruikshank,* and *Reese* contained the seeds of legal doctrine that would later be used to accommodate racial segregation. That does not mean that the earlier decisions were motivated primarily by racism or that later doctrine was predestined.59

The history of the Jim Crow era and early civil rights movement of the mid-twentieth century taught us that arguments centered on states' rights and federalism can be nothing more than a ruse used to excuse racial segregation. But Miller, Waite, and

Bradley did not appear to be mere apologists. Miller, in the *Slaughterhouse Cases,* seemed wary of the possibility that the Fourteenth Amendment would be turned into a weapon used to insulate propertied elites or powerful corporations from state regulation.[60] This will be the subject of later chapters.

Waite and Bradley were also concerned in *Cruikshank* and *Reese* that the enforcement provisions of the Fourteenth Amendment might provide a vehicle for the national government to control elections. And their concern was not merely theoretical. Although Republicans had controlled the government since Lincoln's election in 1860, by the mid-1870s indications were that the party was losing its grip. When Democrats won control of the House of Representatives in 1874, it became obvious that Republicans needed to protect voting rights for blacks in the South if they hoped to maintain control of the federal government. Events a short time later, in the presidential election of 1876, showed that Republican anxiety in this regard was not exaggerated.

In May 1876 the United States began its celebration of the centennial of the Constitution with an exposition in Philadelphia. Grand though it was, the celebration glossed over the fact that the nation had not yet fully healed the wounds of the Civil War. Those wounds festered anew when, even before the celebrating had ended and the exposition had closed, the presidential election that pitted Republican Rutherford B. Hayes against Democrat Samuel Tilden ended in a stalemate.[61]

Democrats saw the election as their first real chance to win the presidency since before the Civil War. Republican success in the intervening years was in no small part due to painting themselves as the party of Lincoln, the party of victory, and the party of the preservation of the Union. The implication, of course, was that anyone who opposed the Republican Party was tainted by disloyalty. For more than a decade the Democrats had been steamrolled by this tactic, which was then called "waving the bloody shirt."

But the political landscape was changing in 1876. The Grant administration, which had been in power for eight years, was so mired in scandal that talk of the war hero running for a third term was quickly cut off. Scandal became a liability to the party, as did the depression of 1873. As the party in power, the Republican Party was likely to receive much of the blame for that economic disaster. Moreover the depression had to have an effect on Northern attitudes toward Republican policies for Reconstruction in the South. Despite shocking reports of lynching, murder, and violence in the South, unemployed and struggling white workers in the North were likely to be more concerned with their own well-being and vote accordingly. In an astounding victory in the congressional elections of 1874, Democrats won control of the House of Representatives. Perhaps they were not being foolhardy in hoping that the bloody shirt was finally wearing thin.

Indeed, the Republican candidate, Hayes, went to bed the night of the election believing that he had lost. He had lost the popular vote by a sizable margin.[62] The initial estimates of the Electoral College vote indicated that he had lost that as well. The next morning many newspapers around the country reported a Tilden victory, and Republicans throughout the country were in despair. Even Hayes virtually admitted defeat to a group of newsmen.[63]

Several of Hayes's lieutenants were not quite ready to give up, however. Late on the night of the election, after studying the returns, General Daniel E. Sickles decided the election was too close to abandon. Sickles realized that winning just a few Southern states would turn the election to Hayes. He and William E. Chandler took it upon themselves to wire party leaders in Louisiana, Florida, and South Carolina instructing them not to concede. Hayes is elected if we have carried South Carolina, Florida, and Louisiana, Sickles wrote, "With your state sure for Hayes, he is elected. Hold your state?"[64] Meanwhile, John C. Reid, managing editor of the *New York Times*, encouraged Republicans not to concede. His paper's headline on November 8 read, "Results Still Uncertain."[65]

Sickles's efforts encouraged and emboldened Southern Republicans, threw the election into chaos, and ignited an epic of political intrigue. The electoral votes of South Carolina, Oregon, Louisiana, and Florida were thrown into doubt. In South Carolina and Oregon, initial returns showed a Republican victory. The task there for Republicans was to hold on to the votes. Louisiana and Florida presented a more difficult problem. In both states the initial count showed a victory for the Democrats, although the margin in Florida was razor thin. Republicans faced the seemingly daunting task of reversing the initial vote.

That was not as hopeless as it might seem. Louisiana and Florida both required votes to be certified by a canvassing or returning board. With the election now in question, both parties sent "visiting statesmen" to assure the fairness of the canvassing. Republicans controlled the canvassing boards in both states, and once local party leaders had grasped the idea that their state could win the election for Hayes, Democrats were practically helpless. Even though the initial counts in both states indicated a victory for Tilden, the canvassing boards had the power to throw out votes on the basis of fraud or irregularities. Taking more than full advantage of that authority, both boards declared a victory for Hayes and certified the Republican electors for the Electoral College.

Frustrated Democrats could do little else than to meet separately and, by various means, certify their own set of delegates to the Electoral College. On December 6, 1876, the day delegates to the Electoral College from all of the states were required to meet in the Capitol and record their votes, Tilden received 184 votes, and Hayes received 165. Both parties claimed the remaining 20 votes, those of Oregon, South Carolina, Florida, and Louisiana. The presence of the disputed delegations froze the election process in a standoff.

With the outcome of the election in doubt, and the Constitution providing no clear instructions for dealing with a stalemate, normal electoral procedures broke down. Already intense sectional and party rivalries intensified. Certain that they had won, some Democratic loyalists even promised men at arms and called on Tilden to take the presidency by force if necessary.[66] Even if such threats were mostly bluff and bravado, the election stalemate undoubtedly "brought the nation to the brink of peril."[67] One hundred and twenty-four years later, writing in the aftermath of the presidential election of 2000, a disputed election in which he played a key role, Chief Justice William Rehnquist described the election of 1876 as a centennial crisis.[68]

It was a crisis not only because of threats of violence but also because the Constitution does not provide much guidance about what should be done in the case of contested electoral votes. The applicable provisions are Article II, Section 1, which is the original provision governing the presidential vote, and the Twelfth Amendment, which amended the process by requiring that the president and vice president be elected separately. Both provide the same directive. "The President of the Senate shall, in the presence of the Senate and the House of Representatives, open all the certificates and the votes shall then be counted." Unfortunately, this language does not answer the crucial question of who was to determine which of the disputed votes to count.

Republicans argued that the president of the Senate had the duty not only to count the votes but also to determine which votes to count. Normally the vice president of the United States served as president of the Senate, but Vice President Henry Wilson had died in 1875. The office of president of the Senate then went to majority leader Senator Thomas Ferry, a staunch Republican.

Naturally the Democrats were not very keen on the idea of Ferry making the determination. Since Democrats now had control of the House of Representatives some argued that the two houses of Congress should together determine which votes should be counted. Tilden himself believed that the dispute should be resolved by another part of Article II, Section 1, that directs the House of Representatives to chose the president if no candidate received a majority. But, again, this provision said nothing about what to do in the case of a dispute.

While the standoff continued, both houses of Congress sent committees to investigate the elections in the South. Meanwhile party officials and members of Congress scrambled to find a solution before inauguration day. Senator George F. Edmunds proposed a constitutional amendment that would authorize the Supreme Court to make the determination. That plan was rejected. Eventually both houses agreed to create a special joint committee charged with the task of devising a solution.

The joint committee proposed that a fifteen-member electoral commission decide the election. Five members of the commission would come from the Democratic-controlled House of Representatives, with three of them being Democrat and two being Republican. Five members would come from the Republican-controlled Senate, with three being Republican and two being Democrat. What made the plan palatable was the inclusion of five members of the Supreme Court. The committee did not choose to include justices for their impartiality. Quite to the contrary, of the justices who were chosen to sit on the Electoral Commission, Stephen Field and Nathan Clifford were staunch Democrats and Samuel Miller and William Strong were just as partisan Republicans. No one expected that these four men would do anything other than vote for their party.

Justice David Davis provided the wild card. Davis, who began his legal career in Bloomington, Illinois, had been a state judge and a friend of Abraham Lincoln. He began his political career as a Whig. However, when Lincoln sought the Republican nomination for the presidency in 1860, Davis became the candidate's chief strategist. In 1862 Lincoln rewarded him with a seat on the nation's high court. Even after his appointment, Davis kept his finger in politics. By 1876 it was well known that he aspired to the presidency and that he was attempting to carve out the image of an independent.[69] This made him attractive to Democrats in Congress, who believed that the addition of Davis gave them some hope. Republicans, unsure of Davis's loyalty, were less happy.

The Electoral Commission Bill specifically designated Justices Field, Clifford, Miller, and Strong to the Electoral Commission and provided that those justices would choose the fifth member from the Court. Everyone understood, however, that the fifth member would be Davis. Fate derailed that understanding.

Prior to ratification of the Seventeenth Amendment in 1913, U.S. senators were chosen by the state legislatures, not by popular vote. Just before the Electoral Commission was finally formed, the Illinois legislature elected Justice Davis to the U.S. Senate. Although he technically could have still accepted a seat on the commission, Davis declined. Astonishingly it was Illinois Democrats who had made Davis's election to the Senate possible and, in doing so, had possibly doomed their party's chances of capturing the presidency. Commenting on the events Republican Party leader and future president James A. Garfield observed, "The Lord came in and removed Davis from the Commission, and with him went the last hope for Tilden's success."[70]

With Davis now out of the picture, the four justices chose Joseph Bradley to fill the last seat on the Electoral Commission. Although all of the remaining available justices were Republicans, Bradley was probably the least objectionable to the Democrats. Yet, in the end, he did the same as all of the other justices and, for that matter, all of the other members of the Electoral Commission. He voted his party line.

Bradley's leanings became immediately apparent with the first key vote of the commission. Florida had submitted three sets of electors. One of them, the Hayes electors, proffered the official certificates that had been signed by the governor. Democrats, however, maintained that the legitimate results of the election had been reversed by the illegal acts of a partisan returning board. The official certificates were illegitimate, they argued, and they urged the commission to look "behind the returns" to allow them to prove it. Republicans countered that the official certificates that had been signed by the governor should be accepted as conclusive and that the commission did not have the power to "go behind the returns" in search of alleged improprieties. After four days of hearing arguments the commission met in executive session on February 6 and 7, 1877, to determine the Florida issue.

Commission member James A. Garfield, who was then a member of Congress, recorded in his diary that while every member explained his view, they all awaited Bradley's explanation. "All were intent because B. held the casting vote," Garfield wrote. "It was a curious study to watch the faces as he read. All were making a manifest effort to appear unconcerned. It was ten minutes before it became evident that he was against the authority to hear extrinsic evidence."[71] Later in the day the commission formally announced its decision not to look behind the returns in the Florida election. The eight to seven vote strictly followed party affiliation, and, although the commission's work was not yet done, an outcome in favor of Hayes was no longer in doubt.

Outraged Democrats claimed that Bradley had earlier indicated that he favored going behind the returns but that something had caused him to change his mind. They claimed that a continuous stream of Republican dignitaries had visited Bradley in the wee hours of the night before the vote to put pressure on him. They also implied that he was influenced by an improper connection with railroad baron Tom Scott and the scheme to build the Texas and Pacific Railroad.

The Democrats' attacks on Bradley became part of the lore of the disputed election of 1876. In 1935 historian Allan Nevins raised the criticism anew when he revealed that Abram Hewitt, then chair of the Democratic National Committee, had compiled a "secret history" of the Electoral Commission.[72] However, later historical accounts of the election have convincingly demonstrated that it is unlikely that any shenanigans took place to secure Bradley's vote.[73] Bradley more likely followed his conscience as well as his party. He explained his vote, in part, on a concern that by going behind the returns, the commission would be trenching upon a power that the Constitution had reserved to the states.[74] This emphasis on the power of the states was at least consistent with the theory of federalism that seemed to be emerging from his and Waite's opinions in cases involving the Reconstruction Amendments. In most instances he expressed a keen respect for state authority, the notable exception being his dissent in the *Slaughterhouse Cases*.

Although the statute creating the Electoral Commission provided that Congress was required to accept its ruling, Democrats, who controlled the House of Representatives, threatened to hold up the commission's decision indefinitely. On February 26, with the election of a president still unresolved, representatives of Hayes and Tilden met in Wormley's Hotel to work out a compromise. In what has become known as the Compromise of 1877, the Hayes camp allegedly agreed to abandon Republican claims to the control of state governments in South Carolina and Louisiana and withdraw federal troops from the South, and tacitly agreed that the South alone should resolve its racial problems. In exchange for this promise of "southern home rule" the Tilden camp allegedly agreed that Democrats would end their filibuster in the House of Representatives and give the presidency to Hayes.[75]

Some accounts of the Compromise of 1877 maintain that the Republicans also promised financial aid for construction of the Texas and Pacific Railroad, the appointment of a Democrat as postmaster general, and federal subsidies to aid Southern rehabilitation.[76] Other accounts question whether there was a "compromise" at all or, at least, whether the compromise involved such explicit details.[77]

Whatever was the agreement, on Friday, March 2, after weeks of threatened filibuster, Congress finally adopted the recommendation of the Electoral Commission. At four o'clock in the morning, with the two houses meeting in joint session, Speaker of the House Thomas Ferry announced that the vote on the disputed presidential race was 185 for Hayes to 184 for Tilden. "Wherefore," Ferry announced, "I do declare that Rutherford B. Hayes of Ohio, having received the majority of the whole number of votes is duly elected President of the United States for four years commencing on the 4th day of March, 1877."[78]

Republican leaders who did not want to wait through the weekend to cement their victory persuaded Hayes to take the oath of office during a White House dinner on Saturday, March 2. During the inauguration on Monday, March 4, Chief Justice Waite administered the oath a second time. The presidency was then securely in Republican hands. To the Democratic faithful, however, the election became known as the "Great Fraud," and Hayes as "His Fraudulency."

The Hayes victory was hard won. A cartoon in *Harper's Weekly* showed a battered Republican elephant leaning on a crutch. The elephant wears a laurel wreath on his head, but his body is bandaged, battered, and bruised. Beneath the elephant is the caption, "Another Such Victory And I Am Undone."[79] Although the Republican Party was not quite undone, its hope of reconstructing the South in a way that assured political and social rights for blacks probably was. The election of 1876 demonstrated, above all, that the years of Republican dominance were over. Whatever were the details of compromise that gave Hayes the presidency, at the very least it marked the symbolic end of Reconstruction.[80]

Modern writers imply that the Supreme Court played a pivotal role in settling the disputed election of 1876. Writing more than 125 years later, after the Court he led gave the disputed presidential election of 2000 to Republican George W. Bush, Chief Justice William Rehnquist observed that it was quite natural for Congress to turn to the justices of the Supreme Court as members of the Electoral Commission of 1877. The judiciary was chosen by default as the tiebreaker, he wrote. "This was a dispute; disputes are traditionally decided by courts."[81] Another modern writer, Roy Morris Jr., also draws a comparison to the election of 2000. As in that election, the controversy in the election of 1876 involved the state of Florida, he observed, "and it, too, ultimately was decided by the vote of a single Republican member of the U.S. Supreme Court."[82] Rehnquist's and Morris's observations leave an impression that the Supreme Court played the deciding role in the election of 1876. John Anthony Scott goes a step further, explicitly stating, "That the Court adjudicated the disputed election should not surprise us."[83]

The implication that the Court asserted its power to decide the presidential election of 1876 ignores the fact that, unlike the presidential election of 2000, the Supreme Court *as an institution* was not involved at all. Rather, Congress turned the dispute over to a fifteen-member commission that included five of the nine justices. Those five justices were selected on the basis of partisanship, not for their judicial impartiality.

The implication also gives a false impression about the attitude of the majority of the justices sitting on the Court in 1876 regarding the reach of judicial power. The legacy of the *Slaughterhouse Cases* indicated that the majority would be hesitant to overturn the act of a state legislature. In *Reese* they declared part of an act of Congress unconstitutional but did so in a way that deferred to legislative authority. Recall Chief Justice Waite's statement in *Reese* that "To limit the statute in the manner now asked for would be to make new law, not to enforce an old one."[84] Even when Congress expanded the jurisdiction of the federal courts through various statutes enacted during Reconstruction, the majority refused to take full advantage of this new power.[85]

The civil rights cases of the first three years of Waite's tenure suggested that the majority of the Court tended to be conservative in the sense of looking backward for their cues. They were intent on resisting the temptation to see the Reconstruction Amendments as an opportunity to make revolutionary changes in the legal system upon which they were weaned or in the system of federalism they knew prior to the Civil War. Similarly they resisted the idea that the amendments were a vehicle to create new rights. *Reese* demonstrated that the majority's method of legal reasoning tended to be formalistic, even to the point of ignoring obvious facts.

They obviously appreciated that the Reconstruction Amendments were intended, in some way, to guarantee the political and civil rights of blacks and at least integrate black citizens into political society. At the same time, however, they were not inclined to stretch themselves to give full force and effect to that guarantee. It remained to be seen whether the Court would continue to display these tendencies after the Compromise of 1877.

Chief Justice Morrison R. Waite. Courtesy of the Library of Congress, Prints and Photographs Division, Washington, D.C.

The Waite Court. Standing from left to right: William B. Woods, Joseph P. Bradley, Stanley Matthews, Samuel Blatchford. Front row from left to right: Horace Gray, Samuel F. Miller, Morrison R. Waite, Stephen J. Field, John Marshall Harlan. Courtesy of the Library of Congress, Prints and Photographs Division, Washington, D.C.

"The Electoral Commission, 1877." From *Frank Leslie's Illustrated Newspaper*, March 10, 1877, 9. Courtesy of Rare Books and Special Collections, Thomas Cooper Library, University of South Carolina

"The Louisiana Murders." From *Harper's Weekly*, May 10, 1873, 396. Courtesy of Rare Books and Special Collections, Thomas Cooper Library, University of South Carolina

"The Disputed Prize." From *Harper's Weekly*, May 10, 1873, 396. Courtesy of Rare Books and Special Collections, Thomas Cooper Library, University of South Carolina

"Stanley Matthews—His Narrow Escape." From *Harper's Weekly,* June 11, 1881. Courtesy of Rare Books and Special Collections, Thomas Cooper Library, University of South Carolina

3

After the Compromise

In the wake of emancipation Radical Republicans were determined to use the might of the federal government to guarantee full equality for blacks. This wing of the party successfully urged the Republican-dominated Congress to enact laws designed to achieve that goal. The last of these ambitious Reconstruction statutes was the Civil Rights Act of 1875, which prohibited racial discrimination in public places such as inns, taverns, or railroad cars and made violation of its provisions a federal crime.[1]

Even before the new civil rights bill was enacted, it was becoming evident that Republican domination of Congress was coming to an end and America's resolve to assure equality for blacks was waning. In the meantime the Supreme Court had already demonstrated that it was inclined to narrowly construe the powers granted to Congress by the Thirteenth, Fourteenth, and Fifteenth amendments. Its 1876 decisions in *U.S. v. Cruikshank* and *U.S. v. Reese* revealed a majority that was skeptical of any law that appeared to create a new right or significantly alter the structure of American federalism. The addition of three new justices in 1880 and 1881 raised a question of whether the Court would continue on this track. One strong indication of the majority's intentions came when challenges to the Civil Rights Act of 1875 reached the Supreme Court in 1883.

Challenges to the law began to appear almost the moment it became effective. Not all of them came from the South. Tennessee provided one, but the others came from Kansas, Missouri, and, more surprisingly, California and New York.[2] These cases, when appealed to the Supreme Court, were combined and became the *Civil Rights Cases*.[3] The challengers had maintained that by prohibiting racial discrimination in public transportation and public places, Congress had exceeded the power granted to it in the Thirteenth and Fourteenth amendments. When the Supreme Court agreed by a vote of eight to one, Justice Joseph Bradley was assigned with writing the opinion.

Bradley emphasized that the Fourteenth Amendment is prohibitory in character. Section 1 commands that "no state shall" deny any person equal protection of the laws or life, liberty, or property without due process. Section 5 gives Congress the power to enforce this provision, Bradley agreed, but it does not invest Congress with the power to legislate upon subjects that are within the domain of the states. Rather Congress's power is limited to correcting or nullifying "state action" that violates the command of Section 1. For Bradley, the Civil Rights Act's prohibition of racial discrimination went far beyond this. It was not corrective legislation, but rather more like a general municipal code that regulated "all private rights between man and man in society." To uphold this law, he argued, "would be to make congress take the place of state legislatures and to supersede them."⁴

In Bradley's opinion, the Thirteenth Amendment, by contrast, was more than a mere prohibition on state action. It was an absolute declaration that slavery or involuntary servitude shall not exist in any part of the United States. Taking advantage of this distinction, government attorneys argued that the enforcement provision of the Thirteenth Amendment gave Congress the power to enact any legislation necessary and proper for abolishing "all badges and incidents of slavery." Racial discrimination in public accommodations, conveyances, and public amusements, they reasoned, tended to fasten upon blacks just the type of badge of slavery the amendment prohibited.⁵

Bradley might have agreed that Congress had the power to prohibit badges of slavery, but he did not agree that racial discrimination in accommodations, conveyances, and amusements amounted to a badge of slavery. "The long existence of African slavery in this country gave us very distinct notions of what it was, and what were its necessary incidents," he wrote. And in one long paragraph he described what they were. Among them were compulsory service, inability to make contracts or hold property, and more severe punishment for crimes. The framers of the Thirteenth Amendment intended to guarantee to blacks the fundamental rights that appertained to the essence of citizenship, he concluded. They did not intend to give Congress the authority "to adjust what may be called the social rights of men and races in the community."⁶

Justice John Harlan was the only dissenter in the *Civil Rights Cases*. When it came to colorful characters, Harlan was an easy match for the likes of Field, Bradley, and Miller. Born to a slaveholding Kentucky family in 1833, Harlan seemed an unlikely defender of equal rights for the races. His father was a Whig lawyer and successful political figure who served as a state legislator, state attorney general, and U.S. attorney. After graduating from Center College and studying law at Transylvania University in Kentucky, Harlan was set to follow in his father's footsteps. He joined the law practice and was admitted to the bar in 1853. Later he successfully ran for several local public offices, eventually becoming a trial judge in Franklin County, Kentucky.⁷

At six feet, two inches tall, Harlan was an imposing physical figure. He was also imposing as a man of strongly held convictions and the willingness to express them. What makes Harlan especially interesting, however, is that he also possessed the ability to change them. Harlan came of age on the eve of the Civil War in the border state of Kentucky. From his father he inherited a belief in a strong Union. Yet he also was convinced that slaves were property, and that the government should not interfere with the rights of slaveholders. Although it must have been a difficult place and time for him, he stuck to both convictions. He joined the Union army, becoming a colonel in the Tenth Kentucky Volunteer Infantry. All the while, he continued to preach against the abolition of slavery.

When his father died before the war ended, Harlan returned to his home, took over his father's law practice, and resumed his political career. He opposed ratification of the Thirteenth and Fourteenth amendments and the enactment of the Civil Rights Act of 1866. After losing on all counts, however, he joined the ranks of his former opponents and began defending Republican policies. In 1871 he ran a losing campaign as Republican candidate for governor of Kentucky. When detractors charged him with being a weather vane he responded, "Let it be said that I am right rather than consistent."[8]

Harlan's path to the Supreme Court ran through his friend and law partner Benjamin Bristow. By 1874 both men were important figures in the reform wing of the Kentucky Republican Party. Bristow's reputation on the national scene was already well established. He had served as an assistant U.S. attorney and was the first person to hold the new office of solicitor general of the United States. Bristow was serving as secretary of the treasury in the Grant administration when Harlan and others pushed him for the 1876 Republican nomination for president. During the Republican convention it became clear that the contest was between Rutherford B. Hayes and James G. Blaine. As leader of the Kentucky delegation, Harlan had been holding the state's votes for his friend. When chances of Bristow's success began to look slim, however, he threw the state's votes to Hayes. Harlan's actions, and Kentucky's vote, helped seal the victory for Hayes. Soon after Hayes won the general election, he rewarded Harlan with a nomination to the Supreme Court.[9] The new justice was sworn in on December 10, 1877. He served on the Court until his death on October 14, 1911.

Harlan brought with him to the Supreme Court the tendency to sometimes appear inconsistent. On the subject of civil rights, for instance, he supported equal rights for blacks in his dissents in the *Civil Rights Cases* and *Plessy v. Ferguson* (1896) yet voted with the majority to uphold increased penalties for adultery between members of different races in *Pace v. Alabama.* At times Harlan seems so unpredictable that historian Tinsley E. Yarbrough titled his biography of Harlan *Judicial Enigma*. Another biographer, Linda Przybyszewski, explains that Harlan did not believe in equality of the races at all. He firmly believed in the superiority of the white race. His support of equal treatment for blacks was the result of a belief that the white race must temper its superiority with a particular kind of Protestant virtue. The virtue he envisioned contained elements of paternalism and pride: the idea that by treating blacks unfairly or denying them political and civil rights, whites reduced their own dignity and ultimately their own superiority.[10]

Whatever the values that drove it, Harlan's dissent in the *Civil Rights Cases* marked the beginning of his reputation as a defender of equal rights. Harlan criticized the majority's "narrow and artificial" reading of the Thirteenth and Fourteenth amendments, calling it a "subtle and ingenious verbal criticism" that sacrificed their true substance and spirit. The constitutional amendments were "adopted in the interests of liberty," he stated, "and for the purpose of securing, through national legislation, if need be, the rights inhering in a state of freedom and belonging to American citizenship." The letter of the law is its body, Harlan observed, but this sense, or reason, of the law is its soul, and it should not be construed to defeat the ends the people desired to accomplish when they ratified the amendments.[11]

The majority, in contrast, seemed consumed with the fear that the Civil Rights Act of 1875 was the first step down a slippery slope, the bottom of which had the federal government replacing the states as the source of "all municipal law." "If this legislation is appropriate for enforcing the prohibitions of the [Fourteenth] amendment, it is difficult to see where it is to stop." Bradley further asked, "Why may not congress, with equal show of authority, enact a code of laws for the enforcement and vindication of all rights of life, liberty, and property?"[12] But Bradley had only to think back to *United States v. Reese* to see that this slippery slope was not the inevitable result of the civil rights legislation. In *Reese* the court ruled that the Fifteenth Amendment did not create a new right to vote but only a new right to be free from racial discrimination in voting, still subject to the conditions the states placed on all voters. Harlan understood that the Civil Rights Act of 1875 did something similar. It did not substitute Congress's judgment for municipal law. It did not impose an unrestricted right to the services of public conveyances, accommodations, and amusements. It only required that the rules a state might make to govern these services, whatever they may be, shall not be applied so as to discriminate on account of race, color, or previous condition of servitude.[13]

Unlike the majority, who were guided by antebellum concepts of federalism, Harlan believed that the Reconstruction Amendments significantly changed the relationships between the national government and the states.[14] He also disagreed with the majority's conclusion about the nature of the rights that the Civil Rights Act guaranteed. For Harlan, the right to be free from discrimination in public conveyances, accommodations, and entertainment was not merely a social right as the majority suggested. He made it clear in his explanation of Congress's powers to enforce the Thirteenth and Fourteenth amendments that he believed it was a civil right that deserved the full protection of the Constitution.

Harlan looked first at Congress's power under the Thirteenth Amendment. "Was nothing more intended than to forbid one man from owning another as property?" he asked. "Were the states, against whose solemn protest the institution [of slavery] was to be destroyed to be left perfectly free . . . to make or allow discrimination against that race . . . in the enjoyment of those fundamental rights that inhere in the state of freedom?" The questions for him were, of course, rhetorical. The Thirteenth Amendment was intended to eradicate the "burdens of disabilities which constitute badges of slavery and servitude," he observed, and it delegated to Congress the power to enact appropriate legislation to do so.[15]

That racial discrimination in public conveyances, accommodations, and amusements amounted to such badges of servitude was, in Harlan's view, evident in the nature of those businesses. Conveyances, particularly railroads, were public highways, supported by the state, regulated by the state, given privileges from the state, and owing duties to the state and the public. Because of this relationship, he said, and because the freedom and power to move about is an essential element of freedom in general, the right of a "colored person" to use an improved public highway, upon the terms accorded free individuals of other races, is fundamental to the essence of freedom.[16] Harlan offered similar observations regarding public accommodations and amusements. Under typical state laws, an innkeeper who has sufficient room is required to provide accommodations for a paying guest, and because public amusements were typically licensed their authority to operate came from the public.[17]

These observations also underlay Harlan's argument that Congress had the power under the Fourteenth Amendment to prohibit racial discrimination. He reminded the majority that in *Munn v. Illinois* the Court ruled that property becomes clothed with public interest when used in a manner to make it of public consequence and affect the community at large. So affected with public interest, they cease to be *juris privati* only. For Harlan, this meant not only that they were subject to regulation but also that they incurred public responsibilities. This led him to conclude that "in every material sense applicable to the fourteenth amendment, railroad corporations, keepers of inns, and managers of places of public amusement are agents of the state." When they engaged in discrimination it was therefore precisely the kind of state action the Fourteenth Amendment prohibited.[18]

John Harlan would become better known for his dissent thirteen years later in *Plessy v. Ferguson*, the case that established the "separate but equal doctrine" and opened the door for official state segregation in the South. In the most significant part of the dissent Harlan began with an observation: "The white race deems itself the dominant race in this country. And so it is, in prestige, in achievements, in education, in wealth, and in power." He then followed the observation with a comment about the meaning of civil rights. "But in view of the constitution, in the eye of the law, there is in this country no superior, dominant, ruling class of citizens. There is no caste here. Our Constitution is color-blind, and neither knows nor tolerates classes among citizens."[19] Harlan's dissents in *Plessy* and the *Civil Rights Cases* thus established his reputation as a defender of civil rights for blacks.

The Waite Court majority, by contrast, is typically criticized for being complicit in the Compromise of 1877 and the subsequent "abandonment of the freedmen." Referring to the Court as the "Guardian of the Compromise of 1877," C. Peter Magrath writes: "Only the determined use of federal force could have given him [the freedmen] an element of political security, and after 1877 any willingness to sustain such force totally disappeared in the North. Instead it wanted reunion; the Hayes-Tilden election crisis provided the excuse for the desired accommodation—an accommodation that had as one of its essential elements the remission of the Negro's destiny to the states. The Supreme Court saw to it that the bargain was not violated."[20]

This criticism rings true in some respects. Certainly Bradley's concluding remarks in the *Civil Rights Cases* reveals an underlying attitude about race and rights that did not bode well for the goal of achieving full equality for blacks. Reflecting a sentiment that had become fairly common among Republicans by the early 1880s, Bradley said, "When a man has emerged from slavery, and by the aid of beneficent legislation has shaken off the inseparable concomitants of that state, there must be some stage in the progress of his elevation when he takes the rank of mere citizen, and ceases to be the special favorite of the laws."[21]

But the Waite Court's record on equal rights for blacks was more nuanced than Magrath's criticism and Bradley's concluding remarks imply. Bradley's opinion itself left open some role for the federal government to protect some kinds of rights. Although he ruled that the Civil Rights Act of 1875 was unconstitutional, Bradley also said that the earlier Civil Rights Act of 1866 was the kind of corrective legislation that Congress had the power to enact. The 1866 law guaranteed a list of rights that most everyone of the time would have classified as civil rights: the right to sue and be sued, make contracts, give evidence, and be subject to taxes and penalties. It further provided that anyone who, under *color of law,* statute, ordinance, regulation, or *custom,* denied another person of these rights on the basis of race or color would be subject to federal prosecution. It was constitutional, in Bradley's view, because the Thirteenth Amendment gave Congress the power to furnish redress against state laws and proceedings *and customs having the force of law.*

In theory Bradley's observation that state action included private acts done under color of law or according to customs having the force of law left ample room for federal intervention in cases involving a state's negligence or refusal to protect blacks against private discrimination. He thus joined other judges of the era in recognizing the federal government's right to intervene to protect blacks against what Pamela Brandwein has called "state neglect."[22] In practice, the Waite Court itself leaned in this direction only with respect to two rights, the right to vote and jury service.

Recall from chapter 2 that in *United States v. Cruikshank* in 1876 the Court adopted a painfully narrow interpretation of Congress's power to intercede in racial violence in the South. That same year, in *United States v. Reese* it ruled the Fifteenth Amendment did not give Congress the power to assure fair elections generally, but only to assure elections free from racial discrimination. The violence that produced *Cruikshank* was not directly linked to voting. But some Klan violence in the 1870s—whippings, beatings, and even lynching of blacks who asserted their rights—clearly was.[23] And violence did not end with the Compromise of 1877. In 1884 the Court had another opportunity to review the limits of Congress's power to address racial violence in the South and assure fair elections.

It began when a Georgia Klansman named Jasper Yarbrough, along with seven cohorts and family members, engaged in repeated and vicious attacks on black citizens. Yarbrough and his group were part of an organization known as the Pop and Go Club, who were pledged to intimidate blacks who wanted to exercise their right to vote. In the summer of 1883 they made numerous night "excursions," dragging blacks out of their homes, beating and whipping them, and killing at least one man. In October Yarbrough and his group were convicted of violating a federal law that prohibited conspiracy to use intimidation or violence to prevent any person from exercising the right to vote.[24]

Because this prohibition was the same as those at issue in *Cruikshank* and *Reese,* the defendants may have thought there was a good chance the Supreme Court would overturn the convictions. Instead, in *Ex parte Yarbrough* (1884) the Court decided to limit the impact of its earlier decisions. Recognizing the precedent, Justice Miller admitted that it may be true that acts that are merely private, not sanctioned by the laws of the state or committed by one exercising the authority of the state, are not normally within the scope of congressional authority or the Fourteenth Amendment. But it is quite a different matter, he observed, "when congress undertakes to protect the citizen in exercise of rights conferred by the Constitution of the United States, essential to the healthy organization of government itself." For Miller, freedom from violence, corruption, and intimidation in the election of the legislature and executive branches was essential to the success of a republican government. If the states could not or would not assure elections free from racial violence, the federal government had the authority to step in.[25]

The majority of justices on the Waite Court tended to admire a system of American federalism akin to that which existed before the Civil War—one in which people generally looked to the states to protect their rights. *Ex parte Yarbrough*, however, revealed Miller's understanding that a state could not guarantee individual rights when the very political institutions designed to do so were corrupted by prejudice and violence.[26] The need to protect the efficacy of the institutions of democratic government within the state could justify increased levels of congressional protection of the right to vote. Another group of cases in 1880 demonstrated that the same logic might permit an increased level of federal intervention with respect to jury service as well.

A West Virginia law that expressly prohibited blacks from serving on juries did not present much of a problem in this regard. In *Strauder v. West Virginia* a black man was tried and convicted of murder by an all-white West Virginia jury. Before the trial began, Strauder petitioned to have his case removed to the federal court under a federal statute that allowed removal of any case against any person who is denied, or cannot enforce, in the judicial tribunals of the state any civil rights guaranteed by the laws of the United States. Strauder claimed that as a result of West Virginia's prohibition against blacks serving on juries, he had been denied the right to trial by a jury impaneled without discrimination against his race. The Supreme Court agreed.[27] This was state action in its most virulent form, and the Court had little difficulty finding that it fell within Congress's authority to pass laws enforcing the Fourteenth Amendment.

In neighboring Virginia the exclusion of blacks from jury service was not written into law. Blacks were technically eligible for jury service, but in Patrick County, at least, the county judge in charge of putting together jury panels systematically excluded them. When two black men accused of murdering a white man asked to have their cases removed from the state court to the federal court, the Supreme Court refused. Writing for the majority in *Virginia v. Rives,* Justice Strong ruled that this type of de facto discrimination did not trigger the removal statute. Because the county judge, not Virginia law, was the source of racial discrimination in this case, the accused had an adequate remedy under state law for the judge's misdeeds. They could appeal their case to the state's highest court. If they failed at that level, they then had a right to further appeal to the U.S. Supreme Court.[28]

Strong was right. The defendants did have a remedy. But it required an arduous appeal through the state court system and then possibly to the U.S. Supreme Court, a route that few would have the resources to undertake. The remedy Strong envisioned was a great disappointment for those who hoped to provide blacks access to the federal courts when entrenched racial discrimination made it impossible or unlikely that they could enforce their rights in the state court system. Nevertheless two other cases involving jury service decided that same year appeared to give some teeth to the majority's rationale in *Virginia v. Rives*. In *Ex parte Virginia* a county judge who had systematically excluded black citizens from the jury list was convicted of violating the Civil Rights Act. The Court upheld the conviction.[29] Then, in *Neal v. Delaware*, the Court dismissed the indictment and overturned the conviction of a black man charged with rape and convicted by an all-white jury.

Although the state's lawyers had conceded in *Neal v. Delaware* that blacks had always been excluded from jury service, the chief justice of the Delaware Supreme Court had refused to dismiss the indictment. Blacks were not excluded because of racial discrimination, he said, but because "of the fact that the great body of black men residing in this State are utterly unqualified by want of intelligence, experience, or moral integrity to sit on juries." Calling this a "violent presumption," Justice John Harlan ruled that the actions of these officers, who were entrusted with the duty of selecting juries, denied blacks equal protection of the law. Furthermore, he said, the failure of the state high court to address the wrongs those officers had committed was a denial of a right secured by the Constitution and laws of the United States to the persons accused of crimes.[30]

While the Court allowed Congress to prevent private discrimination, when it came to voting and jury service, other cases demonstrated that it was not willing to go farther. About the same time as the Yarbrough case, R. G. Harris and a group of assailants took several prisoners from the custody of a Tennessee sheriff and then beat them to death.[31] Harris was indicted for violating a federal law that Congress hoped would alleviate Klan violence by prohibiting "conspiring or going in disguise" with the intention of depriving any person of civil rights and equal protection of the law. On appeal, the Supreme Court followed the same logic that it had used in *Cruikshank* and the *Civil Rights Cases*. The law is unconstitutional, it said, because it applied to private individuals rather than the state and because the U.S. system of federalism left enforcement of criminal law to the states.[32]

It is not surprising that, after the Compromise of 1877, the Waite Court continued to display the same tendencies regarding civil rights that it had before. It continued to look backward, continued to resist the idea that the Reconstruction Amendments created new rights, continued to be excessively formalistic, and continued to idealize an antebellum ideal of federalism. This version of traditionalism did not render the Reconstruction Amendments and enforcement laws inoperative, but it did yield a very narrow interpretation of the civil rights guaranteed to blacks.

Many cases involving women, American Indians, Chinese, and Mormons provide a different twist in that they come out of the West, from territories not yet admitted to statehood. They did not raise concerns of federalism, or the encroachment by the federal government of the powers of the states, and thus shed a different light on how justices of the Waite era thought about the nature of equality and the requirements of the Constitution. Before returning to equality, however, it is worthwhile to trace the Waite Court's response to problems arising from the revolution in commerce and westward expansion.

4

Romancing the Rails

On March 1, 1877, while Rutherford B. Hayes was traveling by special train to his inauguration, Chief Justice Waite announced one of the most significant cases of the era. In *Munn v. Illinois* the Court upheld an Illinois law that set maximum rates that grain elevators in the city of Chicago could charge for storage.[1] The firm of Munn and Scott, which owned one of the elevators, complained that the state's regulation of the rates they could charge deprived them of their liberty and property without due process of law, and thus violated the Fourteenth Amendment. The Supreme Court disagreed. Writing for the majority, Chief Justice Waite reasoned that states could regulate "businesses affected with public interest." The decision was not unanimous, however. In one of his most well known opinions, Justice Stephen Field vehemently dissented. As a result, *Munn* became a focal point in a fierce debate about the extent of the Constitution's protection of property, the nature of individual liberty, and the role of the state in providing for the general welfare and protecting the rights of the community.

The debate was shaped in a large degree by rapid changes in the economic and social landscape. America in the late 1870s was evolving from a nation with predominantly local economic systems to a system that was national and interconnected. It was a revolution in commerce that changed entirely the way that people did business. The revolution depended on a new system of transportation that centered on railroads. Consequently railroads are often found at the center of the debate. In fact, *Munn* was just one of eight related cases that have come to be called the Granger Cases. All of the others involved state efforts to regulate railroads, and even the facts that led to the *Munn* case were linked to railroads. Before turning to the *Munn* decision itself in the next chapter, therefore, this chapter focuses on some earlier legal disputes that revolved around building and operating railroads.

In essence, *Munn* was the culmination of a passionate and volatile relationship between the people of midwestern states and the railroads. It began as a courtship. In the early stages railroad builders expected and received a variety of benefits from government suitors. A railroad's corporate charter was the most fundamental of these government benefits because it gave the railroad a franchise to build and operate a line within the state. It was also a common practice for states to delegate to railroad builders the state's power of eminent domain: that is, the power to forcibly take another's private property for use as its right-of-way. In addition, states gave municipalities the authority to provide financial aid to railroad builders through the issuance of government bonds. It was also common for railroad builders to receive financial aid in the form of land grants, though usually the grants came directly or indirectly from the federal government. All of these government favors were justified by the idea that railroads served a public purpose.

The public purpose justification was especially evident with regard to the delegation of eminent domain and the issuance of government bonds. In his 1873 treatise, *The Law of Railways*, Isaac Redfield defined eminent domain as that "superior right, which of necessity resides in the sovereign power, in all governments, to apply private property to public use, in those great public emergencies which can reasonably be met in no other way."[2] Redfield, who was trying to explain the origins of eminent domain, exaggerated the limits on the power. Nevertheless his description of the power as one to be used in great public emergencies highlights the inherent tension it creates in a society, such as ours, that places a high premium on the right of private property.

Under American law the state is not restricted to using this power "in great public emergency" but rather for a "public use," and the person who is deprived of property is entitled to just compensation. Just what constitutes a public use, however, is difficult to say and is still debated today.[3] But there is one category of activity that undeniably falls within the definition. As Redfield put it, "One of the chief occasions for the exercise of this right is, in creating the necessary facilities for intercommunication, which in this country is now very generally known by the name of Internal Improvement."[4] Among these internal improvements were canals, ferries, bridges, wharves, and public highways.

Railroads joined this category almost from the time of the invention of the locomotive. The earliest legal decisions questioning the status of railroads tended to equate railroads to a public highway. Citing numerous state court opinions, Redfield concluded, "That railways are but improved highways, and are of such public use as to justify the exercise of the right of eminent domain, by the sovereign, in their construction, is now almost universally conceded."[5] This justification was so universally conceded that one critic of railroad policy observed in 1886 that "no railroad of greater importance than a mere switch ever has been or ever can be built without invoking the sovereignty of the government [eminent domain] in its behalf."[6]

This did not necessarily mean that the power had to be delegated to the railroad companies. The state could have just as well used its eminent domain power to create a public right-of-way or public easement, which then could have been operated by a given railroad. By the time railroads were being built, however, there was ample precedent for states delegating the power to private companies for building bridges and dams, starting ferry services, or achieving some other public goal.[7] To the charges that a private company should not be given the authority to seize another person's property to achieve its own private goals, courts often responded that the goals were not private. Rather, the company was standing in for the public by advancing the public interest or enforcing a public right.[8] In one of the earliest cases involving a railroad, the North Carolina Supreme Court ruled that "the [railroad] corporation is a franchise, like a ferry or any other. As to the public, it is a highway, and in the strictest sense *publici juris*."[9]

During a railroad building boom after the Civil War and rapid expansion in the West, the public purpose justification played another role with respect to railroads. Convinced that a route through their community would assure prosperity, municipalities got into the business of financing railroad construction. In the 1860s and 1870s it became common for municipalities to try to attract a railroad by offering to invest in the company or issue municipal bonds to support its construction. In theory the bonds, usually sold at a discount to eastern financiers, would help attract the cash necessary to build the railroad. They would be paid back in taxpayer dollars. And therein lay the potential conflict. Taxation was similar to eminent domain in that American tradition allowed taxes to be levied only for a public purpose.[10]

As might be expected, the courts resolved the potential conflict by importing from eminent domain law the idea that building railroads constituted a public purpose.[11] Consequently by 1873 Redfield was able to conclude that the weight of authority is "that a railway is so far in the nature of an improved highway, that legislatures may empower towns and counties to subscribe for stock in such companies whose roads pass through such towns or counties."[12] The U.S. Supreme Court agreed that "unless restrained by its own constitution, the legislature of a state has the right to authorize a municipality to take stock in a railroad, borrow money to pay for it, and levy a tax to pay the loan."[13]

By the time Waite took office it was clear that railroads satisfied the requirement of public purpose, but the definition of public purpose was still not fully settled.[14] In the 1875 case *Loan Association v. Topeka*, for example, the Court ruled that the town of Topeka, Kansas, did not have the authority to issue bonds to finance a company that manufactured equipment for building bridges. Justice Miller, who wrote the opinion, emphasized the relationship between bonds and taxation, observing that in all but rare instances, contracts creating debts to be paid in the future imply an obligation to pay by taxation. Because the right to tax can only be exercised for a public use, Miller reasoned that bonds issued to aid private enterprise that are not of a public character, such as a manufacturing plant, were not valid.[15] *Loan Association v. Topeka* demonstrated that there were limits to the type of business government could finance, but the opinion had a limited impact.[16] The Court did not thereafter show any particular hesitancy in recognizing public purpose when states issued bonds to encourage economic development.[17]

States did have the authority to limit the ability of state and local officials to borrow money and did so by means of both constitutional provisions and legislation. Legal disputes involving the interpretation of such restrictions would normally be matters for the state courts. Federal courts often became involved, however, because many of these disputes were between a midwestern town or county and a lender or financier whose business was located in an eastern state. The U.S. Constitution gives federal courts jurisdiction in such cases because they involve diversity of citizenship: conflicts between citizens of different states.[18] In diversity cases of the time, the federal courts usually looked to rulings of the appropriate state court for guidance, but the U.S. Supreme Court carved out its own doctrine in bond cases.[19]

Gelpcke v. The City of Dubuque, an 1864 dispute over the payment of municipal bonds, involved a common scenario. In violation of Iowa law, Dubuque issued bonds to a purchaser. Ordinarily the purchaser of those bonds, being party to the illegal contract, would have no rights to collect the value of the bonds. Typically, however, the original purchaser would sell the bonds, and the question then became whether this subsequent purchaser, or subsequent "holder," had a right to collect.

In state court proceedings the *Gelpcke* case raised the question of whether the bonds were invalid because the statute authorizing Dubuque to issue them violated the Iowa Constitution. In a split decision the Iowa Supreme Court first ruled that the statute did not violate the Iowa Constitution. Later, however, in a unanimous decision the Iowa Supreme Court reversed itself and ruled that the bonds did violate Iowa's Constitution. Then, having decided that the bonds were invalid in the first place, the Iowa high court ruled that the subsequent holder had no rights.[20]

On appeal, the U.S. Supreme Court took the bold and unusual step of refusing to follow the Iowa Supreme Court's interpretation of its own state constitution.[21] Just two years earlier Justice Noah Swayne, writing for the majority of the U.S. Supreme Court, ruled that federal courts were bound to follow the latest decision of a state's high court.[22] In *Gelpcke,* however, he changed his mind. Swayne was undoubtedly moved by the fact that the Iowa court had reversed itself.[23] More significant, he categorized the subsequent buyer as a "bona fide holder." Given that status, Swayne concluded that subsequent buyers had a right to presume the bonds were issued under proper authority.[24]

The legal concept of bona fide holder assumes a degree of innocence.[25] The idea behind it is that a subsequent purchaser of a bond, having no way of knowing that the bond may be illegal or unauthorized, should be protected by law. Once the bond is in the hands of the bona fide purchaser, therefore, the law presumes that it was issued under proper authority. Although there are good reasons for following this presumption, especially with respect to private borrowing, Justice Swayne's use of it in *Gelpcke* had the practical effect of undermining the state's power to limit government borrowing. It did not matter if bonds were issued in violation of the state constitution or statutes. It did not matter if municipal leaders fraudulently certified the bonds. Once in the hands of a bona fide holder, the bonds were presumed valid.

Justice Samuel Miller dissented in *Gelpcke,* as he would in many other bond cases over the next several decades. Miller emphasized that, regardless of whether they had jurisdiction to hear such cases, the federal courts did not have the power to change state law.[26] The bona fide holder rule, he would later argue, produced a situation in which a state's constitutional or statutory limits on the ability of municipal officials to put their citizens in debt could be disregarded with impunity.[27]

The Supreme Court built on the *Gelpcke* precedent in scores of cases from the 1860s through the 1880s. Some predated Waite, but many disputes began after the depression of 1873 and reached the Supreme Court just as Waite took office and shortly thereafter. For the most part they demonstrated that Miller's concerns were well-founded. In cases involving state and municipal bonds the Court tended to interpret state laws in a way that protected bondholders.

States employed several methods to limit the authority of public officials to commit their citizens to debt. One was an outright ban on borrowing for certain purposes. Although this method might appear foolproof, several Supreme Court opinions in the early 1870s reduced its effectiveness. In *Township of Pine Grove v. Talcott*, for example, the Court ruled the legislature could authorize a township to issue railroad bonds even though a provision of the Michigan Constitution prohibited the state itself from subscribing to bonds.[28]

One exception to this trend demonstrated that outright prohibitions could be effective. On March 30, 1874, less than a month after Waite became chief justice, the Court decided *Mayor of Nashville v. Ray*.[29] Nashville's municipal charter did not allow the city to borrow money. To get around this, city officials, rather than issuing bonds, issued "checks" that served the same purpose and could similarly be sold on a discount to holders. The Court's reaction to this scheme, bordering on fraud, demonstrated that there was some limit to the bona fide holder doctrine. This time the Court held that the checks were not valid. Justice Miller, who wrote the majority opinion, noted that government officials were unlike private borrowers in that they borrow not for themselves, but for the public. Without limits on their power to borrow, fraudulent issues, speculations, or embezzlements on the part of public officials could create a vast amount of public indebtedness without any corresponding public benefit. Miller warned that recognizing the validity of fraudulent documents such as the Nashville checks would have had the effect of giving corrupt officials the power to involve a community in irretrievable bankruptcy.

In other cases involving official malfeasance that was only slightly less unpalatable, however, the Court was likely to uphold the validity of bonds under the bona fide holder rule. In *Town of Venice v. Murdock*, for example, it validated bonds even though public officials had forged taxpayers' names and certified a fraudulent list of approving voters in the public record.[30] *Town of Venice v. Murdock* was one of a dozen cases decided in 1876 upholding the validity of bonds and was typical of the Court's tendency over the years to liberally apply the bona fide holder rule.[31] Justice William Strong, who wrote many of the decisions in bond cases, captured the logic of the rule. Bondholders in distant markets could not be expected to know whether a proper vote had taken place, he reasoned. To require otherwise would "impose a clog upon their salableness [*sic*]." And since the bonds were valuable only because they could be sold, the legislature could not have meant to impose such a barrier. The town officials' certification of the vote was, for Strong, conclusive evidence that the condition of the statute had been met.[32]

Historian Charles Fairman later observed that in these bond cases, the Supreme Court threw its weight on the side of railroad promoters and investors by an aggressive assertion of federal judicial power.[33] But Strong and the majority saw themselves in a much more traditional light. They could tie their reasoning to a long tradition, going back at least as far as *Fletcher v. Peck* in 1810, that favored a system of commerce based on the sanctity of contract.[34] For those who favored the bona fide holder rule, the Court's "principled resistance to every form of attempted repudiation of debt" played a crucial role in the nation's commercial development.[35]

Justice Miller, who was often joined in dissent by Justice Davis and Justice Field, denounced the underlying rationale of the bona fide holder rule and its assumption of the innocence of the purchaser. For him, it made no sense to assume that a purchaser of bonds could not ascertain whether the bonds conformed to the law. It would be easy to determine, for example, that a municipality had violated a state law that prohibited it from issuing bonds that would require a tax of more than 1 percent of the taxable property within its boundaries to repay the debt.[36] The records of the bond issue are all public and accessible, he observed. A purchaser had but to write to the township clerk or county clerk to know precisely the amount of the issue of the bonds and the value of the taxable property within the township.[37]

The legislature's intention to place a limit on a city's power to borrow money should not be disregarded with impunity, Miller concluded. In any other class of cases the rule of law would require that, before buying these bonds, the purchaser must look into those matters upon which their validity depended. "But in favor of a purchaser of municipal bonds all this is to be disregarded, and a debt contracted without authority, and in violation of express statute, is to be collected out of the property of the helpless man who owns any property in that district."[38]

On one plane the disagreement between Miller and the Court's majority illustrated that a major question in these bond cases was who would be required to pay for the misdeeds of public officials.[39] The majority's theory was based on the belief that eastern financiers had no way of knowing that the commercial paper they had purchased was improperly issued. Besides, it was important to the whole system of finance that lenders have strong assurance that debt on those bonds in which they had invested be honored. Miller was more skeptical about the innocence of bondholders, whom he described not as investors but as "gambling stockbroker[s] of Wall Street."[40]

On another plane, however, the bond decisions reflected that the relationship between midwesterners and the railroads had turned sour. Some municipalities, hit hard by the depression, may have been motivated to challenge the validity of bonds because they were unable to pay. But by the 1870s midwesterners were simply becoming less enchanted with railroad promoters. That disenchantment led to court battles when newly elected officials tried to repudiate what they thought to be the ill-advised and illegal investments of their predecessors. Whatever their motives, most of them failed. In the vast majority of cases the Court followed or expanded on *Gelpcke*'s bona fide holder rule.

Miller's dissents were based not only on abstract legal reasoning but also on his own life experience. As one of the pioneers and civic leaders of Keokuk, Iowa, he had seen firsthand his community's early growth and potential. He had shared its desire to become a transportation hub for the Midwest, and he had heard the predictions of prosperity that came with a railroad line. Keokuk's experience was common. Although the railroad eventually connected the town to the rest of the rail system, its railroad line came only after rival communities had secured the more favorable routes. Keokuk did not become a hub for trade along the Mississippi River, nor did it become a key point along a railroad trunk line. Marginalized and mired in debt, the community withered.[41]

In the late 1860s many Iowans, and other midwesterners, found themselves in the same condition and blamed bondholders for their troubles. Republicans, like Miller, "portrayed bondholders as parasites who, like antebellum slaveholders, lived off the labors of others; Democrats lumped bondholders and African Americans together with other groups who, they believed, received special favors from the federal government."[42] Having found a common enemy, they began to elect state and local officials who promised to repudiate bond debt.[43]

Indebtedness in the form of municipal bonds was not the only problem for Iowans. Like other midwesterners, they were caught in an entirely new system of commerce. The circumstances of the eastern Iowa river towns dramatically illustrates the shift. These towns' hopes of becoming commercial hubs depended on their developing into dominant links to Mississippi River traffic. They thought that railroads would deliver goods to them for transfer to river barges and shipment to St. Louis. Instead, railroad companies like the Milwaukee, the Illinois Central, the Northwestern, the Rock Island, and the Burlington laid track from Chicago to the Mississippi River and beyond. Reaching directly into the interior of the states, these "trunk lines" bypassed the river towns, rendering them mere way stations along the route.[44] As such, they eventually became victims of what they believed to be unfair and discriminatory railroad practices.

Railroad practices in the East and Midwest were driven by a peculiar combination of competition and monopoly, and both might drive the business of any one company. Where a company controlled a strategic location or was the only means of transportation to a particular place, it had all the characteristics of a monopoly. That was usually the case for transportation from one small town to another or from small towns to centers of commerce, which became known as short haul shipping. When it came to transportation from center of commerce to center of commerce, which was called long haul shipping, shippers could choose from a number of alternative routes. As a result, competition for long haul shipping tended to be fierce and sometimes destructive.

Naturally, railroad managers tried to reduce the impact of that competition. A large company might run one route at a loss in order to undercut the fares of a competitor. It might provide special fares to larger customers or for a particular type of product. Sometimes competing lines entered into a pooling arrangement in which they cooperated on fixing rates and prices. Railroad managers maintained that there were reasonable economic justifications for these practices, and some historians agree. But even one of the more moderate of railroad critics, Charles Francis Adams Jr., observed that railroad practices "led directly to systematic discriminations and wild fluctuations."[45]

To reformers, the most blatantly arbitrary and unfair pricing practice was that of charging low rates for the long haul and high rates for the short haul. The favorable long haul rates applied to shipments from one terminal city to another. Shippers from towns along the line were charged the higher short haul rates. Usually these rates were set proportionally higher, but sometimes the short haul shipper would be charged not just more dollars per mile but actually more dollars total than the person shipping from the farther point.[46]

Railroad economists would argue that the difference between long haul prices and short haul prices was justified. Competition to get long haul business forced the railroads to charge the lowest rates they could. Meanwhile, costs from stopping and unloading or pulling partial carloads made the short haul business more expensive to provide. Arthur T. Hadley added that if a railroad could not offer long haul service at the cheaper rate, it would not be able to provide the service along the route at all. Without the long haul business, he reasoned, service for the short haul shippers might not exist. Thus, despite being charged the higher price, short haul shippers and small towns actually benefited from rate discrimination.[47]

This kind of reasoning was a hard sell to small town shippers who suffered the effect of railroad rate-making practices. They were concerned not so much with the logic of railroad economics or the rise and fall of particular companies or railroad magnates, but rather with the impact that railroad practices had on multiple facets of their lives. James F. Hudson captured the feeling when he complained that railroads "hold a greater power over the fortunes and prosperity of individuals and communities than we have ever intrusted to our government."[48]

In the late 1860s business leaders from such communities took the lead in calling for state control over the railroads. Rate discrimination and favoritism served as their clarion. By the early 1870s farmers, loosely organized under the auspices of the Grangers, joined the bourgeoning reform movement. The terms "Grange" and "Granger" were the popular name of the Patrons of Husbandry, a farmers' alliance that came into being in 1867. Although it began as a cooperative movement to encourage education and trade among farmers, the Grangers quickly developed a political presence.

The Granger movement grew at an astonishing rate, and in 1873 and 1874 farmers' organizations placed a significant number of sympathetic representatives in the legislatures of Illinois, Iowa, Minnesota, and Wisconsin. Working with merchants, shippers, and civic leaders, they helped enact laws that set maximum rates railroads could charge for shipping, created railroad commissions, and prohibited rate discrimination. The Grangers' influence in passing reform legislation has probably been exaggerated.[49] Nevertheless the image of the Grangers as an agrarian revolt captured the popular imagination, and the movement gave its name to *Munn v. Illinois* and the related Granger Cases.

Economic self-interest undoubtedly played a role in the railroad reform movement. Small town merchants, shippers, or farmers may not have been able to articulate in the language of economics their complaints about railroad rate making, but they understood the feeling of being gouged. Although most reformers agreed that the railroads had a right to make a profit, they also believed that companies did not have the right to set rates arbitrarily without regard to fairness.

Raw self-interest was not the only concern in what became known as "the railroad problem." Fear also played a role. Railroads were transforming the country from a commercial system made of regional and local economies to a system dominated by a national economy. Even under the old system outside forces, like the weather or price of grain, impacted on the livelihood of small town merchants and farmers. Now, swift transportation allowed farm products to be sold at distant locations. Massive storage facilities that mixed one farmer's produce with another's allowed financiers to speculate in futures.[50] In this new national commercial system outside forces, over which they had no control, had an even greater impact on the well-being of farmers and small town shippers. Many of them were motivated by a desire to take back some control of their own economic destiny.[51]

Taking back control did not mean turning back in time. As historian Charles Postel has demonstrated, many reformers of the late nineteenth century were not opposed to the idea of progress. Rather than seeing the railroad and other modern developments as destructive, they often linked modernization to the promise of unimagined progress that could provide faster, cheaper, and hopefully more equitable access to national and world markets.[52] Their goal was a political and economic system that assured them a fair share of that bounty.

Reformers intuitively understood that individuals could not achieve that fairness or take back control of their economic destiny on their own. They formed organizations to educate farmers on modern agricultural techniques. They formed businesses or cooperatives in an attempt to take control of the distribution of their own products. These businesses were sometimes organized as corporations, which Victoria Saker Woeste has called benevolent trusts.[53] Many, however, hoped to use government as a means of taking back control.

Granger leader D. W. Adams told his followers that against the railroads, "the people, in their individual capacity, are powerless and only through their united action as sovereigns can they obtain redress."[54] In the minds of many railroad reformers government alone had the strength to counterbalance the power and privilege of the railroad corporation, and it could do so by enacting legislation regulating railroad rates and other practices.

There was plenty of precedent in American history for regulating prices and business practices. Mills, markets, taverns, and inns, as well as hackmen (cabbies), draymen (truckers), and various professions, were just some of the businesses and occupations that states commonly regulated.[55] Even so, on some theoretical level, the idea of regulating railroad rates and business practices ran afoul of American society's traditional respect for the rights of private property. For this reason the Granger laws and the Granger Cases are often depicted as a conflict between governmental power and private rights, or as one opponent of regulation described it: "the power of the community to regulate business against the right of the citizen to enjoy the rewards of his enterprise."[56]

Americans have always had a degree of distrust of governmental power. In fact, a distrust of power, a distrust of elites, and a distrust of government were characteristic of the Age of Jackson—the pre–Civil War years in which most reformers as well as railroad leaders came of age. By emphasizing a paradigm that pitted government power against property rights, railroad advocates and opponents of regulation sought to emphasize that tradition and cast regulation in the worst possible light.

The debate over economic regulation was not just a matter of the government's assertion of power being in conflict with an individual's property rights, however. Reformers saw it more as a matter of weighing an individual's claim of property rights against the rights of the people or the rights of the community. Although this may seem like an overly fine distinction, it is not. Instead it linked economic regulation to another American tradition that is just as long-standing and deeply held as property rights. That tradition, as we shall see, is popular sovereignty.

This was evident in the Illinois constitutional convention of 1869–70, which enacted the constitutional reforms that set the stage for *Munn*. From the opening days of discussions, reform-minded delegates like William Allen, a prominent Democrat from the southern part of the state, promised not to acquiesce to "a standing wrong against the rights of my people."[57] Similarly Abel Harwood complained that monied monopolies seriously affected the interests of the people.[58] During subsequent debates about building canals or public warehouses, limiting the state's borrowing authority, and railroad rate making, delegates referred to the rights of the people scores, perhaps even hundreds, of times. More informative than how *often* they used the phrase, however, is *how* they used it.

On their most simple level the phrases "rights of the community" and "rights of the people" were used to convey a speaker's sense of the greater good. In one of numerous examples, Joseph Medill, part owner of the *Chicago Tribune*, maintained that the convention would be derelict in its duty if it failed to enact provisions protecting the rights of the people, public good, and public safety against the unrestricted avarice of monopoly.[59] But the more significant use of the phrase the "rights of the people" linked it with popular sovereignty. Henry W. Wells explained that the power to regulate railroads derived from the rights of the people as sovereign. "I believe it to be the right of the people, in their capacity as sovereigns . . . to fix what tolls shall be reasonable for these railroad companies to charge for transportation of freight and passengers. The railroad companies have their charters, but, behind, superior to them, are the rights of the people which require them [the railroads] to exercise their franchises consistently with the public [well-being]."[60]

Popular sovereignty was said to give the people, as the creators of corporations, the power to control their creation. As Reuben M. Benjamin, a Harvard-educated lawyer from Bloomington, Illinois, pointed out, a legislature, being a mere agent of the people, could not bargain away the people's rights. "The corporation which accepts from the Legislature exemption from governmental control, knowing that it is dealing with an agent bound by duty not to impair a public right, does so at its own peril. Nay, more; the corporation which accepts from the Legislature a grant of any essential attribute of sovereignty should be treated both in morals and in law as a party to a fraud upon the inherent rights of the people."[61] It followed for Benjamin and other reformers that no department of government—be it legislative, executive, or judicial—could bargain away, abandon, or diminish the powers entrusted to it by the sovereign people.[62] Under this theory the rights of the people took precedence over a corporation's claim that rate regulations would violate its vested rights or rights under its corporate charter.[63]

The flip side of the belief that popular sovereignty justified state regulation of railroads and other corporations was reformers' fear that the growing political power of wealthy corporations threatened popular sovereignty itself. This fear also found expression in the Illinois constitutional convention, where William P. Peirce, for example, warned the delegation, "One of the greatest dangers to our republic is the great and rapidly increasing wealth, the great extension and the consolidation of railroad corporations and chartered monopolies."[64] Corporate power as a threat to popular sovereignty as well as individual liberty was also a persistent theme of the Granger movement.[65]

The Illinois constitutional convention adopted, and the people ratified, reform measures that gave the legislature broad powers to regulate railroads and warehouses. In the following years the Illinois legislature passed several laws that were typical of the Granger laws enacted in other midwestern states. One required that railroads charge uniform rates for any class of goods. This "antidiscrimination provision" also specifically outlawed the practice of charging higher rates for a short haul than for a long haul. A second act created a Board of Warehouse Commissioners, which was given the power to prescribe maximum rates. A third set maximum rates for passenger service. Another, which was destined to become the subject of the Supreme Court's opinion in *Munn v. Illinois,* set a maximum rate that could be charged for storing grain in Chicago's grain elevators.[66]

As might be expected, much of the opposition to the Granger laws came from railroad leaders. Some of these were practical complaints. Railroad leaders argued that public authorities, be they legislatures or commissions, were not competent to determine proper rates and that the rates they set would be unfair.[67] The resulting rates, they predicted, would drive out capital and make it impossible for railroads to meet their obligations to bondholders.[68] Railroad leaders anticipated future battles in the state legislatures and used these practical arguments to help make their case.[69] Writing to a community leader of Parksville, Missouri, James M. Walker, president of the Chicago, Burlington, and Quincy, explained that "the present hostility of the legislatures in the Western states toward railroads" made it impossible for his company to build a new route to Parksville.[70] To another community leader he wrote, "I cannot at the present time encourage your hope or think that our people will invest any money in any additional road in your state or perhaps elsewhere in the West."[71]

The railroad leaders' most significant contention was that the Granger laws violated their "exclusive right to fix the rate of transportation."[72] Sometimes they insisted that they derived this right from their charters.[73] But they also believed that both rate regulation and antidiscrimination provisions violated their property rights. In this vein Robert Harris wrote, "They [the legislature] have made a clear issue in the position assumed that they have the right to take away from the owners of the roads their property absolutely if they saw fit. And they seemed to have seen fit."[74] To this John N. Denison added sarcastically, "I suppose that there is no limit to the rights of the sovereign people."[75]

Although railroad leaders hoped to repeal or revise the Granger laws, they did not trust state legislatures. Railroad historian Thomas C. Cochran noted, "Railroad men generally expected more favorable consideration from courts than from legislatures or commissions, more from judges than from juries, and more from the highest courts than from inferior ones."[76] Letters between these men show that they also preferred federal courts to state courts.[77] They also reveal that railroad leaders understood the legal issues involved and that they intended to initiate a campaign to bring regulation within the protections of the Fourteenth Amendment. Regarding one suit brought against the Chicago, Burlington, and Quincy, Walker gave the following directive to company lawyers: "No pains must be spared upon this defense. It will take a great deal of time and much labor, perhaps more than any suit the company has had. . . . The first suggestion that I have to make is whether this case cannot be removed to the United States Court under the 14th Amendment and the law under and in pursuance thereof."[78]

Railroad lawyers steadfastly advised their clients that the Granger laws would not pass constitutional muster and polished the legal theories upon which the railroads would rely. Their advice set off a flurry of lawsuits in both the state and federal courts. The affected companies employed two tactics to get their cases into court: they either ignored the Granger legislation, thus forcing the states to sue for enforcement, or they initiated lawsuits that directly challenged the validity of the laws.[79] Either way, the railroad lawyers' first contention in all the Granger Cases except *Munn* was that the state's effort to legislate rate regulation violated the Article I, Section 10, guarantees that no state shall pass any law "impairing the obligation of contracts."

In contract clause doctrine, franchises and acts of incorporation were considered a contract between the state and the corporation it had created.[80] In theory a subsequent law placing new conditions on the corporation would alter the terms of its franchise, thus impairing the obligation of that contract. In *Chicago, Burlington, and Quincy Railroad Company v. Iowa* railroad lawyers maintained the Granger laws did just that. In this and the other Granger Cases the railroads' grants were silent on the subject of who had the rate-making power. Yet lawyers argued that the company's right to determine the rates it would charge was an inherent part of its contract. The Supreme Court summarily rejected this contention. "Railroad companies are carriers for hire," Chief Justice Waite reasoned. "They are incorporated as such, and are given extraordinary powers, in order that they may better serve the public in that capacity." As such, he concluded, they are "subject to legislative control as to their rates of fare and freight, unless protected by their charters."[81]

Railroad attorneys thus failed to accomplish one of their primary goals. They had hoped to convince the Court to adopt a rule that the reasonableness of a company's rates was a matter for judicial, rather than legislative, determination. In *Chicago, Burlington, and Quincy* Chief Justice Waite noted that a court might determine the reasonableness of rates in absence of any legislative regulation on the subject. But if a legislature decided to enact maximum rates, it had the same power to do so with respect to a corporation as it did with respect to individuals in a similar business.[82]

Even when the charter had an express provision allowing the company to determine reasonable rates, as in *Peik v. Chicago and North-Western Railway Co.*, subsequent legislation regulating rates might not violate the contract clause. The reason was that contract clause doctrine included several exceptions to the inviolability of the corporate franchise. The most important of these recognized the state's right to include a provision in the grant reserving to itself the power to later revise the agreement. In *Peik* the Court noted that the existence of such a reserve clause meant the state had the power to pass subsequent legislation that set maximum rates.

A state's reliance on reserve clauses was, however, also subject to limitations. Under standard contract clause doctrine of the time, even a reserve clause would not give a state the power to defeat or substantially impair the essential object of the grant or any rights vested under it.[83] Under traditional doctrine the notion of what constituted "the essential object of the grant" was broad enough to make the contract clause a useful tool for protecting existing corporations.[84] A corporation might turn to the contract clause to claim that its franchise was exclusive and that the state could not offer a new grant to a competitor. It might claim exemption from taxation or from subsequent state regulation. The contract clause was so useful in this regard that some contemporary observers noted that the clause, more than any other provision of the Constitution, was a source of excessive and angry controversy. Others charged that the contract clause was the bastion of corporate privilege and a shield for corporate power.[85] Despite its usefulness in any particular case, however, traditional contract clause doctrine did not provide what railroad leaders wanted most—a constitutional condemnation of state rate-making authority in general.[86]

To address this limitation, railroad attorneys in the Granger Cases proposed a subtle but important variation on the rule that a state cannot deprive a corporation of the essential object of its grant. Attorneys for the Chicago and Northwestern Railroad proposed the new theory to challenge the validity of a Wisconsin maximum rate law. There they argued that "this act . . . takes the income, and thus deprives the company of the beneficial use of its property, and the means of performing its engagements with its creditors, *as if the road was confiscated.*"[87] Justice Stephen Field seemed to agree.[88] But the majority of the Court did not.

Nevertheless the railroads' tactic of equating rate regulation with confiscation in this fashion blended the contract clause argument with the idea that regulation of rates effectively took the railroad's private property without due process of law and therefore violated the Fifth and Fourteenth amendments.[89] As we shall see in the next chapter, this had important implications for the development of constitutional doctrine.

The railroad's claim that regulation amounted to confiscation also highlighted the degree to which railroad supporters and reformers disagreed at the very most fundamental level: the question of whether regulation was consistent with American traditions and the American system of government. Where reformers maintained that the traditions of popular sovereignty and democracy justified or even required regulation, railroads argued that the traditions of individual liberty and limited government prohibited it. Charles B. Lawrence, attorney for the Chicago and Northwestern Railroad, warned that "the idea that the legislature has the general power to set maximum rates is at war with every principle of free government, and all those provisions of our American Constitution which were designed to protect the natural rights of man against legislative aggression."[90] Another of the Chicago and Northwestern's lawyers, John Cary, maintained that the Granger legislation amounted to "communism pure and simple," which, if not checked, would "ultimately overthrow not only the rights of property, but personal liberty and independence as well."[91]

While it was not unusual for opponents to cast the Granger laws as the product of an agrarian revolt, radical agrarianism, or communism, the roots of railroad reform were anything but radical. Historian George H. Miller has convincingly demonstrated that the call for reform originated in the business communities of small town America. Moreover the theoretical underpinnings of reform can only be described as radical if we are willing to describe the American Constitution itself as radical. The theory of inalienable popular sovereignty that was so evident in the Illinois constitutional convention derives from one of the most revered ideals of the founding of the United States.[92]

The principle of popular sovereignty or the rights of the community also was well entrenched in American constitutional doctrine. The most famous statement of this principle is found in Chief Justice Taney's opinion in *Charles River Bridge Co. v. Warren Bridge* Co. (1837). Rejecting the Charles River Bridge Company's claim that its charter implied an exclusive right to operate a bridge over the Charles River, Taney reasoned that "the object and end of all government is to promote the happiness and prosperity of the community by which it is established, and it can never be assumed that the government intended to diminish its power of accomplishing the ends for which it was created."[93] For Taney, the presumption in favor of the state was not just a matter of governmental power versus individual liberty. It was also a matter of balancing property rights against the rights of the community. "While the rights of private property are sacredly guarded," he observed, "we must not forget that the community also have rights, and that the happiness and well being of every citizen depends on their faithful preservation."[94]

The notion that a legislature could not bargain away the attributes of a state's sovereignty also found expression in traditional constitutional law in cases interpreting the meaning of the contract clause. Thomas M. Cooley, the most renowned constitutional scholar of the time, pointed out that "the State could not barter away, or in any manner abridge or weaken, any of those essential powers which are inherent in all governments, and the existence of such in full vigor is important to the well being of organized society; and that any contracts to that end, being without authority, cannot be enforced under the provisions of the [contract clause]."[95] Among those essential powers Cooley listed the police power, the power of eminent domain, and the taxing power.[96]

Several cases from the early Waite Court years illustrated that with regard to the taxing power, there was a limited exception to this general rule. By then it was well-settled law that a state could exempt a corporation from taxation or limit the taxes of a corporation if the state received consideration in return.[97] *Morgan v. Louisiana* (1874) illustrated that the Court was inclined to apply this exception sparingly, however. In *Morgan* a railroad that had received an exemption from taxation was sold and consolidated with another line. The new company tried to claim a tax exemption on its entire business. The Court ruled that immunity from taxation is a privilege and does not automatically transfer from the railroad to a buyer. The power to tax, Justice Field reasoned, is an exercise of a sovereign attribute of the state. The entire community has an interest in it, and it will not be presumed to be abandoned.[98]

Cooley was firm that a legislature could not bargain away the police power of the state even by an express grant. That left open the question of whether economic regulation, especially regulation of rates and prices, fell within the normal police powers of the state. The history of economic regulation in the early United States makes it clear that most people and legislators thought it was. Americans accepted the distinction between the right of property and the rules of conduct under which property may be used.[99] Licensing, building and regulating public markets, controlling prices or quality of common goods, use of and access to waterways, eminent domain law, public trust doctrine, and the law of nuisance are common examples of states regulating the economy in the public interest. And the list goes on. Although the state's power to interfere with property was not unlimited, nineteenth-century Americans certainly considered regulation normal.[100]

Regulation was also considered normal in nineteenth-century legal doctrine. Judges and commentators gave states wide latitude regarding economic regulation. Moreover they justified regulation not only in terms of balancing government power against individual liberty but also in terms of protecting the rights of the public. Historian Harry Scheiber thus concluded that American judges and legal commentators have given sustained, explicit, and systematic attention to the notion that the public, and not only private parties, have "rights" that must be recognized and honored if there is to be rule of law.[101] He and others commonly use Massachusetts Chief Justice Lemuel Shaw's opinion in *Commonwealth v. Alger* (1851) to support the point: "We think it is a settled principle, growing out of the nature of a well ordered civil society, that every holder of property, however absolute and unqualified may be his title, holds it under the implied liability that his use of it may be so regulated, that it shall not be injurious to the equal enjoyment of others having an equal right to the enjoyment of their property, *nor injurious to the rights of the community.*"[102] Defining the reach of state power to regulate the economy, including regulation of rates and prices, was a matter primarily left to the states themselves. This general rule applied to railroads as much as any other business, and, although many states gave companies flexibility to set their own rates, regulation of railroad rates was a normal practice.[103]

Both common practice regarding economic regulation and legal doctrine indicate that if by "radical" we mean an agent of change, the term more accurately applies to railroad lawyers than proponents of rate regulation. The lawyers who represented the railroads in the Granger Cases were among the most distinguished lawyers in America. They must have realized that under contract clause doctrine, as it stood, they really did not have very good cases. Yet they pressed on, in all likelihood because they had a purposeful and calculated desire to change the status of the law. They wanted to establish a doctrine that the Constitution guaranteed a fundamental right to be free of the type of price regulations created in the Granger laws. Such a doctrine would remove the issue of regulation from the political process.[104] Hindsight tells us that the due process clause of the Fourteenth Amendment, rather than the contract clause, would provide the vehicle for change—and that *Munn v. Illinois* would be provide the first proving ground.

5

THE LAST GASP OF THE RIGHTS OF THE COMMUNITY

Munn v. Illinois differed from the other Granger Cases in that it did not involve a railroad, and it did not involve a corporation. The defendant in this case was Munn & Scott, a partnership that owned and operated grain elevators along the Chicago River. The case began when Munn and Scott was charged with violating an Illinois law that set maximum rates that elevator owners could charge for storing and handling grain.

For those of us who have seen grain elevators dotting the countryside as we drive across rural America, the conflict may not seem very important. But Chicago's grain elevators were different, and their importance to the national market in farm goods cannot be overstated. They were both a product and a symbol of the commercial revolution that was taking place in the late nineteenth century.

In this system of commerce the sale and storage of grain were not local transactions as they had been in the past. Most of the grain produced in the Midwest in the 1870s made its way to the Chicago lakefront. There it was held for shipment by railroad or via the Great Lakes and the St. Lawrence River to eastern markets. All of the grain that reached this gathering point was stored in fourteen immense elevators owned by nine business firms, of which Munn & Scott was one. Most of the firms were directly connected to a particular railroad, often leasing the elevator from the railroad company.

From the farmers' point of view this new system fundamentally changed the way farm goods were marketed. The tendency to store grain in immense facilities concentrated in one location, combined with the ability to disperse it quickly through a web of railroad routes, allowed buyers to hold their grain hoping for the highest price. It essentially created a new business of speculating in grain futures. With speculation affecting the price of grain, farmers, whose livelihood had always been at the mercy of the weather, now faced another obstacle over which they had no control.

Adding to the farmers' dissatisfaction was the fact that cooperation among the nine Chicago firms allowed them to fix the prices they charged for storage of grain. These factors motivated the Grangers to push for regulation of Chicago's grain elevators. But collusion was not the only complaint leveled against the elevator owners, and the Grangers were not the only group calling for regulation. Complaints also came from shippers who claimed that the elevator companies often underweighed their shipments and undervalued the quality of their grain. They also came from traders in grain futures. For them, the elevator firms' practice of overstating the amount and quality of grain they held, and their refusal to allow inspection, turned investment strategy into nothing more than a gamble. The staunchest proponent for regulating the elevators was not the Grangers but the Chicago Board of Trade, which wanted a uniform system of inspection.[1]

Whatever the validity of complaints against the elevator firms, there is no doubt that the new market system created a bottleneck of commerce in the Chicago harbor. Nor is there any doubt that control of that bottleneck gave the owners of Chicago's elevators a stranglehold on the flow of commerce in the Midwest.

When *Munn v. Illinois* reached the Supreme Court in 1877, William G. Goudy and John N. Jewett, the lawyers for Munn & Scott, portrayed their clients in a more favorable light. The elevator companies did not have a stranglehold on commerce, they said. Rather, they were an essential cog in a national market of grain. Goudy and Jewett used this image to make a point that would be minor in the *Munn* decision but would become more important later. They maintained that the Illinois maximum rate law violated Article I, Section 8, of the Constitution, which gives Congress the power to regulate interstate commerce. Although the Court summarily rejected this commerce clause claim, in hindsight it may have been the company's most reasonable point. Modern scholars, as did even some contemporary reformers, have maintained that a uniform federal law would have been a more appropriate method of regulating the transportation industry, especially railroads, than was scattered state regulation.[2] Eventually Congress would pass the Interstate Commerce Act, but that did not happen until 1887, near the end of Waite's term.[3]

The most important issue in *Munn*, however, was whether the state regulations violated the Fourteenth Amendment guarantee that no state shall deprive any person of life, liberty, or property without due process of law. This theory was similar to the argument that the Louisiana butchers had raised, and the Supreme Court had rejected, in the *Slaughterhouse Cases*. The butchers had maintained that the Fourteenth Amendment, taken as a whole, gave federal courts the authority to protect individual liberty and property from arbitrary, partial, and unjust legislation of state governments. Taking a slightly different approach, Goudy and Jewett focused on only one clause of the amendment—the due process clause.

The concept of due process, sometimes referred to as "the law of the land," predates the Fourteenth Amendment. It traces its roots to the Magna Carta and is found in most state constitutions. It is also important to know that the guarantee is also found in the Fifth Amendment, which provides that "No person shall be . . . deprived of life, liberty or property, without due process of law." Although standard constitutional doctrine of the time held that the Fifth Amendment did not apply to the states, the guarantee of due process of law was part of the U.S. Constitution for almost a century before *Munn*. Its most fundamental meaning was that no person could be deprived of life, liberty, or property without the benefit of proper judicial hearing and procedure. In *Munn*, however, company attorneys argued that due process promised more than a trial according to settled judicial procedure. The guarantee, they said, was also meant to protect private rights from arbitrary government interference.

This theory concentrated on the substance of legislation rather than the procedure by which the law was enforced. Substantive due process, as it thus came to be called, would give the federal judiciary the authority to overrule state legislation that interfered with individual rights. The idea that the people have a right to resist arbitrary assertions of government power that threatened individual liberty is undoubtedly part of the American tradition, but there was little legal precedent to support the theory of due process and judicial power the company attorneys were proposing. They pointed to Daniel Webster's famous statement in the *Dartmouth College* case of 1819. The meaning of due process, Webster had reasoned, "is that every citizen shall hold his life, liberty, property, and immunities under the general rules which govern society. Everything which may pass under the form of [legislative] enactment is not considered the law of the land."[4] They could refer the Court to Thomas Cooley's treatise, *Constitutional Limitations,* which maintained that legislation could not interfere with vested rights beyond what was allowed by "settled maxims of law" and safeguards for the protection of individual rights.[5] They could also draw upon some state court opinions to support their argument. The most well known of these was *Wynehamer v. The People,* an 1856 case where New York's highest court ruled that a statute prohibiting the sale and possession of, and authorizing the destruction of, alcoholic beverages violated due process of law.[6]

Other than that, there was little support for the argument. The U.S. Supreme Court had used the concept of substantive due process only once—applying it to the Fifth Amendment's due process clause in the infamous *Dred Scott* case.[7] Justice Bradley had adopted the theory in his 1873 *Slaughterhouse* dissent,[8] but Justice Miller's opinion for the majority in that case conspicuously ignored the substantive due process argument. Miller did the same in the *State Railroad Tax Cases,* decided just a year before *Munn.* When railroad attorneys had argued that an Illinois plan for taxing railroad property took company property without due process, Miller's only response was, "The validity of the statute is not seriously questioned here on the ground of any conflict with the Constitution of the United States."[9]

Weaknesses aside, Jewett and Goudy were committed to their strategy. It would be easy enough for them to establish the general proposition that property rights fell among those liberties the Constitution was intended to protect. Nobody would disagree with that basic contention. The Fifth Amendment, the Fourteenth Amendment, and the contract clause all contained provisions that protected property. The task that would test the company attorneys' skill was to show that setting maximum rates for grain elevators and railroads constituted the type of government activity that violated their clients' property rights.

The key was to convince the Court that regulation of rates amounted to confiscation. From a relatively recent Fifth Amendment case in which a government-sponsored canal project had flooded an individual's adjacent land, they offered the principle that destroying the value of property constituted confiscation.[10] Rate regulation, they said, had the same effect. John Jewett best captured their argument: "It is not merely the title and possession of property that the Constitution is designed to protect, but along with this, the control of the uses and income, the right of valuation and disposition, without which property ceases to be profitable, or even desirable."[11]

Jewett and Goudy's argument embodied an attitude toward property rights that one present-day observer, Mary Ann Glendon, calls an "illusion of absoluteness."[12] The illusion lay in their presumption that an owner has absolute dominion over his or her property. In other words, Jewett and Goudy rejected the idea that the owner's dominion over property can be limited by the rights of the community. Goudy made this abundantly clear. Ignoring the long tradition of economic regulation for the good of the community, including rate and price regulation, he maintained that "for the first time since the Union of these States, a legislature of a State has attempted to control the property, capital and labor of a private individual, by fixing the prices he may receive from other private persons, who choose to deal with him."[13] Rather than balancing individual property rights against the rights of the community, Jewett postured the dispute as one of individual property rights versus government power. Legislation fixing prices represented an arbitrary and irresponsible power, he argued, a power practically to annihilate private property by destroying the value of its use.[14]

To the extent that they predicted the Court would reverse the position it had taken four years earlier in the *Slaughterhouse Cases* and invalidate the Granger laws, the company attorneys had badly miscalculated. Writing for a seven to two majority in *Munn v. Illinois*, Chief Justice Waite upheld the Illinois grain elevator regulations. Nevertheless the Court had faced a barrage of legal arguments from some of the nation's most prominent attorneys. In the process of explaining why the Court had upheld the regulations, the chief justice made some concessions.

The opponents of regulation could find some solace in the fact that Waite did not deny the theory of substantive due process. Statutes regulating the use of private property do not necessarily deprive the owner of property without due process of law, Waite wrote. "Under some circumstances they may, but not under all."[15] The chief justice admitted that the state has limited authority to interfere with property that is exclusively private. But when property is "affected with public interest," he continued, it ceases to be *juris privati* only and is thus subject to more extensive regulation for promotion of the general welfare.[16]

Waite's reasoning seemed sensible enough, and he had age-old authority to back it up. The proposition traced back to the seventeenth-century writings of English jurist Lord Chief Justice Hale, who ruled that owners of wharves, cranes, or other conveniences used by the public must charge reasonable and moderate rates because those conveniences are affected with public interest. Ferries and warehouses joined the list of types of property Lord Hale said could be affected with public interest, and subsequent British and American authorities applied the rule to other businesses like mills, turnpikes, and roads.[17] For Chief Justice Waite and the six other members of the Court who voted to uphold the Illinois rate regulation, it was clear that the Chicago elevators were businesses affected with public interest.

Company lawyers must have been especially dismayed that Justice Bradley voted with the majority to uphold the regulation. In the past, Bradley had shown an inclination to vote against state regulation. He had joined Field and Strong dissenting in the *Slaughterhouse Cases,* and in his separate opinion in that case had done the most to articulate the idea that the due process clause of the Fourteenth Amendment gave the Court power to oversee the substance of state legislation. Now, in *Munn,* only Field and Strong dissented. Not only had Bradley switched his vote, as it turned out, he was the member of the Court most responsible for developing the "business affected with public interest doctrine." In a memo "Outline of my views on the subject of the Granger Cases," Bradley acquainted Chief Justice Waite with the works of Lord Hale.[18]

In the *Slaughterhouse Cases* Bradley and Field had agreed that the Fourteenth Amendment's guarantee of liberty included a right to choose a trade or calling. They agreed that government regulation of business could infringe upon this right to a degree that it violated the Constitution. They also agreed that monopoly posed a threat to individual liberty and a free society. The extent to which they had agreed in the earlier case makes their disagreement in *Munn* even more enlightening, and, by writing his memo to the Chief Justice, Bradley left an unusually vivid source of his views.

The disagreement between Bradley and Field begins with their differing definitions of "business affected with public interest." Field's interpretation of the phrase conformed to his belief that regulation was appropriate only when aimed at government-created monopolies or applied when government enhanced the usefulness or value of a business's property.[19] He pointed out that the writings of Lord Hale and many of the cases upon which Waite and Bradley relied involved companies that operated under an exclusive franchise—either by prerogative of the king or contract with the state. The elevators in *Munn,* he argued, were private companies with no such exclusive franchise. To apply the rule to this kind of company would leave the state with an unlimited power to regulate private property. There would be no way to tell which business was affected with public interest and which business was not.[20]

Although Waite and Bradley failed to articulate a general rule, on one point they were very clear. Whatever might be the boundaries of the "affected with public interest doctrine," the Chicago elevators fell within it because they operated as virtual monopolies. In this sense the two justices saw the facts of *Munn* and the facts of the *Slaughterhouse Cases* as having much in common. In neither case did the company have an actual monopoly, but in both they dominated some essential element of a particular business. All of the butchers in New Orleans had to ply their trade in the Crescent City Company's slaughterhouse. Similarly all grain shipped through Chicago had to be stored in the elevators owned by a few firms that cooperated to fix prices. The only significant difference between the two situations was the source of their privileged position. The New Orleans slaughterhouse obtained its privilege by virtue of a government franchise; the Chicago elevator companies attained theirs through private ownership and cooperation. This made all the difference in the world to Field but no difference at all to Waite and Bradley.

Waite used the company attorneys' own commerce clause argument to explain why. "[The elevators] stand, to use again the language of counsel, in the very 'gateway of commerce,' and take a toll from all who pass. Their business most certainly 'tends to a common charge, and is become a thing of public interest and use.' Every bushel of grain for its passage 'pays a toll, which is a common charge,' and, therefore, according to Lord Hale, every such warehouseman 'ought to be under public regulation, viz., that he take but a reasonable toll.' Certainly, if any business can be clothed 'with public interest,' and cease to be *juris privati* only, this has been."[21] Likewise for Bradley, the source of a monopoly was of little consequence. The important thing for him was that the public could not stand on equal footing with companies such as railroads and Chicago grain elevators.

Despite the company attorneys' success in painting themselves as defenders of liberty and guarding against government oppression, Bradley did not forget that the heart of this dispute was a fundamental disagreement about the meaning of liberty and democracy. And, because he was writing a memo for himself, Bradley did not mince words. "Unrestricted monopolies as to those things which people must have and use, are a canker in any society, and have ever been the occasion of civil convulsions and revolutions," he wrote. "A people disposed to freedom will not tolerate this kind of oppression at the hands of private corporations or powerful citizens."[22]

The majority opinion in *Munn* is most remembered for Chief Justice Waite's adoption of the "affected with public interest" formula, and that aspect of the opinion has been criticized in terms of both style and substance. Later commentators complained that Waite's opinion lacked art or lacked fervor. The chief justice may not have been a great stylist, but his own self-effacing manner probably had a hand in instigating this kind of criticism. To Stephen Field, Waite once wrote, "The difficulty with me is that I cannot give the reasons I wish I could." And writing to Justice Horace Gray, he asked, "Can't you tell me the secret of your style. I wish I had it—Simple words properly used express so much."[23]

More important, criticism of the "affected with public interest" formula was also aimed at substance. This grew out of the experience with the formula in the 1920s and 1930s when judges who were more opposed to regulation flipped the formula on its head. Instead of using it to justify regulation, as Waite had, these later justices maintained that state regulatory authority was appropriate only for a limited set of businesses designated as those affected with public interest. Thus the affected with public interest formula came to serve as a limit on state regulation until the Court repudiated it in *Nebbia v. New York* (1934).[24]

But there was more to Waite's opinion than the "affected with public interest" formula. His reasoning also reflected a personal discomfort with the absolutist version of property rights that Jewett and Goudy favored, and a keen appreciation of the ideals of popular sovereignty and the rights of the people.

Waite's reluctance to accept substantive due process and discomfort in accommodating the absolutist view of property rights were put on display when he tried to explain guidelines for applying the "affected with public interest" formula. "Property does become clothed with public interest," Waite wrote, "when used in a manner to make it of public consequence, and affect the community at large."[25]

So broad was this definition that it caused Justice Stephen Field, a champion of the absolutist view of property rights, to complain, "If this be sound law, if there be no protection, either in the principles upon which our republican government is founded, or in the prohibitions of the Constitution against such invasion of private rights, all property and all business in the State are held at the mercy of a majority of its legislature."[26]

Despite this strong language, even Field agreed that businesses were subject to the police power of the state. Unlike the majority, however, he did not believe that regulation of rates fell within the police power. Field did not give us much help in determining why he reached that conclusion. The police power, he said, extended to "Whatever affects the peace, good order, morals, and health of the community."[27] In applying it, he continued, the state must be guided by the doctrine that the right to use one's property is limited only by the requirement that it not be used to injure others. On the basis of these principles he then concluded that "the compensation which owners of property, not having any special rights or privileges from the government in connection with it, may demand for its use," does not fall within that power.[28] Perhaps the most important factor leading Field to this conclusion was the presumption from which he started. Constitutional provisions intended for the protection of property, he insisted, should be liberally construed.[29] His implication was that the Court should be wary of any statute that interfered with individual liberty.

Contrary to Field, the majority of the Court believed that, in most instances, property rights would be adequately protected without judicial interference. Of course Waite could not deny that a state might abuse its power. But for protection against that potential abuse, he argued, "people must resort to the polls, not to the courts."[30] Bradley agreed and in the process revealed respect for popular sovereignty reminiscent of the debates in the Illinois constitutional convention. "The right to regulate rates and to declare what are reasonable and what are not, must be regarded as reserved to the legislature." Any other rule, he noted, "would be subversive to the authority which the people have confided to the legislature for their protection."[31]

Waite and Bradley did not propose that the Court abdicate to unbridled majority rule. Rather, their emphasis on popular sovereignty led them to presumptions different from Field's. In contrast to Field, Waite would assume that the legislation is valid unless proven otherwise. "Every statute is presumed to be constitutional," he wrote. "The court ought not to declare one to be unconstitutional unless it is clearly so. If there is doubt, the express will of the legislature should be sustained."[32] While he admitted that a state regulation might deprive an individual of property without due process of law, he would uphold regulation "if a state of facts *could* exist that would justify such legislation" and would declare a regulation void only "if *no state of circumstances could exist* to justify such a statute."[33]

The majority's presumption found solid roots in conventional contract clause doctrine of the time. It could be traced back to the majority ruling in the 1837 *Charles River Bridge* case, which was discussed in the previous chapter. There the

Court ruled that in interpreting the meaning of a state-granted charter, every legal presumption should be in favor of the state's power to protect the rights of the public.[34] Waite reiterated this idea in *Munn*, observing that "when one becomes a member of society, he necessarily parts with some rights or privileges which, as an individual not affected by his relations with others, he might retain."[35] "Under the police powers," he continued, "the government regulates the conduct of its citizens one towards another, and the manner in which each shall use his property, when such regulation becomes necessary for the public good."[36]

The majority's presumption in favor of state legislation certainly disappointed railroad leaders and their attorneys, who had hoped to move the question of what constituted reasonable rates and regulations from the legislative arena to the judicial. Field captured their position, and their distrust for the democratic process, in his dissent. "Government can scarcely be free where the rights of property are left solely dependent on the will of the legislative body without any restraint," he warned.[37] And, in his mind, it was the Court's duty to ensure that this did not happen.

For railroad leaders, who placed much more faith in appellate courts than in elected legislatures, the majority decision inflicted a brutal blow. They had dreamed that the decision would establish an unequivocal right to be free of government regulation. More realistically, they hoped it would produce a doctrine that the reasonableness of government rates and regulations was inherently a judicial question and that courts would presume that rate regulations amounted to an unconstitutional form of confiscation. Instead, the Supreme Court's decision in *Munn* reaffirmed the right of state legislatures to regulate.

John Jewett, one of the attorneys for Munn & Scott, warned that the opinion "has sent a chill of apprehension through the very heart of the business enterprise of the nation."[38] Robert Harris, president of the Chicago, Burlington, and Quincy Railroad, also detected a dire omen in *Munn*. Ignoring the fact that the nation was still in the throes of an economic depression that began in 1873 and that the depression was caused in part by overexpansion of railroads and other railroad practices, he blamed the Court's decision for the drop in value of railroad stock. Harris predicted that the Court "has turned over this vast property to the whim of a legislative committee." "If this is good law," he complained, "then corporate property is the only property that has no protection [from legislative interference]."[39]

Reformers, as would be expected, found comfort in the decision. Two years later delegates to the California Constitutional Convention pointed to *Munn* as proof that they had the authority to regulate railroad rates and fares.[40] And even a decade later a reform-minded governor of Minnesota reminded the legislature that while the expediency of railroad regulation might be doubted, the right of the state to regulate was no longer in question.[41] Editors of the *Minneapolis Tribune* were even more confident: "The power to regulate roads has been confirmed by the United States Supreme Court in the Granger Cases, there is no turning back and the ground will never be retraced."[42]

The second part of the *Tribune*'s observation would prove to be wrong. By the mid-1890s, after the Waite era, the Court would reject *Munn* and replace it with a doctrine of substantive due process that took inspiration from Field's dissent. This new doctrine would give much of what railroad and corporate leaders had wanted. Under it, all state regulation of rates would be suspected of being a confiscation of property that violated the Fourteenth Amendment. The Court would thus become the final arbitrator of the validity of rates. Reflecting a distrust of the democratic process, the Court would start from a presumption that rate regulation violated individual liberty. It would also develop a narrow definition of the police powers of the state—that range of legitimate state authority to interfere with liberty.[43] Because of its emphasis on entrepreneurial liberty, this new doctrine is often referred to as laissez-faire constitutionalism.

Although laissez-faire constitutionalism did not become entrenched until after the Waite era, constitutional history tends to treat *Munn* as a stepping-stone in the development of that doctrine. Interest in the case tends to be directed toward Waite's "affected with public interest" formula.[44] Modern treatment of the case also highlights Waite's caveat that some regulation may violate due process, and Field's dissent that all legislation should be presumed to do so. Chief Justice Waite's biographer points out that instead of being remembered as a victory for public regulation, *Munn* is thus more often viewed as the ideological forerunner to an era that emphasized economic liberty and saw the Court as a bulwark protecting business against interference of state regulation.[45] From this perspective it is common to conclude that the Court quickly moved away from the *Munn* doctrine.

Over time historians and legal scholars have developed two narratives about the nature, significance, and path of this move away from the *Munn* doctrine. The earliest version describes the change as a virtual coup d'état in which, in the years following the Waite era, the Supreme Court used the Fourteenth Amendment to attach laissez-faire economic theory to the Constitution. The most recent version of the narrative developed in the 1980s. It holds that there was no coup, but rather that the change reflected the Court's attachment to long-standing American traditions that emphasize individual liberty and limited government. In both versions of the narrative *Munn* plays the part of a first step in the evolution of the substantive due process doctrine. The modern version adds an implication that the path taken was a natural, almost inevitable progression.[46]

Analyzing *Munn* in its own context, rather than as part of the evolution of laissez-faire constitutionalism, puts a different spin on the majority decision. It demonstrates that Waite, while concerned about the American constitutional tradition relating to liberty, was even more influenced by another constitutional tradition that runs equally deep. It was a tradition that emphasized popular sovereignty and that placed property rights in the context of balancing individual freedom and the needs of a democratically governed society. From this perspective *Munn*, instead of being a stepping-stone for development of a doctrine that emphasized economic liberty, might better be described as a last gasp for the antebellum legal tradition that emphasized rights of the community as a limit on property.

Last gasp may be something of an exaggeration, however. From the perspective of long-term history, it is true that the Supreme Court eventually did move away from

Waite's reasoning and rejected the constitutional tradition based on popular sovereignty for a doctrine that idealized an absolutist right of property. Instead of balancing property rights against the rights of the community, it used a model of individual rights versus government power, and it narrowly defined the reach of that power.[47] But the demise of the Court's respect for the rights of the community was more of a drawn-out sigh than a sudden gasp. Although it is difficult to pinpoint precisely when it happened, many accounts place the moment thirteen years later in *Chicago, Milwaukee, & St. Paul Railway v. Minnesota*.[48]

It is also commonly, and mistakenly, believed that *Munn* immediately came under attack from attorneys for railroad, industrial, and financial interests. Perhaps Justice Miller helped fuel that idea when he complained a year later, in *Davidson v. New Orleans*, that the Court's docket "is crowded with cases in which we are asked to hold that state Courts and state legislatures have deprived their own citizens of life, liberty, or property without due process of law." This proliferation of cases, he said, was the result of "some strange misconception of the scope of this provision of the fourteenth amendment."[49]

Miller further complained that attorneys were viewing the Fourteenth Amendment as a means of bringing to the Supreme Court "the abstract opinions of every unsuccessful litigant in a State court [about] the justice of the decision against him, and of the merits of the legislation on which such a decision may be founded."[50] His stern criticism certainly conveyed a warning to business attorneys who might be looking for a new means to fight economic regulations enacted by state legislatures.[51] But it also embraced an attitude toward the Fourteenth Amendment that traced back to the Court's earlier opinions in the *Slaughterhouse Cases, Reese, Cruikshank,* and *Munn*. It conveyed a message that the majority was not inclined to use the Reconstruction Amendments to expand the Court's power. It displayed a nostalgic view of federalism that tended to idealize the pre–Civil War balance of state versus federal power. Most of all, it reaffirmed the majority's belief that the Reconstruction Amendments did not create new rights.

In *Davidson* this last point was evident in how Miller explained the concept of due process of law. The case involved a Louisiana statute that was intended to improve sanitation and decrease the incidence of disease in New Orleans by draining swamps and assessing landowners for the cost of the work.[52] Davidson argued that the city's assessment on his land unfairly required him to pay for these public improvements. The tax, he said, thus violated the Fourteenth Amendment by depriving him of his property without due process of law. Miller rejected the claim by first noting that the Fifth Amendment, which also prohibits the federal government from taking property without due process of law, had been part of the Constitution for nearly a century. This type of taxing scheme would be valid under the Court's interpretation of the Fifth Amendment, he observed, and there was no reason to believe that ratification of the Fourteenth Amendment had changed the nature and meaning of due process.

Miller did not reject the idea that a tax or a regulation could violate the due process clause. To do so, he said, would render the due process guarantee inoperative by allowing a state to "make any thing due process of law which, by its own legislation, it chooses to declare such."[53] The extent of his recognition of what is today called substantive due process was thus consistent with *Munn*. And Miller gave it a limited application, just as Waite had done in *Munn*.[54] Guided by a presumption that state law is valid and an expansive view of the legitimate powers of the states, he concluded that a tax imposed upon property for the public benefit could not be said to deprive the owner of his property without due process of law.[55]

In 1878 the Court issued only one other opinion involving a claim that economic regulation violated the Fourteenth Amendment. In *Railroad Company v. Richmond* a company that had received a charter to run a railroad through Richmond, Virginia, complained that a city ordinance prohibiting operation of steam locomotives down a particular street took its property without due process of law. The court rejected the argument. Writing for the majority, Chief Justice Waite reasoned that "all property within the city is subject to the legitimate control of the government, unless protected by 'contract rights,' which is not the case here. Appropriate regulation of the use of property is not 'taking' property, within the meaning of the constitutional prohibition."[56]

After the Court had disposed of *Davidson v. New Orleans* and *Railroad Company v. Richmond* in 1878, roughly six years would pass before its docket was actually crowded with cases in which it was asked to hold that state economic regulation deprived citizens of life, liberty, or property without due process of law. Railroad and business attorneys instead turned back to the contract clause to protect their clients' interests. In at least one instance attorneys even went out of their way to assure the Court that "the company does not invoke the aid of the Fourteenth Amendment to the Constitution, but submits that the statute . . . impairs the obligation of the contract contained in its charter and is therefore unconstitutional and void."[57]

Although contract clause claims did not provide all that corporate and business attorneys hoped for, they did occasionally yield successful results in the years after *Munn*. In *New Jersey v. Yard* (1877), for example, the Court enforced a provision in a railroad's charter that limited the amount of tax the company could be assessed.[58] And in *Edwards v. Kearzey* (1878) it ruled that state law protecting homesteads from foreclosure could not be applied to contracts entered into before the law took effect.[59] But the limitations of the contract clause, as a general restriction on state economic regulations, showed through even in these victories. These decisions did not alter the fact that the contract clause applied only to contracts already in existence, not future regulation, and that states could reserve the right to modify or dissolve corporate charters.

In addition the Court continued to apply principles for interpreting the contract clause that it had developed earlier. One was the presumption that a charter must be construed most favorably for the interests of the public. The outcome in *Fertilizing Company v. Hyde Park* (1878) turned on this rule of construction. This case involved an ordinance that had the effect of prohibiting the company from operating a fertilizing plant in the village of Hyde Park, Illinois. The company had received a charter from the state to operate a plant that turned offal and other by-products of Chicago slaughterhouses into fertilizer. When the plant began operations it sat in an uninhabited area south of the village. As Hyde Park grew, however, the plant became "an unendurable nuisance to the inhabitants for many miles around its location."[60] Some justices were sympathetic to the company's claim that the ordinance had the effect of confiscating its property without compensation.[61] But Justice Noah Swayne, who wrote the majority opinion, pointed out that the company's charter did not contain a provision expressly exempting it from claims of nuisance. Applying the rule of construction that a charter should be construed most strongly against the corporation, he concluded that the charter's silence on the matter was fatal to the company's claim.[62]

The Court also continued to apply the principle that a legislature could not barter away the essential powers of sovereignty, such as the police power.[63] In *Beer Company v. Massachusetts* (1878) a corporation that had received a charter to manufacture beer claimed that a subsequent state prohibition law violated the contract clause. In an earlier case, *Bartemeyer v. Iowa* (1874), the Court had ruled that prohibition of alcoholic beverages fell within the legitimate police powers of the state.[64] But that case involved an individual who claimed that the prohibition violated the Fourteenth Amendment by taking his property without due process of law.

The fact that these two businesses brought their cases under different clauses of the Constitution was insignificant to Justice Bradley. Writing for the majority in *Beer Company v. Massachusetts,* Bradley reasoned that Beer Company's possession of a charter could not be construed as exempting the corporation from legitimate controls to which an individual citizen would be subject. The right of both the corporation and individual were held subject to the police power of the states. While Bradley did not attempt to define the police power, he noted that protecting the lives, health, and property of citizens and preservation of good order and public morals "belong emphatically to that class of objects which demand the application of the maxim, *salus populi suprema lex* (the welfare of the people is the supreme law)."[65]

Munn, as it turns out, was a more serious setback for railroad and business leaders than is generally thought. The Court had firmly staked its place in a tradition that emphasized that the right to use one's property is limited by rights of the community and held fast to the presumption that state regulations of business practices are presumed to be valid. As might be expected, however, lawyers for the business elite did not give up. Changes in the Court's personnel in the early 1880s encouraged them to try again.

6

TOO BIG TO BE
ALLOWED TO FAIL

Eighteen seventy-seven was a tumultuous year in the United States, and it was not a good year for railroads. In July, a little more than a half year after the disputed presidential election and the Supreme Court's decision in *Munn*, the country faced its first nationwide labor uprising. It began on July 19, 1877, in the Baltimore and Ohio Railroad's Camden Yards in Martinsburg, West Virginia, and in locations just outside of Baltimore.

Several days earlier John W. Garrett, the Baltimore and Ohio Railroad president, had announced that the company would cut wages by 10 percent. This was the second time in eight months that workers had seen their wages cut, and, although the company justified the cuts as an economic necessity, that economic necessity did not keep it from paying a 10 percent dividend to its stockholders. The Baltimore and Ohio was not the only railroad to reduce wages. One after the other, all of the major railroads in the East cut wages by the same amount. Many Americans suspected the trend was not mere coincidence but rather part of an agreement that the railroads had negotiated earlier in the summer.

Organized labor was not a significant force in the mid-nineteenth century. Railroad workers had tried to organize a Trainmen's Union in response to the first wave of wage reductions, but the union failed to garner enough strength to be much of a factor. In Martinsburg, however, engineers, firemen, and brakemen agreed to fight the reduction by abandoning their trains along the tracks or refusing to move trains from the depot. When the company tried to bring in replacements, striking workers blocked the way and forced the replacements to back off. At the behest of Baltimore and Ohio officials, West Virginia governor Henry M. Matthew ordered the state militia to Martinsburg to restore order, protect railroad property, guard strikebreakers, and get the trains running.

The governor's action only made matters worse. When a company of militia accompanied the first train out of the Martinsburg depot, strikers threw a switch to derail it. A guard who noticed that the switch was set in the wrong position leaped off the train and confronted a young striker who was protecting it with a pistol in hand. When the striker, William P. Vandergriff, fired several shots, guards who were riding on the train responded with a volley of rifle fire that tore through Vandergriff's arm and thigh. After having his arm amputated, Vandergriff died several days later, the first casualty of the strike.[1] He was not the last.

It must have been disturbing for Americans to watch how spontaneously and quickly the strike spread. Just twenty years earlier it might have taken a letter, newspaper, or package sent from New York more than a month to reach San Francisco. Yet within days the strike had spread from coast to coast. On July 19, the day after the incident in Martinsburg, railroad workers in Newark, Ohio, walked off the job. They did the same in Chicago on that same day, in Pittsburgh on July 21, in New York City and St. Louis on July 22, and then in cities like Kansas City, Missouri; Galveston, Texas; and San Francisco.[2] In many cases workers from other industries joined the railroad workers' cause.

In most every city the strike turned violent, and in almost every instance railroad officers and state officials called in the state militia, then asked the president to send federal troops, to quell it. Events in Pittsburgh in late July provide an example. Jeering crowds were at the station when a unit of the state National Guard arrived in Pittsburgh. In an effort to move the troops out of the station where they had arrived, officers ordered the troops to fix bayonets and charge. The guardsmen's charge further enraged the strikers and their supporters. Jeers turned to threats and stone throwing. In panic, officers ordered the soldiers to fire directly into the crowd. A few minutes later twenty people lay dead and many more wounded. That was only the beginning of the violence.

Reports of the "massacre" brought thousands of protesters to the streets. The crowd that formed overwhelmed the guardsmen, drove them into a roundhouse, and surrounded it. The protesters then turned on railroad property and burned just about everything in sight: freight cars, company buildings, grain elevators, and even the Union Depot. Unable to get the crowd under control, state officials called for federal help. The violence had already begun to fizzle of its own accord, however, when on July 26 three thousand U.S. Army regulars and six thousand state militiamen boarded special trains outfitted with Gatling guns and moved along the Pennsylvania Railroad's main line to Pittsburgh. Four days later General Winfield S. Hancock reported to the War Department that the city had been occupied and that the Pennsylvania Railroad was operating.[3]

President Hayes was hesitant to use federal troops against striking railroad workers. It is true that as governor of Ohio, Hayes had used the state militia to end a strike of coal miners.[4] It is also true that there was precedent for using federal forces in labor disputes. Andrew Jackson, for one, had used the army in 1834 to end a strike against the Chesapeake and Ohio Canal.[5] Moreover Congress had the authority under Article I, Section 8, of the Constitution to call forth the militia to "suppress insurrections, and repel invasions" and had enacted laws giving the president the power to assist states in suppressing "domestic insurrection."[6] But Hayes, who was selected by the commission that resolved the deadlocked election of 1876, had only been in office a few months. The allegation that Tom Scott, president of the Pennsylvania Railroad, had played a part in negotiating the compromise that put Hayes in office must have made the president sensitive to the possibility of being seen as a tool of the railroads.[7]

He was also sensitive to the Republicans' promise to reduce federal presence in the Southern states where troops had often been used to keep order during the Reconstruction era. Besides, the army was already stretched thin and had other priorities. As one historian observed, "The peacetime army's primary tasks were to subdue Native Americans not strikers, and to maintain order on the frontiers not railroad centers."[8] As if to emphasize that point, the day before the strike began eastern newspapers reported that General Oliver O. Howard was engaged in a battle with the Nez Perce that marked the beginning of Chief Joseph's famous retreat to Canada.[9]

Whatever the reason, the Hayes administration refused to send federal troops against strikers unless state governors submitted a request that satisfied certain requirements. A governor was required to expressly declare that domestic violence or insurrection existed within the state, that state militia could not suppress it, that the legislature could not be assembled in time to address the question, and that federal troops were therefore necessary to restore order.[10] Other justifications for sending troops were used. Some of the president's advisers maintained that strikers were obstructing the mail. Others claimed that the president had authority to send the troops because the strike interfered with interstate commerce.[11] But Hayes chose the cautious approach, and most historians agree it served him well.[12]

Railroad managers found more enthusiastic support in the federal courts. When the Great Strike swept into the Midwest, federal judges of the Seventh Circuit acted quickly to protect struggling railroads that were operating under what most people today would refer to as federal bankruptcy proceedings. Technically these companies had been placed in receivership.[13] Judge Thomas S. Drummond of Chicago declared that any strike against or interference with the Indianapolis, Bloomington and Western, a railroad under receivership in his court, would be considered a violation of federal law. Instructing U.S. marshals to protect the company property, he warned that anyone who interfered would be held in contempt of court.[14] He then asked U.S. Attorney General Charles Devens to send troops to protect government property. Soon Federal District Judges Walter Q. Gresham of Indianapolis and Samuel Hubbel Treat of Springfield, Illinois, who also presided over railroad receiverships, followed suit. The judges' threats were not idle. Authorities arrested several strikers and strike leaders who were charged with and convicted of contempt of court.[15]

Judges Drummond, Gresham, and Treat have been described, with some accuracy, as antilabor judges. They clearly aligned the federal courts on the side of railroad management during the strike of 1877. Perhaps more significant, they demonstrated the potential for the federal judiciary to be a potent force for breaking strikes.[16] The Seventh Circuit's contempt orders were the precursor of the labor injunction, a device that the courts would employ later in the century, most famously in *In re Debs* (1895).[17] But Drummond and his fellow judges did not pull out of thin air the idea of using contempt of court against strikers. Their method was a logical offshoot of a growing body of law relating to federal receiverships.

Although the political, economic, and social influence of railroads and their leaders was undeniable, the 1870s and 1880s were actually not very good years for many railroad companies. The depression of 1873, overbuilding, large fixed debt, fraud, and competition often proved disastrous. Between 15 and 30 percent of the nation's railroad mileage was in court-ordered receivership at any given time.[18] In other industries, when a business was unable to pay its bills, creditors would initiate bankruptcy proceedings in the state courts. The business would be put into receivership and run by a receiver for the benefit of the creditors, or its assets would be sold and the proceeds distributed among its creditors.

Railroads were different. Diversity of citizenship usually placed them in the federal courts. Although Congress had the power to pass bankruptcy law, no federal statute was in effect until 1898. With no statutory rules in place, federal courts were left to create rules of their own.[19] In the eyes of the most influential of federal judges, railroad receiverships created a unique problem. Because the railroads had become the most important link in the system of transportation and commerce, these judges reasoned that it was in the public interest to keep them running rather than selling them off and distributing the assets. The result was a system that one writer appropriately calls "friendly receiverships."[20]

Several features of "friendly receiverships" made them unique and controversial. First, the request to be put into receivership came not from debtors who hoped to protect their investments but from management who hoped to perpetuate the company and their control of it. Second, it was common for the court to appoint as its receiver not a disinterested third party but rather a person from the railroad's management. Third, the courts' desire to keep the company viable created a situation in which protecting the interest of creditors was only a secondary interest, and some investors suffered loss more than others.[21]

In 1884 Jay Gould, president and controlling owner of the Wabash, St. Louis, and Pacific Railway, prevailed upon U.S. District Court Judge Samuel Hubbel Treat to put his company in receivership. The Wabash receivership allowed Gould to maintain control of the railroad and reduce the company's debt at the expense of stockholders and bondholders. Perhaps because of Gould's reputation as one of the era's most notorious robber barons, the Wabash receivership brought the "friendly receivership" to public attention and has become the symbol of its potential for abuse.[22] Although the Wabash receivership immediately became controversial, legal disputes growing out of it did not reach the Supreme Court until 1892. By then federal courts already employed the "friendly receivership" as a means of dealing with railroad bankruptcy.[23]

The Waite Court had given its approval in 1877 to the most fundamental element of friendly receiverships—the use of receiver's certificates. This device was important because it provided the means by which a receiver could raise new money to keep the railroad in operation. The problem the receiver faced was that existing bondholders already had a first lien on the company's property. They had little incentive to renegotiate their contracts on less favorable terms or to invest more. The presence of these "senior creditors" also discouraged outsiders from investing new money in the company since a new investor's claim against the railroad would be secondary to the claim of the existing bondholders. To solve the dilemma federal courts gave receivers the authority to borrow money and issue to the new creditor a guarantee—the receiver's certificate—that superseded even the first liens of earlier bondholders. The creation of this new class of "super senior creditors" encouraged new investment but also drastically diminished the contractual rights of the older bondholders.[24] In *Wallace v. Loomis* (1878) Justice Bradley reasoned that, although it should be exercised with caution, this tradeoff was justified by the court's duty to preserve and manage the property that was in its charge.[25]

Business historian Bradley Hansen has observed that the courts gave this super senior status only to certificates issued by receivers of railroads. "Receiver certificates of other types of corporations were not so privileged."[26] The rationale for this special treatment was familiar. "A railroad, and its appurtenances, is a peculiar species of property," Justice Samuel Blatchford observed. "The franchise and rights of the corporation which construct it were given, not merely for private gain to the corporators, but to furnish a public highway." It followed that all persons who chose to deal with the corporation as a creditor did so with the knowledge that, if the railroad went into insolvency, the court would have a duty to do what was necessary to serve the public.[27]

Using language similar to what he wrote in *Munn,* Chief Justice Waite expressed a slightly different version of public interest rationale. "Every member of a political community must necessarily part with some of the rights which, as an individual, not affected by his relation to others, he might have retained. Such concessions make up the consideration he gives for the obligation of the body politic to protect him in life, liberty, and property. Bankruptcy laws, whatever may be the form they assume, are of that character."[28] Whatever the rationale, the practical effect of the new receiverships was that the contractual rights of earlier creditors and bondholders became subordinate to the public interest in keeping railroads operating.[29]

The federal courts' objective to keep distressed railroads running manifested itself in other ways as well. In *Fosdick v. Schall* (1879) the Supreme Court upheld a receivership plan requiring a railroad to pay its bondholders and secured creditors only after paying debts recently incurred to continue operation. This included debts incurred during the past three months for labor and services, and for the purchase of engines, cars, wood, and supplies.[30] The rule upheld in *Fosdick* may also have been motivated in part by the Court's desire to assure that suppliers who continued to do business with a distressed railroad were treated fairly. Historian Charles Fairman tells the story of how Judge Harry C. Caldwell, the judge issuing the original order, became concerned for the well-being of suppliers after he learned that a woodcutter had hanged himself after a bankruptcy court refused to pay him for what amounted to a year's work supplying wood to a railroad.[31]

Such altruism was not evident in *Barton v. Barbour* (1881).[32] There the Supreme Court gave its sanction to a rule that no one could sue a railroad in receivership without first obtaining permission of the court handling the receivership. In *Barton v. Barbour* the Court applied that rule to a passenger injured when a sleeping car derailed and was thrown off the track and over an embankment. Justice William Woods, writing for the majority, emphasized concern for the ability of a court to carry out its duty regarding the receivership. "If a receiver is to be suable as a private proprietor of the railroad would be, or as the company itself whilst carrying on the business of the railroad was, it would become impossible for the court to discharge its duty."[33] In Woods's view that duty depended on the court maintaining complete control of the priority of claims against the company. If an injured passenger could sue to recover damages, he worried, then every conductor, engineer, or brakeman could also sue to recover wages.[34] In justifying his conclusions, Woods used the case as an opportunity to emphasize again the importance of railroads to the public. The public, he said, "retain rights of vast consequence in the road and its appendages, with which neither the company nor any creditor or bondholder can interfere."[35] Nor, presumably, could any potential litigant.

Although the rule that a receiver could not be sued without leave of the court was not new, the circumstances in which the rule was applied were. Under traditional bankruptcy rules a receiver's duty was to wind up the affairs of the defunct company and distribute the assets. The receiver did not have authority to enter into new contracts, and it was not the receiver's duty to keep the company operating long term. Even under those traditional circumstances this rule, which allowed a company to escape responsibility for its debts, duties, and negligence, posed potential for abuse.

Dissenting in *Barton v. Barbour,* Justice Miller maintained that the new style of railroad receivership, the purpose of which was to keep the railroad running, made the potential for abuse even more dangerous. Miller complained that railroad receiverships had become all too common. He noted that of the fifty or more railroad corporations that had owned the many thousands of miles of railway in his judicial circuit, hardly half a dozen had escaped receivership. The receivers, he observed, usually operated the railroads in their own way, with occasional suggestions from the court. They paid back some money to the debts of the corporation, but quite as often added to them. While operating the company, they made contracts and incurred obligations that they often failed to perform. For Miller, the majority's opinion sanctioned a system that deprived individuals of the right to sue railroads for that failure to perform.[36]

Miller had long been skeptical of railroad receiverships. He and other critics believed that, in addition to allowing companies to escape obligations to individuals and creditors, receiverships also provided railroads a means to escape taxes and other debts to the states. He emphatically made this point in his dissenting opinion in *Woodson v. Murdock* (1874). The case involved a section of the Missouri constitution, ratified in 1865, that read, "The General Assembly shall have no power, for any purpose, to release the lien held by the state upon any railroad."[37] When, two years later, the General Assembly passed a law accepting $5 million in full payment for the $7 million debt the Pacific Railroad owed to the state, the U.S. Supreme Court upheld the agreement. The state constitutional provision prohibited release of the lien, Justice Strong reasoned, not reduction of the debt.[38]

For Miller, this strained interpretation made a mockery of the constitutional provision. The people's intention in passing it was clearly to make the railroads "pay their bonds—pay them in full—or lose their roads, their property and franchises," he stated.[39] It was only through "the ingenuity of casuists and linguists, the nice criticisms of able counsel, the zeal which springs from a large pecuniary interest," that the plain language of the state constitution could be so disregarded. And if such plain language could be frittered away by judicial interpretation, he warned, "then the courts and constitutions become but feeble barriers to legislative corruption."[40]

The presence of corruption was not all that worried Miller, however. He was also concerned with what the case said about the influence of money in the political system. If the people were left with little hope in the safeguards of written constitutions, he warned, "These instruments themselves, supposed to be the particular pride of the American people, and the great bulwark to personal and public rights, must fall rapidly into disrepute if they are found to be efficient only for the benefit of the rich and powerful."[41]

The disagreement between Miller and the majority in these bankruptcy cases foretold of future debates regarding the nature and purpose of "friendly receiverships." The most vehement of contemporary critics complained that federal judges had acted in the interest of Jay Gould and other railroad magnates.[42] Historians have tended to tone down that criticism in varying degrees. Some maintain that federal judges were predisposed to create a system that favored large-scale national businesses.[43] Others say that the new rules favored railroad managers over creditors.[44] Still others, tracking the reasoning judges themselves used, suggest the new rules made the contractual rights of bondholders and creditors subordinate to the public interest.[45] But some historians observe that the federal judges who developed the new rules were simply filling a vacuum. Given the importance of railroads to the public and Congress's failure to pass federal bankruptcy legislation, they had little choice but to find ways to address a pressing problem.[46]

Whatever their motivation, it is important to recognize that it was the emergence of a national economy that caused federal judges to be put into the position of making new bankruptcy rules. The rules they created contained subtle but significant changes in the federal bankruptcy system that existed at the time. Yet federal judges did not start from scratch. Rather they molded familiar legal concepts from the law of equity into a new doctrine. When Congress did eventually pass a federal bankruptcy act in 1898, it incorporated many, but not all, of the characteristics that the courts had developed.[47]

The doctrine of "friendly receiverships" reflected an undisputed fact of American life in the last part of the nineteenth century. Railroads had become a crucial link, if not *the* crucial link, in the new system of commerce. The Supreme Court majority's conclusion that it was in the public interest to keep faltering railroads running should sound familiar to readers in the twenty-first century. In 2009 the government spent trillions of dollars to shore up faltering banks and lending institutions. It then helped organize a bankruptcy designed to keep General Motors Corporation in operation. The government's response to the prospect of the business crisis of 2009 may have been different than the response in the nineteenth century. But the justification is the same. The companies, it is said, are too important to the commercial system to be allowed to fail.

Most people may have been resigned to accept that justification even if they were not fully convinced. Begrudging acceptance of the justification does not mean that they like the policy, however. Justice Miller observed the obvious when he complained about the inherent unfairness of allowing railroad entrepreneurs to walk away from debt, saddling creditors, suppliers, and taxpayers with the leavings. Some railroad owners certainly suffered in the wake of receivership. As the melee over the Wabash receivership showed, however, public perception was more drawn to the image of railroad tycoons making unfathomable amounts of money, then being relieved of much of their debt and other obligations.

Complaints about the unfairness of railroad receiverships, like complaints growing out of the use of state and local bonds to support railroad construction, were part of a broader growing disenchantment with the railroad business. Reformers also worried about the growing power of railroads and other elite corporations in both commerce and politics. Nothing illustrates this more than the disputes that developed over the federal government's financial aid for the construction of the transcontinental railroads.

7

Sinking Fund

In 1867 Francis Train, a powerful director of the Union Pacific Railroad, devised a surefire way to make some money. Train established a trust company, Crédit Mobilier of America, which was completely owned by a small group of directors of the Union Pacific. The group soon became known as the Pacific Railroad Ring. Because they controlled the board of directors of the Union Pacific, the ring was able to award building contracts to Crédit Mobilier, giving wildly favorable terms and paying exorbitant prices for the work. They used this scheme to siphon money out of the Union Pacific and into the coffers of their own company. In actuality, the primary function of the Crédit Mobilier Company was to shift money—money that came from the U.S. treasury and the pockets of the Union Pacific's minor shareholders. As railroad reformer Charles Francis Adams Jr. put it, "They receive money into one hand as a corporation, and pay it out into the other as a contractor." The profit they kept for themselves.[1]

When it came to light, the Crédit Mobilier scheme became the era's foremost symbol of corporate greed, corporate corruption, and corporate power. It brought to the surface an already growing public concern that, after making vast fortunes for promoters, financiers, and entrepreneurs, the Pacific railroads would not be able to repay the enormous sums of money the government had loaned to them to build their railroads. Tales of business and political corruption made the Crédit Mobilier scandal sensational, but the reaction to it also fueled an already intense debate about the status of corporations in American politics and society, and ultimately about the status of corporations in American constitutional law. That debate first reached the Supreme Court in 1875, about one year after Waite's appointment as chief justice. The legal contest lasted four years and produced several cases that tested Congress's efforts to assure that the Pacific railroad companies paid back the loans. It finally concluded when, in 1879, two years after *Munn v. Illinois*, the Court ruled on the *Sinking Fund Cases.*

One might have thought that building and operating railroads provided a good means for making money without an underhanded scheme like Crédit Mobilier. This was especially true of the Union Pacific Railroad and Central Pacific Railroad, the two companies Congress engaged to build the first transcontinental railroad. The building of the first transcontinental railroad is a success story deeply embedded in American lore. A marvel of engineering, persistence, and drive, it was initially a source of great national pride. Beginning at the Mississippi River, the Union Pacific worked its way westward across the Great Plains and Rocky Mountains. At the same time the Central Pacific worked its way eastward, blasting and cutting through the rugged Sierra Nevada. When the two railroads met at Promontory Summit, Utah, on May 10, 1869, Americans were empowered by the feeling that, more than ever before, they lived in a nation that stretched from coast to coast.[2]

Congress provided the builders of the transcontinental railroad with two forms of aid. One came in the form of land given to the railroads as right-of-way and land grants.[3] The other, which is more important to the Crédit Mobilier scandal, was a subsidy in government bonds. Under this plan, Congress promised to give to the railroads bonds valued at between $16,000 and $48,000 per mile of track laid. In effect, these bonds constituted a loan from the federal government to the railroad at 6 percent interest. The plan provided some means for partial repayment of the loans over time, and it required the companies to eventually repay the principle and interest in full when the bonds matured thirty years after the railroad was completed.[4]

Estimates of the amount of money the railroads received vary widely. Whatever the actual figure, however, there is no doubt that it represented an extremely large amount of money by nineteenth-century standards. Some members of Congress later complained it was more than $100 million.

Large as it was, the government subsidy may have been only enough to prime the pump. Railroad entrepreneurs faced a problem of converting the government bonds and land into cash. In order to raise the cash they needed, the railroads typically sold the government bonds on the open market for less than face value. They also supplemented the funds they received from the government bonds with private financing. Once construction began, they had to supply enough money to keep the project moving, and their task was complicated by the fact that the government did not give the railroads the land and bonds all at once, but only as the company had completed construction of twenty continuous miles of track.

From the entrepreneurs' point of view, building the transcontinental railroad was a risky venture, and it was accomplished primarily through the savvy, persistence, energy, and skulduggery of men of destiny: men like them. It would have been natural for them to believe that they should be left free to guide the growth of this new transportation industry.

Nobody could doubt the accomplishment. And Americans tend to admire savvy, persistence, energy, and even skulduggery up to a point. But as the new wore off of the transcontinental railroad, the public began to see railroad entrepreneurs as robber barons who, through monopoly and collusion, were bleeding the common people of their economic well-being. Many people also came to believe that railroad entrepreneurs were getting excessively wealthy by feeding at the public trough and feared that the influence of railroad interests in politics threatened the liberty and political authority of the people. This was the mood of much of the country when the Crédit Mobilier scandal hit the news.

The Crédit Mobilier scheme was not a deeply held secret. In an 1869 article in the *North American Review* Charles Francis Adams Jr. explained in detail how it worked.[5]

But it took the glaring headlines of a political scandal to really draw the American public's attention to how key directors of the Union Pacific were manipulating the company. On September 4, 1872, the *New York Sun* broke the news that Crédit Mobilier had been distributing shares of its stock to influential political figures. Congressmen John B. Alley and Oaks Ames were said to have developed the scheme, but other key figures of the Grant administration were implicated when they received gifts or offers to buy the stock cheap.

In response to these revelations, Congress initiated several investigations. Because it was difficult to prove bribery, however, most of the public officials implicated in the scandal were exonerated.[6] Nevertheless the Crédit Mobilier scandal reinforced the suspicions of a growing number of politicians, civic leaders, shippers, and farmers who were pressing for more forceful government control of railroad and corporate business practices.

News of the scandal could not have come at a worse time for railroad entrepreneurs. Although the political, economic, and social influence of railroads and their leaders was undeniable, the 1870s and 1880s were actually not very good years for many railroad companies. Within months of the breaking of the Crédit Mobilier scandal the country was mired in the depression of 1873. That, along with overbuilding, large fixed debt, fraud, and competition drove many into bankruptcy and court-ordered receivership. Many companies were bankrupt and in court-ordered receivership at any given time.[7] Many of these were local railroads that had been financed with the help of county and municipal bonds. Prevalence of railroad receiverships led many people to worry that states and local governments would never be paid back for what were in effect loans to the railroads. Now people began to worry that the federal government would not be paid back either.

The terms of the government's loan to the Pacific railroads were initially set out in the Pacific Railroad Act in 1862. This act provided that the companies would complete repayment of the bonds with 6 percent simple interest thirty years after completion of the railroad. To secure repayment of the loans the government took a first lien against the companies' property. Under the act, each year 5 percent of the net earnings of the companies would also be applied to repayment of the debt the companies owed. Other than that, the companies were not required to make any cash payments on the principle or interest until the date of maturity, which would be sometime between 1895 and 1899.

The companies were required to keep tracks in good repair and to transport mail, troops, and public stores for the government at reasonable rates. The statute further provided that all compensation due to the companies for services rendered to the government would be applied to the payment of the bonds and the interest.[8]

Two years later Congress amended this law, giving the companies more favorable terms. The amendment of 1864 reduced the amount of earnings that were to be applied to payment of the bonds and interest to half of the money the railroads earned for services rendered to the government. It also allowed the companies to issue private bonds and made the government's lien subordinate to that of the new private lenders. In both the 1862 and 1864 acts Congress expressly reserved the right to alter or revise the terms of the grants.

The Crédit Mobilier scandal motivated an anxious Congress to reconsider these new terms. Critics worried that the Pacific Railroad directors, who had been paying high dividends to themselves and shareholders and siphoning money to their own corporations, would leave the railroads in such a poor financial condition that they would not be able to repay their debt to the government when it became due. Congress responded with the Crédit Mobilier Act of 1873, an awkwardly designed statute that sent mixed signals about how Congress intended to solve the problem. Section 1 of the act directed the secretary of the treasury to withhold all payments the government owed to the railroads for freights and transportation. That, standing alone, might have seemed clear enough. But Congress added Section 2, which gave the companies the right to sue in the Federal Court of Claims "to recover [from the federal government] the price of such freights and transportation" as the court determined was owed to them.[9]

Following the directive of the first section, the secretary of the treasury withheld the entire amount of payments for services rendered by the Union Pacific between February 1871 and February 1874. Given the second section, the company then filed a suit in the Court of Claims to recover the amount owed to it.

At trial the government pointed out that the Union Pacific owed more than $12 million in interest to the government and had never paid any part of it to that date. The Crédit Mobilier Act, it maintained, was intended to allow the government to recover that debt. The company argued that the terms of the 1864 act still applied, and that the government had a right to apply only half of the payment to the interest. It therefore demanded that it be paid half of the amount the secretary of the treasury had withheld. When the Court of Claims ruled in favor of the company, Attorney General Edwards Pierrepont appealed the case to the Supreme Court.

Given the circumstances under which the Crédit Mobilier Act was enacted, it was reasonable to assume that Congress had intended to repeal the changes it made in 1864 and return to the original terms of the Pacific Railroad grant. It would have made sense that Congress hoped to protect the public interest by providing, once again, that all compensation the government owed to the railroads for providing transportation would be applied to repayment of the bonds. That is not how the Court interpreted the new statute, however.

Instead, in *United States v. Union Pacific Railroad Company* (1875) the Court ruled that the Crédit Mobilier Act did nothing more than provide the government and the companies with a procedure for enforcing their respective rights.[10] According to the majority of the Court, nothing in the act actually changed the amount that the government could apply to interest. Section 1 merely allowed the secretary to initially withhold all payments the railroads charged for services rendered to the government. Section 2 then gave the railroads a means by which they could retrieve what money the government ultimately owed to them. Under this interpretation the Crédit Mobilier Act simply provided a procedure for carrying out the terms of the grant as amended in 1864. It did not change substantive rights of the parties, the Court concluded.[11] Only half of the money the government owed to the railroads could be used to pay the railroads' debt and interest on the bonds.

Justice Stephen Field desperately wanted to write the opinion of the Court. Field, one of the most outspoken of the justices, had a well-established reputation as an advocate of entrepreneurial liberty and as a friend of big business in general and railroads in particular. There was no doubt that his links to the business elite of California were strong. He socialized with Central Pacific founder Leland Stanford and had links with another Central Pacific founder, Collis P. Huntington, as well as with Lloyd Tevis, president of Wells Fargo. When riding circuit in California, he joined with members of San Francisco's elite clubs, where the business elite tended to gather and socialize, and where some lived in luxury.

Throughout his time on the bench, Field kept his hands in California politics, and he became the arch enemy of reformers. Although political rivals in his home state frequently linked Field to scandals, reformers did not need scandals to detest him. In their own minds they knew that his sentiments lie with what one critic called "The Pacific Club Set."[12] The *San Francisco Examiner* typified reformers' complaints when it described Field's record as a judge: "In any case where the people or the state, or a private citizen, has been a party on one side, and a rich corporation the opposing party, [Field] has invariably pronounced opinion or given judgment in favor of the corporation."[13] The *Examiner's* assessment may not have been completely accurate, but such was Justice Field's reputation.

Given the level of public excitement about the Crédit Mobilier scandal and the fact that the outcome of *United States v. Union Pacific Railroad Company* would be in favor of the railroad, Chief Justice Waite was inclined to assign it to "someone who would not be known as the personal friend of the parties representing the railroad interest." He decided to temper the potential negative reaction by assigning the case to Justice David Davis. Although strong willed and opinionated, Davis had a reputation for impartiality.

Waite had been chief justice for just a little more than a year when *United States v. Union Pacific Railroad Company* reached the Court. The modest lawyer from Ohio had been appointed in March 1874 to lead a court inhabited, at the time, by men of exceedingly immodest egos. Perhaps that is why Justice Field, the most irascible member of the bench, strenuously argued in conference that he, not Davis, should write the opinion. If Field believed that he could intimidate Waite, however, he was mistaken. Soon after Field had complained about the assignment, Waite responded with a letter to Field that demonstrated the chief justice was both tactful and fully in charge. "There is not doubt of your intimate personal relations with the managers of the Central Pacific," he reminded Field, "and naturally you, more than anyone else on the court, realize the vast importance of the great work that has been done."[14]

The decision in *United States v. Union Pacific Railroad Company* was undoubtedly a victory for the railroad. Justice Davis's short opinion devoted almost two pages to praising the accomplishments of the Pacific Railroad companies. But his opinion ultimately turned on an uninspired and detailed reading of statutory language.

A subsequent case interpreting another section of the Crédit Mobilier Act produced a similar result. Section 4 of the act directed the attorney general to sue companies and individuals who had misused or misdirected assets of the Pacific railroads. The section also provided that the government could initiate a suit in any circuit court of the United States. Following this directive, in the summer of 1873 Attorney General George H. Williams brought suit in the Circuit Court for Connecticut. The government charged that the Union Pacific Railroad, the Crédit Mobilier Company, the Wyoming Coal Company, and some 150 other persons had misdirected funds and defrauded the Union Pacific. When the case came to trial Justice Ward Hunt, who was riding circuit, and District Judge Shipman dismissed the charges. The government appealed the case to the Supreme Court, where it became commonly known as the *Crédit Mobilier Case*.[15]

The Court heard arguments on the case twice. First arguments were on December 13 and 14, 1876, but the justices failed to reach a conclusion regarding the outcome, and on February 28, 1877, the Court ordered a reargument. In the meantime Justice Davis resigned on March 7, 1877, and was replaced by John Harlan on December 10, 1877. The reargument did not take place until November 26 and 27, 1878, almost two years later.[16]

Like the first case, the *Crédit Mobilier Case* ended in a victory for the railroad. But the Court again refrained from addressing any grand constitutional issues. Once again the decision turned on a technical reading of the statute and the circumstances to which it was being applied. And, once again, Chief Justice Waite assigned the opinion to a person who was not perceived to be a friend of the railroad and corporate interests.

Justice Samuel Miller was, quite to the contrary, exceedingly skeptical of the system of finance that had grown out of government aid in support of railroad construction. Miller, as mentioned previously, was one of the early settlers of Keokuk, Iowa, a Mississippi River town that saw its dreams of becoming a hub of railroad commerce unfulfilled. He had experienced firsthand the allure of the railroad's promise of prosperity and the disappointment when it failed to pan out. As the circuit judge for much of the Midwest, he had observed that the practice of government assuming debt to help finance a railroad was as likely to produce calamity as prosperity.[17]

He had also seen firsthand railroads taking advantage of the new type of "friendly receivership" that allowed companies to continue operating at the same time that they avoided fully paying their debts to private individuals and governments.[18] For Miller, the system of railroad financing had resulted in "the gradual formation of a new kind of wealth in this country, the income of which is the coupons of interest and stock dividends." He believed this system had created "a class of individuals whose only interest or stake in the country is the ownership of these bonds and stocks." "They engage in no commerce, no trade, no manufacture, no agriculture," he observed. "They produce *nothing*."[19]

Even Miller's reputation did not insulate the Court from criticism for its *Crédit Mobilier* decision, however. Reformers complained that the majority's formalistic interpretation of the statute defeated the obvious purpose of the law. That may have been true to some extent, but Miller maintained that the fault lay with Congress and seemed genuinely frustrated by what he saw as Congress's flawed attempt to assure that the government would be repaid.

Miller virtually scolded Congress. He pointed out that the Crédit Mobilier Act was predicated on the false assumption that, as a party to a contract with the Union Pacific, Congress could sue for fraud to protect the interests of the nation and for the benefit of the company itself. The Crédit Mobilier scheme may have constituted fraud, he admitted, but the United States could not sue the perpetrators because it was not the party who had been defrauded. Similarly he observed that although Congress might fear that the Union Pacific would not be able to pay its debt to the United States when it became due, the company had not yet defaulted on its obligations and therefore was not liable for any breach of the agreement. It was really the Union Pacific itself, more particularly, the bona fide stockholders who were not part of the scheme who were the victims of Crédit Mobilier.

But Miller went on to observe that the United States was not merely a party to a contract with the Union Pacific. It is also the sovereign, and as sovereign had an obligation to protect the rights of the public. Moreover, he said, Congress had at its disposal ample powers to do so. It could, for example, establish a public trust, which, in order to assure the repayment of the railroads' debt, would gather and hold the government's payments to the railroads. There may be trusts that the United States may enforce against the company, Miller concluded, but he was of the opinion that none were set forth in this statute.[20]

Miller was obviously aware that Congress had been debating just that type of solution. In fact, by the time he was ready to write the opinion in the *Crédit Mobilier Case* Congress had already passed the Pacific Railroad Sinking Fund Act, a plan that put into a public trust fund the money that the government owed to railroads for services such as carrying the mail or troops. The new law was popularly known as the Thurman Act after its sponsor, Senator Allen G. Thurman of Ohio.[21] Thurman had calculated that on the date the Pacific railroads' bonds matured, their annual payments under the 1864 law would have yielded only $15 million. The problem was that the amount of debt remaining unpaid at that time would be more than $119 million. Given the revelations of the Crédit Mobilier scheme and the fact that the companies were sometimes paying huge dividends, Thurman worried that the companies would not be able to make up the $104 million difference when the debt became due.

Thurman's solution was to amend the act of 1864 so that once again all the money the railroads earned from providing services to the government would be applied to secure payment of the debt. He knew that in the *Crédit Mobilier Case,* the Court had overruled Congress's plan to apply all such earnings to payment of the railroads' debt. His plan, however, was different. Under it only half of the amount would be used to immediately pay the outstanding debt. The other half would be held in a sinking fund: an account maintained in trust by the U.S. treasurer and not to be used except to pay the railroads' debt when it became due.[22]

Railroad leaders were not completely opposed to the idea of creating a sinking fund. Collis P. Huntington, for example, offered an alternative piece of legislation that would set up a sinking fund in exchange for an extension of the time when the bonds would become due.[23] Nevertheless, when the Thurman Act passed in its final form, the railroads immediately initiated lawsuits to challenge it. In one suit Albert Gallatin, a shareholder of the Central Pacific, filed a contrived suit against the company in the Federal District Court of California to test the new law. Almost simultaneously the Union Pacific brought suit against the government in the U.S. Court of Claims. When the two suits reached the Supreme Court, they were combined and became the *Sinking Fund Cases*.[24]

Although the first two opinions growing out of the Crédit Mobilier scandal had yielded victories for railroad financiers, both were based upon technicalities. Justice Stephen Field's desire to write the Court's opinion in *United States v. Union Pacific Railroad Company* suggested that the railroad interests yearned for more. In fact, the Crédit Mobilier incident was embedded in a broader struggle about the nature and status of corporations and other large business concerns in American society and law as well about the influence of big business in politics. It was a struggle for control. In the most sweeping of terms reformers maintained that government retained the right to regulate corporations, like the railroads, to assure that they operated in the best interests of the community. Railroad leaders, to the contrary, argued that the Constitution limited the degree to which government could interfere with business practices.

This debate's first major scrimmage in the courts in *Munn v. Illinois* and the other Granger Cases had been a stinging defeat for railroads and the corporate elite.[25] Nevertheless the railroads pulled out all stops in their legal attacks on the Thurman Act. Bolstered by victories in *United States v. Union Pacific Railroad Company* and the *Crédit Mobilier Case*, they hoped this case would establish the kind of legal precedent they wanted. In contrast to Huntington, who had opposed the Thurman Act only because its particular plan for the sinking fund was not financially favorable enough to the railroads, attorneys for the railroads argued that the creation of a sinking fund violated their clients' constitutional rights.

They began with the proposition that by changing the terms of the grants to the Union Pacific and Central Pacific, the Thurman Act violated the Constitution's prohibition against "impairing the obligation of contracts." Although the contract clause of Article I, Section 10, of the Constitution expressly provides that no *state* shall pass any law "impairing the obligation of contracts," they argued that the prohibition applied by implication to the federal government as well. Borrowing from the theory they used in *Munn*, they next argued that the government's plan to divert payments into a sinking fund violated the Fifth Amendment guarantee that no person be deprived of life, liberty, or property without due process of law. Into this mix they added the charge that the Thurman Act simply violated their clients' fundamental rights.

The Court heard arguments on March 19 to 21, 1879. Less than a month later, in an unusually fast time, it announced its opinion upholding the Thurman Act. With public emotion regarding the case running high, Chief Justice Waite decided to take it upon himself to write the majority opinion. Justices Stephen Field, William Strong, and Joseph Bradley read separate dissenting opinions on the same day.

Waite did not reject outright the railroads' constitutional theories. "The United States cannot any more than a State interfere with private rights, except for legitimate governmental purposes," he observed. The Article I, Section 10, prohibition against passing laws "impairing the obligation of contracts" is directed only at the states, Waite observed. But the federal government equally with the states is prohibited from depriving persons or corporations of property without due process of law.[26]

Although Waite thus placed the case within the framework of the Fifth Amendment's due process clause, his analysis that followed was a coagulated mix of due process thinking and principles related to the contract clause. In the Pacific Railroad acts of 1862 and 1864 Congress had reserved the right to alter or amend its contracts with the railroads, he observed. Its power to do so was not unlimited. It could not, for example, take away property already acquired by the corporation. As a party to the contract it did not have the power to repudiate its obligations under the contract, he said. But the change wrought by the Thurman Act did none of these things. It merely represented an attempt to assure that the railroads would be able to meet their obligations under the contract.[27]

Waite emphasized that the U.S. government was not just a party to the contract. It was also the sovereign. As sovereign, it had not only the right but also the duty to see to it that the current stockholders of the companies did not appropriate for their own use that which in equity belonged to others. In his mind that equity belonged to future stockholders and to the public. The Thurman Act takes nothing from the railroads that actually belonged to them, he said. "It simply gives further assurance of the continued solvency and prosperity of a corporation in which the public are so largely interested, and adds another guaranty to the permanent and lasting value of its vast amount of securities."[28]

To determine whether Congress acted properly Waite applied the same presumption that would have been appropriate in a pure contract clause case. It was also the presumption he followed in *Munn*. While admitting that it is the Court's duty to declare an act of Congress void if it is not within the legislative power of the United States, he emphasized, legislation should never be overruled except in a clear case. "Every possible presumption is in favor of the validity of the statute," he wrote, "and this continues until the contrary is shown beyond a reasonable doubt."[29]

In their separate opinions the three dissenting justices offered a variety of skilled lawyerly arguments to get around the reserve clauses in the Pacific Railroad acts of 1862 and 1864. Justice Strong took the position that the contracts relating to the bonds were not part of the Pacific Railroad acts of 1862 and 1864 but rather separate agreements that occurred later.[30] Justice Bradley maintained that while the government could reserve the power to alter, amend, or repeal a corporate charter, it could not reserve the power to violate a contract. Reservation of the power to violate a contract would be repugnant to the contract itself and void.[31] Focusing on the precise language of the reserve clause in the act of 1862, Justice Field maintained that the government's power to alter or amend the contract was limited to assuring that the railroads were built, kept in working order, and secured for postal delivery, military transportation, and other government uses. Since the Thurman Act did not fall into these categories, he concluded that the reserve clauses did not apply.[32]

Far more interesting, however, was how the dissenters maneuvered the question in this case from one involving the contract clause to one involving the Fifth Amendment prohibition against taking property without due process of law. Their reasoning was as simple as it was ingenious. Justice Bradley captured it best. "A contract is property," he said. "To destroy it wholly or to destroy it partially is to take it; and to do this by arbitrary legislative action is to do it without due process of law."[33]

It is hard to understand why Bradley considered the Thurman Act to be arbitrary legislative action. He had, after all, agreed with the majority in *Munn* that businesses affected with public interest were subject to legitimate police powers of the state. Although Bradley did not give a very satisfactory explanation for why the Thurman Act was not an exercise of the police power, all the dissenters took a similar approach. Having asserted that a federal law that wholly or partially destroys a contract would violate the Fifth Amendment prohibition against taking the railroads' property without due process, they then turned to the common law of contract to explain why the Thurman Act did so.

Justice Field, after admitting that the government had specific and limited duties as sovereign, emphasized its role as a party to the contract. "As a contractor it is bound by its engagements equally with a private individual," he wrote, "it cannot be relieved of them by an assertion of its sovereign authority."[34] The authority of interpreting or construing the contract, they all agreed, was not a legislative prerogative. It was a judicial question.[35]

Railroad leaders knew they could depend on Field. Central Pacific manager David Colton made this clear in a letter discussing the case. "Judge Field will not sit in the Gallatin Case [in the U.S. District Court], he wrote, but instead will reserve his best efforts (I have not doubt) for the final determination of the case in Washington before the full bench."[36] Field did not disappoint them. His best efforts may not have yielded the opinion most firmly rooted in law, but they certainly yielded the most forceful of the dissenting opinions.

Field was, at the time, engaged in a serious run for the Democratic nomination for president. He based his candidacy on strength of character, being able to carry the West, and states' rights. This last plank of his platform made its way into his dissent. Field accurately noted that unlike the Union Pacific, which had received its charter from the federal government, the Central Pacific was incorporated by the state of California. It was a creation of the state, he said, and creations of the states cannot be taken from their control. The power to regulate railroads, he continued, is vested not in the federal government but in the states. Field conveniently neglected to remind his readers of his dissent in *Munn,* an opinion in which he expressed a vision of very limited state regulation.[37]

Critics complained that Field had introduced a campaign speech into the body of a judicial opinion. Once his states' rights argument was disposed of, however, Field cut right to the heart of the political dispute that produced the *Sinking Fund Cases.* There is in the country a general feeling against the Pacific railroad companies, he observed. It is an attitude that the railroads had become so powerful that they should "be brought by strongest measures into subjection to the state." But while admitting that a general feeling against the Pacific railroad companies might be justified, Field argued that the power and influence of the railroads did not furnish justification for the government's invasion of its contracts. There is a general principle involved here, he warned. "The law that protects the wealth of the most powerful, protects also the earnings of the most humble; and the law that would confiscate the property of the one would take the earnings of the other."[38] For Field, it did not matter that the "powerful" were corporations. Their rights were the same.

Field's opinion highlighted one aspect of the *Sinking Fund Cases* that is often overlooked. The opinions in the case also reflected a debate about whether corporations are persons entitled to full protection of the Constitution. In arguing for the broadest protection of the corporation, and in comparing the rights of a corporation to the rights of a humble worker, Field painted an image of the anthropomorphic corporation—one having human attributes and therefore human rights.

As a matter of convenience courts often drew analogies treating corporations as persons for specific legal purposes. In order to determine the proper jurisdiction of a diversity suit, for example, federal courts recognized corporations as "citizens" of the state in which they were incorporated.[39] Obviously corporations were not actually citizens. Rather courts used the concept of citizen as an analogy, what judges call a legal fiction. Judges indulged in that fiction as a matter of convenience. As railroad and business attorneys began to argue that their corporate clients' had rights to due process of law, equal protection of the law, and even natural law, however, the benign convenience of the corporate person took on a new and more controversial significance.

The majority's opinion in the *Sinking Fund Cases* expanded somewhat on the conventional legal fiction of the corporate person in that it recognized that a law that takes property from a corporation might violate due process. In contrast to Field, however, Waite was not ready to fully equate a corporation to a human being. "This corporation is a creature of the United States," he said, speaking of the Union Pacific. It is a private corporation created for public purposes. A corporation might own property, but it also was "a peculiar species of property, which is subject to legislative control so far as its business affects the public interest." Furthermore Waite observed that the corporation is not sentient. It does not have a mind of its own; managers make the decisions for it.[40]

Field may have been certain about the anthropomorphic essence of the corporation, but most people were more ambivalent. Justice Miller typified this when he described the history of the Union Pacific Railroad. "In the feeble infancy of this child of its creation" the U.S. government had done all it could to strengthen, support, and sustain it, Miller wrote. "Since it [the Union Pacific] has grown to a vigorous manhood, it may not have displayed the gratitude which so much care called for.

If that be so, it is but another instance of the absence of human affections which is said to characterize all corporations."[41]

This debate about the status of corporations as persons and the degree to which they remained under the control of legislative bodies gave the *Sinking Fund Cases* a lasting importance. Reformers both in and out of Congress could revel in their victory. For railroads and advocates of the corporate elite, however, the *Sinking Fund Cases* proved to be a severe disappointment. Their frustration even made its way into the usually staid proceedings of the Supreme Court. When presenting his dissent orally, Justice Field concluded with this sharp rebuke of Waite and the majority. "He must be dull indeed who does not see that under the legislation and the course of decision of late years, our government is fast drifting from its ancient moorings, from the system established by our fathers into a vast centralized and consolidated government."[42]

Ultimately Field toned down his written decision. But he and others continued to complain of the danger and unfairness of the Court's decision. The Central Pacific's Collis P. Huntington, for example, warned that the opinion "was calculated to fill the country with alarm." With no little sarcasm he asked whether the principle that "neither corporation nor person can acquire any right of ownership or enjoyment in property which the majority of the legislative power cannot at its discretion abridge, annul, or take away under the pretense of giving it to the public is becoming the guiding principle of jurisprudence among us."[43]

The legal disputes arising from the Crédit Mobilier scandal revealed a court still struggling with questions of whether, or to what degree, the Constitution limited government regulation of business, and to what extent the Constitution afforded rights to corporations. Attorneys for the railroads and the business elite hoped to use the opportunity to establish precedent that would insulate their clients from legislative interference. Although disappointed by the result of this round, they did not give up.

8

A Change Is Gonna Come

Historians have maintained that railroad attorneys entered into a deliberate campaign to overturn the effects of *Munn,* the *Sinking Fund Cases,* and their progeny, and that the Court quickly moved away from the principles it had adopted in *Munn.* This observation is accurate enough, but cast in a wide beam from a twenty-first-century light, it leaves some important details in the shadows. By focusing the beam more precisely on the time between *Munn* in 1877 and Chief Justice Waite's death in 1888 we will see, for example, that the corporate elite's campaign to change constitutional doctrine was deliberate in the sense of being resolute and persistent but not in the sense of being precisely organized. It will also reveal that the claim that the Court moved quickly away from the principles of *Munn* and the *Sinking Fund Cases* is a matter of perspective. During this time attorneys for the railroads and the corporate elite undoubtedly made incremental gains that set the stage for their eventual success. But the Court's majority steadfastly resisted the persistent attempts to convince them to fully reject the traditional doctrine. Railroad and corporate attorneys did not achieve their ultimate goal until after Waite had died.

The deliberate campaign also got off to a sputtering start. For roughly six years after the *Munn* decision the Court saw only a handful of cases in which businesses claimed that state regulation violated the Fourteenth Amendment and a few more that made some kind of similar claim. Even though the *Sinking Fund Cases* did not involve state regulation, and therefore did not involve the Fourteenth Amendment, it gave railroad attorneys the opportunity to press their theories again. Rebuked once again, however, railroad attorneys did not force the issue for a few more years. It was only after four new justices joined the Court in 1881 and 1882 that attorneys again began to press for changes that would insulate business from government regulation.

There is little doubt that some members of the business elite sensed an opportunity in 1880 to mold the Court into an institution more sympathetic to their interests. Justices Clifford, Hunt, and Swayne were so feeble that it was hard to imagine they would be able to hold on to their seats much longer. President Hayes, who decided not to run for reelection, would be out of office in January 1881, and it looked like his successor would get two or possibly three appointments.

His eventual replacement, Republican James Garfield, faced strong opposition from a rejuvenated Democratic Party and its candidate, General Winfield S. Hancock. In addition, Garfield had only lukewarm support among some elements of his own party, particularly in New York. Fearing that their candidate would lose the state, Garfield's campaign strategists sought to secure approval, and the all important financial support, from New Yorkers like railroad entrepreneur Jay Gould and corporate lawyer William W. Phelps. In a remarkable exchange of letters Whitelaw Reid, one of Garfield's trusted advisers, explained to the future president that he could expect the support of these men only if they could be assured that he disapproved of the "revolutionary course of the majority of the Court" in *Munn* and the *Sinking Fund Cases,* and that he would appoint men who held views similar to Justices Field and Strong.

Garfield refused to give specific assurances, saying that to do so would be improper. But his explanation that he believed in the sanctity of contract and in vested rights and would not appoint to the Court any person "whom I did not believe to be entirely sound on these questions" was enough. With the help of generous contributions from the likes of Gould, John D. Rockefeller of Standard Oil, and Chauncey Depew of the New York Central Railroad, he carried the state and won the election.[1]

As it turned out, the first new appointment to the Court was not Garfield's to make. On December 14, 1880, William Strong resigned from the bench, giving lame-duck President Hayes the nomination. Strong was seventy-three years old and in good health both mentally and physically. Justice Miller, for one, thought that the resignation would be a heavy loss for the Court. But Strong had sat on the Court for a decade and was eligible for a pension. According to his daughter, he hoped his resignation would set an example for some of his fellow justices who had become enfeebled.[2] Strong's resignation was a potential loss for the corporate elite. His record reflected sympathy with the theories they favored. He had dissented in the *Slaughterhouse Cases,* joined Field's dissent in *Munn,* and dissented in the *Sinking Fund Cases.*

His replacement was William B. Woods, a respected U.S. circuit judge from Georgia. Woods was born in Newark, Ohio, about thirty miles east of Columbus. Although he grew up on a farm, Woods received a good education. He attended Western Reserve College in Ohio for two years, then transferred to Yale, where he graduated as class valedictorian. After graduating, he studied law with a prominent Newark attorney and was admitted to the bar in 1847.

Woods, who began his political career as a Whig, joined the Democratic Party in the 1850s. He was a staunch supporter of the Union, however. After the attack on Fort Sumter he joined the Seventy-sixth Ohio Volunteer Infantry. He saw action with the Union army at Shiloh and Vicksburg and in Sherman's march to the sea. By the end of the war, Woods had earned the rank of brevet major general.

At the war's end Woods settled in Alabama. Now a Republican, he was elected as a state judge. In 1869 President Grant appointed him the U.S. circuit judge for the Fifth Circuit. Recall that, as circuit judge, Woods sat with Justice Joseph Bradley in the *Cruikshank* case and other cases as well. Justice Bradley thought so highly of Woods that he submitted his name for the seat that became available when Justice David Davis resigned in 1877. John Harlan got that appointment. But Woods had only a few more years to wait. After Strong resigned President Hayes submitted Woods's nomination to the Senate. He was confirmed on December 21, 1880.

The factors that led to Woods's appointment had nothing to do with the struggle between elite corporations and reform. He was the brother-in-law of a U.S. senator. He had Justice Bradley's support. Also, he was attractive to Hayes and the sitting members of the Court because he was from a Southern state, specifically one in the Fifth Circuit, and because he was a skilled and energetic judge. Indeed, Woods became one of the Court's most productive members. In the seven years he sat on the bench, he produced hundreds of opinions, mostly dealing with relatively mundane cases.[3]

Business leaders and the legal community received another surprise when Justice Noah Swayne retired on January 24, 1881. Given that the resignation came less than six weeks before Garfield's inauguration, it would have been reasonable for Hayes, now even a lamer duck, to leave the nomination for his successor. Instead, Hayes nominated Stanley Matthews to fill the seat.

Matthews had ample credentials. The Ohio Republican had studied law under the future chief justice Salmon P. Chase. He was a prominent lawyer and politician who had been a U.S. attorney for the Southern District of Ohio, a judge of the Superior Court of Ohio, and a Republican candidate for the U.S. Congress. In 1877, at the urging of Hayes, the Ohio legislature elected Matthews to fill a vacancy in the U.S. Senate. As a senator, Matthews vigorously opposed the Thurman Act, and, when his term expired, he returned to private practice representing railroad and business interests, including the interests of Jay Gould.

Given their evident interest in shaping the Court, it is easy to suspect that Gould and his friends were behind the nomination.[4] Perhaps they were, but the evidence shows that the New York business elite had tried to influence Garfield, not Hayes. Besides, other factors better explain Hayes's choice. The two men were longtime and close friends, having first met when they both attended Kenyon College in central Ohio. During the Civil War, they served in the same unit in the Union army: the Twenty-third Ohio Infantry. They even claimed a connection through marriage because Matthews's sister was married to the brother of Hayes's wife.[5]

Perhaps the most politically significant connection between the two was that, more than any other person, Matthews was responsible for Hayes's victory in the disputed presidential election of 1876. After Congress set up a commission to determine the outcome of the election, the Republican Party chose Matthews as one of the men to make its case. And afterward, when Democrats in Congress threatened to filibuster the Electoral Commission's decision in favor of Hayes, Matthews set up a meeting to broker a deal with the Democrats. The meeting, which took place in Matthews's quarters in Wormley's Hotel, is said to have produced the Compromise of 1877 that won Hayes the presidency. Modern historians have questioned whether the deal hammered out at Wormley's Hotel was actually an essential element of Hayes's success, but this does not diminish the role that Matthews played or Hayes's appreciation.[6]

One other factor explains Matthews's nomination. Noah Swayne agreed to resign from the Supreme Court only after Hayes promised to nominate Matthews as his successor. Appointed in 1862, Swayne had been on the Court for nineteen years.

Although he had been productive as late as 1878, his mental acuity began to decline after that. He participated in court proceedings and wrote some opinions until he retired in 1881, but by then most people counted him as one of the three incapacitated justices who needed to be replaced.[7]

Even though credentials and contacts adequately explained the choice of Matthews, the nominee's connection to Jay Gould and to railroad interests is what caught the public's attention. Hayes may have seen the nomination as payback to an old friend who had loyally supported him over the years, but many others saw it as a payoff to the robber baron element of the economy that Gould had come to symbolize. On January 27, 1881, one day after the nomination, the *New York Times* ran an article opposing Matthews. The *Times* complained that appointments to the nation's highest court should be based on ability and judicial character, not on intimate personal friendship or partisanship. It also reminded readers that Matthews had opposed the Thurman Act.[8] It took up the latter theme again a few days later, writing that it was natural that the judiciary committee should "view with a critical eye the appointment of Mr. Matthews to the tribunal upon whose decisions may depend the effect of [the Thurman] bill, and in fact the vitality of the generic principle of the power of the Government over the corporations created by it."[9]

Opposition from a number of quarters reflected similar themes. In an open letter to the Senate Judiciary Committee, the New York Board of Trade and Transportation maintained that Matthews's nomination represented an effort of the great railroad corporations "to obtain control of this court of last resort, which has heretofore been the most important bulwark in defending the public interest against the encroachments of corporations."[10] Similarly protesting a resolution in support of his nomination, Democrats in the Ohio legislature described Matthews as "the retained attorney of gigantic corporations" who pleaded their case "against the sacred rights of the people."[11]

It did not help Matthews's case that the chair of the Senate Judiciary Committee was none other than Allen Thurman, the named author of the bill that created the sinking fund. Joining Thurman on the committee were other senators who had fought for the Thurman Act: George Edmunds, Augustus Garland, and former associate justice of the U.S. Supreme Court David Davis.[12] Although his supporters, including Hayes, worked hard to secure the confirmation, by February 15 a discouraged Matthews went home to Ohio. As many had predicted, the committee refused to send the nomination to the floor, and Matthews's appointment died when Congress adjourned.[13]

Hindsight tells us that both Hayes's nomination of Matthews and the vehement opposition to it were predictable. The only mystery in the events surrounding Matthews's appointment to the Supreme Court was why the new president, James Garfield, decided to renominate him. Although both men were Ohio Republicans, they were as often rivals as they were friends. At the end of February, when Matthews's prospects looked dim, Garfield had refused to comment on the possibility of renominating him. Nevertheless he did. The nomination may have been the result of a promise to Hayes or to Swayne. It may have been a payback to

Gould and his associates. Whatever the reason, on March 14, 1881, Garfield submitted Matthews's nomination to the Senate.

Opposition mobilized immediately. The National Anti-Monopoly League, joined with organizations like the Grangers and the New York Board of Trade and Transportation, lobbied the Senate and released public statements opposing Matthews. As modern observers have pointed out, this was the first time that organized interest groups played a role in the confirmation of a Supreme Court nominee. John Anthony Maltese notes that "prior to Matthews, Senate opposition blocked seventeen Supreme Court nominations, but each was a result of partisan politics, sectional rivalries, senatorial courtesy, or lack of qualifications." The Matthews nomination was different, according to Maltese and Scott H. Ainsworth, because the confirmation faced stiff opposition from organized interests, especially the National Grange.[14]

There is no denying that the Grange played an important part in the drama that swirled around Matthews's confirmation, or that the Grange's opposition revealed its causes. Writing to the Senate Judiciary Committee, the National Anti-Monopoly League and the president of the Pennsylvania Grange used almost identical language to explain their opposition. A March 15 letter from the National Anti-Monopoly League, for example, reasoned that the Supreme Court had "heretofore been a barrier to corporate aggression against the rights of the people" and that Matthews's appointment was "an effort to bring the Supreme Court under corporate control."[15]

But just as enactment of the Granger laws in the Midwest had not been entirely due to the efforts of the Granger movement and had not simply reflected a struggle between farmers and the railroads, so it was with the nomination of Stanley Matthews. Opposition came from all corners. The records of the Senate Judiciary Committee are filled with clippings from newspapers around the country that opposed the nomination.[16] Although some stated other reasons, most of the opposition stemmed from Matthews's link to Jay Gould. The *Detroit Free Press,* for example, reported sarcastically that Matthews's nomination actually meant that "Mr. Jay Gould has been appointed to the United States Supreme Court in the place of Judge Swayne."[17]

The Gould taint even caused some railroad leaders to oppose Matthews's nomination. Charles E. Perkins, president of the Chicago, Burlington, and Quincy Railroad, was alert to the possibility that Gould and other eastern railroad financiers might have designs on the Midwest. Perkins had his own favorite to fill the vacant seat on the Supreme Court. It was Charles B. Lawrence, former chief justice of the Illinois Supreme Court who previously represented the Chicago and Northwestern Railway in one of the Granger Cases.[18] As late as July 19, 1881, Perkins was working behind the scenes to sidetrack Matthews's confirmation and install Lawrence as the nominee.[19]

Despite the widespread opposition, Matthews was confirmed—albeit by the narrowest margin in history. On May 9 the Senate Judiciary Committee voted seven to one to report Matthews's nomination to the floor with a recommendation that the Senate vote against confirmation. Ignoring the adverse recommendation, on May 12 the Senate confirmed Matthews's nomination by a vote of twenty-four to twenty-three.[20] According to the *New York Times,* the margin was even closer than that. The *Times* reported that Senator Henry B. Anthony of Rhode Island, who was said to be against confirmation, left the chamber for a few minutes before the vote was taken and did not return until after the count. Had Anthony voted, the *Times* speculated, Matthews would have been defeated by a tie vote.[21] Matthews's friends were said to have been chagrined over the narrowness of his escape from defeat, but it did not matter. Five days later, on May 17, 1881, Stanley Matthews took the oath of office and became an associate justice of the U.S. Supreme Court.

When Garfield was elected, political insiders speculated that he would likely have the opportunity to make four appointments to the Supreme Court. Fate gave him only one. On July 2, 1881, a disappointed office seeker named Charles Julius Guiteau shot the president in the back. With a bullet lodged next to his spine, Garfield hung on to life for about three months. When he died on September 19, 1881, the presidency passed to Vice President Chester A. Arthur.

Even with the addition of Justices Woods and Matthews the Court was effectively shorthanded at the time President Arthur took office. It still included two justices who had held on to their seats after they had ceased to be productive. Adding to the problem was the fact that the Court's jurisdiction, and caseload, had expanded in the years after the Civil War. The Court needed more workhorses, and President Arthur would appoint two of them.

One of the replacements was for Justice Nathan Clifford, a Buchanan appointee who had been on the bench since 1858. Clifford had begun to deteriorate mentally and physically as early as 1874. Afterward, he became increasingly difficult to work with and unproductive. He remained on the Court until he died on July 25, 1881. Clifford's replacement was Horace Gray, who was appointed by President Arthur on December 19, 1881, and confirmed the following day.

Born in Boston, Horace Gray was a child of privilege. He attended private schools in the Boston area, entered Harvard at thirteen years of age, and graduated when he was seventeen. While traveling in Europe after graduation, Gray learned that his family's merchant and shipbuilding business had gone broke. Now faced with the prospect of finding a profession, he entered Harvard Law School. Gray had a talent for law, a penchant for detailed work, and an interest in history. Soon after finishing law school and starting practice he was appointed to the prestigious post of reporter of the opinions of the Massachusetts Supreme Court. In 1864 he was appointed associate justice of the Massachusetts Supreme Court and nine years later became that court's chief justice. Although Gray had a history of reaching milestones at a very young age, he remained a bachelor until he was sixty years old. Then, in 1889, he married Jane Matthews, the daughter of his friend and fellow Supreme Court justice, Stanley Matthews.

Gray, who had served seven years on the Massachusetts Supreme Court at the time of his appointment, was, like Woods, a highly respected jurist. He wrote more than a thousand opinions during his seventeen years on the Massachusetts court and another 450 before he resigned from the U.S. Supreme Court in 1902. Yet because most of them were in routine and mundane cases, historians have found it difficult to pin down his judicial philosophy.[22]

Arthur's second appointment replaced Justice Ward Hunt, who had been unable to participate in Court proceedings during the last five years of his service. Hunt hung on in part because he did not want Hayes to select his replacement, but also because he did not qualify for a pension. When in 1882 Congress passed a special bill providing him with a pension, Hunt resigned soon after. On March 13, 1882, President Arthur nominated another respected federal judge, Samuel Blatchford, to take his place. Blatchford was confirmed a month later, on April 13, 1882.

The son of a New York lawyer, Blatchford graduated from Columbia and began reading law in his father's office. He left to serve as secretary to New York governor William Seward and eventually joined Seward's law practice. Seward, who was a close friend of Blatchford's father, would eventually become an outspoken opponent of slavery and would serve as secretary of state under Presidents Abraham Lincoln and Andrew Johnson. Blatchford's association with him opened doors to a distinguished and powerful list of clients. It also led to his appointment as a U.S. district judge in 1867, then as the U.S. Circuit Judge for the Second Circuit in 1872.

As an attorney Blatchford had developed an expertise in maritime and patent law, and this expertise was reinforced by his service as a judge for the Second Circuit, which covered the southern part of New York. Once on the Supreme Court he was assigned most of the admiralty and patent cases. Blatchford sat on the Court until his death in 1893. In those eleven years he authored 430 majority opinions. Few dealt with significant constitutional issues.[23]

The reconstituted Court, especially the addition of Stanley Matthews, gave elite corporations and their attorneys new hope. From 1883 to 1888, and beyond, the federal courts were bombarded with cases that sought to insulate business from government regulation and even taxation.[24] The increased number of cases showed that a push to overturn the doctrine of *Munn* and the *Sinking Fund Cases* was afoot, but the substance of the cases showed that it did not take the form of a carefully orchestrated campaign.

While all the cases made a general argument that any regulation interfering with a company's ability to conduct business violated the Constitution, they were not tied to any one theory explaining why. Lawyers argued that such regulations violated the contract clause, the Fifth Amendment's due process and takings clauses, the Fourteenth Amendment's due process and equal protection clauses, or natural rights. Sometimes they used more than one theory in the same case.

Perhaps this strategy reflected the attitude of their clients. Historian Thomas C. Cochran observed that, although railroad leaders practiced a general philosophy that governments should aid but not hinder business, they were first and foremost pragmatists. "The question was what worked to the advantage of management of the company? A theory to justify the choice could be developed later."[25]

Although corporation lawyers made some gains during the Waite Court years, their efforts did not produce a pivotal moment that changed constitutional doctrine. In fact, the Court's first relevant opinion subsequent to the new appointments expressly reaffirmed the *Munn* doctrine. *Ruggles v. Illinois* (1883) was actually a contract clause case. A subsidiary of the Chicago, Burlington, and Quincy Railroad claimed that Illinois's general rate law violated a provision of the charter that gave the company the right to set its own rates. The Court rejected that claim. In doing so, Chief Justice Waite took the opportunity to point out that under the rules of *Munn*, the railroad was required to carry at reasonable rates and the legislature was at liberty to fix the maximum of what would be reasonable.[26]

A concurring opinion by Justice Harlan gave corporation lawyers some solace. Although he agreed with the majority in this case, Harlan maintained that the determination of whether rates are reasonable is not solely a matter for the legislative judgment but can also be of judicial cognizance.[27] Justice Field also concurred, but only because "no proof was made that the rate prescribed by the legislature was unreasonable."[28] Within a year Field would change his mind on this score.

No one was more determined than Field to change the doctrine of *Munn* and the *Sinking Fund Cases*. Field had, of course, dissented in both of those decisions. Even before the changes in the Court's makeup he persistently hammered away to embed in the Constitution the general theory of entrepreneurial liberty the business elite favored. *Spring Valley Water-Works v. Schottler*, in 1884, showed he was not likely to let up. The case involved a company chartered in 1858 to supply water to the city of San Francisco. Under its original charter, rates were to be determined by a board of commissioners comprised of two persons chosen by the city or town, two by the water company, and one other chosen by those four. In 1879 California ratified a new constitution that substituted a new method for determining rates. Under the new constitutional provision, the rates or compensation for companies providing water to any city, county, or town was to be fixed annually by the utility's governing body. Spring Valley Water-Works argued that the new constitutional provision violated the contract clause and took its property without just compensation.

When the majority of the Court rejected the company's claims, Field dissented. The facts provided an ideal forum for him to state a theory of the limits of a state's rate-making authority and regulatory authority in general. To define those limits, Field melded natural law and the Constitution, and the Spring Valley Water-Works situation allowed him to employ an "in the state of nature" argument that would have made John Locke and Adam Smith proud.

"It is a general principle of law, both natural and positive, that where a subject, animate or inanimate, which otherwise could not be brought under the control or use of man, is reduced to such control or use by individual labor, a right of property in it is acquired by such labor," Field wrote. What purer example could there be than that of the Spring Valley Water-Works? As Field described it, the company literally converted rain as it fell from the sky and, through expenditures of vast amounts of money, gathered it in reservoirs, then piped it hundreds of miles to the city. Once the water was there, Field maintained, the company had the right to sell its property at such reasonable prices as it could obtain, just as it might have sold grain, fruit, or coal had it brought those articles to market.[29] It did not matter to him that Spring Valley Water-Works was a corporation or that its corporate charter included a reserve clause giving the state the right to alter or amend the contract. Corporations, he said, stand the same as natural persons with regard to the limits of state power.[30]

The state could declare the water of public use, Field admitted. But, if it did, the state had to pay just compensation to the owner of the property. This sounded like an application of the Fifth Amendment guarantee that private property shall not be taken for public use without just compensation. Under standard constitutional doctrine of the time, however, the Fifth Amendment applied only to the federal government, not to the states. That detail did not deter Field, who reasoned that the right to take property for public use was inherent in all governments. This right, he said, was limited only by the "constitutional guaranties" that "just compensation shall be made to the owner of the property, and that this just compensation shall be ascertained by an impartial tribunal." The second of those guarantees is not, of course, in the U.S. Constitution, but it brought Field back to his underlying premise. Because a state board could not be impartial when it came to setting rates, that board must be unconstitutional.

For all the legal razzle-dazzle, Field's *Spring Valley Water-Works* dissent really articulated two simple and related ideas near to the hearts of elite business leaders. It was the embryo of a theory that, because state economic regulation deprives a business of the market-driven price for its goods or services, all regulation amounts to confiscation and is therefore presumed to be unconstitutional. The related theory that followed was that the adequacy of rates, and ultimately of all economic regulation, is inherently a question for the judiciary rather than the legislature.

Chief Justice Waite's opinion for the majority portrayed the company in a different light. He saw it as a virtual monopoly that had availed itself of the privileges granted it by the state. Waite emphasized that changing the makeup of the commission did not violate the contract clause because the company's charter included a reserve clause giving the state that power. Then he responded to the company's claim that the change took its property without due process. "That it is within the power of government to regulate the prices at which water should be sold, by one who enjoys a virtual monopoly of the sale, we have no doubt," he wrote. "That question was settled by what was decided on full consideration in *Munn v. Illinois*." Adding even more weight to his position was the fact that "the objection here is not to any improper prices fixed by the officers, but to their power to fix prices at all."[31]

Field and Waite continued the debate three years later in the Railroad Commission cases of 1886. Arguing that a company's control of rates and policies was indispensable to the successful management of the business of every railway company, Field pointed out the parade of horrible results that legislative interference would likely produce. Once again he failed to convince the majority.[32] Waite reiterated the points he had made many times. A state cannot barter away the power of sovereignty. Regulation is not the equivalent of confiscation but rather a legitimate exercise of the police power. The legislature is under a duty to regulate in the interest of the rights of the community, and abandonment of its power to do so cannot be presumed. Conceding to Harlan's point in *Ruggles,* however, he noted that it was not to be inferred that a state's power to regulate is without limits. "Under pretense of regulating fares and freights, the state cannot require a railroad corporation to carry persons or property without reward; neither can it do that which in law amounts to a taking of private property for public use without just compensation, or without due process of law. What would have this effect we need not now say."[33]

Two years earlier *Butchers' Union Slaughter-House & Live Stock Co. v. Crescent City Live-Stock Landing & Slaughter-House Co.* (1884) provided an example of the role the contract clause continued to play with respect to a state's authority to regulate. *Butchers' Union* was a continuation of the battle that the Court had seen in 1873, when the *Slaughterhouse Cases* upheld a charter giving the Crescent City Company the exclusive right to operate a slaughterhouse in New Orleans. In 1879 the state of Louisiana enacted a new constitution, one section of which allowed municipalities to regulate slaughterhouses and prohibited monopolies in the industry. When New Orleans subsequently approved other slaughterhouses, the Crescent City Company claimed the new constitutional provision violated the contract clause. All of the justices agreed that it did not, but for different reasons.

Taking a standard contract clause approach, Justice Miller's opinion for the majority pointed out that Crescent City Company's claim (that its grant to operate the New Orleans slaughterhouse was permanent) would tie the hands of future legislatures. Regulation of slaughterhouses fell squarely within the police powers of the state, Miller continued, and the company's claim thus clearly ran afoul of the doctrine that the police powers of the state cannot be bargained away by contract.

What was significant about the case, however, was that four justices—Bradley, Harlan, Woods, and Field—took the opportunity to state that the Fourteenth Amendment placed a limit on the state's police power. Tracking the reasoning of the dissents in the *Slaughterhouse Cases*, they agreed that the original charter was itself unconstitutional because by creating a monopoly in the butchering trade it denied other butchers the right to pursue a lawful profession.[34]

Although most of the justices agreed in the abstract that there was a limit to the police power of the states, the Waite Court was exceedingly hesitant to find that a state had exceeded that limit. In the years between 1883 and 1888 numerous economic regulations were challenged on the grounds that they were unconstitutional, but the Court upheld almost all the statutes. Laws awarding multiple damages for a railroad's failure to maintain fences, regulation of milldams, a variety of taxes and tolls for doing business, assessments and liens to pay for reclamation of swamplands, and laws prohibiting certain kinds of mortgages were all upheld.[35]

This trend continued right up to the end of Chief Justice Waite's tenure, when the Court upheld a Kansas prohibition law. By this time it was well settled that states could prohibit the sale of alcoholic beverages, but the Kansas law went beyond that. It prohibited not only the sale and manufacture for sale but also manufacture for one's own use. Declaring all places that manufacture, sell, or give away alcohol to be public nuisances, it also directed law enforcement officers to close them and destroy the liquor, bars, bottles, glasses, and other property.

Justice John Harlan, who wrote the opinion upholding the act, maintained that the authority to determine whether the manufacture of alcohol for sale or for personal use was injurious to the community rested in the legislature. Speaking of the police power, he said, "we cannot shut out of view the fact, within the knowledge of all, that the public health, the public morals, and the public safety, may be endangered by the general use of intoxicating drinks; nor the fact established by statistics accessible to every one, that the idleness, disorder, pauperism, and crime existing in the country are, in some degree at least, traceable to this evil."[36]

Harlan, whose brother and nephew struggled with alcoholism, had personal experience with the danger of intoxicating beverages and little sympathy for those who abused them.[37] But as tempting as it may be to attribute his opinion to personal beliefs, Harlan's conclusion rested more on his traditional view of the authority of the states to guard the interests of the public and his view of the role of courts. He rejected the defendant's contention that enforcement of the statute amounted to a taking of property without just compensation. The questions in this case did not arise under the state's power of eminent domain, he noted, but rather under what were strictly the police powers of the state.[38] For him, it was up to the legislature to determine how the police power should be applied. Certainly the court had the duty to overrule any law that, under the pretense of protecting the public health, morals, or safety, actually violated the Constitution, he reasoned. "But every possible presumption is to be indulged in favor of the validity of the statute."[39]

Justice Stephen Field wrote a dissenting opinion in which he disagreed with the majority's reasoning that the provision prohibiting manufacture for export would not violate the commerce clause. He also stated that the provision for destruction of property violated the due process clause. By any account the law in *Mugler v. Kansas* (1887) went to the fringes of a line between regulation and confiscation. The state had declared that businesses that sold or manufactured alcoholic beverages were a public nuisance and ordered their property destroyed. Field argued that declaring property a nuisance without affording the owner a hearing amounted to confiscation.[40]

Eventually, after Waite's death, the Court would move in Field's direction. In the Minnesota milk rate case of 1890 the Court subtly revised *Munn*'s presumption of the validity of state legislation. Writing for the majority, Justice Samuel Blatchford stated, "The question of the reasonableness of a rate charged for transportation by a railroad company is eminently a question for judicial investigation."[41] Then, in the 1898 case *Smyth v. Ames*, it added force to the idea that regulation could amount to confiscation when it ruled that the due process clause guaranteed that businesses receive a fair return on the value of the property they employ for the public convenience.[42] At the same time the Court began to hone a theory called "liberty of contract," which subjected all regulation, not just rate making, to the challenge that it violated the due process clause of the Fourteenth Amendment.[43]

But repeated efforts between 1883 and Waite's death in 1888 did not produce the kind of constitutional protections from government regulation that the corporate elite wanted. Throughout the Waite era, the Court refused to equate regulation with confiscation. It refused to interpret the Fourteenth Amendment as providing a general restriction on government regulation of business. In cases challenging the validity of regulations it continued to rely on the antebellum legal tradition that emphasized the right of the community as a limit on property. The ideas and theories railroad and corporate attorneys pressed were gradually becoming part of constitutional discourse, but their elevation to constitutional doctrine would have to wait until after the Waite era.

Advocates for the railroad and corporate elite appeared to have had better success with their efforts during the Waite era to achieve another goal. Because most elite businesses were corporations, they hoped to convince the Court to adopt the principle that corporations are entitled to the full protection of the Constitution, just as if they were natural persons. In the *Sinking Fund Cases,* and even before that, they had made some progress in that the majority was willing to recognize that a state could not confiscate corporate property any more than it could confiscate the property of a natural person. But this concession did not provide much more protection to corporations than the standard contract clause doctrine that a state could not deprive a corporation of the essential object of its charter. Besides, although the majority of justices in the *Sinking Fund Cases* were ambivalent about the status of the corporation, they were definitely unwilling to adopt the anthropomorphic corporation portrayed in Field's dissent.

Soon after the appointments of the new justices between 1880 and 1882, Field tried again to convince them. The California Constitution of 1878–79 revised the formula for assessing property values for purposes of taxation. Under the new formula, taxes for most kinds of property were based on the property's actual value less the amount of any mortgages held against the property. Railroads "and other quasi public corporations" were assessed differently. Their property taxes were based on the actual value of the property—without any deduction for the amount of mortgages held against the property.

Although this new scheme for assessing property undoubtedly treated railroads differently from other individuals or companies, the state offered a reasonable rationale for doing so. Farmers and small businesses were thought to be paying double taxation: once taxed on the full value of their property, including the amount of their mortgage, they then paid to their banks the amount the bank was taxed on the value of the mortgage. Delegates to the constitutional convention wanted to relieve farmers and small businesses of the perceived double taxation, but they worried that a plan that allowed all taxpayers to reduce their assessment by the amount of their mortgages would also allow railroads to escape paying their fair share of taxes. The railroad mortgage was a different breed of credit from the mortgage on a farm, they argued. Rather than a loan, it was a way of raising capital. Moreover railroad mortgages tended to be held by out-of-state interests that were not subject to state taxation.[44]

Predictably dissatisfied with the new scheme, railroads withheld taxes for 1880–81 and sued in California courts to test the validity of the new law. After some legal maneuvering the cases were removed to the Federal Circuit Court for the District of

California—the court over which Justice Stephen Field presided when he rode circuit. Field and Judge Lorenzo Sawyer chose two of the disputes, *San Mateo v. Southern Pacific Railroad Company* (1882) and *Santa Clara v. Southern Pacific Railroad Company* (1883), as the lead cases.[45]

Field announced his theory of corporate equal protection when he took jurisdiction of the cases and, in doing so, hinted at what he thought would be the outcome of the disputes. Lecturing the parties about the issues to be decided, he advised them to prepare to address the question of whether the Fourteenth Amendment applies to corporations as well as natural persons. If so, he said, the case would turn on the meaning of the equal protection clause. That clause, Field noted, was designed to cover all cases of possible discrimination and partial legislation against any class; the problem with the California tax scheme, he later said, was that the difference in taxes was based not on the nature of the property but on the character of the owner.[46]

Field's instructions postured the cases as a direct clash between competing visions regarding the rights of the community and the nature of corporations. The legal dispute thus echoed the debate that had dominated the early stages of the California constitutional convention that had produced the tax scheme in question. There, reformer delegates had successfully made the case that the state had not only the power but also the duty to control corporations. While debating the provisions on corporations during the convention, delegates often emphasized the need for controlling corporations. Volney E. Howard, a delegate from Los Angeles, captured their concerns in a nutshell: "Have the community no power to defend themselves?" he asked. "If not, then we had better turn this government over to the Central Pacific Railroad Company, if they are willing to pay the expense, for it is the practical government of the state, and this country, and the most grasping unprincipled government at that."[47]

The majority of convention delegates believed that the community did have the "power to defend themselves." Far from being radical, their arguments tracked typical beliefs of the time, beliefs that were reflected in standard legal and constitutional doctrine. Corporations were creatures of the state, they reasoned. The community gave corporations extraordinary rights and allowed them to use the powers of the state, like eminent domain, to benefit the public good. The community, in turn, had the right to control its creation. In this vein the first line of the proposed section on railroads declared, "All railroads, canals, and transportation companies shall be common carriers and subject to legislative control."[48] Finding encouragement in *Munn v. Illinois,* the convention also proposed a railroad commission with the power to set rates and charges for the transportation of passengers and freights. And, of course, it designed the tax scheme that became the issue in the *San Mateo* and *Santa Clara* cases.

What reformers won in the state convention they lost in the federal circuit court, where Justice Field and Judge Sawyer declared that because the California property tax treated certain corporations differently than natural persons, it was therefore unconstitutional.[49] A corporation consists of an association of individuals united for some lawful purpose, Field reasoned. Whatever affects the property of the corporation necessarily affects the property of those individuals who comprise it, he continued, and it would be unthinkable to conclude that the right of these individuals to be free from discrimination ceases when they become members of a corporation. This argument, which modern observers call the "associational theory" or "partnership justification," tracked normal constitutional thinking of the time. Standard doctrine, under both the contract clause and later the due process clause, held that a corporation could not arbitrarily be deprived of its property.[50]

Field did not merely want to reiterate the idea that the courts should be mindful of the rights of those individuals who make up a corporation, however. He wanted to instill an idea that corporations are no different from natural persons and therefore must be afforded the same rights as anyone else. To do this he turned to the concept of equal protection. Adoption of the Fourteenth Amendment meant that all persons within a state's jurisdiction could claim equal protection under the law, he said. This meant "equal security to every one in his private rights—in his right to life, to liberty, to property, and to the pursuit of happiness." It may be difficult to imagine how a corporation pursues happiness, but that did not matter to Field. The important point to him was that the guarantee of equal protection meant that a state could subject no one, corporation or natural person, "to any greater burdens or charges than such are imposed upon all others in like circumstances." With characteristic flair he declared that the Constitution serves as a perpetual shield against all unequal legislation by the states, "whether directed against the most humble or the most powerful; against the despised laborer from China, or the envied master of millions."[51]

Field's opinions represented a major setback for California reformers. The state of California joined the counties in appealing the cases to the U.S. Supreme Court. While the appeal was pending, however, the Southern Pacific Railroad continued to withhold taxes and was soon able to force the state into a settlement in which the railroad essentially set its own terms. For many reformers, the episode confirmed their worst fear—"that a power had grown up in the state greater than the state itself."[52]

Ultimately in *Santa Clara County v. Southern Pacific Railroad* (1886) the Supreme Court confirmed the result of the circuit court rulings.[53] But it did so on the basis of a peculiarity in the California law. The majority conspicuously refused to address the sweeping constitutional theories upon which Field had based his circuit court opinions.

The cases would have gone down in history as relatively unimportant tax cases except for an exchange of memos between Chief Justice Waite and Bancroft Davis, the court reporter in charge of preparing the Court's opinions for publication. Recalling instructions that the chief justice had given to the attorneys arguing the *Santa Clara County v. Southern Pacific Railroad* case, Davis wrote: "In the opening the Court stated that it did not wish to hear argument on the question whether the Fourteenth Amendment applies to such corporations as are parties in these suits. All the judges were of the opinion that it does. Please let me know whether I correctly caught your words and oblige." Waite gave the following reply: "I think your [memo] in the California Rail Road Tax cases expresses with sufficient accuracy what was said before the arguments began. I leave it to you to determine whether anything need be said about it in the report inasmuch as we avoided meeting the constitutional question in the decision."[54]

Davis used his discretion to insert the following statement into the official published report. "Mr. Chief Justice Waite said: The court does not wish to hear argument on the question whether the provision in the Fourteenth Amendment to the Constitution, which forbids a state to deny to any person within its jurisdiction the equal protection of the laws, applies to these corporations. We are all of the opinion that it does."[55]

Later judges would use the preface to the *Santa Clara* opinion as the seminal precedent for a doctrine that a corporation is a person for purposes of the Fourteenth Amendment. In the 1898 case *Smyth v. Ames*, for example, Justice Harlan accepted the proposition without hesitation.[56] The standard interpretation today is that the *Santa Clara* case established a doctrine of corporate personhood that eventually gave corporations most of the rights held by natural persons. One modern application of the doctrine holds that corporations are protected by the First Amendment guarantee of freedom of speech.[57]

Historians and critics of that doctrine have pointed out that a comment from the court's reporter is not a legitimate source of precedent. They have also recognized that the implication of Waite's response is not clear-cut and that the assumption that he meant to give corporations all the rights of natural persons ignores nuances in the Court's debates about corporate rights that continued right up to the *Santa Clara* case. Just two years earlier in *Spring Valley Water-Works*, for example, Waite himself emphasized that "the Spring Valley Company is an artificial being, created by or under the authority of the legislature of California."[58]

The idea that the *Santa Clara* opinion stands as precedent for a theory of expansive corporate personhood also ignores the fact that the debate about the extent of corporate rights continued in the years immediately following. Corporate taxpayers continued to press the idea of corporate equal protection, and the majority of the court continued to reject it, more than once noting that corporations are artificial beings. Even Field was inconsistent at times about the nature of the corporation. In *Pembina Consolidated Silver Mining & Milling Co. v. Pennsylvania*, a case decided shortly before Waite's death, Field insisted that corporations were persons entitled to the guarantees of the Fourteenth Amendment. But he justified this proposition with the rationale that a corporation was nothing more than an association of individuals. Even more revealing, he recognized in that case that an out-of-state corporation is a creature of the state that had created it.[59]

Nevertheless Waite's offhand remark has mutated or been molded into a key moment in the establishment of a doctrine of corporate personhood that guarantees to corporations virtually all of the rights the Constitution guarantees to persons made of flesh and blood. Field helped push the Court in that direction by continuing to cite *Santa Clara* and *Pembina* as definitive authority for the proposition that a corporation is a person within the meaning of the Fourteenth Amendment.[60]

Despite considerable efforts by lawyers for elite corporations, the Waite Court after 1881 resisted pressure for a fundamental change in the constitutional doctrine that it had followed in *Munn* and the *Sinking Fund Cases*. Lawyers seeking change did make subtle gains in the sense of attaching their ideas to the constitutional discourse. But that is as far as they got. At least in cases involving economic regulation, the majority of the justices on the Court continued to follow what they saw as the traditional course: the course exemplified in cases like *Munn* and the *Sinking Funds Cases*. These cases tended to recognize the fundamental power of government to regulate business and have some degree of control over corporations. However, the revolution in commerce and growth of the national market intensified the question of which government, state or federal, was the appropriate regulator.

9

INTERSTATE COMMERCE

The commercial revolution and emergence of a national economy posed new challenges for the traditional thinking about federalism and interstate commerce. The Waite Court responded with a body of precedent that perplexed even the most esteemed experts of the time. Article I, Section 8, of the Constitution gives Congress the power to regulate commerce "with foreign nations, among the several states, and with the Indian tribes." In its simplest terms this means that the power to regulate interstate commerce belongs to the federal government. The power to regulate local, or intrastate, commerce belongs to the states.

During the first century of the nation's existence, however, Congress did not enact much legislation regulating commerce. Prior to the end of the nineteenth century the states played the predominant role in regulating economic matters. Disputes over the meaning of the commerce clause therefore did not usually raise questions about the limits of Congress's power. They were more likely to involve claims that state legislation had run afoul of the commerce clause. This aspect of the commerce clause doctrine, usually referred to as the "dormant commerce power," required the Court to distinguish state regulations that were appropriate exercises of the traditional police power of the states from those that placed an impermissible burden on interstate commerce.[1]

In fairness, the Waite Court did not begin with a blank slate. The Supreme Court's commerce clause doctrine traced back to *Gibbons v. Ogden* in 1824, where Chief Justice John Marshall championed a broad view of Congress's power. In *Gibbons* the Court ruled that a New York law granting a monopoly to operate steamboats in the state's waters was unconstitutional because it was in conflict with a congressional law governing trade in coastal waters.[2] But *Gibbons* did not address the question of to what degree Congress's power was exclusive. If Congress had not enacted legislation covering a given aspect of interstate commerce, if its power remained dormant, could a state regulate that subject?

In *Wilson v. Black Bird Marsh Co.* (1829) Marshall ruled that in the absence of federal legislation, a state did have some authority to enact local legislation that had a tangential impact on interstate commerce. A state's authority was limited, however. Explaining this, Marshall tried to draw a line between state legislation that interfered with interstate commerce and legislation that, while having an impact on interstate commerce, represented the legitimate powers of the state to protect the health, safety, and welfare of its citizens.[3]

Later the Court developed a basic formula for dealing with this balancing act. In *Cooley v. Board of Wardens* (1851) it ruled that where the subject of regulation was national in scope and demanded uniform regulation, Congress's power over interstate commerce was exclusive. A state could not interfere with it even if Congress had not acted. If the subject could impact on interstate commerce but was local in its character, however, a state could regulate until such time as Congress passed legislation on the same subject. Then the federal legislation preempted the state law.[4]

The *Cooley v. Board of Wardens* formula offered future courts an underlying principle. But applying the formula was a difficult matter, often producing conflicting results. As the American economy became more national and interconnected in the years after the Civil War, tensions arising from the concept of Congress's dormant commerce power that had percolated in the early years showed signs of exploding. The Waite Court faced the task of applying the doctrine to new circumstances.

State taxation of businesses that dealt in interstate commerce and transportation proved to be the most vexing source of conflict with the dormant commerce power during the Waite era. Of course a state had the power to tax property, including inventory of goods, located within its jurisdiction. And the fact that goods had moved in interstate commerce did not necessarily exempt them from state taxation. But there was always a question of whether a tax on such goods really amounted to a tariff on imports from another state. The earliest rule governing taxation of goods that had moved from state to state came from *Brown v. Maryland* (1827), where the Marshall Court ruled that a state could not tax an item in interstate commerce so long as it remained in its original package.[5]

The Waite Court modified this "original package doctrine" with what seemed to be a rule that a state could tax goods before they started their journey or voyage and after they had reached their final resting place but not in between.[6] This was not always easy to determine, however. One example, *Coe v. Town of Errol* (1886), involved a New Hampshire town's tax on logs. The logs were being floated down the Androscoggin River, which meandered from Maine into New Hampshire then back into Maine. Their eventual destination was Lewiston, Maine, but they were stored near Errol, New Hampshire, during low-water season. Some of the logs had been cut in New Hampshire. The Court ruled that these had not yet begun their interstate journey and were thus subject to the New Hampshire tax. Others had been cut in Maine. These, the Court ruled, were still on their interstate journey and were thus exempt.[7]

State efforts to tax nonresident businesses and salesmen, or to require that they obtain a special license, produced similarly muddled doctrine. Although all of the justices agreed that a state could not discriminate against a nonresident business, determining when discrimination occurred was not always self-evident.

Licensing out-of-state drummers provides an example. Drummers were a type of salesmen used to expand a company's market by showing potential customers samples of their product and taking orders for delivery. The Court split over a

Tennessee law that required all drummers to pay a fixed fee for the privilege of doing business in Memphis. Justice Bradley and the majority believed that the license discriminated against out-of-state businesses and thus ruled that the fee was illegal. Chief Justice Waite, joined by Field and Gray, believed that the licensing of drummers was a legitimate tax, no different than a tax on companies having a fixed place of business within the city.[8] However, when Maryland required a nonresident drummer to pay a fee based on the company's total amount of stock in trade, Waite, Field, and Gray joined the majority in condemning the law as a tax on commerce among the states.[9]

Taxation of railroads and canals raised an especially thorny problem for the dormant commerce power. As Justice Miller pointed out, unlike banks or factories whose businesses affect commerce only remotely or incidentally, the railroad business—the transportation of persons and property—is itself commerce.[10] Although railroads had already become a national industry by the 1870s, there was no intimation from the Court that state regulation of railroads *necessarily* interfered with interstate commerce.

Baltimore & Ohio Railroad Co. v. Maryland (1875) provides one example. The case involved a grant from Maryland to the Baltimore and Ohio Railroad to build a branch across the state line to Washington, D.C. The grant stipulated that every six months the company pay to the state of Maryland one-fifth of the entire amount it received for transporting passengers between Baltimore and the District of Columbia. Despite the obvious interstate nature of this particular enterprise, the Supreme Court ruled that the imposition of this tax or fee did not interfere with interstate commerce. The state, it said, has a right to control and profit from the use of its public highways.[11] The question of how far that right could be stretched before a state tax did interfere with interstate commerce remained unanswered.

When Waite took the bench the question of what kind of tax a state might impose on transportation companies was far from settled.[12] Throughout the Waite era the Court continued to grapple with determining whether a tax constituted a legitimate levy on corporate or business property located within a state or constituted an impermissible tariff on goods transported through that state. In 1885, for example, it ruled that Pennsylvania's taxation of a company that ferried passengers and freight from Gloucester, New Jersey, to Philadelphia unduly interfered with interstate commerce. The company was incorporated in New Jersey, and all of its property was located in New Jersey, except for one dock that it leased in Philadelphia. Admitting that the state could tax the company on the value of the dock lease, the Court nevertheless concluded that the Pennsylvania tax, calculated on the entire gross receipts of any company doing business in the state, amounted to a tax on transportation and thus invaded the exclusive power of Congress to regulate interstate commerce.[13] Then, in 1887, the Court overruled a Pennsylvania tax on the gross receipts of an interstate steamship company that was incorporated within the state of Pennsylvania.[14]

Modern readers who might be confused by these fine distinctions will find some comfort in knowing they are not alone. Frustrated by apparent inconsistency, Samuel

Miller reminded his fellow justices that the ultimate purpose of the commerce clause was to prohibit a state from compelling citizens of other states to pay to it a tax for the privilege of having their goods transported through that state by ordinary channels of commerce.[15]

State taxation was not the only source of perplexing commerce clause doctrine. Thomas M. Cooley explained in the 1883 edition of his influential *Treatise on Constitutional Limitations* that there were numerous other examples of legitimate state power to enact regulations affecting commerce. That continued to be the case long after the Waite era and remains true today. Among those regulations Cooley highlighted were "quarantine regulations and health laws of every description."[16] Following this general rule, the Waite Court in 1886 upheld a Louisiana law that required vessels heading from the Gulf of Mexico to New Orleans to stop at a quarantine station and pay a fee for inspection.[17]

Yet even quarantine and health regulations could run afoul of the dormant commerce power. In 1877 the Court overruled a Missouri law that prohibited bringing "Texas, Mexican, or Indian" cattle across state lines. While admitting that a state may pass sanitary and quarantine laws and may prevent the spread of disease, it concluded that the Missouri statute was not one of those such laws but rather a prohibition on an entire class of goods moving in interstate commerce. As such, it was an intrusion on the exclusive domain of Congress.[18]

State efforts to control immigration, although often couched as laws intended to protect the health, safety, morality, and economic well-being of the state, tended to interfere with the dormant commerce power. In an 1837 case, *City of New York v. Miln*, the Court upheld a section of an immigration law that required ship captains to provide a list of all passengers along with place of birth, age, occupation, and other information.[19] When the state also required that the master of the vessel pay a fee or bond for each passenger, however, the Court was more inclined to view the law as an interference with Congress's power.[20] This was especially evident when the court suspected or determined that the true purpose of the statute was to discourage immigration altogether or discourage immigration of a particular group.

In 1876 the Court overruled a New York law that required masters of each vessel landing in New York either to pay an excessively expensive bond for every passenger who was not a citizen of the United States or, alternatively, to pay a fee of $1.50 for each foreign passenger. The state argued that the law served a legitimate purpose of indemnifying the people of the state from "the consequences of the flood of pauperism emigrating from Europe."[21] Justice Miller, writing for the majority, was not impressed. The transportation of immigrants to the United States, he observed, "has become a part of our commerce with foreign nations, of vast interest to this country, as well as to the immigrants who come among us to find a welcome home within our borders."[22] Miller observed that rather than poverty, some immigrants brought wealth. But even more important to him, they brought the "labor which we need to till our soil, build our railroads, and develop the latent resources of the country in its minerals, manufactures, and its agriculture."[23] The policy regulating such commerce, he concluded, falls within the sole authority of Congress.

Miller's view that Congress had the sole authority to make policy regarding immigration was even more self-evident in another case read on the same day. *Chy Lung v. Freeman* overruled a California law that authorized the state commissioner of immigration to determine whether any passengers of a ship fell into the category of undesirables that included "lunatic, idiotic, deaf, dumb, criminals, and *lewd or debauched women.*"[24] The commissioner could prohibit these passengers from disembarking unless the master of the vessel posted a bond of $500 in gold.

Chy Lung was one of a group of twenty-two Chinese women who were denied entry under the statute, and it was obvious to Miller that the true purpose of the California law was to discourage Chinese immigration. The statute, Miller observed, was skillfully framed to place in the hands of a single state official "the power to prevent vessels engaged in foreign trade, say with China, from carrying passengers."[25] This led him to conclude: "The passage of laws which concern the admission of citizens and subjects of foreign nations to our shores belongs to Congress, and not to the States. It has the power to regulate commerce with foreign nations: the responsibility for the character of those regulations, and for the manner of their execution belongs solely to the national government." If it were otherwise, he warned, "a single State can, at her pleasure, embroil us in disastrous quarrels with other nations."[26]

Undoubtedly one aspect of *Chy Lung* was the prohibition of state discrimination against Chinese immigrants. However, any thought that the Court was embarking on a course that used the commerce clause as a tool to promote racial equality was erased two years later when, in *Hall v. Decuir*, it overruled a Louisiana statute that prohibited racial segregation on riverboats on the Mississippi River. Writing for the majority, Chief Justice Waite emphasized that the decision said nothing about the state's right to prohibit such discrimination within it own boundaries.[27] But he reasoned that even though it purported to prohibit discrimination only within Louisiana, this statute necessarily influenced the conduct of interstate carriers along the entire course of their voyage.[28] To allow each state the liberty to regulate in this manner, he continued, would result in confusion, great inconvenience, and unnecessary hardship.[29]

Concern about state regulations causing confusion, inconvenience, and unnecessary hardship did not stop the Court from upholding all sorts of regulations that differed from one state to another. Historian James Ely has observed that with respect to railroads, the consummate transportation industry, the Court generally allowed states broad leeway to protect the safety of passengers and the public.[30] Fence laws, liability laws, limits on train speed, laws requiring the use of safety equipment, and laws prescribing qualifications of engineers and conductors serve as examples.[31] But there were also numerous exceptions. A law that required carriers to provide freight cars upon written application of shippers, laws that prohibited shipment or required a license for shipping alcoholic beverages, state laws prohibiting running trains on Sundays, and some state flood control projects ran afoul of the dormant commerce power.[32]

Even constitutional scholars of the time were at a loss to explain the doctrine. One of the most prominent, Thomas M. Cooley, complained that "the line of distinction between that which constitutes an interference with commerce, and that which is a mere police regulation is sometimes exceedingly dim and shadowy, and it is not to be wondered that learned jurists differ when endeavoring to classify the cases which arise."[33]

Perhaps those learned jurists could not be faulted for producing an exceedingly dim and shadowy doctrine. In the years following the Civil War America's social order and economy were in a state of flux. When it came to regulating economic matters, traditional thinking about the nature of American federalism had emphasized the role of the states. Inconsistency in commerce clause doctrine occurred when judges tried to apply that old tradition to the new national economy, or perhaps tweak the old tradition to fit the new economy.

Railroads symbolized the problem, and they were part of the problem. In the late nineteenth century railroads were the engine that drove the nation toward a new national economy. But the industry got its start in a time when the American economy was rural and local. With the exception of the transcontinental routes, railroads were organized on the state level. They were incorporated by the states and often subsidized by the states or municipalities. States provided them with rights of way and often the power of eminent domain. The earliest railroads were thought of as something like a farm-to-market road or a mode of regional transportation like a canal or turnpike. Even though some early railroad lines crossed state boundaries, it was natural for American legislators and judges to assume that the states would regulate the terms and conditions of their operation.

The Waite Court had followed this assumption in the 1877 Granger Cases. Recall that these cases, which were decided along with *Munn v. Illinois,* tested the power of several midwestern states to regulate the rates railroads could charge for their services. Everyone understood that the states had the power to regulate rates for the transportation of people and property carried entirely within the state. A related question was whether states also had the authority to regulate rates for the transportation of people and property "taken up outside the state and brought within it or taken up within the state and carried without."[34] The Court ruled in the Granger Cases that they did. Its most explicit statement came when upholding a Wisconsin rate regulation in *Peik v. Chicago & North-Western Railway Co.* Any impact of Wisconsin's rate law on interstate commerce was indirect and incidental, the majority reasoned. Congress does have the power to control interstate rates, but, until it did so, Wisconsin may regulate the fares of companies operating in the state.[35]

When the Court made its decisions in the Granger Cases on March 1, 1877, a push for enacting federal regulation of railroad rates was already germinating. Rates, more than fencing laws, liability laws, and safety laws, tended to affect interstate commerce. This was especially evident in debates about the volatile issue of rate discrimination. Complaints about rate discrimination, along with the habit among the major trunk lines of entering into "pooling" or price-fixing agreements, provided the catalyst for congressional action. They were a major aspect of what became known as "the railway problem."

Although railroad critics attacked both pooling and rate discrimination as being unfair and monopolistic, the railway problem also existed for the railroads. Different sectors of the railroad industry could simultaneously be highly competitive and monopolistic.[36] Businesses that wanted to ship freight from one major trade center, like Chicago, to another, like New York, had a variety of choices of routes and companies. Consequently competition for long haul shipping tended to be cutthroat. In order to attract business in this competitive environment, the great trunk lines—those routes that ran across the country from center of commerce to center of commerce—sometimes had to offer rates that barely covered their fixed costs. From the industry point of view the competition was so fierce that it threatened to put a company into bankruptcy, and various state attempts to regulate rates only made the situation worse.[37] Industry advocates had only to direct attention to the rate of railroad bankruptcies in the 1870s and 1880s to make their point.

It is simplistic to characterize the railway problem as a battle between railroad companies, on one side, and small town shippers and farmers, on the other. The problem was much more complex.[38] It is safe to say, however, that even though the Court ruled in the Granger Cases that states had the power to regulate rates, a growing number of Americans were coming to believe that the existing system of building, operating, and regulating railroads was unsatisfactory. An important part of that existing system was the tradition of state regulation. But it had become apparent that the railroad industry had burst through the limits of states' abilities to regulate railroads effectively and efficiently, and perhaps strained the boundaries of the states' constitutional powers.[39]

The first serious proposal for federal regulation of the railroads was introduced in the House of Representatives in 1878.[40] Named the Reagan Bill, after John H. Reagan, chair of the House Committee on Commerce, it proposed prohibiting short-haul price discrimination, outlawing pooling, and requiring railroads to publish their rates, and it directed that enforcement of rate regulations would be through the courts. The Reagan Bill seemed to reflect the interests of farmers and short haul shippers. Thus the earliest explanations maintained that the National Grange got the movement for federal legislation under way.[41] But historians have convincingly demonstrated that the support for federal regulation of the railroads came from a wide variety of places—from independent oil producers, to New York merchants, to Southern business interests, to the railroads themselves.[42] In the end it seems that most people favored federal regulation of the railroads. In the decade it took for the Interstate Commerce Act to emerge from Congress, the major debate was not about whether federal regulation was appropriate but rather over the specific form it would take.

This was the political atmosphere when, in 1886, the Supreme Court was asked to reconsider its commerce clause ruling in *Peik* and the other Granger Cases. *Wabash, St. Louis, and Pacific Railway Co. v. Illinois* tested an Illinois statute that prohibited rate discrimination.[43] The Illinois Supreme Court had ruled that the Wabash, St. Louis, and Pacific violated the statute when it charged one shipper fifteen cents per hundred pounds to ship freight from Peoria, Illinois, to New York City and on the same day charged another shipper twenty-five cents per hundred pounds to ship similar goods from Gilman, Illinois, to New York City. Facing a maximum $5,000 fine and three times actual damages to the shipper harmed, the railroad appealed. It contended that because the Illinois statute affected the shipment of goods from within the state to New York, it interfered with the Constitution's mandate giving Congress the power to regulate interstate commerce.

Illinois admitted that the state's prohibition of rate discrimination affected interstate commerce but claimed that it fell into that class of commercial regulations that were within the state's power until such time as Congress chose to exercise its power over the subject.[44] The state had plenty of precedent to back it up, not the least of which was *Peik* and the Granger Cases. But the majority of the Court believed otherwise.

The vote was six to three to overrule the Illinois prohibition of rate discrimination.[45] Although the Waite Court's personnel had changed substantially since the Granger Cases, that alone does not explain the reversal of direction. Justice Samuel Miller, who nine years earlier had voted to uphold state regulation of railroad rates, now wrote the majority opinion overruling the Illinois law.

Miller addressed his apparent inconsistency head-on. He recognized that the general language of the court in *Munn, Peik,* and the other Granger Cases indicated that states retained the power to regulate railroad rates until Congress had acted. He admitted that he had concurred with those opinions, and he said he was prepared to accept his share of the responsibility for them.[46] Miller explained, however, that the question of whether the state retained the authority to regulate rates for freight in a way that impacted interstate commerce "did not receive very elaborate consideration" and was not fully considered in the Granger Cases. The main question in those cases, which overshadowed all others, was the right of the state in which a railroad company did business to regulate the price at which companies would carry passengers and freight. To explain further, he recalled that all the railroad companies had strenuously and confidently denied that any legislative body whatever had a right to limit the tolls and charges to be made by carrying companies for transportation.[47]

The question in *Wabash, St. Louis, and Pacific* was not whether *any* legislative body had a right to regulate, but rather *which* legislative body had the power. It was a question of federalism. And Miller now accepted a new, more nationalist interpretation of the Constitution's sharing of power between the national and state governments. He argued that the commerce clause was intended to secure the right of continuous transportation from one end of the country to the other. In modern times, Miller said, that right is essential to freedom of commerce from restraints that the states may choose to impose on it.[48]

The dissenters took a different approach to the question of what level of government had the power to regulate. Justice Bradley remained consistent with his vote in *Munn* by observing that "the very being of the [Wabash, St. Louis and Pacific], the very existence of their railroad, the very power they exercise of charging fares and freights are all derived from the state." If the state created the company and its franchise, he reasoned, it surely may make regulations as to the manner of using them.[49] Bradley admitted that the regulation of railroads, as a medium of transportation, affected interstate commerce. But he concluded that "the state does not lose its power to regulate the charges of its own railroads in its own territory simply because the goods or persons transported have been brought from or are destined to a point beyond the state in another state."[50]

Miller may have agreed with Bradley's view of federalism when the Court decided the Granger Cases in 1877. If so, he had changed his mind by 1886.[51] Perhaps the maturing national economy had something to do with that. Railroad transportation was of a national character, he reasoned, and the type of regulation Illinois had attempted "can only appropriately exist by general rules and principles, which demand that it should be done by the congress of the United States under the commerce clause of the constitution."[52]

Congress finally enacted the Interstate Commerce Act on January 14, 1887. It was a compromise measure that prohibited pooling, regulated short haul rate discrimination, and provided for enforcement through a newly created Interstate Commerce Commission.[53] At first glance it may seem that Congress passed the law in response to the Supreme Court's decision and that the Waite Court had taken it upon itself to initiate a change in public policy.[54] Tempting as it is, that conclusion does not appear to be accurate. Less than three months had passed between the Court's decision and enactment of the legislation. Moreover Congress had been working on the measure for years, and at the time the Court decided the *Wabash, St. Louis, and Pacific* case competing bills had already passed in the Senate and House of Representatives.[55]

Enactment of the Interstate Commerce Act was a pivotal moment in that it was the beginning of Congress's involvement in actively regulating the economy. The Supreme Court consequently was more often asked to determine the reach of Congress's power. From a few years after Waite's death until 1937 it tended to narrowly interpret that power. It held, for example, that the commerce power could be applied to regulate activities that constituted the trading of goods across state lines, not to the process of manufacturing goods that might be shipped in interstate commerce. Similarly it held that the commerce power extended only to activities that had a direct effect on interstate commerce, not to activities that affected it indirectly.[56] In 1937 this narrow interpretation set up a clash with President Franklin Delano Roosevelt, whose approach to solving the problems of the Great Depression was based on broad federal regulation of the economy.[57]

This all began after the Waite era, however. The Waite Court did not face questions of whether a federal regulation was constitutional but rather questions of whether state regulations tended to interfere with interstate commerce. Considerations of federalism had been at the heart of the Waite-era decisions on the commerce clause. Federalism was not completely lost in the years thereafter, but it became melded into a debate over whether, or the degree to which, government should be involved in regulating the economy at all.

10

THE BIG COUNTRY

After the end of the war with Mexico in 1848, President James Polk bragged that the acquisition of former Mexican territories of California and New Mexico "constituted of themselves a country large enough for a great empire."[1] Combined with the acquisition of the Oregon Territory from the British and the admission of Texas as a state, the United States had acquired sovereignty over more than a million square miles of new territory. The country now stretched from coast to coast.

Much of the land west of the Mississippi was considered to be unclaimed and thus part of the public domain. It was land owned by the United States and not yet sold, dispersed, or transferred into private hands. The untapped wealth of this territory offered enormous opportunity and potential for profit. It is not surprising, therefore, that it was also the source of great conflict and that numerous disputes over how to use these new public lands spilled over into the federal courts. The Waite Court handled its share, but it is not possible to explain the Waite Court decisions without looking back at some of the earlier cases that set the stage.

Although it may have been popular to think of the West as unclaimed or unsettled, not all of it was. In the Treaty of Guadalupe Hidalgo, which ended the war with Mexico, the United States agreed to honor the rights of people who had received grants of land from the Mexican government. Some of these huge land grants became the subject of legal disputes that will be discussed later in this chapter. But first it is important to recognize that Native Americans occupied a significant amount of land west of the Mississippi, and their claims to the land were often recognized by treaty with the U.S. government.

American Indian use and claims to the land were not static.[2] Some tribes were located in territory they had occupied for generations. Some migrated onto lands occupied by other tribes. The U.S. government had forcibly moved others to the West. The most well known episode of this policy was the infamous "Trail of Tears," which occurred in the 1830s when the government removed the Cherokee from their lands in Georgia to Indian Territory in and around Oklahoma. The purpose of the Cherokee removal was to open lands in the Southeast to white settlers. When the same pressure to open lands to white settlers moved west of the Mississippi River, the federal government began a policy of entering into treaties that set aside territories of land as American Indian reservations and opened the rest for development. Although it was sometimes maintained that reservations were established to preserve certain lands for Indians, they also became a means of confining Indians to certain territory.

By the 1870s the amount of territory reserved or set aside for Indian tribes began to rapidly shrink. Under continuing pressure to open more land for white settlement, the exploitation of minerals, and the growth of railroads, Congress entered into a policy of abrogating, or nullifying, existing treaties. Often this abrogation took the form of a sale, with the tribe renouncing its claim to the land in exchange for money. But in most instances the tribes were actually coerced into the agreements.[3]

As a result of this policy, the 1870s and 1880s witnessed a series of "Indian uprisings." Perhaps the most famous occurred after gold was discovered in 1874 within the boundaries of the Sioux reservation in the Black Hills. When the Sioux refused to sell the reservation, the U.S. Army was ordered to remove them. In the summer of 1876 George Custer led his army to the most heralded defeat in U.S. military history when he and all of his men were killed at the Battle of Little Bighorn. Congress later accomplished what the army could not. When it cut off food and supplies to the reservation, the Sioux eventually gave in and sold the land.[4]

Congress was responsible for Indian land policy, and, by and large, the Supreme Court acquiesced. That was the Court's posture before, during, and after the Waite era. In an 1870 case, before the Waite era, the Court recognized that Congress had the power to abrogate treaties with Indian tribes.[5] Three decades later, in *Lone Wolf v. Hitchcock* (1903), the Court refused to question Congress's new policy under the Dawes Act to end communal ownership of reservations, allot tribal lands to individual members, and open the surplus to homesteading and settlement.[6] The Waite Court did not do anything different, and Stephen Field may have best captured its attitude. "It is to be presumed that in this matter the United States would be governed by such considerations of justice as would control a Christian people in their treatment of an ignorant and dependent race," he wrote. "Be that as it may, the propriety or justice of their action towards the Indians with respect to their lands is a question of governmental policy and is not a matter open to discussion [in the courts]."[7]

The Waite Court did have some impact in cases involving Indians' lands. For example, it rejected settler and railroad claims to Indians' lands in cases where Congress had not clearly extinguished the Indians' title.[8] But these cases did not test congressional Indian policy. They were battles among settlers, miners, land speculators, and railroad companies about how to divvy up the spoils.[9]

Justices of the Waite Court were perhaps no different than most Americans in succumbing to the temptation to treat this new territory in the West as raw and unclaimed. Some of the most intense political debates of the second half of the nineteenth century were linked to the question of how to best use or develop it. This certainly was not the first time the nation was faced with the question of how to develop new territory, but now acquisition of the new territory occurred at the same time that the economy was evolving from one that was rural and local into one that was national and interconnected. Added to this was the growth of a land reform movement that took hold in the 1840s and reached its zenith with passage of the Homestead Act of 1862.

Before the 1840s the federal government tended to treat public lands as a necessary and convenient source of revenue. Thus federal policy was to survey the land, then sell it at auction, usually in large blocks to speculators and land companies. By the late 1840s, however, reformers like George Henry Evans, Horace Greeley, and George Julian urged that the public domain should be used to provide cheap or free land to a class of "actual settlers." They based their arguments, in part, on concepts of morality and justice, the idea that every man had a right to a share of the soil. "The lands belong to the people," they said, and the public domain should be freely granted to them in small tracts.[10] But there was also an element of politic philosophy in the movement. Julian linked it to Thomas Jefferson's old theory that for democracy to flourish, independent farmers are needed to balance the power of connected elites. The independent farmers that the homestead policy would produce, he said, "are everywhere the basis of society and true friends of liberty."[11]

Legislation from the 1840s through the 1860s turned federal policy in the direction of land reform. The first steps were preemption and donation acts that directed the government to dispose of surveyed public land by selling small plots to settlers who were willing to settle on it and cultivate it.[12] Reformers' crowning achievement was the Homestead Act of 1862, which provided free homesteads to any person who was the head of a family or twenty-one years of age and who was a citizen or filed a pledge of his or her intention to become a citizen. Although the land was free to those who conformed to the requirements of the law, there were fees to be paid.[13] Congress seemed to be moving toward a policy that favored dispersing public land in small blocks to actual settlers, but congressional policy had one very major loophole in this respect. It did not prohibit the government from continuing to sell public domain for revenue, giving away large land grants, or allowing speculators and land companies to accumulate large blocks of land that had been in the public domain.

Land reformers of the late 1840s and 1850s were quite aware of this failing. Horace Greeley and the National Land Reform Association advocated banning sales of public land to speculators. George Julian called for an end to the policy of "frittering away" public lands by grants to states and private corporations for the benefit of "special objects."[14]

The Homestead Act was simply superimposed on an already existing land policy. Paul Wallace Gates, who spent a lifetime studying land policy, referred to the result as an "incongruous land system."[15] Some aspects of the system promised distribution of land to actual settlers, but others provided ample opportunity to accumulate large blocks and remove vast quantities of land from the public domain that might otherwise have been available for homesteading. Added to this mix was the presence of enormous Mexican land grants, which the U.S. agreed to uphold in the treaty ending the war with Mexico. The result was a policy that seemed well designed to produce conflict.

This was nowhere more apparent than in disputes growing out of Mexican land grants in the territory acquired from Mexico and in disputes involving grants from the U.S. Congress to aid in construction of the railroads. These disputes often found their way to the federal courts. The U.S. Supreme Court alone handled hundreds of such cases, most of them complex and many dealing with minutia of specific statutes. Simply counting to determine which side was victorious in most of these cases is not a very profitable method of finding a pattern or general policy preference. Some of the decisions favored railroads or large landowners; some favored settlers. A better means of understanding the Court's sentiment is to compare the presumptions of law the Court applied in various circumstances.

With respect to claims brought by homesteaders and settlers, the Court tended to interpret the law strictly and narrowly. In *Frisbie v. Whitney* (1869), one of the early California land disputes, it established the rule that settlers had no legal or equitable right to the land upon which they had settled until they had satisfied all conditions imposed by the appropriate law.

Frisbie v. Whitney involved a large section of land in California known as the Suscol Ranch. General Mariano Guadalupe Vallejo had claimed the Suscol Ranch under grants from the Mexican government in 1843 and 1844. In March 1862, however, the U.S. Supreme Court ruled that the original grant was invalid, and the land thus reverted to public domain.[16]

By that time, however, Vallejo had sold or distributed most of it. When the Court made its decision, a significant portion of the Suscol Ranch was no longer raw land. It included the towns of Benicia and Vallejo, a navy yard, a depot of the Pacific Steamship Company, and hundreds of acres of cultivated land. The Court's decision threw the ownership of all of this into mayhem. Speculators and settlers who had been following the proceedings flooded onto the land that the Court had now declared vacant. Some staked homestead claims to raw land, others to land that had already been improved and cultivated by people who had acquired it from Vallejo.

A year later Congress responded to the confusion. It passed a law that allowed people who had acquired property from Vallejo, but lost any right to it when the Court determined his grant was invalid, to buy that same property from the federal government for a very nominal price. But the one-year delay inevitably resulted in disputes between people who had purchased land from the holders of the invalid Mexican grant and those who had quickly claimed the land after the grant was declared invalid but before Congress enacted the legislation. *Frisbie v. Whitney* was one of those disputes.[17]

Neither of the parties came to this case with clean hands. Frisbie, who was Vallejo's son-in-law, claimed to have acquired the land from Vallejo. He did not actually occupy it, however, but rather leased it to a tenant farmer. Whitney was a settler who, upon learning that the Court had declared Suscol Ranch to be public domain, moved himself, his wife, and their two children to a quarter section of land within the Suscol Ranch. He built a three-room house and staked a claim. In the process, however, Whitney displaced a tenant who was occupying and cultivating the land.

Typically homestead and preemption laws required that a settler occupy the land, cultivate and improve it, have it surveyed if the government had not already done so, and file a claim. The settler also had to pay for the land or, in the case of a homestead claim, pay a small administrative fee to the government. When Whitney attempted to file his claim and pay the required fee, federal land officers refused to accept his application. They said, first, that no surveys had been made to identify the exact boundaries of the claim. Second, they refused to accept the application because Congress had passed the law for the benefit of the Vallejo claimants, and since Whitney had yet to pay the fee and obtain a certificate of entry, his claim was invalid.

Whitney filed a suit in which he argued that his act of settling on public domain and cultivating and improving it gave him an equitable interest in the property. The first court to hear the case agreed. The land had been opened for settlement, it observed. Once the settler had begun the process, the land could not be taken from him and transferred to another against his consent, even by an act of Congress.[18]

The Supreme Court disagreed and ultimately ruled that Frisbie, who traced title to the Vallejo grant, had the superior right to the land. Whether that outcome was just is debatable. The one thing that is certain is that the Court's reasoning, which was grounded on a strict construction of the statutes related to homesteading and preemption claims, had a far-reaching impact. Whitney had not registered his claim or paid the required fee, the Court observed, and until he had satisfied all the conditions imposed by the law, he had no legal or equitable right to the land.[19]

The Court's reasoning in *Frisbie v. Whitney* had major implications for the advocates of land reform. While reformers hoped to maximize the amount of public domain available for homesteading, the Court's decisions in disputes between settlers and people claiming title under Mexican land grants tended to reduce it. Another case decided just before Waite took office illustrated this tendency even more. It involved the preemption claim of a man who settled in what was to become Yosemite National Park. At the time Congress created the park, a pioneer named James Mason Hutchings had already staked a homestead or preemption claim in the valley and refused to leave. The subsequent legal proceedings to force him off the land eventually reached the U.S. Supreme Court as the *Yosemite Valley Case*.[20]

The presence of George Julian, one of the most prominent and persistent proponents of land reform, on Hutchings's legal team revealed the significance of the case. In the mind of land reformers the government's attempt to remove Hutchings from his preemption claim threatened to water down their achievements. The case was similar to *Frisbie v. Whitney* except it did not involve a dispute between competing private parties claiming the land, but rather a dispute with the government itself. As was true in the earlier case, Hutchings had settled on the land, occupied it, and improved it. He had, in fact been one of the earliest white settlers in the Yosemite Valley. But he had not filed his survey and paid the required fee.[21]

Hoping to reverse or limit the impact of the *Frisbie v. Whitney* precedent, Julian argued that this was enough to give Hutchings an equitable title to the property. The pioneer settler, he maintained, has been favored in law, and the government was bound by good faith to protect settlers who had cultivated and improved the land.[22] He concluded that there is no justice in the argument that a preemptor, after having made valuable improvements on a claim and complied with all the conditions of title that were within his power, may nevertheless be driven from his possession, his improvements confiscated, and his land conveyed to another.[23]

The Court rejected Julian's theory and, following the trend started in *Frisbie v. Whitney*, strictly interpreted the requirements of the statute. Writing for the majority, Stephen Field ruled that until a settler had satisfied *all* the conditions of the law, he or she had no right against the government. Settling on the land did not give the settler a right but rather only a privilege. It was a privilege that preempted other claims if the government offered the land for sale; that is, a privilege to purchase them in that event in preference to others.[24]

The U.S. Supreme Court decided *Frisbie v. Whitney* and the *Yosemite Valley Case* shortly before Waite took office, but similar disputes continued well into the Waite Court years. Many were linked to the Suscol Ranch and other Mexican land grants.[25] One of these cases, *Hosmer v. Wallace* (1879), was a typical dispute between two men who claimed the same parcel of land. Hosmer was a homesteader who arrived on his claim in 1856, built a house, and cultivated the land. Six years later, in 1862, Wallace, who claimed title to the same land under a Mexican land grant, had Hosmer evicted.

The grant to which Wallace tied his claim was an enormous floating grant—not unusual under Mexican law—in which the grantee was given the right to choose a specific parcel of land from a much larger area. At the time Wallace had Hosmer evicted, Wallace's claim to the land was not yet perfected, or complete. There remained conditions that he had to fulfill before the U.S. government fully recognized his claim. Most significant, he had not carved the specific plot he planned to claim out of the larger area from which he had a right to choose.

Three years later, in 1865, the U.S. Land Commission upheld the validity of the Mexican grant and Wallace's claim to the specific parcel he carved out of it. The property upon which Hosmer had made his homestead had been within the borders of the large floating grant but was not included within the parcel Wallace ultimately received. Hosmer, claiming that Wallace had had no right to evict him, was now trying to get it back.

In *Hosmer v. Wallace* the U.S. Supreme Court refused to recognize that Hosmer had any right to the land. Writing for the majority, Justice Stephen Field concluded that even though the grant was a floating grant, the boundaries of which could not be easily determined, and even though the specific tract was later ruled to be outside the grant, Hosmer had no right to be there in the first place. The law allowed homesteaders to make claims only on land that was part of the public domain, Field reasoned. The land Hosmer claimed was not public land, open to settlement, until 1865, when the U.S. government ultimately determined that it was not covered by the grant.[26]

During the Waite era the Court continued to follow the pattern of strictly construing homestead and preemption laws. Although it usually worked to the disadvantage of settlers, occasionally the Court's formalistic interpretation of homestead and pre-emption law worked to their benefit. While the Court held to the proposition that, until they complied with every requirement, settlers did not have a right to the land, it also recognized that settlement on the land did create a legally enforceable right of preference, or a right of first claim if the government should offer the land for sale. The Court also ruled that this right was transferable.[27] It ruled in *United States v. Schurz* (1880) that once the Department of Interior had granted a patent, the document that formally transferred property from the government to a private individual, to a settler, it could not subsequently withhold delivery of the patent to that settler.[28] And in *Wirth v. Branson* (1878) it ruled that a settler who had complied with all the requirements of the law, including the survey and payment, but had not yet received a patent was to be regarded as the equitable owner of the land. A subsequent grant of the same land to another was therefore void.[29]

The line of cases from *Frisbie v. Whitney* through the Waite era demonstrated that the Court was inclined to strictly interpret claims based on preemption and homestead laws and require settlers to satisfy all the conditions, formalities, and technicalities of the law in order to obtain a property right in the land. In contrast, the Court did not apply the same strict interpretation to people claiming enormous blocks of land under Mexican land grants. Disputes over land grants in California, Texas, and New Mexico reached the Court during the Waite years, but here, once again, the Court was presented with a precedent established before Waite took office. For the most part it followed that precedent, at least until the late 1880s when it added its own touch. In order to explain that development, however, it is necessary to go back to the 1855 case *Frémont v. United States*.

As part of the 1848 Treaty of Guadalupe Hidalgo, ending the war with Mexico, the United States promised, "Property of every kind now established [in the ceded territory], shall be inviolably respected." Most commentators agreed that these terms guaranteed that all grants of land made by the Mexican government were to be considered valid to the same extent that they would have been valid if the territory had remained under Mexican rule.[30] What this meant in practice, however, was open to interpretation. Congress attempted to sort out the problem with the California Land Act of 1851.[31] Over objections of grant holders, who would have preferred a plan that allowed them to simply register their claim and presume its validity, the California Land Act required grant holders to appear before a commission to prove their claim. By placing the burden of proof on people who claimed to hold Mexican grants, the new law seemed to create a presumption that favored designating as much land as possible as public domain that would then be available for settlement.

That presumption changed with the U.S. Supreme Court's decision in *Frémont*. The case involved John C. Frémont's claim to a rancho called Las Mariposas.[32] In 1847 Frémont, the famous explorer and politician, purchased the rights to this grant from Juan B. Alvarado. The original 1844 Mexican grant to Alvarado was generous. It was a floating grant that gave Alvarado the exclusive right to lay out a rancho of ten square leagues (approximately 44,784 acres, or 70 square miles) from within a larger specified area estimated to be as much as 900 square miles. But the grant also included a number of explicit conditions. Alvarado was forbidden to sell the property, and he was required to inhabit it within a year, survey the property, and place landmarks. Mexican law required that Alvarado obtain a patent from the local alcalde and file a crude map called a *diseño* with the supreme government. At the time Frémont presented his claim to the U.S. Land Commission in 1852, neither he nor Alvarado had done anything to meet these conditions.[33] In fact, Alvarado had violated the express condition that he could not sell the land. All arguments aside, it is fair to say that the letter of the Mexican law had not been followed with respect to this grant.

Existing precedent indicated that the Court would rule that Frémont's claim was invalid. In earlier cases involving claims in Florida and Louisiana, it had required that claimants strictly comply with the letter of Spanish law under which the grants were made.[34] But the Court concluded that Mexican law was different. In an opinion written by Chief Justice Taney, the Court applied informal "Mexican customs and usages" and "the common or unwritten law of every civilized country" to hold for Frémont. Taney had written some of the earlier cases that required strict compliance; nevertheless he distinguished Frémont's claim by noting that the earlier precedent involved Spanish law, which had made the conditions "conditions precedent" to ownership. Here, he reasoned, the Mexican government had granted the land outright. Because the grant conveyed a present and immediate interest, the conditions imposed on Alvarado were only "conditions subsequent."[35]

Frémont set the tone for cases involving Mexican land grants. Rather than strictly construing Mexican law, the Court was inclined to use the concept of "custom and usages" to favor claimants. In the 1860s the U.S. Supreme Court held that the words "five leagues more or less" supported a grantee's claim for eleven leagues. It validated a grant of two leagues even though the document had been altered, changing it from one league to two. And it validated a grant even though it was dated after the time Mexican authorities said they had quit issuing grants.[36] It should be pointed out that American speculators and adventurers, not former Mexican citizens, were usually the beneficiaries of these rulings.[37]

That pattern continued into the Waite era. This did not mean that all grants were validated. The Court rejected some claims in cases of fraud, for example, or in cases where a claimant failed to establish proper proof that a grant existed.[38] The Court's presumption, however, leaned in favor of the validity of the claim. And when a claimant was able to procure a patent from the U.S. government—even through fraud—that presumption was virtually unrebuttable.[39]

The Waite Court handled hundreds of Mexican land grant cases, not only from California but from Texas and New Mexico as well.[40] It is striking how many of these disputes went on for decades or reemerged long after they were thought to have been settled. A series of disputes over valuable lots in San Francisco provides one example. The San Francisco conflict began in 1852 with title to the lots a hopeless mess. Some people traced ownership under a Mexican law that gave land to pueblos or towns. Others claimed ownership under the right of preemption. The conflict lasted for years, with city ordinances, state statutes, state court decisions, and decisions from federal courts all coming into play. Finally when, on March 8, 1866, Congress passed a law entitled "An Act to Quiet Title to Certain Lands Within the Corporate Limits of the City of San Francisco," many thought the dispute was settled.[41]

Perhaps Waite-era justices were therefore somewhat exasperated when decades later they received more cases involving the San Francisco lots. In two of those cases, *Hoadley v. San Francisco* (1876) and *City and County of San Francisco v. Scott* (1884), the Court refused to decide the outcome of the disputes on the merit of the respective parties' claims. In the first of these cases the Court reasoned that Hoadley's claim to several valuable lots was not based on the congressional Act to Quiet Title but rather on an ordinance of the city of San Francisco.[42] With language similar to what today would be described as "no federal question doctrine," the Court refused to take jurisdiction of the case because the claims Hoadley raised did not arise under the laws of the United States. The Court subsequently used this approach to avoid ruling on other California cases, with Chief Justice Waite usually writing the opinion.[43] This trend of refusing to accept jurisdiction appeared to be a relatively benign development, and not out of line with the Court's tendency in other areas. However, it became extremely significant in a series of land disputes coming from New Mexico and Colorado.

In 1876 the United States Freehold and Immigration Company filed a suit to eject a settler named John C. Tameling from a 160-acre homestead upon which he had settled in Colorado. The company claimed the land under the Sangre de Cristo grant, a Mexican land grant originally given to Carlos Beaubien. Tameling's attorneys did not challenge the validity of the grant but instead argued that the Sangre de Cristo grant fell into the category of an individual grant and was thus limited under Mexican law to eleven leagues. Because the company's claim far exceeded that amount, they argued, the land in question was not its property.

When the case reached the Supreme Court, Justice Davis avoided interpreting Mexican law. Instead, he emphasized that the surveyor-general had approved the boundaries of the grant and had recommended confirmation without a limitation as to the quantity. Furthermore Congress had approved the recommendation. The question of the grant's boundaries was a matter for Congress, he said, "and we deem ourselves concluded by the actions of that body." The limitations of Mexican law did not matter at all, in Davis's opinion, because Congress's act had passed title from the United States as if the terms of the grant were de novo (completely new).[44]

With *Tameling v. United States Freehold and Emigration Company* (1877) the Court had effectively taken itself out of the business of interpreting Mexican law as it applied to grants in New Mexico and Colorado. But another 1887 case, *United States v. Maxwell Land Grant*, is more notorious and more clearly demonstrates the implications of this precedent.[45] Perhaps the notoriety of the *Maxwell Land Grant* case came from the sheer size of the claim. When the company received a patent from the U.S. government in 1879, it was for 1.7 million acres.[46]

Notoriety also may have come from the nature of the land and the length of time that people had been contesting rights to it. The struggle began in 1841 when

Mexican governor Manuel Armijo granted a parcel of land in north-central New Mexico to Carlos Beaubien and Guadalupe Miranda. At the time Armijo gave the land away, Jacirilla and Pueblo Indians occupied much it, using it for hunting and agriculture. Between 1858 and 1867 Beaubien's son-in-law, Lucien B. Maxwell, consolidated most of the claim and ran the land in the fashion of a Mexican hacienda or patronage system in which workers did not own land but tended specific plots, had access to common areas, and paid the patron a part of their production. This informal property system, which was based on a common understanding of traditional rights, was familiar in Mexico but produced confusion when the territory became part of the United States.[47]

Another factor that caused confusion was that the boundaries of the claim were not precise. Maxwell sold his family's claim in 1869 to a consortium of European investors that eventually became the Maxwell Land Grant Company. By that time, homesteaders, settlers, miners, and entrepreneurs occupied, worked, and laid claim to some of the same land. One, Richard D. Russell, was typical. Russell, a Union army veteran, had been stationed in New Mexico during the Civil War. Upon his discharge, the U.S. government granted him a homestead of 160 acres. Russell and his wife settled in the Stonewall Valley in southern Colorado in 1871. They built a house, ran a cattle ranch and small farm, and raised a family of four sons and two daughters on the homestead.[48] It is understandable that Russell would not idly sit by and allow the Maxwell Land Grant Company to claim land he thought was his.

The company's attempts to assert its ownership by trying to evict settlers or trying to force them to pay for the land upon which they had settled ran into fierce opposition. Mexicans who had settled under Maxwell's hacienda system joined American homesteaders in resistance that culminated in 1875 in a period of violence known as the Colfax County War.[49]

Later the U.S. government entered the legal fray, partially because it disputed the company's right to land in the northern portion of the claim, much of which was in Colorado. By 1880 the government opened areas of this disputed region to settlement, and at least 107 settlers had filed homestead claims.[50] In support of the government's decision to designate the disputed region as public domain, the attorney general filed suit asking the federal court to set aside that portion of the Maxwell Land Grant Company's patent that sat in Colorado. The suit reached the U.S. Supreme Court in 1887.

The government's case rested on two theories. First, the government claimed that the grant's boundaries were extended into Colorado as the result of a fraudulent survey. Government attorneys pointed out that the survey setting the boundaries of the grant traced back to one done by W. W. Griffin for the Maxwell Land Grant Company in 1870. But the fact that the original survey was done for the company and contained mistakes was not enough to convince the Court that fraud had been involved.[51] Applying a typical presumption, Justice Miller reasoned that the Court would not void a written instrument for fraud unless the evidence was clear, unequivocal, and convincing.[52]

The government next claimed that the original grant to Beaubien and Miranda had been a personal grant, which, under Mexican law, could not exceed eleven leagues, or roughly 97,000 acres. Congress, the government attorneys claimed, could therefore not have intended to include in the patent to the company the roughly 265,000 acres that sat north of the New Mexico border. The opposing attorneys sparred over the question of whether the original grant was an individual grant, to which the eleven-league limit applied, or an *empresario* grant, to which it did not. Justice Miller spent some effort addressing the issue. In light of the precedent of *Tameling*, that Congress has the power to determine the size of a grant, the outcome should have been obvious. It really did not matter if the grant was an individual or *empresario* grant. If Beaubien and Miranda had claimed land in excess of the amount available to them under Mexican law, that land was the property of the United States, and Congress had the unrestricted authority to give it away. Starting from that point, Miller could do little else than conclude that the Court did not have the authority to set aside the act of Congress that gave the company its patent.[53]

Settlers were not all convinced that the Court's decision ended any chance they might have had to keep the land they believed was theirs. They continued to resist the company's attempts to remove them. In August 1888, more than a year after the decision, hundreds of enraged settlers surrounded Animas County Sheriff W. T. Burns, a group of company agents, and Pinkerton detectives staying in the Pooler Hotel in Stonewall, which was located in what is today Colorado. After the sheriff refused warnings to leave town, shots rang out. Both sides opened fire from behind barricades, but the homesteader Richard D. Russell was caught in the middle. A bullet hit him in the shoulder, passed through his body and out his abdomen. Russell died five days later, joining two other settlers who were killed in the Stonewall Valley War. Settlers reacted to Russell's death by burning down the Pooler Hotel, but the Stonewall Valley War marked the end of settler resistance.[54]

Like the Court's interpretation of Mexican customs and usages in *Frémont*, its delineation of the limits of its own authority in *Tameling* and *Maxwell Land Grant Co.* resulted in generous treatment of individuals claiming property under Mexican land grants. Similar generosity was evident in cases involving federal grants of land to railroad companies.

Although specific railroad grants from the U.S. or state governments differed in some details, most shared common characteristics. The grants were made either directly to the railroad or to a state or territory to be used for the purpose of building a railroad. The grants did not usually specify a particular route, but rather required that a railroad be constructed from one place to another. The government gave railroads land for a right-of-way. And it also granted the railroads large blocks of land with the idea that the land would be used to finance construction or provide raw materials. Typically these grants gave the railroads the land in alternating twenty-section parcels on either side of the right-of-way. If property within these parcels was already claimed through homestead, preemption, or purchase, the railroad could choose an equal amount of "lieu lands" from the public domain. Before any land was actually transferred, however, the railroad was required to form a company, lay out a route, file a route plan, and build sections of the road. Usually the railroad received some land after a specified distance of the line was completed and received the rest as construction progressed.[55]

One source of conflict regarding railroad grants involved the question of who possessed what rights to the land during the time between the date Congress made the grant and the time the railroad met the conditions of the grant and thus started to receive the land. It is important to emphasize that this question did not apply only to right-of-way. It also applied to vast, but vaguely identified, expanses of land granted to the railroads as sources of revenue and raw materials. Railroad attorneys argued that these grants were grants in praesenti—that is, they took effect immediately and vested a property right at the moment the act of Congress was passed, even though the land had not yet been identified.

Decisions before the Waite era rejected this theory. In *Rice v. Minnesota & N.W. R. Co.* (1861) a divided court ruled that the railroad obtained no rights to the property until it had completed twenty miles of the railroad. Following the tradition that emphasized rights of the community, Justice Nathan Clifford applied the presumption of the *Charles River Bridge* case: "whenever privileges are granted to a corporation, and the grant comes under revision in the courts, such privileges are to be strictly construed against the corporation, and in favor of the public."[56] Justice Samuel Nelson later provided another rationale for rejecting the railroads' theory, explaining, "Until the line of the railroad was definitely fixed upon the ground there could be no certainty as to the particular sections of lands falling within the grant."[57]

In two cases decided early in 1875, during the first year of Waite's tenure, the Court completely reversed this rule. Now writing for the majority, Justice Stephen Field, de-emphasizing the conditional nature of the grant, ruled that federal land grants to railroads were indeed in praesenti.[58] In other words, at the moment Congress passed the statute that created the grant, the railroad obtained a property right in land, even though it had not yet satisfied the conditions of the grant and even if the location of that land was not clearly identified. This right was superior to that of homesteaders, preemptors, or anyone else who laid a claim to the land during the interim between the time Congress made the grant and the time the railroad filed for specific routes or claims or made progress toward satisfying the conditions of the grant.

In advocating the in praesenti rule Field apparently meant that the company's rights started when Congress passed the legislation creating the grant. He was not so happy a year later when the Court ruled that the company's rights were fixed in place at that moment in time. *Newhall v. Sanger* was linked to a long-running conflict that revolved around a disputed Mexican land grant in California known as the Moquelamos grant.[59] During the time that the validity of the Mexican grant was under dispute, Congress passed the Pacific Railroad acts of 1862 and 1864. These statutes, typical of railroad grants of the time, allowed railroads to claim certain lands from the public domain. On January 31, 1865, the Western Pacific Railroad

Company filed a route and claimed lands, some of which lay within the disputed Moquelamos grant. Less than a month later, on February 13, 1865, the U.S. Supreme Court declared that the Moquelamos grant was invalid.

When the railroad tried to claim the former Moquelamos land as part of its grant, however, a majority of the Court ruled that the railroad did not have a right to the land in question. Writing for the majority, Justice Davis observed that when Congress passed the acts of 1862 and 1864, it gave the company the right to choose land only from the public domain. At that time the land in question was part of a disputed Mexican land grant and therefore not part of the public domain. It did not matter that the grant was later declared invalid. The company's rights were fixed at the time it received the grant, and it could choose only from the public domain as defined at that time.[60]

The Court had reached the same conclusion a few weeks earlier in *Leavenworth, Lawrence, and Galveston Railroad Company v. United States*. This case involved a scramble for land in southern Kansas that had been ceded by an 1825 treaty to the Great and Little Osage tribes. In 1867 the government purchased some of the lands back and removed the Indians. Then, in 1869, Congress opened the former Osage land to white settlement. Relying on this, hundreds of people settled in the area, made improvements, and paid the purchase price on their claims. The problem was that the Leavenworth, Lawrence, and Galveston Railroad claimed some of the same land. The company traced its right to an 1863 grant of land from Congress to the state of Kansas for the construction of a railroad. In 1864 the Kansas legislature chose the Leavenworth, Lawrence, and Galveston to build the line. The company did not locate a route and file its claim until January 1868, after the U.S. government had removed the Osage, but that did not matter to the majority of the Court. Once again the majority ruled that the railroad could pick only from the land that was public domain at the time it received its grant.

Referring to the Indians as "a disturbing element" of Kansas's population, Justice Davis's opinion for the majority put a nineteenth-century spin on the equities involved. Davis maintained that just because Congress removed the Indians from Kansas to procure land for settlement, it did not mean that Congress had also contemplated obtaining title from any tribe in order to convey it to the railroad. "The policy of removal—a favorite one with the government, and always encouraged by it—looked to the extinguishment of the Indian title for the general good," he wrote, "and not for the special benefit of any particular interest."[61]

Stephen Field, always an advocate for the railroads, dissented in both cases. He maintained in *Newhall* that the land claimed under the Moquelamos grant was always public land. The fraudulent claim did not suspend or change its status.[62] In *Leavenworth, Lawrence, and Galveston Railroad Company* he observed that Indian claims to land in the United States were limited to the right of occupancy. Congress retained ownership of Indian lands subject only to the right of occupancy, and Congress could thus convey title to those lands to a new owner with the same condition: that it was subject to the Indians' right of occupancy.[63] More generally, Field argued that the Court's decisions were unfair to the railroads, which in anticipation of receiving public lands had expended millions of dollars in construction of railroads and opened the wilderness to settlement.[64]

The precedent of *Newhall* and *Leavenworth, Lawrence, and Galveston Railroad Company* did not last very long. The Court rather quickly retreated from its position that a railroad's rights were fixed as of the time it received the grant. In 1879 the Court limited the *Newhall* precedent by ruling that it applied only to the company's right to sections of land along its route but did not limit the company's rights to choose lieu lands.[65] A few years later, in a case involving the same Moquelamos grant, the Court virtually reversed itself. *Newhall* had not taken into account that the Moquelamos grant was a floating grant, the justices reasoned. Since all of the massive territory claimed was not needed to satisfy the grant, the government could consider it public land that was available for the benefit of the railroad.[66]

Except for the anomaly of *Newhall* and *Leavenworth, Lawrence, and Galveston Railroad Company* the in praesenti rule generally worked in favor of the railroads. In one sense the rule was a reasonable policy choice. Congress's purpose in providing the land grants to railroads was to allow the companies to raise the money needed for construction of the lines. At a time when a fledgling railroad might have little more to offer than hope and the land granted, the in praesenti rule added weight to the grant. Perhaps it was a choice that favored using the public domain to fuel the ongoing revolution in commerce. But it was also a choice fraught with social costs. And it was a choice that vividly displayed the judiciary's preferences toward use of the public domain.

Because most grants gave railroads flexibility in choosing the specific route, the status of land that lay along any of the possible routes was in question until the railroad filed a final route plan. Vast quantities of the public domain were tied up for months and even years. Until there was a route plan on file, settlers and other businesses had no legal notice of the railroad's claim. Some of these people may have been taking a calculated risk, but the rule also worked a hardship on innocent homesteaders, preemptors, or purchasers who settled on land between the time of the grant and the time of filing the route plan. Nevertheless until 1884 the Court continued to rule that a railroad's rights to specific lands existed from the day Congress passed legislation creating its grant.[67] In 1884 it modified the precedent by ruling that, until it filed a route plan, a railroad had no right to have lands set aside and reserved from settlement.[68]

Court doctrine was kind to railroads claiming land grants in other ways as well. An offshoot of the in praesenti rule held that although all grants provided that the railroad's failure to meet the conditions forfeited the grant, forfeiture was not automatic.[69] This meant that even in the case of a failed venture, a railroad kept the rights under the grant, including the land, until Congress or the attorney general took positive action to forfeit it. This interpretation seemed to be an invitation to political shenanigans. More clearly, it had the effect of once again throwing the status of vast quantities of land into limbo.

Most railroad land grants provided that, within a certain time, the company was required to divest itself of the land it had claimed from the public domain. Congress included this provision in order to avoid monopolies of public lands by large corporations or single individuals and to encourage immigration and settlement.[70] In this vein the Pacific Railroad Act provided that if within three years the company failed to "sell or dispose of" the land it had claimed under the grant, the land would revert to the public domain and be available for preemption and settlement. In *Platt v. Union Pacific Railroad Co.*, however, a six to three majority of the Court decided that the railroad's act of mortgaging its property to secure a loan constituted "selling or disposing of the land" and satisfied this requirement of the grant. Justice William Strong, who wrote the opinion, began his rationale with the observation that the construction of a railroad through mountains and uninhabited desert for thousands of miles "was most uninviting to private capitalists."[71] Although he recognized the suitability of Congress's policy to avoid monopoly and encourage settlement, he emphasized that "this policy was manifestly subordinate to the higher object of having the road constructed and constructed with the aid of the land grant."[72] The Union Pacific would not have accomplished this primary purpose without the ability to mortgage the lands.

Dissenting along with Clifford and Miller, Justice Bradley emphasized that the object of the act was to encourage speedy settlement of the land along the line of the railroad. As a result of the majority's opinion, he wrote, "the company, by one sweeping deed of trust, or mortgage, could cover the whole domain as with a blanket, and thus prevent settlement thereon until lands, by advance of prices, would be out of reach to actual settlers."[73] This, he concluded, would entirely defeat the object of the act.

Platt resulted from the conflict between settlers and railroads that was not uncommon in the West. Sometimes the conflict turned violent, as it did at a place called Mussel Slough, in California. The Mussel Slough incident began in 1869 when, in anticipation of receiving a federal patent for the land along its final route, the Southern Pacific Railroad encouraged homesteaders to settle a part of southern California land that lay along its projected route. Because the company had yet to receive a patent, it could not sell the land outright. Instead, it invited settlers to enter the lands and promised them an option to buy at prices averaging $5 an acre. Acting on these promises, settlers flocked to the rich but arid valley, irrigated the land, and turned the valley into a productive agricultural region. In 1877, after it had received a patent from the federal government, the Southern Pacific reneged on its promise to the original settlers and instituted a policy of selling the land on the open market at prices ranging from $25 to $40 per acre.

On May 11, 1880, a delegation of the original settlers confronted a federal marshal who was charged with the duty of evicting settlers. Tempers flared, the confrontation erupted into gunfire, and seven men were killed. That incident thrust the situation at Mussel Slough into the spotlight. It became a political rallying cry and the inspiration for several muckraking novels, including Frank Norris's *The Octopus*.[74]

Although the Mussel Slough dispute never reached the Supreme Court, it was the subject of a lawsuit in the U.S. Circuit Court for the District of California in *Southern*

Pacific R. C. v. Orton (1879).[75] As is often true with legal opinions, the issues raised in *Orton* had little to do with what settlers would have considered the issues of the dispute. Settlers complained of deceit, broken promises, and the inequity of encouraging them to improve the land and then charging them prices based on the value of those improvements. But the posture of the case allowed the court to ignore the company's early promises. Judge Lorenzo Sawyer summarily disposed of the settler's claim. The settler, Orton, "was an naked trespasser without right," he wrote. "Whatever the rights of the railroad company may be, [h]e is a total stranger to the title."[76] Sawyer's answer to the question of what were the rights of the railroad company reflected his unmistakable sentiment in favor of railroad grants. Considering the vast interests involved and the securities resting on Southern Pacific title, he stated, "there, certainly, ought to be a very clear cut case to justify a court annulling the rights hitherto supposed to have been acquired by the plaintiff [Southern Pacific]."[77]

Justice Stephen Field expressed the sentiment even more frankly. In *United States v. Burlington and Missouri River Railroad Company* (1879) the federal government sought to invalidate patents totaling 1,200,000 acres issued to the railroad. The Burlington and Missouri River Railroad's grant gave the company the right to claim ten alternate sections of land from along the line of its route, provided that the land had not already been disposed of or claimed as a homestead or preemption. Most railroad land grants also provided that if sufficient land was not available along the route, the railroad could choose other public land in lieu of the alternate sections. The Burlington and Missouri River Railroad's grant did not contain such a provision. Justice Stephen Field nevertheless ruled that the company had an implied right to choose lieu lands. "This view . . . would commend itself to Congress by its intrinsic equity," he reasoned, "for by it each road gets the largest quantity of land the statute permits."[78]

Congressional land policy may have been incongruous or inconsistent in terms of how it would encourage settlement of the West, but Court decisions displayed a significant preference for distributing the public domain in large parcels rather than small homesteads. With respect to the simple question of who benefits, the public land cases seem to stand in contrast with cases like *Munn v. Illinois* and the *Sinking Fund Cases,* where the Court seemed to rule against the interests of railroads and the corporate elite. The land cases show that this did not mean the Court opposed the idea of people accumulating enormous wealth or the idea of government helping them do it. Perhaps the members of the Court, like many other American leaders of the time, were more influenced by the idea of using the public domain as means to fuel the ongoing revolution in commerce.

The West has been depicted in the movies as "Big Country." While the history of settlement of the lands west of the Mississippi is complex, its bigness and openness can have a tendency to magnify and clarify conflicts. In law, clarity also may come from the fact that much of the West had not yet been admitted to the Union as states. It remained organized as territories and was thus completely under the jurisdiction of the federal government.

11

Equal Rights

Tales of the Old West

In cases involving civil rights for blacks the Waite Court tended to look backward for its cues; it was reluctant to create new rights, was influenced by an antebellum ideal of federalism, and was hesitant to expand its own authority. These tendencies traced back to *Cruikshank* and *Reese* in 1876 and continued through the *Civil Rights Cases* and beyond.

One other characteristic of the Waite Court that also helps explain its decisions in the area of civil rights was its tendency to indulge in excessively formalistic or hyperformalistic reading of a statute. This tendency was put on display in the 1883 decision in *Pace v. Alabama*. The Alabama statute in question made adultery and fornication a crime. If a white couple was convicted of the offense, they each were to be fined not less than one hundred dollars and also "may be imprisoned" at hard labor for not more than six months. If "any white person and any negro" were convicted of the same offense, each "must . . . be imprisoned in the penitentiary or sentenced to hard labor for not less than two nor more than seven years."

When Tony Pace, a black man, and Mary J. Cox, a white woman, appealed their convictions, claiming the second section of the statute denied them equal protection of law, the Supreme Court disagreed. In a terse opinion Justice Stephen Field pointed out that the two sections of the law were separate. One section of the law prescribed a punishment for an offense committed by persons of different sexes, he observed. The other prescribed a punishment where the two sexes are of different races. The different penalties were for different crimes, he reasoned. "The punishment of each offending person, whether white or black, is the same."[1]

It was also the same for each offending person, whether man or woman. Ironically, by this reasoning *Pace* may have been the only decision of the era to recognize equal treatment of women. Recall that in 1873 the Court upheld an Illinois prohibition against women practicing law in the state.[2] It was true that Waite, along with Davis and Miller, later supported a proposal to allow women to practice before the U.S. Supreme Court. Waite himself was said to be sympathetic to the women's rights movement and to have believed that "if a woman does a man's work and does it as well as he can, she ought to have a man's pay."[3] Nevertheless he wrote the 1874 opinion in *Minor v. Happersett* denying that the Fourteenth and Fifteenth amendments gave women the right to vote.[4] Few other cases involving the rights of women reached the Supreme Court during the Waite era. However, in *Virginia v. Rives* and *Ex parte Virginia* the majority accepted as common knowledge that a state could deny women the right to sit on a jury.[5]

Dissenting in the last of the jury cases, *Neal v. Delaware*, Chief Justice Waite pointed out the obvious. The defendants in these cases were not asking to sit on a jury; they were asking for the right to be tried by a jury that included members of their own race. For Waite, accepting this proposition would allow "Chinamen, Indians, resident foreigners," or even women to insist that people of their race and gender be summoned as jurors in cases affecting their interests. Such a drastic change in the law was unnecessary, he observed, because "[n]o one can truly affirm that [these classes of people] though excluded from acting as jurors, are not equally protected by the laws of the State as are those who are allowed to serve in that capacity."[6] Waite's optimism about how these disfavored groups were likely to be treated by both state and federal governments was, given the tenor of the times, naive.

Nothing demonstrated this more clearly than *Baldwin v. Franks*, an 1887 case that asked the Court to revisit the same section of the Enforcement Act it had overruled four years earlier in *United States v. Harris*.[7] Where *Harris* had involved Klan violence against blacks in the South, *Baldwin* involved mob violence against Chinese in the West.

The incident that produced *Baldwin v. Franks* took place in Nicolaus, California, a small agricultural town located about twenty-five miles from Sacramento. Like many California towns at the time, Nicolaus had an active anti-Chinese club. On February 6, 1886, members of the club sent out a warning to Chinese residents that they should leave the area or suffer the consequences. When the Chinese refused to leave, the club decided to "encourage" them. In the middle of the night of February 18, 1886, a mob of masked men broke into the residences of the town's Chinese farm workers. The mob forced the Chinese down to the Feather River, loaded them on a barge, and, to the applause of a crowd that had gathered, sent them downriver toward Sacramento.[8]

Nicolaus was not an isolated incident or even the most violent incident of the time. From the early days of the Gold Rush, Chinese were the victims of prejudice-induced murder, arson, assault, robbery, and burglary.[9] But anti-Chinese hysteria reached its high point in 1885 and 1886. Riots in Rock Springs, Wyoming, and Squak Valley, Washington, resulted in the death of dozens of Chinese workers, and mob action in many western cities drove Chinese residents from their homes. Conditions had become so bad that the Chinese government sent its vice-consul to investigate the incident at Nicolaus and the scenes of other incidents. Outraged that the U.S. government had done nothing to aid and protect the victims, the Chinese government and Chinese business leaders hired legal counsel and encouraged some victims to take action. Following their lead, John Sing swore out a complaint charging that Thomas Baldwin and fifteen other Nicolaus men had conspired to deprive him and other Chinese residents of their right to equal protection of the laws.

Although Chinese workers were not citizens, they did have significant legal rights—at least on paper. In treaties with China, the Burlingame Treaty in 1868 and the Treaty of 1880, the United States agreed that Chinese residents "shall be accorded all the rights, privileges, immunities, and exemptions which are accorded to the citizens and subjects of the most favored nations." In addition, the Treaty of 1880 provided if Chinese residents living in the United States should meet with "ill treatment at the hands of any other persons," the government of the United States would exert all its power to devise measures for their protection and to secure to them those rights, privileges, immunities, and exemptions.[10]

Despite the promises of the Burlingame Treaty and the Treaty of 1880, however, anti-Chinese zealots frequently employed state law to harass and discriminate against Chinese residents. Challenges to some of these anti-Chinese measures produced a body of law that was already in place before *Baldwin v. Franks* reached the courts. At various times California imposed special taxes on Chinese or immigrant workers and barred Chinese from certain jobs or required that they get a special license.[11] When Californians ratified a new constitution in 1880, it included a provision prohibiting any corporation from hiring Chinese in any capacity and another that prohibited employing Chinese in public works. It delegated to municipalities the power to remove Chinese from their boundaries or confine them to certain districts. It also denied Chinese the guarantee to own property and included them among people who were denied the right to vote.[12]

The discriminatory impact of other laws was indirect or depended on how the law was applied. A favorite technique was to enact regulations aimed at the conditions of living in Chinatowns or aimed at the businesses toward which Chinese gravitated. In 1870, for example, California enacted a law requiring every lodging house to provide at least 500 cubic feet of air per inhabitant. Anyone found sleeping in a lodge that violated the law was subject to a fine. To give the statute more effect, San Francisco passed an ordinance directing jailers to crop the hair of every male prisoner to a uniform length of one inch. The city leaders undoubtedly knew that for Chinese, wearing their hair in a braided queue had spiritual meaning, and intended the law as a form of harassment.

When Ho Ah Kow was convicted for violating the cubic air ordinance, he sued the sheriff under an 1870 federal civil rights statute. In 1879, while riding circuit in California, Justice Stephen Field overruled Ho Ah Kow's conviction. Field called the queue-cutting ordinance "hostile and spiteful" legislation, unworthy of a brave and manly people. It was unconstitutional, he said, because it interfered with the Burlingame Treaty and thus violated the sphere of authority reserved to the federal government. It was also unconstitutional because it amounted to discriminating legislation by a state against a particular class of people and was thus forbidden by the Fourteenth Amendment.[13]

At the time he wrote his opinion in what became known as the Queue Case, Field was actively engaged in his campaign to become the Democratic Party's nominee for president. The opinion gave him the reputation as a friend of the Chinese, and, given the strong anti-Chinese sentiment among California Democrats, it did not do much to help his cause. Unable to secure enthusiastic support in his home state, Field's bid for the nomination in 1880 failed. He tried again four years later, meeting with even less success.

The Queue Case, like many other cases challenging anti-Chinese legislation, was decided in the Ninth Circuit, which covered the Pacific Coast. In the early 1880s, however, three cases testing statutes aimed at Chinese laundries made it to the Supreme Court. In the first of these the Court had no hesitation upholding an ordinance that prohibited operating a laundry between the hours of 10:00 P.M. and 6:00 A.M. Stephen Field, who wrote the opinion, noted that the statute discriminated against no one. All people engaged in the business were treated alike. Given that operating a laundry produced a potential fire hazard, regulation of the hours of business was well within the police power of the state.[14] The ordinance at issue in the second case also limited the hours of operation, but only in certain sections or districts of the city. Although opponents of the ordinance argued that it was actually aimed at laundries operating in Chinatown, Field again upheld it as a legitimate exercise of the police power. He ruled that there was not enough evidence in the ordinance and in the record of its enactment to sustain the allegation of a discriminatory purpose.[15]

The facts of the third case went one step further in the direction of overt discrimination. Once again the ordinance itself was benign. It prohibited anyone from operating a laundry within the city of San Francisco without first having obtained consent of the board of supervisors, and made violations punishable by a fine and imprisonment in the county jail. Laundry operator Yick Wo, who ran a well-established laundry, was denied permission by the board and convicted of violating the ordinance. The city admitted that, of the two hundred people who had been denied consent, only one was not Chinese. Meanwhile, eighty white petitioners were granted permission to carry on the same business under similar conditions. This was too much for Justice Matthews, who, writing in *Yick Wo v. Hopkins* (1886), observed that "no reason for [this discrimination] exists except hostility to the race and nationality to which the petitioners belong." Although the law was fair on its face, he wrote, its administration made unjust and illegal discriminations. It thus constituted a denial of equal protection that violated the Fourteenth Amendment.[16]

The record of Chinese success in the courts was mixed when *Baldwin v. Franks* reached the courts, but the Court's decision in *Yick Wo v. Hopkins,* having come just one year earlier, gave the Chinese laborers who had been driven out of Nicolaus some hope that their charges against Baldwin and the rest of the mob would stick.

Unlike *Yick Wo,* however, the case against Baldwin did not involve discrimination by law or under the authority of law. It was the result of a purely private act. Because of this, attorneys hired by the Chinese government and Chinese business leaders appeared in federal court and swore out a warrant charging members of the Nicolaus mob with violating Section 5519 of the Revised Statutes of 1875. This statute made it a federal crime for private individuals to conspire to deprive any person or class of persons of the equal protection of the laws.

Hall McAllister, the attorney hired to represent Chinese interests, knew that the Supreme Court had ruled in *United States v. Harris* that Section 5519 was unconstitutional. But he also knew that the logic of the *Harris* decision began with the majority's view of federalism, specifically their steadfast belief that ordinary criminal law fell within the province of the states and was not a legitimate subject for congressional legislation. What made *Baldwin v. Franks* different, he theorized, was that the rights of Chinese residing in the United States were established by treaty. Relations with other nations, and specifically the power to enter into treaties, he emphasized, unmistakably fell within the powers of the federal government. In the 1880 treaty with China the United States expressly promised to "exert all its power to devise measures" to protect Chinese residents and to secure to them the rights to which they were entitled. McAllister thus proposed that, when applied to prosecute private violence against Chinese residents, Section 5519 was a valid exercise of Congress's power and duty to enforce the treaty.

To reinforce his case, McAllister also charged that the Nicolaus mob had violated a second section of the 1875 law. Section 5536 made it a crime to "conspire to prevent, hinder or delay the execution of any law of the United States." The 1880 treaty qualified as a law of the United States, McAllister argued. The mob violence against Chinese residents represented a conspiracy to prevent compliance with the treaty, and Congress certainly had the power to pass laws ensuring compliance with its own treaties.[17]

McAllister's argument provided a palatable enough version of federalism to satisfy the Court's most ardent states' rights advocate, Stephen Field. Furthermore the entire Court agreed the U.S. government had the power to provide for the punishment of any individuals who were guilty of depriving Chinese residents of any of the rights, privileges, immunities, or exemptions guaranteed to them by the treaty.

Even so, McAllister lost his case. The vote was seven to two, with the chief justice writing for the majority and Field and Harlan dissenting.[18] Although the Court's concerns about federalism appeared to be satisfied, the majority was troubled by McAllister's proposition that his clients could enforce the treaty by turning to a statute that had previously been declared unconstitutional. In Waite's opinion, this proposition would only be valid if the statute was made up of parts that were separable. Section 5519 was not. The Court's ruling in *Harris* had rendered the statute void, and, unless *Harris* was overruled, Section 5519 could not be used as a tool to enforce the federal government's obligation under the treaty.

Rejecting also the charge that the mob had violated Section 5536 by conspiring to prevent the United States from executing the treaty, Waite reasoned that the statute was aimed at conspiracies that directly interfered with government action. The mob violence in this case was not directed at the government but against the Chinese residents of Nicolaus. The Chinese residents had a right to seek protection of the federal government, but Section 5536 would come into play only if the mob had interfered with the government in its attempt to provide that protection.[19]

Stripped bare of federalism concerns, *Baldwin v. Franks* can only be explained as a hyperformalistic interpretation of the statutes involved. In one sense the opinion joins *Reese, Cruikshank,* and *Harris* as examples of the Waite Court majority's resistance to allowing the federal government a role in protecting rights of minorities from the acts of private individuals. But it stands out as an example of how unwilling the Court was to stretch itself to protect the rights of minorities.

In a dissenting opinion Justice Harlan chided the majority by examining the practical impact of its formalistic reasoning. "It would seem from the decision in this case that if Chinamen, having a right under the treaty, to remain in our country, are forcibly driven from their places of business, the government of the United States is without power to protect them against such violence, or to punish those who in this way subject them to ill treatment."[20]

The Fourteenth Amendment guarantee that no state shall deny any person equal protection of the law does something more than prescribe the duty and limit the power of the states, Harlan continued. It guarantees that the rights of individuals be guarded and protected against lawless combinations of individuals, acting without direct sanction of the state. "The denial by the state of equal protection of the laws to persons within its jurisdiction may arise as well from the failure or inability of the state authorities to give that protection as from unfriendly enactments."[21] Harlan had seized the opportunity to, once again, explain his alternative view of the duty both the states and the federal government owed to provide every person the equal protection of the laws.

The "Chinese problem," as it came to be called, was just one form of the racial and ethnic conflict that was part of America's westward expansion. Where Chinese in America tended to be imported laborers, Mexicans and American Indians had a deeper connection to the region and had interests rooted in an established culture and in the land itself. Consequently much of the history of tension between Anglo settlers and Mexicans and Indians involved the kind of land disputes discussed in chapter 10. Over time, however, Mexicans in the Southwest were subjected to many of the same forms of discrimination as Southern blacks. Identifying that discrimination as something that might violate the guarantees of the Fourteenth Amendment or various civil rights statutes was complicated by a number of factors. Most significant, Mexicans were categorized as white or treated as white for purposes of the law.[22] Discrimination against them before the twentieth century tended to be culturally based and informal. In part for these reasons, cases claiming that Mexicans had been denied civil rights, the right to vote, or the right to sit on a jury did not reach the federal courts during the Waite era.

Like the rights of Chinese, the rights of American Indians traced back to treaties. In the case of American Indians, however, the link was complicated by a long history of the federal government's relations with Indian tribes and the existence of numerous treaties with various tribes. Treaties notwithstanding, by the late nineteenth century the government had ceased to deal with the tribes as independent sovereign nations. They were treated instead as something of a hybrid between sovereign and dependent. Even while genuflecting to treaties, the federal government formulated "Indian policy" unilaterally. The Supreme Court played only a supporting role. As Stuart Banner aptly demonstrates, there was a huge gap between the law expressed in Court decisions and the law in practice. The Court served merely as a conscience center of government, he writes, too far from the frontier to have much real influence and largely ignored in the field.[23] Nevertheless in two cases during the Waite era the Court addressed questions about the status of individual Indians in American society and the extent of the federal government's authority within Indian reservations.

In 1885 Congress enacted legislation giving the federal government jurisdiction over crimes committed on Indian reservations. If Indian tribes had been treated as sovereign, it would have stood to reason that their own laws would govern criminal acts committed within the reservation. Otherwise, criminal law would normally be the subject of state jurisdiction. Casting aside any concern about treading on state authority, the Supreme Court upheld the statute. Justice Miller's opinion reasoned that because the reservations are set apart from the state, federal jurisdiction posed no threat to the operation of state laws.

To a great extent, however, Miller's opinion was steeped in a peculiar blend of confusion and paternalism. He recognized that Indian tribes were a separate people with a semi-independent position but emphasized that their status was difficult to define. They are not states, not nations, and not possessed with the full attributes of sovereignty. Although unsure of their precise status, Miller was sure of one thing. "These Indian tribes *are* wards of the state," he wrote in *United States v. Kagama* (1886). "They are *dependent* on the United States." Thus he concluded that "the power of the federal government over these remnants of a race once powerful, now weak and diminished in numbers, is necessary to their protection, as well as to the safety of those among whom they dwell."[24]

Although the Court remained somewhat confused about the status of Indian tribes, it was certain about the status of individual Indians. In *Elk v. Wilkins* it ruled that an Indian born a member of an Indian tribe within the United States is not a citizen within the meaning of the first section of the Fourteenth Amendment. The Fourteenth Amendment reads: "All persons born or naturalized in the United States, and subject to the jurisdiction thereof, are citizens of the United States and of the State wherein they reside." John Elk was born on a reservation but had severed his relations with his tribe and lived among whites. He claimed to be a citizen, and thus to have the right to vote, by virtue of having been born in the United States. The Court took a different approach to interpreting the amendment, emphasizing the conditional clause "and subject to the jurisdiction thereof." The majority began with the proposition that Indians owed immediate allegiance to their tribes, which was "an alien though dependent power." Born on a reservation, Elk was in a geographical sense born in the United States. Given his presumed allegiance to the tribe, however, he had not been born in the United States and subject to the jurisdiction thereof. He could not therefore claim citizenship by virtue of birth. Like the subject of a foreign country, he could attain it only through the process of naturalization.[25]

Justice John Harlan, joined by Justice Woods, dissented in *Elk v. Wilkins*. In one eloquent run-on sentence Harlan described what he considered to be the failings of the majority's opinion. "If [Elk] did not acquire national citizenship on abandoning his tribe and becoming, by residence in one of the states, subject to the complete jurisdiction of the United States, then the fourteenth amendment has wholly failed to accomplish, in respect of the Indian race, what, we think, was intended by it; and there is still in this country a despised and rejected class of persons with no nationality whatever, who, born in our territory, owing no allegiance to any foreign power, and subject, as residents of the states, to all the burdens of government, are yet not members of any political community, nor entitled to any of the rights, privileges, or immunities of citizens of the United States."[26]

The phrases "Chinese problem" and "Indian policy" capture in shorthand two of the social, economic, political, and constitutional conflicts that were part of America's westward expansion. Joining these was the "Mormon Question." The phrase referred to the conflict over the role of the Mormon church in the Utah Territory and, more precisely, over the practice of polygamy. Polygamy had become a tenet of the Mormon faith in 1843, when Mormon leader Joseph Smith received the "Revelation of Celestial Marriage." Although "the Principle," as it came to be called, was kept secret for a number of years, it eventually added fuel to anti-Mormon feelings. Harassment of and violence against Mormons became common in Illinois and Missouri, where they had settled. In 1844 a mob murdered Smith, who was being held in a Nauvoo, Illinois, jail. Three years later, following a new leader, Brigham Young, Mormons began a migration westward to the Great Salt Lake Basin in what is now Utah.[27]

Polygamy was not the only cause of anti-Mormon feelings. In the eyes of some of their neighbors, Mormons were seen as outsiders. To some they seemed threatening because their organization, dedication, and strict obedience to their leaders gave them unusual economic and political strength in their communities. Perhaps these characteristics helped Mormons successfully create vibrant settlements in some incredibly inhospitable parts of Utah. By the time Congress organized the Utah Territory in 1850, Mormons were in firm control of the territorial legislature. The Utah legislature granted corporate status to the church, permitted the corporation to acquire and control unlimited amounts of property, and allowed the church to govern marriages of its members. Buoyed with these privileges, the Mormon church and its patriarchs became not only a dominant religious power but also a political and economic power that controlled the territory. The extent of Mormon political and economic power, the jealousies and fears it produced, certainly goes far toward explaining anti-Mormon feelings in the nineteenth century. But the target of those feelings was the practice of polygamy, and polygamy eventually provided the topic for constitutional debate.[28]

Reformers, preachers, novelists, and politicians railed against polygamy as early as the 1850s, and condemnation of polygamy was in full display at the first national convention of the Republican Party in 1856. Likening polygamy to slavery, the party's platform called for the abolition of these "twin relics of barbarism."[29] Reformers complained that polygamy was incompatible with Christian morality, incompatible with republican government, and barbaric and archaic in practice. They also argued that the practice victimized women, reducing white women to the level of beasts.[30]

Pressure for federal legislation to prohibit plural marriage eventually produced results in 1862, when Congress passed the Morrill Act outlawing bigamy and polygamy in the territories.[31]

Advocates who thought the Morrill Act would end polygamy and break what they perceived to be a Mormon stranglehold on Utah business and politics were sorely disappointed. Mormon control of Utah's territorial and local government and local law enforcement rendered the statute virtually unenforceable. It remained so until 1874, when Congress reduced the powers of territorial judges and gave U.S. attorneys the authority to appoint jury pools. With new powers in hand, federal prosecutors began to indict Mormon leaders and other polygamists. After working its way through the legal system, their first conviction for violation of the Morrill Act's prohibition of polygamy came to the U.S. Supreme Court in 1879 as *Reynolds v. United States*.[32]

George Reynolds, who had been convicted under the act, argued that he should have been acquitted because of his belief that plural marriage was his religious duty. The Court unanimously disagreed. Chief Justice Waite admitted that under the First Amendment guarantee of freedom of religion, Congress could not pass a law that prohibited the free exercise of religion in the territories. But he concluded that a law prohibiting polygamy did not do this. Polygamy had always been prohibited in every state of the Union, he observed. It was a primitive practice linked to despotism and inconsistent with republican government.[33] There was no doubt that Congress had the authority to outlaw the practice generally, Waite reasoned. Therefore the issue in this case was whether a person who knowingly violated an otherwise valid law should be considered not guilty because he entertained a religious belief that the law was wrong. To answer the question, Waite drew a distinction between belief and action. The First Amendment deprived Congress of power over mere opinion, but left it free to prohibit actions that violated social duties or were subversive of good order.[34] To excuse Reynolds of the acts of polygamy because of his religious belief would be to make the professed doctrines of religious belief superior to the law of the land, and in effect to permit every citizen to become a law unto himself or herself. Government could exist only in name under such circumstances.[35]

Decided in 1879, *Reynolds* is remembered as the first case to interpret the First Amendment guarantee of freedom of religion. But Reynolds's attorneys made another argument—one that the Court ignored. Congress interfered not only with religious practice, Reynolds's attorneys maintained, but also with local autonomy. This did not raise an issue of federalism in a technical sense. Utah was a territory, not a state. The subjects were similar, however, in that they both involved imposing the will of the national government on a local majority. Congress undoubtedly had significant authority to legislate for the territories. However, Reynolds's attorneys reminded the Court that political and constitutional tradition held that the authority to enact laws relating to the social and domestic life of a territory's inhabitants, as well as its internal police, was reserved to the people dwelling in the territory.[36]

Unfortunately, the most direct legal precedent for this proposition was Chief Justices Taney's discredited 1857 opinion in the *Dred Scott* case.[37] But Reynolds's attorneys also based their arguments on the theories of popular sovereignty to which a majority of the Court generally subscribed. The greatest threat to popular sovereignty, they maintained, was an excess of centralized power. Migration to a territory did not strip citizens of the United States of their rights to govern themselves, they argued. It did not give the federal government the power to treat them as mere colonists, dependent on the will of the center.[38] Despite their attachment to a version of federalism that emphasized state authority, the justices of the Waite Court ignored this argument and upheld Reynolds's conviction.

Reynolds was not the end of the campaign to eliminate polygamy and punish those who practiced it. In 1885 the Court upheld a federal law denying polygamists the right to vote. In doing so it addressed the theory of local autonomy it had ignored in *Reynolds*. "The people of the United States, as sovereign owners of the national territories, have supreme power over them and their inhabitants," Justice Matthews wrote. Under the Constitution, the right of local self-government belongs to the states and to the people thereof. For Matthews, the personal and civil rights of people residing in the territories were amply protected by the principles of constitutional liberty that restrained the federal government, and their political rights, including the right to vote, were privileges held at the legislative discretion of Congress.[39]

Then, after the Waite era, *Late Corporation of the Church of Jesus Christ of Latter-Day Saints v. United States* (1890) upheld provisions of a new law, the Edmunds-Tucker Act, which abolished the church corporation and directed the U.S. attorney general to confiscate the church's property.[40] The theory supporting this action was similar to foreclosure. The church corporation was a charitable franchise, Justice Bradley reasoned. By engaging in the "barbarous custom" of polygamy, the Mormon church had abandoned its charitable purpose and forfeited its right to the charter. This led him to conclude that dissolution of the corporation and confiscation of its assets were "the most appropriate means of vindicating the sovereign dominion of the people of the United States, themselves a Christian people."[41]

In September 1890 the Mormon church ended its resistance. Mormon President Wilford Woodruff reported that he had received a communication from God advising that the church should abandon its defense of polygamy in order to assure its survival. Soon after he issued a manifesto to that effect, criminal prosecutions against polygamists ceased. Those who had been convicted received pardons, and church property that had already been confiscated was returned.[42]

The Compromise of 1877 and the seating of new justices in the early 1880s did not produce a fundamental change in the Court's attitudes toward civil rights and the Reconstruction Amendments. The majority continued to appreciate that the Reconstruction Amendments were intended, in some way, to guarantee the political and civil rights of blacks and at least integrate black citizens into political society. The Court's continued attachment to a nostalgic ideal of federalism, however, severely limited the authority of Congress to give full force and effect to that guarantee.

From the vantage point of more than 125 years later, it is hard to understand the seriousness of the Court's fear of allowing the federal government to infringe on the sphere of authority that had traditionally been reserved to the states. We live in an era when a clear distinction between state and federal spheres of authority has become blurred. Few people today are surprised by federal involvement in crime control or federal regulation concerning education, health, personal injury disputes, marriage, or any number of other matters governing the social relationships within the states. In addition, we have experienced the Jim Crow era of the first half of the twentieth century, an era when the clarion of states' rights was nothing more than an excuse for allowing racist public policy to flourish in the South.

It would be a mistake to lump the civil rights decisions of the Waite Court into the same category as those of the Jim Crow era and dismiss them as being racist and nothing more. As Michael Les Benedict put it, "No feat of revisionism can turn the Waite Court of the 1870s and 1880s into a firm and unflinching defender of black peoples' rights, but the fact is that modern criticism distorts our constitutional history."[43] It distorts it by failing to distinguish the Waite Court decisions from the decisions of later courts. Moreover it distorts it by overlooking the impact of factors other than race: separation of powers, public welfare, popular sovereignty, and federalism. There is nothing to suggest that the Waite Court's attachment to nostalgic federalism, popular sovereignty, or separation of powers was anything but principled. It was based in part on a common belief that the states were the best guarantors of individual liberties, and that power centralized in a national government posed the greatest threat to popular sovereignty and individual liberty. The same ideals were reflected in *Munn v. Illinois* and other cases dealing with economic matters.

Still, there seems to be something else at play in the decisions involving civil rights. As civil rights disputes reached into the 1880s and spread to Chinese, American Indians, and Mormons, the decisions at times revealed a sentiment common among men who were America's leaders in the late nineteenth century. It was an unabashed certainty of their own superiority: superiority of their race, superiority of their gender, and superiority of their Protestant version of Christianity.

Certainty of their own superiority showed in Justice Bradley's impatience in the *Civil Rights Cases* that former slaves had yet to progress to the rank of citizen. It is evident in the opinion of Justice Field, "that dissimilarities in physical characteristics, language, manners, religion, and habits will always prevent assimilation of [Chinese] with our people."[44] It was obvious in Justice Miller's explanation that Illinois could prohibit Myra Bradwell from practicing law because "[t]he natural and proper timidity and delicacy which belongs to the female sex evidently unfits it for many occupations of civil life,"[45] and his belief that Indian tribes were wards of the state dependent on the protection of the United States.[46] It was just as obvious in Waite's and Bradley's statements that polygamy was an archaic, odious, and barbaric custom.[47] Even Harlan, often thought of as the Court's champion of civil rights, believed in the superiority of the white race.[48] Although this sentiment does not, by itself, explain the likes of the *Civil Rights Cases, Baldwin v. Franks, Kagama,* or *Reynolds,* it was present in all of them. And the civil rights decisions of the time are better understood by realizing that it was an important aspect of the worldview of the justices who sat on the bench during Chief Justice Waite's tenure.

Conclusion

Legacy of the Waite Court

On October 27 and 28, 1887, about five months before Chief Justice Waite's death, the Court heard arguments in a case involving August Spies and several other men who had been convicted of murder by an Illinois trial court. The defendants had appealed to the Illinois Supreme Court, which upheld the conviction. Now they were appealing to the U.S. Supreme Court, claiming that the state of Illinois had denied them a trial by an impartial jury, had violated their right against self-incrimination, and had convicted them on the basis of evidence obtained through an unlawful search. On this particular day the defendants were not arguing the merits of their claims but rather asking the Court to issue a writ of error—that is, asking it to take the case on appeal. The issues the defendants raised are common in today's federal courts, but that was not true in 1887. And there was nothing common about the facts behind this case. Known as the *Anarchists' Case*, it was the last desperate legal maneuver of labor activists who had been convicted of murder and sentenced to die for their role in the Haymarket Affair.[1]

The Haymarket Affair was a product of widespread labor unrest in May 1886. Strikers picketed nationwide in a coordinated effort to attain an eight-hour workday. In Chicago, much of the city's industry was shut down as strikers picketed the city's factories and millworks. One exception was the McCormick Reaper Works, where police guarded strikebreakers who were keeping the factory operating. On May 3 the police guards fired into a crowd of strikers who were threatening the strikebreakers as they left the plant. The police attack killed at least six of the strikers and wounded many more. Labor leaders responded by calling for a mass protest the next day at Haymarket Square. The meeting, while peppered with fiery speeches, was generally peaceful. After it had gone on for some time, however, a police captain ordered the speakers to cease and the crowds to disperse. When the last speaker, Samuel Fielden, objected, police began to move in. At that moment someone threw a bomb into the ranks of the police, who responded by opening fire into the crowd.[2]

The bomb killed eight officers and wounded sixty-seven others, along with an unknown number of civilians. No one knew who threw it, but the state of Illinois decided to blame it on eight anarchists who were quickly tried and convicted of the murder of one of the policemen. History has demonstrated that general hysteria, fear of perceived radicalism in the labor movement, and antiforeigner sentiment played more of a role in the convictions than did the evidence. But despite a lack of evidence and improprieties in the investigation and trial, the Illinois Supreme Court upheld the convictions. The anarchists then appealed to the U.S. Supreme Court.

Startling though it may be to a modern observer, the Supreme Court decided to stay out of the matter. On November 2, 1887, reasoning that there was no federal question involved, the Court announced its decision to reject the defendants' request for appeal.[3] With the federal appeal out of the way, the state of Illinois acted quickly, scheduling the execution just nine days later. The day before the scheduled execution Illinois governor Richard Oglesby commuted the sentences of two of the men, Samuel Fielden and Michael Schwab, changing them to life in prison. Another of the defendants, Louis Lingg, avoided execution by committing suicide in his cell. One of the men, Oscar Neebe, had received a fifteen-year prison sentence. But on November 11, the four remaining defendants—Augustus Spies, Albert Parsons, Adolph Fischer, and George Engle—were led to the gallows and hanged. In 1893 another Illinois governor, John Altgeld, decided that the convictions had been a miscarriage of justice and pardoned Fielden, Neebe, and Schwab.

The Haymarket Affair has remained controversial. Assuming, however, that the convictions and the executions of the four defendants were miscarriages of justice, it is tempting to conclude that the Supreme Court could have done more. Perhaps it could have. But the Court's decision to reject the anarchists' appeal fit cleanly into the contemporary legal precedent. While in modern times we have come to expect the Supreme Court to produce scores of new opinions every year on topics involving the rights of persons accused of crime and civil liberties in general, standard constitutional doctrine of Waite's time gave it more limited occasion to hear criminal cases.[4]

Its occasion to hear appeals of criminal cases coming from the states was limited even more by the fact that the Waite Court continued to follow the precedent, established in *Barron v. Baltimore* in 1833, that the Bill of Rights did not apply to the states.[5] Moreover in *Hurtado v. California* (1884) it reaffirmed its commitment to that precedent.[6]

The *Hurtado* case began in February 1882 when Joseph Hurtado was arrested for murder. Following the procedure set out in the California Constitution and statutes, the district attorney filed a document called "an information," which officially charged Hurtado with the crime. California law did not require that the charges first go to a grand jury. The prosecutor's independent determination that there was enough evidence against the accused was all that was necessary for the case to go to trial.

After being convicted and sentenced to die, Hurtado appealed to the U.S. Supreme Court, arguing that California's procedure violated the Fifth and Fourteenth amendments. At the time the argument had a serious hole, however. The Fifth Amendment contains the guarantee that no person shall be denied life, liberty, or property without due process of law. It also contains the explicit guarantee that "[n]o person shall be held to answer for a capital, or otherwise infamous crime, unless on a presentment or indictment of a grand jury." But under standard precedent of the time the Fifth Amendment did not apply to the states. The Fourteenth Amendment applies to the states and contains the guarantee that no state shall deny any person of life, liberty, or property without due process of law. But the Fourteenth Amendment does not contain the explicit guarantee that no person shall answer to a capital or infamous crime unless on indictment by a grand jury.

Hurtado's attorneys hoped to solve this dilemma by melding the two amendments. They argued that in the Anglo-American understanding of justice, the right to a grand jury had historically been considered an essential cog in the operation of due process of law. Accordingly, they said, the Fourteenth Amendment's general guarantee of due process includes the more specific guarantee of a right to a grand jury.

In 1884 the majority of the Supreme Court was not convinced. Justice Matthews, who wrote the opinion for the Court, pointed out that Hurtado's argument failed in several ways. He first noted that the Fifth Amendment contained two distinct guarantees: due process and the grand jury. The framers of the Fourteenth Amendment were well aware of this, he reasoned. Yet they chose to include the due process guarantee and not to include the right to a grand jury. The right to a grand jury was not an essential element of due process of law, Matthews concluded. For him, this case was not about abuse of government authority. Rather, it involved a rule of law, "enacted by the [state] legislature which was a just and reasonable expression of the public will, and of government as instituted by popular consent and for the general good."[7]

Dissenting in the *Hurtado* case, Justice Harlan took the majority's logic to its most extreme conclusion. If the right to a grand jury was not an essential element of due process of law, he said, neither would be the other guarantees of the Bill of Rights. The guarantee not to be put twice into jeopardy for the same offense, the right against self-incrimination, the right to a speedy trial by an impartial jury, or the right to confront witnesses, all of which are universally considered to be fundamental principles of liberty and justice, would be excluded from enforcement against the states. Harlan was not willing to accept that conclusion.[8]

Hurtado was an early foray into a long-running dispute about the meaning of the due process clause of the Fourteenth Amendment and whether, or to what degree, it applied the Bill of Rights to the states. The majority held fast to the old precedent from *Barron v. Baltimore*, ruling that states are not required to use a grand jury. That particular aspect of the *Hurtado* decision has never since been overruled, and consequently the Fifth Amendment guarantee of the right to a grand jury still does not apply to the states. But over time the Supreme Court has applied most of the other provisions of the Bill of Rights to the states.

The process has been neither smooth nor complete. In the 1930s and 1940s Justices Benjamin Cardozo and Felix Frankfurter subscribed to the idea that the due process clause of the Fourteenth Amendment only extends to the states those guarantees that are "implicit [essential] in the concept of ordered liberty."[9] For them, some provisions of the Bill of Rights fell into that category, others did not. Justice

Black vehemently disagreed. Black believed that the Fourteenth Amendment guarantee that no state shall deprive any person of life, liberty, or property without due process of law meant that all of the Bill of Rights applied to the states, nothing more and nothing less. His theory was that the phrase "due process" is synonymous with the phrase "bill of rights" and thus incorporates the Bill of Rights into the Fourteenth Amendment. It has thus come to be called the "incorporation doctrine."

The Supreme Court has never fully accepted either Cardozo and Frankfurter's theory of ordered liberty or Black's incorporation doctrine. Instead of applying the Bill of Rights to the states by means of one sweeping theory of the meaning of due process, the Court has applied most of its guarantees one step at a time. There are exceptions, one of the most notable being the Second Amendment guarantee of the right to bear arms. While most of the cases that have applied guarantees of the Bill of Rights to the states came after the Waite era, the Waite Court did set the precedent for the Second Amendment. In *Presser v. Illinois* (1886) it ruled that the Second Amendment is a limitation only upon the power of Congress and the national government, and not upon the states.[10]

Of course the Supreme Court had much broader jurisdiction in matters involving federal crimes than it had with respect to state criminal prosecutions. It is true that not nearly as many activities were the subject of federal criminal law in the nineteenth century as they are today. Nevertheless Congress had considerable authority to enact criminal statutes.

Congress could, for example, enact criminal laws pursuant to the powers granted to it in Article I, Section 8. Thus in *Ex parte Jackson* (1877) the Court ruled that the power to establish post offices and post roads was broad enough to include regulation of the mail. Consequently it upheld a defendant's conviction for sending prohibited lotteries through the mail.[11]

Not all criminal cases raised issues that would be categorized today as civil liberties, and there were not enough of these cases to produce a definite pattern.[12] But some opinions of the Waite era contained seeds of the theories that are familiar today. In an early example of the exclusionary rule and the idea that the Constitution protects an individual's right of privacy, *Boyde v. United States* (1886) prohibited the use of evidence that federal customs officials had obtained under a regulation that required importers to produce their invoices. Even though the officials had not forcibly obtained the evidence, the Court ruled that the officials' actions violated the Fourth Amendment prohibition against unreasonable search and seizure and the Fifth Amendment guarantee against self-incrimination.[13]

Because Article IV gives Congress the authority to govern the territories, the Court also heard appeals in civil liberties and criminal cases coming from the territorial courts. The First Amendment guarantee of freedom of religion was at issue in *Reynolds v. United States* and the polygamy cases described in chapter 10. But the territories also produced cases such as *Wilkerson v. Utah* in 1879, where the Court held that the death sentence does not violate the Eighth Amendment prohibition of cruel and unusual punishment.[14] Westward expansion was bound to increase the number of these cases. Appeals from Utah alone raised questions of whether the Sixth

Amendment right to a trial by jury required that juries in the territories be made up of twelve members, whether a defendant must be present during jury selection, and about what constitutes a voluntary confession.[15]

Recall also that ratification of the Thirteenth, Fourteenth, and Fifteenth amendments had the effect of expanding the number of appeals in cases involving civil liberties and criminal law. Each of these amendments contained a provision giving Congress the authority to enforce them by enacting appropriate legislation. The effect of these enforcement provisions was prominent in the accounts of cases from *Cruikshank* and *Reese* to the *Civil Rights Cases*. We have also seen that from the *Slaughterhouse Cases* through *Munn* and beyond, the Court was pressured to interpret the Reconstruction Amendments in a way that would expand its federal question jurisdiction to cover economic liberties.

Expanded jurisdiction of the federal courts in the areas of civil rights and civil liberties increased the Court's workload, but it was only part of the story. When considering all kinds of cases, the Supreme Court's docket and workload exploded during the Waite era. The increase in the number of cases coming to the Supreme Court has been well documented. In 1850 the Court heard 253 cases. That number more than doubled just after the Civil War, reaching 636 in 1870. After 1880 it grew even faster, reaching 1,563 in 1888.[16]

Historians have paid significant attention to the Court's heavy workload in the Waite years. Overwork undoubtedly imposed a heavy toll on individual justices. Charles Fairman comments that by the time Congress enacted a court reform measure in 1891, "both Waite and Miller would have collapsed from overwork and died."[17] Overwork also resulted in a backlog of the docket. Waite himself complained relief was necessary for the Court, but that there also was an even more urgent need of "relief for the people against tedious and oppressive delays."[18]

Implicit in the historical emphasis on the workload is the idea that overwork had a negative impact on the Court's decision making and perhaps motivated the Court to avoid expanding rights for fear of creating more work for itself. No doubt workload did have an impact. But the history of the Waite Court demonstrates that the Court's resistance to expanding its own authority also stemmed from a principled belief among the majority that the Court played an important but limited role in American democracy.

Whatever may have been its impact, the Court's workload was a serious concern, causing members of the Court, as well as members of Congress, to call for reform of the federal judiciary. One plan, favored by Justice Field and others, would have divided the Supreme Court into three separate chambers and increased the number of justices.[19] Chief Justice Waite opposed that particular plan, but actively lobbied for some kind of relief.

Although Waite did not live to see the accomplishment, in 1891 Congress provided some relief with the Circuit Court of Appeals Act.[20] The new law made the federal circuit courts intermediate courts of appeals, and ended the practice of the justices riding circuit. Then, enactment of the "Judges' Bill" in 1925 ended the practice of automatic appeal to the Supreme Court and gave the Court discretion over the cases it decided to take.²¹ The result was a federal judicial system more similar to what we have today.

Causes of the Waite Court's increasing workload varied. It could be explained in part by the country's rapidly increasing population. Perhaps more significant was the nation's geographic growth, especially the addition of large new territories that came under the jurisdiction of the federal government. Added to this was the impact of the commercial revolution, which expanded interstate commerce, increased the likelihood of cases coming to the federal courts under diversity jurisdiction, and increased the number and types of disputes that might reach the federal courts. Most of these cases involved common disputes. Although some undoubtedly were important, they were not matters involving constitutional issues or issues that might mold the nation's political and social institutions. The vast majority involved commercial litigation such as disputes over contracts, mortgages, negligence, stock, and insurance. Added to this were numerous cases involving admiralty or maritime law, patents, copyrights, and trademarks.²²

The Bell Telephone cases, although not typical of what the Court faced, highlighted the problem of increased workload more than any other case could. It was a consolidation of six cases, coming from the lower federal courts, that each challenged Alexander Graham Bell's 1876 patent to the telephone. Arguments before the Supreme Court took twelve days between January 24 and February 8, 1887. When a divided Court ruled in favor of Bell, Chief Justice Waite assigned the opinion to himself. He worked on it incessantly from that time until March 5, 1888, when he wrote to Bancroft Davis, the court reporter, "I have at last finished the opinion."²³ The opinion, along with its statement of facts and arguments of the attorneys, takes up an entire volume of the United States Reports.²⁴

Eighteen days later Waite was dead. The chief justice was seventy-one years old when he died and not in the best of health. He had suffered a physical breakdown in December 1884 and spent two months recovering in Florida. On Saturday, March 18, 1888, after walking home from a reception, he became seriously ill. He insisted on going to court the following Monday to read the decision in the Bell Telephone cases. Once there, however, he lacked the strength to carry on. Doctors diagnosed a severe case of pneumonia and confined Waite to bed. He died on March 23, 1888.²⁵

Morrison R. Waite's reputation had improved over time. The reaction to his appointment as chief justice in 1874 had ranged from disappointment to outright disdain. In death he was hailed as a personable leader and a man of high moral character.²⁶ The eulogies reflected mild, perhaps even begrudging, admiration. The *American Law Review* wrote, for example, "He did nothing to lower the dignity of the great office which it was his lot for fourteen years to fill."²⁷ Although his contemporaries did not consider Waite to be a brilliant intellectual, he was admired as a skilled administrator who kept the Court functioning efficiently.²⁸

Waite's biographer C. Peter Magrath saw something more in the chief justice, however. Writing in 1963, he maintained that Waite is a vastly underrated figure in American constitutional history. According to Magrath, Waite's weakness was a lack of artistic ability, not intellectual shallowness. Waite, he said, was consistent and tenacious in espousing a judicial philosophy based on the idea that the people acting through legislatures know their own best interest.[29]

The legacy of the Waite Court has not been so positive as that of the chief justice himself. Even Magrath describes the Waite period as the "Unheroic Era."[30] What that means is not self-evident, but two related attitudes that are typically expressed about the Waite Court come to mind. One is that the Waite Court is often considered to be transitional. Although it presided in an era wedged between the Civil War and the Gilded Age, an era that faced the prospect of major changes in constitutional doctrine, few of those changes were complete until after the Waite era. This leads to the second related attitude. The Waite Court is often criticized for its role in setting the groundwork for two controversial constitutional doctrines. In the area of civil rights the court is thought to have initiated a constitutional doctrine that eventually allowed racial segregation to flourish during the Jim Crow era. In the area of economic regulation it is thought to have opened the door for the era of laissez-faire constitutionalism.

There is no doubt that the Waite Court was transitional in the sense that it found itself applying law to the changing circumstances brought about by the legacy of the Civil War, a revolution in commerce, and the consolidation of westward expansion. Sometimes, as was the case in developing rules governing railroad receiverships, it responded by adopting novel doctrine. It also applied old doctrine to new circumstances. Sometimes this had serious political consequences, as was the case with its use of the bona fide holder rule in railroad bond cases. Occasionally the Waite Court reversed the course of existing precedent, as it did when it applied the in praesenti rule to railroad land grants. Or, as in cases involving land grants, it expanded earlier precedent. In that particular example it made the precedent even more favorable to land speculators, railroads, and others claiming large parcels of land in the West. In some instances the Waite Court struggled to fill a vacuum. When Congress was slow to use its authority to regulate interstate commerce, for example, the Court tried to adapt old commerce clause doctrine to meet the changes in the economic and social system.

The Waite Court was also transitional in the sense that it preceded the more controversial era under Chief Justice Melville W. Fuller (1888–1910), an era that saw more dramatic changes in doctrine. It was transitional, in other words, in its place in time. Even though it faced legal disputes that grew from the drastic changes in America's social, political, and economic order, however, the Waite Court tended to look backward for its cues. Its attitudes toward the powers and duties of government were shaped by the system of federalism the justices had known before the Civil War. And even in the light of the post–Civil War amendments, it hesitated to find new rights in the Constitution. In terms of attitude, therefore, it is more accurate to describe the Waite Court as traditional.

This is an important distinction because describing the Waite Court as transitional tends to leave the impression that later changes in legal doctrine were virtually inevitable. With respect to the subjects of civil rights and economic regulation, the two topics for which the Court is sometimes criticized, it leaves the impression that constitutional doctrine developed in a natural progression from ratification of the Reconstruction Amendments, through the Waite era, and beyond. By isolating the history of the Waite Court, we have seen that this impression is not accurate.

With respect to cases involving race, the Waite Court is usually described as transitional because it is said to have set the law on the path to the Jim Crow era, a time in which segregation of the races was enforced by state law. Of course the case that is most clearly linked to the onset of the Jim Crow era, *Plessy v. Ferguson*, did not occur until 1896, eight years after Waite's death.[31] In *Plessy* the Court ruled that states could enact laws that officially enforced segregation of the races, so long as they provided equal facilities for both races. This "separate but equal doctrine" provided the basis for subsequent laws that segregated schools and other public facilities and prohibited blacks from using the same water fountains, bathrooms, or swimming pools as whites. It eventually led to laws such as poll taxes, literacy tests, and other devices used to deprive blacks of the right to vote.

According to the narrative of transition, however, the Waite Court started the law down this path when in *Reese* and *Cruikshank* it narrowly interpreted the power of Congress to enforce the Reconstruction Amendments. It continued through the *Civil Rights Cases* (1883), which overruled Congress's attempt to prohibit racial discrimination in public places. In doing so it established the "state action doctrine," holding that the Fourteenth Amendment gave Congress the power to prevent discrimination by states but not discrimination by private individuals.

There is no doubt that the Waite Court's record from *Reese* and *Cruikshank* through the *Civil Rights Cases* was a great disappointment to people who hoped to use the power of the federal government to assure full equality for blacks. Future courts would be able to find in these opinions the building blocks for the Jim Crow–era decisions, but that outcome was not preordained.

For one thing, it takes a huge leap to get from the state action doctrine (a rule that the federal government cannot enact laws that prohibit private discrimination) to the separate but equal doctrine (a rule that states may enact laws that require segregation of the races). For another, the state action doctrine that came out of the Waite Court did not completely rule out the possibility of federal law prohibiting private discrimination. Modern studies have shown that the Justice Department continued to enforce civil rights laws throughout the era.[32] It is also clear that the Waite Court did allow the federal government to prohibit some private discrimination in two areas: voting and jury service. In addition, even the majority opinion in the *Civil Rights Cases* recognized, or struggled with, what Pamela Brandwein has called state neglect.[33] It left open the possibility that the federal government might step in when a state failed to satisfy a duty to prevent private discrimination.

Beginning with *Brown v. Board of Education* in 1954, decisions of the civil rights era put an end to the separate but equal doctrine.[34] But the state action doctrine has held on for more than 125 years. As a result both the Court and Congress have occasionally wrapped themselves into mental contortions to overcome its presupposition that the enforcement provision of the Fourteenth Amendment does not give the federal government authority to curb private discrimination. One example is reflected in the Court's handling of restrictive covenants. These are private real estate agreements that were used to prohibit blacks from living in certain neighborhoods. In *Shelley v. Kraemer* (1948) the Court recognized that such agreements were private discrimination and therefore constitutionally permissible. At the same time, however, the majority held that any attempt to enforce such a covenant in state courts would constitute state action and would thus violate the Fourteenth Amendment.[35]

Another example occurred when Congress enacted the Civil Rights Act of 1964. Faced with the rule that the enforcement clause of the Fourteenth Amendment did not give it authority to prohibit discrimination in transportation, inns, restaurants, or other public services, Congress claimed that it had the authority to do so under its power to regulate interstate commerce. That approach worked at the time. Applying an extremely broad interpretation of the commerce clause in the 1964 cases *Heart of Atlanta Motel v. United States* and *Katzenbach v. McClung*, the Court upheld the Civil Rights Act of 1964.[36] But envisioning a day when the commerce clause would be interpreted more narrowly, Justice William O. Douglas maintained that the Court should address the state action doctrine straight on. In a concurring opinion Douglas argued that basing the legislation squarely upon the Fourteenth Amendment would put an end to all obstructionist strategies for perpetuating racial discrimination and "finally close the door on a bitter chapter of American history."[37]

More recent developments demonstrate that Douglas's concern was well-founded. In *United States v. Morrison* (2000) the majority of the Court reaffirmed the state action doctrine and narrowed the reach of the commerce clause to rule that the Federal Violence Against Women Act was unconstitutional.[38] *Morrison* reinforces the idea that, if in 1964 the Court had wanted to expand the federal government's power to prevent private discrimination, perhaps it should have overruled or reinterpreted the state action doctrine.

It is difficult to understand why the state action doctrine has been so firmly entrenched in constitutional doctrine. Perhaps the doctrine's persistence traces to the narrative of transition and the sense of inevitability it projects. And perhaps a closer look at the Waite era origins of the state action doctrine would have provided means to change it.

With respect to economic regulation, the narrative of transition maintains that the Waite Court set the stage for laissez-faire constitutionalism. The march in that direction is said to have begun with Chief Justice Waite's concession in *Munn v. Illinois* that in some cases economic regulation might deprive an owner of his or her property without due process of law, but not in all. Bolstered by this concession and Justice Stephen Field's vigorous dissent, the Court is said to have quickly moved away from the doctrine it had established in *Munn* and toward an era during which the Fourteenth Amendment became a tool for protecting business interests from government interference.

Isolating the Waite Court era reveals that, with respect to economic regulation, the Waite Court actually held fast to tradition. Borrowed from contract clause doctrine, it was a tradition that recognized that private property, while to be sacredly guarded, was held subject to the rights of the community. Furthermore it was a tradition that emphasized that questions of economic regulation were, for the most part, matters for legislative determination. It therefore followed the established rule of interpretation that in such disputes a court should apply a presumption in favor of the state legislature, which is presumed to be acting in the interests of the community.

By seeking to create a right to be free from government regulation, attorneys for the corporate and business elite proposed a radical change in this tradition. They would eventually be successful. They would see the day when the Fourteenth Amendment stood as a barrier to economic regulation. They would see the day when legal doctrine favored an absolutist right of property and when, instead of balancing property rights against rights of the community, the court thought in terms of individual rights versus government power and narrowly defined the reach of that power.[39] During the laissez-faire era from the early 1890s to 1937, the Supreme Court would reverse the presumptions that guided the Waite Court, instead presuming that economic liberty was the general rule and restraint the exception, and that the power to abridge that freedom could only be justified by the existence of exceptional circumstances.[40] But the change did not actually begin until after Melville W. Fuller became chief justice, and, in order to accomplish it, the Fuller Court had to overrule or reverse the most fundamental features of the Waite-era precedent.

Although the laissez-faire era ended in 1937, the history of the Waite Court continues to offer some important lessons with respect to economic regulation and the Constitution. The standard interpretation among today's historians portrays the laissez-faire era as resulting from a gradual, almost inevitable evolution of a constitutional tradition that emphasizes individual liberty.[41] In many ways this interpretation has been motivated by a desire to better understand the laissez-faire era, the reaction to it, and the Constitution's role in America's evolving social and political order. But treating the laissez-faire era as the inevitable product of constitutional tradition has had practical implications as well. Some modern legal scholars have called for a return to the principles that guided laissez-faire constitutionalism. They admire the laissez-faire model that weighs economic liberty against government power and applies the presumption that economic liberty is the rule and regulation the exception. Furthermore they maintain that this model represents a return to tradition that runs from the framing of the Constitution, through the Jacksonian era, and up to the end of the laissez-faire era in 1937.[42]

Isolating the Waite era has demonstrated that the opposite is true. Rather than being an inevitable continuation of tradition, the theories that drove laissez-faire constitutionalism were a revolutionary break with long-standing constitutional tradition—a tradition that emphasized popular sovereignty and the rights of the community.

One unexpected result of concentrating on the Waite era is that the chief justice stands out as more of an intellectual leader than he is commonly portrayed.[43] Others have recognized Waite's impact on the direction of constitutional doctrine, but they tend to portray Waite as a man simply struggling to guide an overworked court and tied to a belief that judges should play a limited role in a democracy. Felix Frankfurter described Waite as having "a touch of the commonplace about him." Yet he admired the chief justice for his understanding that one of the greatest duties of a judge is "the duty not to enlarge his authority."[44] Similarly C. Peter Magrath observed that Waite held to a simple faith that the people, acting through their legislatures, know their own best interest and that judges should therefore be reluctant to upset legislative decisions.[45]

Waite's decision making was driven by more than simple deference to the legislative branch, however. He certainly did not demonstrate any particular deference to Congress in cases involving civil rights. Rather than thinking of the Waite Court legacy in terms of attachment to a particular legal doctrine or theory regarding the role of judges, it may be more fruitful to think of it in terms of tendencies. During the Waite era a majority of the Court tended to idealize the balance of federalism that existed before the Civil War, it tended to interpret law in a formalist way, it hesitated to agree that the Reconstruction Amendments created new rights, it was committed to the ideal of popular sovereignty, and it was attached to a theory of property that recognized the rights of the community. These tendencies reveal that, for better or worse, the Waite Court viewed its role as that of a keeper of tradition.

Notes

SERIES EDITOR'S PREFACE

1. 113 N.Y. 378 (1856).
2. 60 U.S. (19 How.) 393 (1857).
3. 83 U.S. (16 Wall.) 36 (1873).
4. *Munn v. Illinois*, 94 U.S. (4 Otto.) 113 (1877); *Peik v. Chicago & North-Western Railway Co.*, 94 U.S. (4 Otto.) 164 (1877).
5. *The Sinking Fund Cases*, 99 U.S. (9 Otto.) 700 (1879).
6. *Hepburn v. Griswold*, 75 U.S. (8 Wall.) 603 (1870); *The Legal Tender Cases*, 79 U.S. (12 Wall.) 457 (1871), with Justice Field's dissent at 634.
7. James W. Ely Jr., *The Chief Justiceship of Melville W. Fuller, 1888–1910* (Columbia: University of South Carolina Press, 1995); Walter F. Pratt Jr., *The Supreme Court under Edward Douglass White, 1910–1921* (Columbia: University of South Carolina Press, 1999); William G. Ross, *The Chief Justiceship of Charles Evans Hughes, 1930–1941* (Columbia: University of South Carolina Press, 2007).

INTRODUCTION: TRADITIONAL COURT, TURBULENT TIMES

1. Robert Sobel, *Panic on Wall Street: A Classic History of America's Financial Disasters—With a New Explanation of the Crash of 1987* (New York: Truman Talley Books, 1988), 167.
2. *New York Times*, September 19, 1873.
3. Sobel, *Panic on Wall Street*, 184.
4. Ibid., 192 (provides statistics).
5. *New York Times*, March 5, 1874 (oath of office); Donald Grier Stephenson Jr., *The Waite Court: Justices, Rulings, and Legacy* (Santa Barbara, Calif.: ABC-CLIO, 2003), 110 (Waite's death).
6. *United States v. Lopez*, 514 U.S. 549 (1995); *United States v. Morrison*, 529 U.S. 598 (2000).
7. *Barron v. Baltimore*, 32 U.S. (7 Pet.) 243 (1833).
8. *Hurtado v. California*, 110 U.S. 516 (1884).
9. Eric Foner, *Reconstruction: America's Unfinished Revolution 1863–1877* (New York: Harper and Row, 1988), 529; William M. Wiecek, *Liberty Under Law: The Supreme Court in American Life* (Baltimore: Johns Hopkins University Press, 1988), 101.
10. Charles Lane, *The Day Freedom Died: The Colfax Massacre, the Supreme Court, and the Betrayal of Reconstruction* (New York: Henry Holt, 2008).
11. Michael A. Ross, *Justice of Shattered Dreams: Samuel Freeman Miller and the Supreme Court during the Civil War Era* (Baton Rouge: Louisiana State University Press, 2003), 202–3. Ross also maintains that Miller's opinion could be viewed as a vote of confidence for Louisiana's biracial legislature.
12. Pamela Brandwein, *The Supreme Court, State Action, and Civil Rights: Rethinking the Judicial Settlement of Reconstruction* (Cambridge: Cambridge University Press, forthcoming). The author graciously allowed me to read her draft manuscript before its publication.
13. Michael Les Benedict, "Preserving Federalism: Reconstruction and the Waite Court," *Supreme Court Review* (1978): 39–79; Pamela Brandwein, "A Judicial Abandonment of Blacks?

Rethinking the 'State Action' Cases of the Waite Court," *Law and Society Review* 41 (June 2007): 343–81.

14. Robert J. Kaczorowski, *The Politics of Judicial Interpretation: The Federal Courts, Department of Justice and Civil Rights 1866–1876* (New York: Oceana Publications, 1985), 227.

15. Harry N. Scheiber, "The Road to *Munn:* Eminent Domain and the Concept of Public Purpose in the State Courts," in *Perspectives in American History: Law in American History*, vol. 5, ed. Donald Fleming and Bernard Bailyn (Cambridge, Mass.: Charles Warren Center Studies in American History, Harvard University, 1971), 329–402; William J. Novak, *The People's Welfare: Law and Regulation in Nineteenth-Century America* (Chapel Hill: University of North Carolina Press, 1996).

16. *Charles River Bridge Co. v. Warren Bridge Co.*, 36 U.S. (11 Pet.) 420, 547 (1837).

17. *Chicago, Milwaukee, & St. Paul Railway v. Minnesota*, 134 U.S. 418 (1890); *Smyth v. Ames*, 169 U.S. 466 (1898); *Lochner v. New York*, 198 U.S. 45 (1905).

18. Charles W. McCurdy, "Justice Field and the Jurisprudence of Government-Business Relations: Some Parameters of Laissez-Faire Constitutionalism, 1863–1897," *Journal of American History* 61 (1975): 970–1005. For a more detailed historiography covering both interpretations of the era, see William M. Wiecek, *The Lost World of Classical Legal Thought: Law and Ideology in America 1886–1937* (New York: Oxford University Press, 1998).

19. Randy E. Barnett, *Restoring the Lost Constitution: The Presumption of Liberty* (Princeton, N.J.: Princeton University Press, 2004).

20. Mary Ann Glendon, *Rights Talk: The Impoverishment of Political Discourse* (New York: Free Press, 1991).

21. William M. Wiecek, "Reconstruction of Federal Judicial Power," *American Journal of Legal History* 13 (1969): 333–59, 342.

22. Stephenson, *Waite Court*, 52.

Chapter 1: Waite, Waite, Don't Tell Me

1. C. Peter Magrath, *Morrison R. Waite: The Triumph of Character* (New York: Macmillan, 1963), 15. Chase had died on May 7, 1873.

2. Michael A. Ross, *Justice of Shattered Dreams: Samuel Freeman Miller and the Supreme Court during the Civil War Era* (Baton Rouge: Louisiana State University Press, 2003), 213–15, provides a detailed account of Justice Miller's campaign for the seat.

3. Magrath, *Morrison R. Waite*, 11.

4. *Nation*, January 15, 1874.

5. "Tone of the Western Press," quoted in *New York Times*, January 21, 1874.

6. *New York Times*, January 21, 1874.

7. Ross, *Justice of Shattered Dreams*, 215.

8. *Nation*, January 22, 1874, quoted in Magrath, *Morrison R. Waite*, 17.

9. *Nation*, January 22, 1874.

10. For this and the following account of Waite's early life, I have relied upon Magrath, *Morrison R. Waite*, 23–74.

11. *New York Times*, January 24, 1874.

12. Magrath, *Morrison R. Waite*, 57–58, 72–73.

13. Charles Fairman, *Reconstruction and Reunion 1864–88, Part Two*, Oliver Wendell Holmes Devise History of the Supreme Court of the United States (New York: Macmillan, 1987), 7:80.

14. *Mechanic's and Trader's Bank v. Union Bank*, 89 U.S. (22 Wall.) 276 (1874).

15. See *Freeland v. Williams*, 131 U.S. 405 (1889).

16. *The Slaughterhouse Cases*, 83 U.S. (16 Wall.) 36 (1873). Two recent works provide wonderful details about the facts, issues, and debates involved in the *Slaughterhouse Cases:* Ronald M. Labbé and Jonathan Lurie, *The Slaughterhouse Cases: Regulation, Reconstruction, and the Fourteenth*

Amendment (Lawrence: University Press of Kansas, 2003); and Ross, *Justice of Shattered Dreams*, 189–211. I have also borrowed heavily from my earlier description of the case in Paul Kens, *Justice Stephen Field: Shaping Liberty from the Gold Rush to the Gilded Age* (Lawrence: University Press of Kansas, 1997), 118–25.

17. Labbé and Laurie, *Slaughterhouse Cases*, 61.

18. Ibid., 6.

19. Ibid., 73–74; Fairman, *Reconstruction and Reunion*, 6:1322.

20. Labbé and Laurie, *Slaughterhouse Cases*, 42–51.

21. See William J. Novak, *The People's Welfare: Law and Regulation in Nineteenth-Century America* (Chapel Hill: University of North Carolina Press, 1996).

22. Ross, *Justice of Shattered Dreams*, 196.

23. Labbé and Laurie, *Slaughterhouse Cases*, 103–36; Fairman, *Reconstruction and Reunion*, 6:1324–27.

24. Labbé and Laurie, *Slaughterhouse Cases*, 183–94.

25. Ross, *Justice of Shattered Dreams*, 1–13, describes Miller's life in Barbourville and his evolving antislavery views.

26. Ibid., 19–50, describes the rise and fall of Keokuk.

27. Ibid., 30, 65–79; Donald Grier Stephenson Jr., *The Waite Court: Justices, Rulings, and Legacy* (Santa Barbara, Calif.: ABC-CLIO 2003), 20–22.

28. Ross, *Justice of Shattered Dreams*, 49.

29. See *Gelpcke v. The City of Dubuque*, 68 U.S. (1 Wall.) 175 (1864); Ross, *Justice of Shattered Dreams*, 89–93.

30. *The Slaughterhouse Cases*, 83 U.S. at 61, 62.

31. *Barron v. Baltimore*, 32 U.S. (7 Pet.) 243 (1833).

32. *The Slaughterhouse Cases*, 83 U.S. at 71.

33. Ibid., at 71–72.

34. Ibid., at 80.

35. Carl Brent Swisher, *Stephen J. Field: Craftsman of the Law* (1930; repr., Hamden, Conn.: Archon Books, 1963), provides the biography of Field's early years. I have borrowed much of the description below from two of my earlier writings, Kens, *Justice Stephen Field;* Paul Kens, "Introduction," *Journal of Supreme Court History* 29 (2004): 1–21. Field's memoir has been republished in two forms. The first is Stephen J. Field, *Personal Reminiscences of Early Days in California* (1877; repr., New York: Da Capo Press, 1968). It has also been republished in two issues of the *Journal of Supreme Court History:* Stephen J. Field, "Personal Reminiscences of Early Days in California," ed. Paul Kens, *Journal of Supreme Court History* 29 (2004): 22–119; George C. Gorham, "The Story of the Attempted Assassination of Justice Field by a Former Associate of the Supreme Bench of California," ed. Paul Kens, *Journal of Supreme Court History* 29 (2005): 105–94.

36. Kens, "Introduction," 2–3.

37. Ibid., 4.

38. Kens, *Justice Stephen Field*, 4–5.

39. *The Slaughterhouse Cases*, 83 U.S. at 89, Field dissenting.

40. Ibid., at 96, Field dissenting.

41. Ibid., at 97, Field dissenting.

42. Ibid., at 122, Bradley dissenting.

43. This was, in part, because of Miller's narrow interpretation of privileges and immunities. Miller notes in his opinion for the majority that the butchers' attorneys had not pressed the due process claim. Ibid., at 80.

44. Labbé and Laurie, *Slaughterhouse Cases*, 186–94.

45. *The Slaughterhouse Cases*, 83 U.S. at 88–89, Field dissenting.

46. *Munn v. Illinois*, 94 U.S. 113 (1877).

47. *The Slaughterhouse Cases*, 83 U.S. at 111, Field dissenting.
48. Ibid., at 121, Bradley dissenting.
49. Ibid., at 116, Bradley dissenting.
50. For background on Bradley, I have relied most heavily on Ruth Ann Whiteside, "Justice Joseph Bradley and the Reconstruction Amendments" (Ph.D. diss., Rice University, 1981). I also used Stephenson, *Waite Court*, 94–97; Clare Cushman, ed., *The Supreme Court Justices: Illustrated Biographies, 1789–1995*, 2nd ed. (Washington, D.C.: Congressional Quarterly, 1995), 201–5. See Whiteside, "Justice Joseph Bradley," 17–19, for reference to Bradley's connection to Frederick Frelinghuysen.
51. Whiteside, "Justice Joseph Bradley," 35–36, 49–61, 83–86.
52. Stephenson, *Waite Court*, 97.
53. Whiteside, "Justice Joseph Bradley," 86–104.
54. Ibid., 66.
55. Grant had one appointment by virtue of a congressional statute restoring the Court to nine members. He had the other by virtue of the retirement of Justice Robert Grier. Stephenson, *Waite Court*, 24–26; Whiteside, "Justice Joseph Bradley," 105–36.

56. Jonathan Lurie, "Mr. Justice Bradley: A Reassessment," *Seton Hall Law Review* 16 (1986): 343–75, 373; Cortlant Parker, "Mr. Justice Bradley of the United States Supreme Court," in *Proceedings of the New Jersey Historical Society* 11 (2nd series, 1892), 157.
57. Lurie, "Mr. Justice Bradley," 373, citing scrapbooks compiled by the clerk's office of the U.S. Supreme Court (quoting the *New York Morning Journal*, February 5, 1890) (available in the National Archives Records, Washington, D.C.).
58. Charles Fairman, "What Makes a Great Justice? Mr. Justice Bradley and the Supreme Court 1870–1892," *Boston University Law Review* 30 (1950): 49–102, 85. Fairman actually uses the phrase "final fact," but that seemed confusing.
59. *The Slaughterhouse Cases*, 83 U.S. at 120, Bradley dissenting.
60. Ibid., at 123, Bradley dissenting.
61. The Senate confirmed him three days after he was nominated. For the background on Swayne, I have used Cushman, *Supreme Court Justices*, 171–75.
62. *The Slaughterhouse Cases*, 83 U.S. at 129, Swayne dissenting.
63. Ibid.
64. Fairman, "What Makes a Great Justice?" 78.
65. Ross, *Justice of Shattered Dreams*, 203, 210, goes even farther, arguing that Miller hoped to prevent his more conservative colleagues from turning the Fourteenth Amendment into a weapon with which they could defend propertied elites.
66. *The Slaughterhouse Cases*, 83 U.S. at 78.
67. *Bradwell v. Illinois*, 83 U.S. (16 Wall.) 130 (1872); see Jane M. Friedman, *America's First Woman Lawyer: The Biography of Myra Bradwell* (Buffalo, N.Y.: Prometheus Books, 1993).
68. *Bradwell*, 83 U.S. at 133–37, argument for the plaintiff in error.
69. Ibid., at 141. Bradley professed sympathy for the movement to give women the right to vote.
70. *Bartemeyer v. Iowa*, 85 U.S. (18 Wall.) 129 (1874).
71. Ibid., at 138.
72. Chief Justice Chase died on May 7, 1873. Cushman, *Supreme Court Justices*, 195.
73. Magrath, *Morrison R. Waite*, 274.

Chapter 2: Freedom Detoured

1. See *City of Boerne v. Flores*, 521 U.S. 507 (1997). The modern debate involves the question of whether an act of Congress is enforcement of a right guaranteed by the Constitution or whether it amounts to interpretation of the Constitution or creation of a new right.

2. *United States v. Cruikshank*, 92 U.S. (2 Otto.) 542 (1876); *United States v. Reese*, 92 U.S. (2 Otto.) 214 (1876); Enforcement Act of May 31, 1870 16 Stat. 140, reprinted in Charles Fairman, *Reconstruction and Reunion 1864–88, Part Two*, Oliver Wendell Holmes Devise History of the Supreme Court of the United States (New York: Macmillan, 1987), insert between 7:136 and 137.

3. Charles Lane, *The Day Freedom Died: The Colfax Massacre, the Supreme Court, and the Betrayal of Reconstruction* (New York: Henry Holt, 2008), 265–66, provides an appendix with careful attention to the number of dead.

4. Ted Tunnell, *Crucible of Reconstruction: War, Radicalism and Race in Louisiana 1862–1877* (Baton Rouge: Louisiana State University Press, 1984), 153.

5. For descriptions of violence before the Colfax massacre, see ibid., 153–60; for descriptions of violence occurring afterward, see George C. Rable, *But There Was No Peace: The Role of Violence in the Politics of Reconstruction* (Athens: University of Georgia Press, 1984), 129–43.

6. Tunnell, *Crucible of Reconstruction*, 157.

7. Ibid., 171.

8. The town of Colfax was named after Grant's vice president, Schuyler Colfax. Robert M. Goldman, *Reconstruction and Black Suffrage: Losing the Vote in Reese and Cruikshank* (Lawrence: University Press of Kansas, 2001), 44.

9. The following account of the Colfax massacre relies most heavily on Goldman, *Reconstruction*, 44–51. Other sources I used include Joe Gray Taylor, *Louisiana Reconstructed: 1863–1877* (Baton Rouge: Louisiana State University Press, 1974), 267–72, which refers to the incident as the Colfax Riot; Rable, *But There Was No Peace*, 126–29; Tunnell, *Crucible of Reconstruction*, 189–93. See also Lane, *Day Freedom Died*, an excellent account that was not published until after I had written this chapter.

10. See Goldman, *Reconstruction*, 44–49, for details of the massacre.

11. Ibid., 51; Fairman, *Reconstruction and Reunion*, 7:264.

12. Goldman, *Reconstruction*, 54.

13. Ibid., 58; Fairman, *Reconstruction and Reunion*, 7:269.

14. For differing views of Bradley's motives, see Goldman, *Reconstruction*, 58–59; Lane, *Day Freedom Died*, 205–11. Pamela Brandwein, *The Supreme Court, State Action, and Civil Rights: Rethinking the Judicial Settlement of Reconstruction* (Cambridge: Cambridge University Press, forthcoming), ch. 4, emphasizes the importance of Bradley's circuit court opinion.

15. Fairman, *Reconstruction and Reunion*, 7:272.

16. Although ironic, David Dudley Field's argument was not totally inconsistent with his brother's dissent in the *Slaughterhouse Cases*. David Dudley Field maintained that the enforcement provisions of the Reconstruction Amendments allowed Congress to do nothing whatever beyond providing judicial remedies in the federal courts for parties aggrieved by deprivation of their rights. Michael Les Benedict, "Preserving Federalism, Reconstruction and the Waite Court," *Supreme Court Review* (1978), 39–79, 65, citing Philip B. Kurland and Gerhard Casper, eds., *Landmark Briefs and Arguments of the Supreme Court of the United States* (Washington, D.C.: University Publications of America, 1975), 6:441–43.

17. Fairman, *Reconstruction and Reunion*, 7:272; Goldman, *Reconstruction*, 80–81.

18. Act of May 31, 1870, to Enforce the Right to Vote and for Other Purposes, 16 Stat. 140; *Cruikshank*, 92 U.S. at 556.

19. Fairman, *Reconstruction and Reunion*, 7:270–72; Goldman, *Reconstruction*, 80–81.

20. Goldman, *Reconstruction*, 52.

21. *Minor v. Happersett*, 88 U.S. (21 Wall.) 112 (1875).

22. *Cruikshank*, 92 U.S. at 555–56.

23. Ibid., at 556.

24. Ibid., at 542. I have simplified and combined the language of the first, second, ninth, and tenth counts of the indictment.

25. Ibid., at 552–53.

26. Ibid., at 554.

27. Ibid., at 557.

28. Ibid., at 557–59. Fairman, *Reconstruction and Reunion*, 7:226, maintains that the most lasting legacy of *Cruikshank* was establishing the idea that penal statutes must be sufficiently definite to give the accused fair notice or warning of the charges.

29. *Cruikshank*, 92 U.S. at 559, Clifford dissenting.

30. *Cruikshank* actually arrived at the Supreme Court as an appeal from the circuit court decision arresting the trial court's judgment. The order of the circuit court arresting judgment was affirmed, and the case remanded, with instructions to discharge the defendants. Justice Clifford wrote a separate concurring opinion. Ibid., at 559.

31. *United States v. Reese*, 92 U.S. (2 Otto.) 214 (1876).

32. Ibid., at 238–39, Hunt dissenting; Goldman, *Reconstruction*, 65–67.

33. *Reese*, 92 U.S. at 217.

34. Fairman, *Reconstruction and Reunion*, 7:244–49; Justice Nathan Clifford concurred with the outcome in *Reese* but would have ruled that the indictments were faulty because the government had failed to show that Garner had the means to pay the tax, and that Reese and Fouchee had refused to let him vote because of his race. *Reese*, 92 U.S. at 222, Clifford concurring.

35. Ibid., at 221.

36. Ibid., at 242, Hunt dissenting.

37. Ibid., at 245, Hunt dissenting.

38. Donald Grier Stephenson, *The Waite Court: Justices, Rulings, and Legacy* (Santa Barbara, Calif.: ABC-CLIO, 2003), 99–104; Clare Cushman, ed., *The Supreme Court Justices: Illustrated Biographies 1789–1995*, 2nd ed. (Washington, D.C.: Congressional Quarterly, 1995), 206–10.

39. C. Peter Magrath, *Morrison R. Waite: The Triumph of Character* (New York: Macmillan, 1963), 129–30, citing Waite to John T. Waite, April 2, 1876; see also Waite to Richard Waite, March 28, 1876, Letterbooks (as cited in Magrath, *Morrison R. Waite*).

40. Magrath, *Morrison R. Waite*, 131, citing *New York World*, March 28, 1876; *Richmond (Virginia) Enquirer*, March 28, 29, 1876; *Louisville (Kentucky) Courier-Journal*, March 28, 31, 1876; *Atlanta Constitution*, March 30, 1876.

41. Magrath, *Morrison R. Waite*, 130–31; Goldman, *Reconstruction*, 108–9.

42. *New York Times*, March 29, 1876.

43. Ibid. The *Times* mistakenly refers to the opinion as *United States versus Ruse*.

44. Magrath, *Morrison R. Waite*, 131.

45. Tunnell, *Crucible of Reconstruction*, 193.

46. The Waite Court, however, at least seemed willing to apply the formula consistently. It rejected a white shop owner's claim that a Louisiana statute prohibiting race discrimination denied him equal protection of the law. *Walker v. Sauvinet*, 92 U.S. (2 Otto.) 90 (1875).

47. Robert M. Goldman, *A Free Ballot and a Fair Count: The Department of Justice and the Enforcement of Voting Right in the South 1877–1893* (New York: Fordham University Press, 2001); Richard M. Valelly, *The Two Reconstructions: The Struggle for Black Enfranchisement* (Chicago: University of Chicago Press, 2004); Xi Wang, *The Trial of Democracy: Black Suffrage and Northern Republicans, 1860–1910* (Athens: University of Georgia Press, 1997); Brandwein, *Supreme Court, State Action, and Civil Rights*.

48. Benedict, "Preserving Federalism," 39–79.

49. The exceptions are the qualified prohibition on suspending the writ of habeas corpus in Article I, Section 9, the provisions that no state shall pass bills of attainder, ex post facto laws, or laws impairing the obligation of contracts in Article I, Section 10; and the guarantee of a republican form of government in Article IV, Section 4.

50. Eric Foner, "Moments of Change: Transformation of American Constitutionalism—The Strange Career of the Reconstruction Amendments," *Yale Law Journal* 108 (1999): 2003–2009, 2006.

51. Christopher Waldrep, "Joseph P. Bradley's Journey: The Meaning of Privileges and Immunities," *Journal of Supreme Court History* (forthcoming 2009), provides insight into Bradley's development. Brandwein, *Supreme Court, State Action, and Civil Rights,* notes that Bradley was attempting to develop a theory of the Reconstruction Amendments as a whole.

52. *United States v. Cruikshank,* 25 F. Cas. 707, 714 (C.C.D. La. 1874).

53. Ibid., at 710.

54. Ibid., at 710, 714.

55. Ibid., at 711.

56. Ibid., at 712.

57. Ruth Ann Whiteside, "Justice Joseph Bradley and the Reconstruction Amendments" (Ph.D. diss., Rice University, 1981), 47–48.

58. *Cruikshank,* 25 F. Cas. at 714. This is part of a longer quote in which Bradley also states the limits of federal power. This thinking led Bradley to develop what Pamela Brandwein calls the Fifteenth Amendment exception to the state action doctrine. Brandwein, *Supreme Court, State Action, and Civil Rights.*

59. Michael Les Benedict, "Preserving Federalism, Reconstruction and the Waite Court," *Supreme Court Review* (1978): 39–79; Brandwein, *Supreme Court, State Action, and Civil Rights.*

60. Michael A. Ross, *Justice of Shattered Dreams: Samuel Freeman Miller and the Supreme Court during the Civil War Era* (Baton Rouge: Louisiana State University Press, 2003), 203, 210.

61. The election took place on November 7, 1876. The exposition officially closed on November 10, 1876. See Keith Ian Polakoff, *The Politics of Inertia: The Election of 1876 and the End of Reconstruction* (Baton Rouge: Louisiana State University Press, 1973), 3. I have relied primarily on the following books to write this account of the disputed election: Polakoff, *Politics of Inertia;* Charles Fairman, *Five Justices and the Electoral Commission of 1877,* Oliver Wendell Holmes Devise History of the United States Supreme Court, supplement to vol. 7 (New York: Macmillan, 1988); William H. Rehnquist, *Centennial Crisis: The Disputed Election of 1876* (New York: Alfred A. Knopf, 2004); Roy Morris Jr., *Fraud of the Century: Rutherford B. Hayes, Samuel Tilden, and the Stolen Election of 1876* (New York: Simon and Schuster, 2003).

62. Polakoff, *Politics of Inertia,* 199–200, puts Tilden's lead at a quarter of a million votes.

63. Ibid., 205.

64. Ibid., 201–4.

65. Ibid., 202.

66. A. W. Grizzan to S. J. Tilden, December 1, 1876, and A. W. Robinson to S. J. Tilden, December 25, 1876, Tilden Papers, New York Public Library. There are more such papers in the Tilden Collection.

67. Fairman, *Five Justices,* xv.

68. Rehnquist, *Centennial Crisis.*

69. Cushman, *Supreme Court Justices,* 181–85; Kermit L. Hall, ed., *Oxford Companion to the Supreme Court of the United States* (New York: Oxford University Press, 1992), 218–19.

70. Allen Peskin, "Was There a Compromise of 1877," *Journal of American History* 60 (June 1973): 63–75, 74.

71. Polakoff, *Politics of Inertia,* 287, quoting Garfield Diary, February 6, 7, 1877, in Garfield papers.

72. Allan Nevins, *Abram S. Hewitt* (New York: Harper and Brothers, 1935).

73. Fairman, *Five Justices,* 123–96; Rehnquist, *Centennial Crisis,* 193-200; Polakoff, *Politics of Inertia,* 290.

74. Fairman, *Five Justices*, 97.

75. Polakoff, *Politics of Inertia*, 310–13; Peskin, "Was There a Compromise of 1877," 63.

76. C. Vann Woodward, *Reunion and Reaction: The Compromise of 1877 and the End of Reconstruction* (Boston: Little, Brown, 1951). Peskin, "Was There a Compromise of 1877," 63–75, provides this summary with references.

77. See Peskin, "Was There a Compromise of 1877," 63–75; Michael Les Benedict, "Southern Democrats in the Crisis of 1876–1877: A Reconsideration of *Reunion and Reaction*," *Journal of Southern History* 46, no. 4 (November 1980): 489–524; Ari Hoogenboom, *The Presidency of Rutherford B. Hayes* (Lawrence: University Press of Kansas, 1988), 47–50.

78. Hoogenboom, *Presidency of Rutherford B. Hayes*, 49–50.

79. *Harper's Weekly*, March 24, 1877, 232.

80. Michael McConnell, "The Forgotten Constitutional Moment," *Constitutional Commentary* 11 (Winter 1994): 115–44, maintains that the "Compromise" marked a fundamental reorientation of the Republican Party away from the goals of Reconstruction and toward the goal of economic expansion.

81. Rehnquist, *Centennial Crisis*, 119.

82. Morris, *Fraud of the Century*, 1.

83. John Anthony Scott, "Justice Bradley's Evolving Concept of the Fourteenth Amendment from the Slaughterhouse Cases to the Civil Rights Cases," *Rutgers Law Review* 25 (1971): 552–69, 567–68. Scott takes the position that Bradley changed his mind in the Florida dispute and that he did so with the encouragement of Chief Justice Waite for the purpose of constructing a legal rationale to justify and give force to the Compromise of 1877. For a contrary opinion, see Whiteside, "Justice Joseph Bradley," 253–54.

84. *Reese*, 92 U.S. at 221.

85. *Murdock v. City of Memphis*, 87 U.S. (20 Wall.) 590 (1874). Justices Clifford and Swayne dissented. Justice Bradley also dissented but maintained that there was no federal question jurisdiction at all in this case. The Court decided the case just before Chief Justice Waite took his seat; he did not participate. William M. Wiecek, "Reconstruction of Federal Judicial Power," *American Journal of Legal History* 13 (1969): 333–59, 354, points out that Congress was determined to expand the power of the federal courts to make them partners in implementing Reconstruction policy.

Chapter 3: After the Compromise

1. Charles Fairman, *Reconstruction and Reunion 1864–88, Part Two*, Oliver Wendell Holmes Devise History of the Supreme Court of the United States (New York: Macmillan, 1987), provides a convenient summary of the legislation in an insert between 7:136 and 137.

2. Fairman, *Reconstruction and Reunion*, 7:550–54, provides details.

3. *The Civil Rights Cases*, 109 U.S. 3 (1883).

4. Ibid., at 13.

5. Ibid., at 20.

6. Ibid., at 22.

7. For this biographical sketch of Harlan, I relied primarily upon Clare Cushman, ed., *The Supreme Court Justices: Illustrated Biographies 1789–1995*, 2nd ed. (Washington, D.C.: Congressional Quarterly, 1995), 216–220; Linda Przybyszewski, *The Republic According to John Marshall Harlan* (Chapel Hill: University of North Carolina Press, 1999); Donald Grier Stephenson Jr., *The Waite Court: Justices, Rulings, and Legacy* (Santa Barbara, Ca.: ABC-CLIO, 2003), 110–17; Tinsley E. Yarbrough, *Judicial Enigma: The First Justice Harlan* (New York: Oxford University Press, 1995).

8. Frank B. Latham, *The Great Dissenter: John Marshall Harlan, 1833–1911* (New York: Cowles, 1970), 59; Alan F. Weston, "Mr. Justice Harlan," in *Mr. Justice*, ed. Allison Dunham and Philip B. Kurland (Chicago: University of Chicago Press, 1964), 108–9.

9. Yarbrough, *Judicial Enigma,* 65–115, provides a detailed and fascinating account of Harlan's political rise and his appointment to the Supreme Court.

10. Przybyszewski, *John Marshall Harlan,* see especially 97–98.

11. *The Civil Rights Cases,* 109 U.S. at 26, Harlan dissenting.

12. Ibid., at 14–15.

13. Ibid., at 26–27, 50, Harlan dissenting.

14. Ibid., at 45–46, Harlan dissenting. "The fourteenth amendment presents the first instance of the investiture of congress with affirmative power, by *legislation,* to *enforce* an express prohibition upon the states."

15. Ibid., at 34–35, Harlan dissenting.

16. Ibid., at 39, Harlan dissenting.

17. Ibid., at 40–41, Harlan dissenting.

18. Ibid., at 42, 58–59, Harlan dissenting.

19. *Plessy v. Ferguson,* 163 U.S. 537, 559 (1896), Harlan dissenting.

20. C. Peter Magrath, *Morrison R. Waite: The Triumph of Character* (New York: Macmillan, 1963), 149.

21. *The Civil Rights Cases,* 109 U.S. at 25. Bradley expressed an attitude that had become common among Northern Republicans by this time. See Charles W. Calhoun, *Conceiving a New Republic: The Republican Party and the Southern Question 1869–1900* (Lawrence: University Press of Kansas, 2006).

22. Pamela Brandwein, "A Judicial Abandonment of Blacks? Rethinking the 'State Action' Cases of the Waite Court," *Law and Society Review* 41 (June 2007): 343–81; Brandwein, *Supreme Court, State Action, and Civil Rights: Rethinking the Judicial Settlement of Reconstruction* (Cambridge: Cambridge University Press, forthcoming).

23. See Eric Foner, *Reconstruction, 1863–1867: America's Unfinished Revolution* (New York: Harper and Row, 1988), 182.

24. Robert M. Goldman, *Reconstruction and Black Suffrage: Losing the Vote in Reese and Cruikshank* (Lawrence: University Press of Kansas, 2001), 113.

25. *Ex parte Yarbrough,* 110 U.S. 651, 665, 666 (1884); see Richard M. Valelly, *The Two Reconstructions: The Struggle for Black Enfranchisement* (Chicago: University of Chicago Press, 2004), 244–46; Michael A. Ross, *Justice of Shattered Dreams: Samuel Freeman Miller and the Supreme Court during the Civil War* (Baton Rouge: Louisiana State University Press, 2003), 247–48; see also *Ex parte Siebold,* 100 U.S. 371 (1880); *Ex parte Clark,* 100 U.S. 399 (1880).

26. Ellen D. Katz, "Reinforcing Representation: Congressional Power to Enforce the Fourteenth and Fifteenth Amendments in the Rehnquist and Waite Courts," *Michigan Law Review* 101 (2003): 101–69, 148, 154.

27. *Strauder v. West Virginia,* 100 U.S. 303 (1880); revised Federal Statutes, Sec. 641, is reproduced at 311.

28. *Virginia v. Rives,* 100 U.S. 313 (1880).

29. *Ex parte Virginia,* 100 U.S. 339 (1880). The judge was convicted of violating a provision of the Civil Rights Act of 1875 that was different from the section at issue in the *Civil Rights Cases.* This is mentioned in *The Civil Rights Cases,* 109 U.S. at 15–16.

30. *Neal v. Delaware,* 103 U.S. 370, 393–94, 397 (1880). Brandwein, "Judicial Abandonment of Blacks?" 358.

31. It has always been assumed that the prisoners were black men even though the court reporter's description of them is frustratingly vague. In an admirable bit of sleuthing Pamela Brandwein discovered that the prisoners were actually white men. She notes, however, that the Court may have been under the impression that the men were black. Brandwein, *Supreme Court, State Action, and Civil Rights,* ch. 5.

32. *United States v. Harris,* 106 U.S. 629 (1883).

Chapter 4: Romancing the Rails

1. *Munn v. Illinois,* 94 U.S. 113 (1877).

2. Isaac F. Redfield, *The Law of Railways,* 5th ed. (Boston: Little Brown, 1873), 1:245.

3. *Kelo v. City of New London, Connecticut,* 545 U.S. 469 (2005). The Fifth Amendment uses the term "public use." Courts have sometimes interpreted this as "public purpose," a term that seems to convey expanded power. Kelo went even farther, allowing a city to take private property when it served a "public benefit." The city had condemned homes in order to provide land for office buildings and shopping centers. It justified this redevelopment with the claim that increased taxes and revenue would benefit the public.

4. Redfield, *Law of Railways,* 1:245.

5. Ibid., 1:246, n.2.

6. James F. Hudson, *The Railways and the Republic* (New York: Harper and Brothers, 1887), 111. Hudson believed that the way to solve the railroad problem was to encourage competition by designating railroads as truly public highways. That is to allow all persons to run their trains, for a fee, over a railroad company's tracks. James W. Ely Jr., *Railroads and American Law* (Lawrence: University Press of Kansas, 2001), 36–37, has warned against exaggerating the implications of Hudson's statement. Ely points out that railroads often obtained land for rights-of-way and depots through voluntary purchases and gifts. He also notes that when in 1840 New Hampshire prohibited the use of eminent domain by new railroads, railroad building came to a halt and the legislature relented.

7. Harry N. Scheiber, "The Road to *Munn:* Eminent Domain and the Concept of Public Purpose in the State Courts," in *Perspectives in American History: Law in American History,* vol. 5, ed. Donald Fleming and Bernard Bailyn (Cambridge, Mass.: Charles Warren Center Studies in American History, Harvard University, 1971) 327–402, 339–43, 360–87, explains in detail the history of the eminent domain power and the public purpose doctrine. Scheiber observes that eminent domain performed three functions: a supportive function for public enterprises, a supportive function for private enterprises, and a negative-check function, limiting the police power.

8. For a detailed discussion of the rationale behind this policy and its limits, see ibid., 364–73, 384–87.

9. Ibid., 341, citing *Raleigh & Gaston R.R. v. Davis,* 2 Dev. & Batt. 451, 469 (N.C. 1837). Redfield, *Law of Railways,* 1:250–51, notes that state courts placed limits on a railroad's use of the power. A railroad could not enforce eminent domain to lay temporary tracks, for example, or to erect a building for the manufacture of railroad cars, or to take land for employee housing.

10. Charles Fairman, *Mr. Justice Miller and the Supreme Court 1862–1890* (1939; repr., New York: Russell and Russell, 1966), 209.

11. Scheiber, "Road to *Munn,*" 387.

12. Redfield, *Law of Railways,* 2:434.

13. *Thompson v. Lee County,* 70 U.S. 327, 330 (1865).

14. *Olcott v. The Supervisors,* 83 U.S. (16 Wall.) 678 (1873). In an 1873 case the United States Supreme Court even disregarded a Wisconsin Supreme Court decision that declared that building a railroad was not public use for taxation purposes.

15. *Loan Association v. Topeka,* 87 U.S. (20 Wall.) 655, 659–60 (1875).

16. Justice Clifford dissented, arguing that the Court could nullify an act of a state legislature on the vague ground that they think it opposed to the latent spirit of the Constitution or natural law. Ibid., at 669. Herbert Hovenkamp, *Enterprise and American Law, 1836–1937* (Cambridge, Mass.: Harvard University Press, 1991), 38–41, maintains *Topeka* provided a theory that allowed courts to distinguish general manufacturing from businesses like railroads that provided public service.

17. See *Burlington v. Beasley*, 94 U.S. (4 Otto.) 310 (1877), where the Court allowed a municipality to finance the construction of a steam-powered gristmill.

18. U.S. Constitution, Article III, Section 2.

19. *Swift v. Tyson*, 41 U.S. (16 Pet.) 1 (1842), established the power of federal courts to follow general commercial law instead of state court rulings. This rule stood until it was repudiated in 1938. *Erie Railroad Co. v. Topeka*, 304 U.S. 64 (1938).

20. For a detailed account of the dispute, see Michael A. Ross, *Justice of Shattered Dreams: Samuel Freeman Miller and the Supreme Court during the Civil War Era* (Baton Rouge: Louisiana State University Press, 2003), 89–93.

21. *Gelpcke v. The City of Dubuque*, 68 U.S. (1 Wall.) 175 (1864). Charles A. Heckman, "Establishing the Basis for Local Financing of American Railroad Construction in the Nineteenth Century: From *City of Bridgeport v. The Housatonic Railroad Company* to *Gelpcke v. City of Dubuque*," *American Journal of Legal History* 32 (1988): 236–64, maintains that *Gelpcke* was the logical outgrowth of a long line of cases dealing with the financing of railroad construction.

22. *Burlington and Missouri Railroad Company v. County of Wapello*, 13 Iowa 388, 423–24 (1862) cited in Ross, *Justice of Shattered Dreams*, 89.

23. *Gelpcke*, 68 U.S. at 206; Charles Fairman, *Reconstruction and Reunion 1864–88, Part Two*, Oliver Wendell Holmes Devise History of the Supreme Court of the United States (New York: Macmillan, 1987) 7:296–97.

24. *Gelpcke*, 68 U.S. at 205.

25. Ross, *Justice of Shattered Dreams*, 91, concludes Swayne believed that justice and morality demanded that Dubuque pay its contractual obligation to innocent bondholders.

26. Miller emphasized that these cases did not involve a constitutional question such as whether the state had violated Article I, Section 10, by impairing the obligation of contracts. *Gelpcke*, 68 U.S. at 209–10, Miller dissenting. Justice Swayne had hinted that there was a contract clause issue. *Gelpcke*, 68 U.S. at 206. Some legal historians have thus concluded that the contract clause was later invoked to bar localities from repudiating bonded debt. James W. Ely Jr., "The Protection of Contractual Rights: A Tale of Two Constitutional Provisions," *NYU Journal of Law and Liberty* 1 (2005): 370–403, 379. When a contract for bonds existed before Illinois ratified a constitutional prohibition, the Court ruled that a retroactive application of the new provision would violate the contract clause. *County of Moultrie v. Rockingham Ten-Cent Savings-Bank*, 92 U.S. (2 Otto.) 631 (1876).

27. *Humbolt Township v. Long*, 92 U.S. (2 Otto.) 642, 647 (1876), Miller dissenting.

28. *Township of Pine Grove v. Talcott*, 86 U.S. (19 Wall.) 666 (1874). Although the opinion was read on May 4, 1874, about two months after Waite took his seat, it ends with a notation that the new chief justice did not take part in the decision. See also *Chicago, Burlington, and Quincy Railroad v. Otoe*, 83 U.S. (16 Wall.) 667 (1873), ruling that a constitutional limit on the amount a state could borrow did not apply to municipalities.

29. *Mayor of Nashville v. Ray*, 86 U.S. (19 Wall.) 468 (1874).

30. *Town of Venice v. Murdock*, 92 U.S. (2 Otto.) 494 (1876); see also *County of Callaway v. Foster*, 93 U.S. (3 Otto.) 567 (1876); Ross, *Justice of Shattered Dreams*, 220; *Town of Coloma v. Eaves*, 92 U.S. (2 Otto.) 484 (1876); *Humbolt Township v. Long*, 92 U.S. (2 Otto.) 642 (1876), upholding bonds even though public officials failed to provide voters with notice of the bond election as state law required.

31. *Humbolt Township*, 92 U.S. at 646, Miller dissenting. In several later cases the Court recognized some limits on the bona fide holder rule. It ruled bonds in excess of a state mandated ceiling were invalid because the value of taxable property was on record with the state as the last assessment for state and county taxes. *Buchanan v. Litchfield*, 102 U.S. (12 Otto.) 278 (1880). In a later case where the bonds on their face did not include a certification that the required vote

had been taken, the Court ruled that the bond was invalid. *Katzenberger v. City of Aberdeen,* 121 U.S. 172 (1887). Dissenting in *United States v. County of Clark,* 96 U.S. (6 Otto.) 211, 218 (1878), Chief Justice Waite maintained that the debt on bonds could only be collected from the fund specified for that purpose. However, these opinions did not reflect a significant retreat from the majority's application of the bona fide holder rule.

32. *Town of Venice v. Murdock,* 92 U.S. at 498.

33. Fairman, *Mr. Justice Miller,* 207. As is often the case, the issue was frequently more complex, as suggested by one railroad leader's advice "to take the necessary steps to prevent, if possible, our being required to pay taxes to help build rival roads." A. K. Ackerman to Messes. Griffith and Knight, May 23, 1882, A. K. Ackerman out-letters, Illinois Central, Newberry Library.

34. *Fletcher v. Peck,* 10 U.S. (6 Cranch) 87 (1810).

35. Scheiber, "Road to *Munn,*" 394.

36. *Marcy v. Township of Oswego,* 92 U.S. (2 Otto.) 637 (1876); see also *Butz v. City of Muscatine,* 75 U.S. (8 Wall.) 575 (1869); *Meyer v. City of Muscatine,* 68 U.S. (1 Wall.) 384 (1864).

37. *Humbolt Township v. Long,* 92 U.S. (2 Otto.) 642, 649 (1876).

38. Ibid., at 649, Miller dissenting. Miller used the *Humbolt Township* case as a vehicle for explaining his dissents in all of the other cases decided at this time.

39. See Ross, *Justice of Shattered Dreams,* 218.

40. *Gelpcke,* 68 U.S. at 214.

41. The story of Keokuk is told in Ross, *Justice of Shattered Dreams,* 167–70.

42. Ibid., 169.

43. Some of these public officials refused to pay bondholders even in the face of federal court orders that they do so. This led Justice Miller to complain that the decisions of the Court compelled him, while riding circuit, "to enter an order to commit to jail at one time over a hundred of the best citizens of Iowa," for obeying an injunction issued by a competent court of their own state. *Butz v. City of Muscatine,* 75 U.S. at 587; Ross, *Justice of Shattered Dreams,* 173–74.

44. George H. Miller, *Railroads and the Granger Laws* (Madison: University of Wisconsin Press, 1971), 98–101.

45. Charles Francis Adams Jr., *Railroads: Their Origin and Problems* (1878; repr., New York: G. P. Putnam's Sons, 1886), 119–20.

46. Ibid., 123–26, provides one of numerous descriptions of this phenomenon.

47. Arthur T. Hadley, *Railroad Transportation: Its History and Its Laws* (New York: G. P. Putnam's Sons, Knickerbocker Press, 1896), 114–19; Herbert Hovenkamp, "Regulatory Conflict in the Gilded Age: Federalism and the Railroad Problem," *Yale Law Journal* 97 (1988): 1017–72, 1051–53; Hovenkamp, *Enterprise and American Law,* 153–56, which provides a good explanation of this reasoning; see also Arthur T. Hadley, "Railroad Business under the Interstate Commerce Act," *Quarterly Journal of Economics* 3, no. 2 (January 1889): 170–87, for an explanation or justification of pooling.

48. Hudson, *Railways and the Republic,* 9–10. Hudson wrote this during the debate over formation of the Interstate Commerce Commission, but it captures the feelings of the Granger era as well.

49. Miller, *Railroads and the Granger Laws,* traces in detail the influence of small town merchants and shippers as well as farmers. See also Solon J. Buck, *The Granger Movement: A Study of Agricultural Organization and Its Political, Economic, and Social Manifestations, 1870–1880* (1913; repr., Lincoln: University of Nebraska Press, 1963), 80–122; Gerald Berk, *Alternative Tracks: The Constitution of American Industrial Order, 1865–1917* (Baltimore: Johns Hopkins University Press, 1994), 78; Charles Fairman, "The So-Called Granger Cases: Lord Hale and Justice Bradley," *Stanford Law Review* 5 (1953): 587–678, 598–600.

50. See Miller, *Railroads and the Granger Laws,* 9–23; Edmund W. Kitch and Clara Ann Bowler, "The Facts of *Munn v. Illinois,*" *Supreme Court Review* (1978): 313–43.

51. Berk, *Alternative Tracks,* 77–80.

52. Charles Postel, *The Populist Vision* (New York: Oxford University Press, 2007), 11.

53. Victoria Saker Woeste, *The Farmer's Benevolent Trust: Law and Agricultural Cooperation in Industrial America 1865–1945* (Chapel Hill: University of North Carolina Press, 1998).

54. Annual Address of Worthy Master D. W. Adams, at the last session of the National Grange, held in Charleston, February 1875, in Ezra Carr, *Patrons of Husbandry on the Pacific Coast* (San Francisco: A. L. Bancroft, 1875), 125.

55. William J. Novak, *The People's Welfare: Law and Regulation in Nineteenth-Century America* (Chapel Hill: University of North Carolina Press, 1996).

56. Miller, *Railroads and the Granger Laws,* 181, provides an example of this description.

57. *Debates and Proceedings of the Constitutional Convention of the State of Illinois, Convened at the City of Springfield, Tuesday December 13, 1868,* Ely, Burnham, and Bartlett official stenographers, 2 vols. (Springfield, Ill.: M. L. Merritt and Brothers, Printers to the Convention, 1870), 2:317. Miller, *Railroads and the Granger Laws,* 75–82, discusses the convention.

58. *Debates and Proceedings,* 2:313 (January 27, 1870).

59. Ibid., 2:1629. Speeches during the debates provide some specific examples of this public welfare with respect to railroad regulation. Ibid., 2:1654. See Miller, *Railroads and the Granger Laws,* 75, for background on Medill.

60. *Debates and Proceedings,* 2:1656.

61. Ibid., 2:1642. Benjamin later helped prepare the brief for the state in *Munn v. Illinois.* Miller, *Railroads and the Granger Laws,* 75, 77.

62. *Debates and Proceedings,* 2:1642. See also comments by Hildrup, ibid., 2:1651, and Brownwell, ibid., 2:1664.

63. Ibid., 2:1645 (Medill); Ibid., 2:1642 (Benjamin).

64. Ibid., 2:1645 (Peirce).

65. See, for example, Declaration of Purposes of the National Grange, reproduced in Carr, *Patrons of Husbandry,* 126.

66. *Munn,* 94 U.S. at 114–17, reproduces the statute.

67. R. Harris to W. P. Hepburn, March 20, 1874, Harris out-letters, Burlington Archives, Newberry Library, Chicago.

68. J. M. Walker to "My Dear Counselor" (Hon. Sydney Bartlett), April 18, 1874; J. M. Walker to O. H. Browning, April 20, 1874, J. M. Walker out-letters, Burlington Archives, Newberry Library. Walker suggested that bondholders seek injunctions in the federal courts against the company and the railroad commission.

69. J. M. Walker to J. M. Forbes, March 20, 1874, J. M. Walker out-letters, Burlington Archives, Newberry Library. Predicting some amendment through the legislature "if we can manage to keep along without its being known that RR interests are concerned." Richard C. Cortner, *The Iron Horse and the Constitution: Railroads and the Transformation of the Fourteenth Amendment* (Westport, Conn.: Greenwood Press, 1993), 20, points out that even before *Munn* railroads were successful in the political arena. For example, he notes that in 1875 the Minnesota legislature repealed an 1874 act setting rates and replaced it with a single railroad commissioner with little power.

70. J. M. Walker to W. H. Falconer, March 19, 1874, J. M. Walker out-letters, Burlington Archives, Newberry Library.

71. J. M. Walker to Wm. L. Toole, March 7, 1874, J. M. Walker out-letters, Burlington Archives, Newberry Library. As public relations ploys go, however, Walker could not top the

Chicago, Burlington, and Quincy's general manager, Robert Harris, who used the antidiscrimination provision of a Granger law as an excuse to refuse requests for special rates to religious gatherings. "If we are ever again allowed our freedom," Harris lamented, "we may resume our old practice of favoring such gatherings." Robert Harris to H. Hitchcock, April 1, 1874, Robert Harris out-letters, Burlington Archives, Newberry Library.

72. J. M. Walker to J. N. Denison, July 10, 1874, J. M. Walker out-letters, Burlington Archives, Newberry Library.

73. J. N. Denison to Jacob B. Jewett, October 15, 1873, J. N. Denison out-letters, Burlington Archives, Newberry Library.

74. R. Harris to W. P. Hepburn, March 20, 1874, R. Harris out-letters, Burlington Archives, Newberry Library.

75. J. N. Denison to N. M. Beckwith, April 7, 1873, J. N. Denison out-letters, Burlington Archives, Newberry Library. Denison was at the time the chairman of the board of the Chicago, Burlington, and Quincy.

76. Thomas C. Cochran, *Railroad Leaders 1845–1890: The Business Mind in Action* (New York: Russell and Russell, 1965), 191.

77. See J. M. Walker to O. H. Browning, April 20, 1874; J. M. Walker to Sydney Bartlett, May 14, 1874; J. M. Walker to Judge [illegible], April 14, 1874, J. M. Walker out-letters, Burlington Archives, Newberry Library; J. N. Denison to N. M. Beckwith, April 7, 1873; J. N. Denison to Jacob B. Jewett, October 15, 1873, J. N. Denison out-letters, Burlington Archives, Newberry Library. See also Miller, *Railroads and the Granger Laws,* 174–75.

78. J. M. Walker to O. H. Browning, March 7, 1874, J. M. Walker out-letters, Burlington Archives, Newberry Library. Walker continued, "Beckwith is disposed to think it can be. I enclose you his suggestions" (possibly referring to Warren Beckwith, road master of the Burlington and Missouri River Railroad).

79. Miller, *Railroads and the Granger Laws,* 174–75, provides details regarding the legal tactics.

80. *Trustees of Dartmouth College v. Woodward,* 17 U.S. (4 Wheat.) 519 (1819).

81. *Chicago, Burlington, and Quincy Railroad Company v. Iowa,* 94 U.S. (4 Otto.) 155, 161 (1877). The chief justice also noted that they were businesses affected with public interest as in *Munn.*

82. Ibid., at 161–62.

83. See, as an example, *Holyoke v. Lyman,* 82 U.S. (15 Wall.) 500 (1872).

84. Redfield, *Law of Railways,* 1:50.

85. Ely, "Protection of Contractual Rights," 370–403, 397–99. Ely cites Thomas M. Cooley, *Treatise on the Constitutional Limitations Which Rest Upon the Legislative Power of the States,* 2nd ed. (1871), 280 n.2, as sharply criticizing the use of the contract clause as a shield for corporate charters.

86. Ely, "Protection of Contractual Rights," 401, points out that railroads were seldom able to successfully claim exemption from rate regulation by pointing to the language of their charters.

87. *Peik v. Chicago & North-Western Railway Co.,* 94 U.S. (4 Otto.) 164, 168 (1877). Although it is common today to think of property's constitutional guarantee as including protection of its title, possession, use, and value, in the nineteenth century jurists extended the constitutional protection only to property's possession. Stephen A. Siegel, "Understanding the Nineteenth Century Contract Clause: The Role of the Property-Privilege Distinction and 'Takings' Clause Jurisprudence," *Southern California Law Review* 60 (November 1986): 1–108, 56, 76–77.

88. Field used *Stone v. Wisconsin,* 94 U.S. (4 Otto.) 181, 183 (1877), to express his dissent to all the Granger Cases involving corporations. I say he seemed to agree because Field actually claims that the majority misses an opportunity to define the limits of the power of the states over corporations. He definitely rejected the Court's rationale in *Munn* and thus its application to the cases involving the contract clause.

89. *Peik*, 94 U.S. at 168.

90. Miller, *Railroads and the Granger Laws*, 185, citing C. B. Lawrence's argument in *Peik*.

91. Miller, *Railroads and the Granger Laws*, 185, citing John Cary's argument in *Peik*.

92. Two recent studies that emphasize the importance of popular sovereignty are Christian G. Fritz, *American Sovereigns: The People and America's Constitutional Tradition before the Civil War* (New York: Cambridge University Press, 2008); and Larry D. Kramer, *The People Themselves: Popular Constitutionalism and Judicial Review* (New York: Oxford University Press, 2004).

93. *Charles River Bridge Co. v. Warren Bridge Co.*, 36 U.S. (11 Pet.) 420, 547 (1837).

94. Ibid., at 547.

95. Thomas M. Cooley, *A Treatise on the Constitutional Limitations Which Rest Upon the Legislative Power of the States of the American Union*, 3rd ed. (Boston: Little, Brown, 1874), 283.

96. Ibid., 280–84. Siegel, "Understanding the Nineteenth Century Contract Clause," 41–55, explains that elements of this principle of inalienability were controversial and became even more so toward the end of the century.

97. Cooley, *Constitutional Limitations* (1874), 280–81.

98. Ibid., 280–84; *Morgan v. Louisiana*, 93 U.S. (3 Otto.) 217, 222 (1876) (taxes). The Court applied this presumption in a similar case, ruling that when two companies consolidated, a tax exemption applies only to the part of the new company that received it in the first place. *Central Railroad and Banking Company v. Georgia*, 92 U.S. (2 Otto.) 665 (1875). In a similar vein it ruled that a contract that exempted companies from a state tax did not imply that municipalities could not tax those companies, and that a grant of temporary tax immunity did not imply that a company was permanently exempted from being taxed. *Bailey v. Magwire*, 89 U.S. (22 Wall.) 215 (1874); *Home Insurance Company v. City Councils of Augusta*, 93 U.S. (3 Otto.) 116 (1876); *Tucker v. Ferguson*, 89 U.S. (22 Wall.) 527 (1874).

99. Stephen A. Siegel, "Understanding the *Lochner* Era: Lessons from the Controversy Over Railroad and Utility Rate Regulation," *Virginia Law Review* 70 (1984): 187–263, 197–98.

100. See Scheiber, "Road to *Munn*"; Novak, *People's Welfare;* Gregory A. Mark, "Review of William J. Novak, *The People's Welfare: Law and Regulation in Nineteenth-Century America*," H-Law, H-Net reviews, November 1999, 5 URL: http://www.h-net.msu.edu/reviews/showrev.cig?path=5155944065677, observes that Novak's discussion of official markets demonstrated the naturalness of exchange and of regulation.

101. Harry N. Scheiber, "Public Rights and the Rule of Law in American Legal History," *California Law Review* 72 (1984): 217–51, 219. Philip A. Talmadge, "The Myth of Property Absolutism and Modern Government: The Interaction of Police Power and Property Rights," *Washington Law Review* 75 (2000): 857–909, is another modern observer who takes a similar position.

102. *Commonwealth v. Alger*, 7 Cush. 53, 84–85 (Mass., 1851). Shaw goes on to say: "All property in this commonwealth . . . is derived directly or indirectly from the government, and held subject to those regulations, which are necessary to the common good and general welfare." See Scheiber, "Public Rights," 222–23; Novak, *People's Welfare*, 19–20. It is interesting that Shaw's language begins with a statement very similar to what advocates of laissez-faire constitutionalism would later use to describe the limits of property rights. That language, which was captured by the Latin maxim *sic utere tuo ut alienum non laedas* (so use your property as not to injure the property of others), differs only in that it drops the reference to the rights of the community.

103. Miller, *Railroads and the Granger Laws*, 31. Ely, *Railroads and American Law*, 71–90, recognizes that regulation of rates was common but emphasizes that legislative rate making was often ineffective.

104. I borrowed some of the description and parts of the analysis of *Munn* in this and the next chapter from my own previous writings in Paul Kens, *Justice Stephen Field: Shaping Liberty from the Gold Rush to the Gilded Age* (Lawrence: University Press of Kansas, 1997).

CHAPTER 5: THE LAST GASP OF THE RIGHTS OF THE COMMUNITY

1. Edmund W. Kitch and Clara Ann Bowler, "The Facts of *Munn v. Illinois*," *Supreme Court Review* (1978): 313–43. Kitch and Bowler point out that the most important reform for the Board of Trade was a system of uniform inspection. Rates were a secondary matter. Ibid., 325. Railroad leaders expressed some concern about filling elevators for purposes of speculation. W. K. Ackerman to Capt. W. P. Halliday, September 6, 1881, W. K. Ackerman out-letters, Illinois Central Archives, Newberry Library, Chicago.

2. Herbert Hovenkamp, *Enterprise and American Law, 1836–1937* (Cambridge, Mass.: Harvard University Press, 1991), 136–37, is one writer who makes this point by maintaining that railroad regulation was a problem of federalism.

3. See James W. Ely Jr., *The Chief Justiceship of Melville W. Fuller 1888–1910* (Columbia: University of South Carolina Press, 1995), 61, 90–94.

4. W. C. Goudy, "Brief for the Plaintiff in Error, *Munn v. Illinois*," in *Landmark Briefs and Arguments of the Supreme Court of the United States: Constitutional Law*, ed. Philip B. Kurland and Gerhard Casper (Washington, D.C.: University Publications of America, 1975), 7:511.

5. Ibid., 7:512, citing Cooley, *Constitutional Limitations*, 351 ff.

6. *Wynehamer v. The People*, 13 N.Y. 378 (1856). See James W. Ely Jr., "The Oxymoron Reconsidered: Myth and Reality in the Origins of Substantive Due Process," *Constitutional Commentary* 16 (1999): 315–45, 338–44.

7. *Dred Scott v. Sanford*, 60 U.S. (19 How.) 393, 450 (1857). Goudy did not make reference to *Dred Scott*.

8. *The Slaughterhouse Cases*, 83 U.S. (16 Wall.) 36 (1873), Bradley dissenting.

9. *State Railroad Tax Cases*, 92 U.S. (2 Otto.) 575, 596, 618 (1876).

10. Goudy, "Brief," 515; John N. Jewett, "Brief for the Plaintiff in Error, *Munn v. Illinois*," in *Landmark Briefs and Arguments of the Supreme Court of the United States: Constitutional Law*, ed. Phillip B. Kurland and Gerhard Casper (Arlington, Virginia: University Publications of America, 1975), 7:558, citing *Pumpelly v. Green Bay Company*, 80 U.S. (13 Wall.) 166 (1871).

11. Jewett, "Brief," 557.

12. Mary Ann Glendon, *Rights Talk: The Impoverishment of Political Discourse* (New York: Free Press, 1991), 18–46.

13. Goudy, "Brief," 483.

14. Jewett, "Brief," 549.

15. *Munn v. Illinois*, 94 U.S. 113, 125 (1877).

16. Ibid., at 127.

17. See Charles Fairman, "The So-Called Granger Cases, Lord Hale and Justice Bradley," *Stanford Law Review* 5 (1953): 587–679.

18. *Munn*, 94 U.S. at 127. I have Charles Fairman to thank for bringing Bradley's memorandum "Outline of my views on the subject of the Granger Cases" to light. He reproduces the Bradley memorandum in Fairman, "So-Called Granger Cases," 587-678.

19. *Munn*, 94 U.S. at 146–47, Field dissenting.

20. Ibid., at 139–41, Field dissenting.

21. Ibid., at 132.

22. Fairman, "So-Called Granger Cases," 670.

23. C. Peter Magrath, *Morrison R. Waite: The Triumph of Character* (New York: Macmillan, 1963), 184–85; Felix Frankfurter, *The Commerce Clause under Marshall, Taney, and Waite* (Chapel Hill: University of North Carolina Press, 1937), 79–80, 85.

24. *Nebbia v. New York*, 291 U.S. 502 (1934); Fairman, "So-Called Granger Cases," 656–59; Magrath, *Morrison R. Waite*, 187–88. Fairman charged Waite with bungling the opinion in *Munn* by misinterpreting the significance of Bradley's memo and failing to see that the affected with public interest doctrine could lend itself to contradictory purposes.

25. *Munn,* 94 U.S. at 126.
26. Ibid., at 140, Field dissenting.
27. Ibid., at 145, Field dissenting.
28. Ibid., at 146, Field dissenting. Scheiber, "Road to *Munn,*" 389–91, notes that Field and Cooley favored a more limited use of taxation in support of railroads because they understood the link to justifying greater police power regulations.
29. *Munn,* 94 U.S. at 142–43, Field dissenting.
30. Ibid., at 133.
31. Fairman, "So-Called Granger Cases," 677.
32. *Munn,* 94 U.S. at 123.
33. Ibid., at 132 (emphasis added).
34. *Charles River Bridge Co. v. Warren Bridge Co.,* 36 U.S. (11 Pet.) 420 (1837).
35. *Munn,* 94 U.S. at 124. Waite continued, "A body politic is a social compact by which the whole people covenants with each citizen, and each citizen with the whole people, that all shall be governed by certain laws for the common good."
36. Ibid., at 125.
37. Ibid., at 148, Field dissenting.
38. Jewett, "Brief," 662.
39. R. Harris to Schuylar Colfax, March 12, 1877, R. Harris out-letters, president's office, Burlington Archives, Newberry Library. The actual quote is "if this is good law, then corporate property is the only property that has no protection from the constitutions of the Western States." See also R. Harris to James Wentworth, March 9, 1877, R. Harris out-letters, president's office, Burlington Archives, Newberry Library.
40. *Debates and Proceedings of the Constitutional Convention of the State of California,* C. B. Willis and P. K. Stockton, official stenographers, 3 vols. (Sacramento, 1880), 1:377.
41. The address of Governor Andrew R. McGill, *Minneapolis Tribune,* January 6, 1887, cited in Richard C. Cortner, *The Iron Horse and the Constitution: Railroads and the Transformation of the Fourteenth Amendment* (Westport, Conn.: Greenwood Press, 1993), 22–23.
42. *Minneapolis Tribune,* December 24, 1887, cited in Cortner, *Iron Horse and the Constitution,* 38.
43. See Ely, *Chief Justiceship of Melville W. Fuller,* 57–127.
44. See *New State Ice Company v. Liebmann,* 285 U.S. 262 (1932); *Nebbia v. New York,* 291 U.S. 502 (1934).
45. Magrath, *Morrison R. Waite,* 192–93.
46. For a detailed historiography covering both the traditional and the modern interpretations of the era, see William M. Wiecek, *The Lost World of Classical Legal Thought: Law and Ideology in America 1886–1937* (New York: Oxford University Press, 1998), 253–77; I have also discussed the competing versions in more detail in Paul Kens, "*Lochner v. New York,* Tradition or Change in Constitutional Law," *NYU Journal of Law and Liberty* 1 (2005): 404–31. For early expressions of the modern view, see Charles W. McCurdy, "Justice Field and the Jurisprudence of Government-Business Relations: Some Parameters of Laissez-Faire Constitutionalism, 1863–1897," *Journal of American History* 61 (1975): 970–1005; Charles W. McCurdy, "The Roots of Liberty of Contract Reconsidered: Major Premises in the Law of Employment," *Yearbook of the Supreme Court Historical Society* (1984): 20–33; Howard Gillman, *The Constitution Besieged: The Rise and Demise of Lochner Era Police Powers Jurisprudence* (Durham, N.C.: Duke University Press, 1993).
47. Wiecek, *Lost World of Classical Legal Thought,* 112, notes, "All Justices of the Supreme Court in the last third of the nineteenth century agreed with Madison that the fundamental challenge of American Constitutionalism was mediating between the power of government and the liberty of the individual."

48. *Chicago, Milwaukee, & St. Paul Railway v. Minnesota,* 134 U.S. 418 (1890). See James W. Ely Jr., "The Railroad Question Revisited: *Chicago, Milwaukee & St. Paul Railway v. Minnesota* and Constitutional Limits on State Regulations," *Great Plains Quarterly* 12 (Spring 1992): 121–34.

49. *Davidson v. New Orleans,* 96 U.S. (6 Otto.) 97, 103 (1878).

50. Ibid., at 104.

51. Michael A. Ross, *Justice of Shattered Dreams: Samuel Freeman Miller and the Supreme Court during the Civil War Era* (Baton Rouge: Louisiana State University Press, 2003), 233.

52. Ibid., 232–34.

53. *Davidson,* 96 U.S. at 102. In a concurring opinion Justice Bradley was even stronger in his recognition of what has come to be called substantive due process, writing, "It seems to me that private property may be taken by a state without due process of law in other ways than by mere enactment, or want of judicial proceeding." Yet Bradley also would defer to the "large discretion every legislative power has of making wide modifications in the forms of procedure in each case, according as the laws, habits, customs, and preferences of the people of the particular State may require." Ibid., at 106–7.

54. Miller noted that it is impossible "to define what it is for a State to deprive a person of life, liberty, or property without due process of law, in terms which would cover every exercise of power thus forbidden to the State, and exclude those which are not." He thus concluded that the only way to determine the reach of the due process guarantee was through the gradual process of judicial inclusion and exclusion. Ibid., at 104.

55. Ibid., at 104–5. The state law allowed a property owner to appeal the assessment to the state courts. This means that there was no question of proper procedure. One might argue that this is a significant point, but I have ignored it in order to simplify the account.

56. *Railroad Company v. Richmond,* 96 U.S. (6 Otto.) 521, 529 (1878). The Court first rejected the company's claim that the ordinance violated the contract clause. Justice Strong dissented without comment. 96 U.S. at 529.

57. *Beer Company v. Massachusetts,* 97 U.S. (7 Otto.) 25, 27 (1878).

58. *New Jersey v. Yard,* 95 U.S. (5 Otto.) 104 (1877).

59. *Edwards v. Kearzey,* 96 U.S. (6 Otto.) 595 (1878).

60. *Fertilizing Company v. Hyde Park,* 97 U.S. (7 Otto.) 659, 664 (1878).

61. Ibid., at 680, Strong dissenting.

62. Ibid., at 666. Justice Miller agreed with Strong on the general principle that if the public welfare requires that a company's property be destroyed, the community ought to pay for it by condemning the property, but he ultimately agreed with Swayne that the power of the legislature to abate a nuisance could only be limited by express terms of the contract. Ibid., at 671, Miller concurring.

63. See Chapter 4, text accompanying notes 30–36.

64. *Bartemeyer v. Iowa,* 85 U.S. (18 Wall.) 129 (1874). See Chapter 1, text accompanying notes 71–72.

65. *Beer Company,* 97 U.S. at 32. *Stone v. Mississippi* 101 U.S. (11 Otto.) 814 (1880), applied similar reasoning to a state law prohibiting lotteries.

Chapter 6: Too Big to Be Allowed to Fail

1. Robert V. Bruce, *1877: Year of Violence* (1959; repr., Chicago: Quadrangle Books, 1970), 78.

2. Philip S. Foner, *The Great Labor Uprising of 1877* (New York: Monad Press, 1977), 231–40, provides a chronology.

3. This story is told in ibid., 61–75. I have summarized Foner's account here. The story is also covered in Bruce, *1877,* 159–83. Another view of the causes and impact of the Great Strike

is found in David O. Stowell, *Streets, Railroads, and the Great Strike of 1877* (Chicago: University of Chicago Press, 1999).

4. Ari Hoogenboom, *The Presidency of Rutherford B. Hayes* (Lawrence: University Press of Kansas, 1988), 81.

5. Foner, *Great Labor Uprising*, 40.

6. Gereld G. Eggert, *Railroad Labor Disputes: The Beginnings of Federal Strike Policy* (Ann Arbor: University of Michigan Press, 1967), 27, citing U.S. Revised Statutes, Sec. 5297.

7. Foner, *Great Labor Uprising*, 40; Hoogenboom, *Presidency of Rutherford B. Hayes*, 85.

8. Hoogenboom, *Presidency of Rutherford B. Hayes*, 82.

9. Bruce, *1877*, 73.

10. Eggert, *Railroad Labor Disputes*, 31.

11. Ibid., 41–47; Hoogenboom, *Presidency of Rutherford B. Hayes*, 86.

12. Eggert, *Railroad Labor Disputes*, 47–53; Hoogenboom, *Presidency of Rutherford B. Hayes*, 87, 89–92.

13. Eggert, *Railroad Labor Disputes*, 36.

14. Ibid., 37.

15. Ibid., 35–41. The Hayes administration backed the judges' decisions by sending troops to support the U.S. marshals whenever necessary and by encouraging other judges to follow the policy established in the Seventh Circuit.

16. Hoogenboom, *Presidency of Rutherford B. Hayes*, 89–90; Bruce, *1877*, 258–59.

17. *In re Debs*, 158 U.S. 564 (1895). Courts used the power of an injunction to order unions to end a strike. Debs, president of the American Railway Union, was convicted of contempt of court for failing to put an end to the Pullman strike.

18. Peter Tufano, "Business Failure, Judicial Intervention, and Financial Innovation: Restructuring U.S. Railroads in the Nineteenth Century," *Business History Review* 71 (Spring 1997): 1–40, 24, provides a graph charting railroad receiverships in the late nineteenth century. Gerald Berk, *Alternative Tracks: The Constitution of American Industrial Order, 1865–1917* (Baltimore: Johns Hopkins University Press, 1994), 47, places receiverships at 30 percent in the 1870s, 15 percent in the 1880s, and 25 percent in the 1890s.

19. Tufano, "Business Failure," 11–12.

20. Berk, *Alternative Tracks*, 47.

21. Bradley Hansen, "The People's Welfare and the Origins of Corporate Reorganization: The Wabash Receivership Reconsidered," *Business History Review* 74 (2000): 377–405, 383–86.

22. For a more detailed discussion of the Wabash receivership, see Berk, *Alternative Tracks*, 51–61; Hansen, "People's Welfare," 380–85; Albro Martin, "Railroads and Equity Receiverships: An Essay on Institutional Change," *Journal of Economic History* 34 (September 1974): 685–709, 685–89.

23. Hansen, "People's Welfare," 381, citing *Quincy, Missouri and Pacific Railroad Co. v. Humphreys*, 145 U.S. 82 (1892). The main purpose of Hansen's article is to demonstrate that the theory supporting these new receiverships and many of the rules governing them were developed earlier.

24. The best explanation of how the receiver certificate works is found in Tufano, "Business Failure," 6–19. I have borrowed the terms "senior creditor" and "super senior creditor" from his account.

25. *Wallace v. Loomis*, 97 U.S. (7 Otto.) 146, 162–63 (1878).

26. Hansen, "People's Welfare," 398.

27. *Union Trust Company of New York v. Illinois Midland Rwy. Co.*, 117 U.S. 434, 455–56 (1886).

28. *Canada Southern Ry. Co. v. Gebhard*, 109 U.S. 527, 536 (1883). This case did not involve receiver's certificates but was similar in that bondholders claimed that a Canadian bankruptcy

law that reduced the value of their bonds violated the U.S. Constitution by taking their property without due process.

29. James W. Ely Jr., *Railroads and American Law,* (Lawrence: University Press of Kansas, 2001), 177.

30. *Fosdick v. Schall,* 99 U.S. (9 Otto.) 235 (1879).

31. Charles Fairman, *Mr. Justice Miller and the Supreme Court 1862–1890* (1939; repr., New York: Russell and Russell, 1966), 243–45.

32. *Barton v. Barbour,* 104 U.S. (14 Otto.) 126 (1881).

33. Ibid., at 136.

34. Ibid., at 130.

35. Ibid., at 135.

36. Ibid., at 137–38, Miller dissenting.

37. *Woodson v. Murdock,* 89 U.S. (22 Wall.) 351, 367 (1874); See Michael A. Ross, *Justice of Shattered Dreams: Samuel Freeman Miller and the Supreme Court during the Civil War* (Baton Rouge: Louisiana State University Press, 2003), 222–24; Fairman, *Mr. Justice Miller,* 235.

38. *Woodson v. Murdock,* 89 U.S. at 368–69.

39. Ibid., at 379, Miller dissenting.

40. Ibid., at 381, Miller dissenting.

41. Ibid.

42. See Hansen, "People's Welfare," 385; Berk, *Alternative Tracks,* 51–62.

43. See Berk, *Alternative Tracks,* 16, 47–72.

44. Tufano, "Business Failure," 38.

45. Ely, *Railroads and American Law,* 177.

46. Martin, "Railroads and Equity Receiverships," 685–709.

47. See Tufano, "Business Failure," 11–12. Ely, *Railroads and American Law,* 178, points out that Congress legislated some changes in 1887. Technically this was a system of receivership. No federal system of bankruptcy existed before Congress enacted bankruptcy law in 1898. I have used the word "bankruptcy" in this chapter to convey the idea to nonexpert readers.

Chapter 7: Sinking Fund

1. Charles Francis Adams Jr., "Railroad Inflation," *North American Review* 108 (January 1869): 130–64, 148; for descriptions of the scheme, see John Hoyt Williams, *A Great and Shining Road: The Epic Story of the Transcontinental Railroad* (New York: Times Books, 1988), 84; Albro Martin, *Railroads Triumphant: The Growth, Rejection, and Rebirth of a Vital American Force* (New York: Oxford University Press, 1992), 285–89. The Central Pacific had a similar scheme. Williams, *Great and Shining Road,* 183–84; Stuart Daggett, *Chapters in the History of the Southern Pacific* (New York: Ronald Press, 1922), 75–82.

2. Williams, *Great and Shining Road;* Stephen Ambrose, *Nothing Like It in the World: The Men Who Built the Transcontinental Railroad 1863–1869* (New York: Simon and Schuster, 2000).

3. Chapter 10 discusses land grants.

4. Williams, *Great and Shining Road,* 42–48; Daggett, *Chapters in the History of the Southern Pacific,* 54–56; Charles Fairman, *Reconstruction and Reunion 1864–88, Part Two,* Oliver Wendell Holmes Devise History of the Supreme Court of the United States (New York: Macmillan, 1987), 7:589–90. The statutes are found at 12 Stat. 489 (1862) and 13 Stat. 356 (1864).

5. Charles Francis Adams Jr., "Railroad Inflation," *North American Review* 108 (January 1869): 130–64.

6. Williams, *Great and Shining Road,* 177, 281–83.

7. Peter Tufano, "Business Failure, Judicial Intervention, and Financial Innovation: Restructuring U.S. Railroads in the Nineteenth Century," *Business History Review* 71 (Spring 1997): 1–40, 24, provides a graph charting railroad receiverships in the late nineteenth century. Gerald Berk,

Alternative Tracks: The Constitution of American Industrial Order, 1865–1917 (Baltimore: Johns Hopkins University Press, 1994), 47, places receiverships at 30 percent in the 1870s, 15 percent in the 1880s, and 25 percent in the 1890s.

    8. Act of 1864, 12 Stat. 489, reproduced in Fairman, *Reconstruction and Reunion,* 7:590.

    9. Fairman, *Reconstruction and Reunion,* 7:591.

    10. *United States v. Union Pacific Railroad Company,* 91 U.S. (1 Otto.) 72 (1875).

    11. Ibid., at 91.

    12. See Paul Kens, *Justice Stephen Field: Shaping Liberty from the Gold Rush to the Gilded Age* (Lawrence: University Press of Kansas, 1997), 197–235.

    13. *San Francisco Examiner,* October 27, 1870, October 22, 1879.

    14. C. Peter Magrath, *Morrison R. Waite: The Triumph of Character* (New York: Macmillan, 1963), 258–60, citing Waite to Field, November 7 and 10, 1875, Morrison R. Waite Papers, Library of Congress, Washington, D.C.

    15. *United States v. Union Pacific Railroad Company,* 98 U.S. (8 Otto.) 569 (1879) [*The Crédit Mobilier Case*]. The language of the statute can be found in Fairman, *Reconstruction and Reunion,* 7:599–600. It can also be found in the case, 98 U.S. at 569–70.

    16. After the first argument in December 1876 the vote was apparently five to four with Bradley, Davis, Swayne, and Clifford in the minority. Davis resigned from the Court on March 7, 1877, and Justice John Harlan took his place. Harlan's presence did not make a difference. He voted the same as Davis. Fairman, *Reconstruction and Reunion,* 7:600, citing Waite's docket book.

    17. Michael A. Ross, *Justice of Shattered Dreams: Samuel Freeman Miller and the Supreme Court during the Civil War Era* (Baton Rouge: Louisiana State University Press, 2003), 167-74.

    18. See Chapter 4, notes 26 and 27, and text accompanying these notes.

    19. Ross, *Justice of Shattered Dreams,* 175.

    20. *United States v. Union Pacific Railroad Company,* 98 U.S. at 619. I have paraphrased this conclusion for simplicity. Miller actually says that none are set forth in the bill of equity authorized by the statute.

    21. The Thurman Act became law when President Hayes signed the bill on May 7, 1878. Fairman, *Reconstruction and Reunion,* 7:604–5.

    22. 20 Stat. 56 (1878).

    23. *Nation,* October 30, 1879, 290; Daggett, *Chapters in the History of the Southern Pacific,* 388, n.29.

    24. *The Sinking Fund Cases,* 99 U.S. (9 Otto.) 700 (1879).

    25. *Munn v. Illinois,* 94 U.S. 113 (1877).

    26. *The Sinking Fund Cases,* 99 U.S. at 722.

    27. Ibid., at 724.

    28. Ibid., at 726.

    29. Ibid., at 718.

    30. Ibid., at 732–38, Strong dissenting.

    31. Ibid., at 749, Bradley dissenting.

    32. Ibid., at 756–58, Field dissenting.

    33. Ibid., at 746–47, Bradley dissenting.

    34. Ibid., at 747, Bradley dissenting; Ibid., at 751, Field dissenting; Ibid., at 731, Strong dissenting.

    35. Ibid., at 746, Bradley dissenting; Ibid., at 759–60, Field dissenting.

    36. David Colton Letters, September 20, 1878; *San Francisco Chronicle,* April 18, 1885. Carl Brent Swisher, *Stephen J. Field: Craftsman of the Law* (1930; repr., Hamden, Conn.: Archon Books, 1963), 247, 240, doubts the authenticity of this letter; Magrath, *Morrison R. Waite,* 231, does not.

    37. *The Sinking Fund Cases,* 99 U.S. at 768–69. I have covered Field's run for the Democratic nomination in Kens, *Justice Stephen Field,* 169–236.

38. *The Sinking Fund Cases,* 99 U.S. at 767, Field dissenting.

39. See, for example, *Railway Company v. Whitton,* 80 U.S. (13 Wall.) 270 (1871).

40. *The Sinking Fund Cases,* 99 U.S. at 719, 722–23.

41. *United States v. Union Pacific Railroad Company,* 98 U.S. at 620.

42. Field's oral delivery was reported by the press; see Fairman, *Reconstruction and Reunion,* 7:611; *New York Times,* October 21, 1879.

43. This is from a letter from Huntington to the *Nation* reprinted in the *New York Tribune* and other newspapers nationwide and cited in Magrath, *Morrison R. Waite,* 235. See *Galveston Daily News,* November 7, 1879.

Chapter 8: A Change Is Gonna Come

1. This story is told and some of the letters reprinted in C. Peter Magrath, *Morrison R. Waite: A Triumph of Character* (New York: Macmillan, 1963), 236–43.

2. David N. Atkinson, *Leaving the Bench: Supreme Court Justices at the End* (Lawrence: University Press of Kansas, 1999), 57–58.

3. For background on Woods, I have relied upon Clare Cushman, ed., *The Supreme Court Justices: Illustrated Biographies 1789–1995,* 2nd ed. (Washington, D.C.: Congressional Quarterly, 1995), 221–25; Donald Grier Stephenson Jr., *The Waite Court: Justices, Rulings, and Legacy* (Santa Barbara, Calif.: ABC-CLIO, 2003), 117–21. For another treatment of the changes in court personnel, see Charles Fairman, *Reconstruction and Reunion 1864–88, Part Two,* Oliver Wendell Holmes Devise History of the Supreme Court of the United States (New York: Macmillan, 1987), 7:520–32.

4. Magrath, *Morrison R. Waite,* 236–43, leaves this impression.

5. For the relationship between Hayes and Matthews, see ibid., 243; Cushman, *Supreme Court Justices,* 228–29; Stephenson, *Waite Court,* 124–25; John Anthony Maltese, *The Selling of Supreme Court Nominees* (Baltimore: Johns Hopkins University Press, 1995), 38–39; Scott H. Ainsworth and John Anthony Maltese, "National Grange Influence on the Supreme Court Confirmation of Stanley Matthews," *Social Science History* 20 (Spring 1996): 41–62, 47–48.

6. Ari Hoogenboom, *The Presidency of Rutherford B. Hayes* (Lawrence: University Press of Kansas, 1988), 46–50.

7. Cushman, *Supreme Court Justices,* 175; Stephenson, *Waite Court,* 68; Atkinson, *Leaving the Bench,* 58–59. Although the *Washington Post,* January 27, 1881, Proquest Historical Newspapers (1877–1991), reported that Swayne was forced out, one would wonder what power a departing president would have to do that.

8. *New York Times,* January 27, 1881.

9. Ibid., February 2, 1881.

10. Ibid., February 8, 1881.

11. Ibid., February 11, 1881.

12. Magrath, *Morrison R. Waite,* 244.

13. *New York Times,* February 15, 1881; Magrath, *Morrison R. Waite,* 244; Maltese, *Selling of Supreme Court Nominees,* 41.

14. Ainsworth and Maltese, "National Grange Influence," 41–62.

15. National Anti-Monopoly League to Hon. G. F. Edmunds, March 15, 1881, Records of the United States Senate, Record Group 46, Judiciary Committee, 47th Congress, NA No. 47B-A5, Matthews, Stanley: Nomination as a Justice of the Supreme Court, National Archives; see also Leonard Rhone, Master of the Pennsylvania State Grange, to the Senate Judiciary Committee, March 11, 1881, in the same file of the National Archives.

16. The clippings were submitted by the New York Board of Trade and Transportation Records of the United States Senate, Record Group 46, Judiciary Committee, 47th Congress,

NA No. 47B-A5, Matthews, Stanley: Nomination as a Justice of the Supreme Court, National Archives; see also *Chicago Tribune,* March 18, 1881, reprinting the comments found in other newspapers.

17. Magrath, *Morrison R. Waite,* 244; see also Maltese, *Selling of Supreme Court Nominees,* 43–44, quoting a similar statement in the *New York Sun.*

18. *New York Times,* April 10, 1883, obituary; *Peik v. Chicago & North-Western Railway Co.,* 94 U.S. (4 Otto.) 164 (1877).

19. C. E. Perkins to Hon. James F. Wilson, C. E. Perkins to Mr. Wilson, April 19, 1881, and C. E. Perkins to Mr. Wilson, May 5, 1881, C. E. Perkins out-letters (Personal), Burlington Archives, Newberry Library, Chicago.

20. Ainsworth and Maltese, "National Grange Influence," 49, notes that the vote was thirty-six to thirty-five counting paired senators; Cushman, *Supreme Court Justices,* 229.

21. *New York Times,* May 13, 1881. Another newspaper, however, reported that due to confusion in pairings, there was probably one other vote in his favor. *Washington Post,* May 13, 1881, Proquest Historical Newspapers.

22. Cushman, *Supreme Court Justices,* 231–35; Stephenson, *Waite Court,* 127–33; Atkinson, *Leaving the Bench,* 59–61. Gray joined Bradley and Lamar dissenting in the Minnesota milk rate case. *Chicago, Milwaukee, & St. Paul Railway v. Minnesota,* 134 U.S. 418, 461 (1890).

23. Cushman, *Supreme Court Justices,* 236–40; Stephenson, *Waite Court,* 133–37. With respect to significant opinions on constitutional issues, Blatchford wrote the majority opinions in the Minnesota milk rate case, *Chicago, Milwaukee, & St. Paul Railway v. Minnesota,* 134 U.S. 418 (1890); and *Budd v. New York,* 143 U.S. 517 (1892).

24. Although I have not attempted a precise count, a Westlaw or Lexus search of phrases like "Fourteenth Amendment," "due process," or "Munn" reveals a striking increase in the number of cases.

25. Thomas C. Cochran, *Railroad Leaders 1845–1890: The Business Mind in Action* (New York: Russell and Russell, 1965), 201.

26. *Ruggles v. Illinois,* 108 U.S. 526, 531 (1883).

27. Ibid., at 535–41, Harlan concurring.

28. Ibid., at 541, Field concurring.

29. *Spring Valley Water-Works v. Schottler,* 110 U.S. 347, 373–76 (1884), Field dissenting.

30. Ibid., at 364, Field dissenting.

31. Ibid., at 352–54.

32. *Stone v. Farmer's Loan & Trust Co.,* 116 U.S. 307, 342–47 (1886), Field dissenting.

33. Ibid., at 331.

34. *Butchers' Union Slaughter-House & Live-Stock Co. v. Crescent City Live-Stock Landing & Slaughter-House Co.,* 111 U.S. 746 (1884).

35. See *Missouri Pacific Ry. Co. v. Humes,* 115 U.S. 512 (1885) (multiple damages); *Head v. Amoskeag Manufacturing Co.,* 113 U.S. 9 (1885) (mill dam act); *Sands v. Manistee River Improvement Co.,* 123 U.S. 288 (1887) (toll for floating logs); *Carter v. Greenhow,* 114 U.S. 317 (1885); *Little Rock and Ft. Smith Ry. v. Worthen,* 120 U.S. 97 (1887) (tax cases); *Hagar v. Reclamation District,* 111 U.S. 701 (1884); *Provident Inst. for Savings v. City of Jersey City,* 113 U.S. 506 (1885); *Wurts v. Hoagland,* 114 U.S. 606 (1885) (cases involving reclamation and water lands); *Vance v. Vance,* 108 U.S. 514 (1883); *Gross v. U.S. Mortgage Co.,* 108 U.S. 477 (1883) (rules regarding mortgages). The only cases I found in which a statute was overturned on Fourteenth Amendment grounds were not really economic regulations. *Campbell v. Holt,* 115 U.S. 620 (1885) (retroactively changing statute of limitations takes a vested right); *State of Louisiana ex rel. Folsom v. City of New Orleans,* 109 U.S. 285 (1883) (state law limiting party's ability to collect judgment against city violates due process clause).

36. *Mugler v. Kansas,* 123 U.S. 623, 662 (1887).

37. Tinsley E. Yarbrough, *Judicial Enigma: The First Justice Harlan* (New York: Oxford University Press, 1995), 201–5; Linda Przybyszewski, *The Republic According to John Marshall Harlan* (Chapel Hill: University of North Carolina Press, 1999), 191–96.

38. *Mugler,* 123 U.S. at 668.

39. Ibid., at 661.

40. Ibid., at 675–78, Field dissenting.

41. *Chicago, Milwaukee, & St. Paul Railway v. Minnesota,* 134 U.S. 418 (1890). This statement led Justice Bradley to complain that the majority's decision "practically overrules *Munn v. Illinois.*" Ibid., at 461, Bradley dissenting. See James W. Ely Jr., "The Railroad Question Revisited: Chicago, Milwaukee & St. Paul Railway v. Minnesota and the Constitutional Limits on State Regulations," *Great Plains Quarterly* 12 (Spring 1992): 121–34.

42. *Smyth v. Ames,* 169 U.S. 466 (1898).

43. See James W. Ely Jr., *The Chief Justiceship of Melville W. Fuller, 1888–1910* (Columbia: University of South Carolina Press, 1995), 83–110.

44. I have described this part of the California constitutional convention in more detail in Paul Kens, *Justice Stephen Field: Shaping Liberty from the Gold Rush to the Gilded Age* (Lawrence: University Press of Kansas, 1997), 217–20.

45. *San Mateo v. Southern Pacific Railroad Company,* 13 F. 741, 738.

46. *San Mateo v. Southern Pacific Railroad Company,* 13 F. 722 (C.C.D. Cal. 1882); *Santa Clara v. Southern Pacific Railroad Company,* 18 F. 385 (C.C.D. Cal. 1883).

47. *Debates and Proceedings of the Constitutional Convention of the State of California,* C. B. Willis and P. K. Stockton, official stenographers, 3 vols. (Sacramento, 1880), 1:480, cited in Kens, *Justice Stephen Field,* 218.

48. Ibid., 1:376, cited in Kens, *Justice Stephen Field,* 218.

49. *Santa Clara,* 18 F. at 398; *San Mateo,* 13 F. at 740, 741, 748.

50. *San Mateo,* 13 F. at 743–44; *Santa Clara,* 18 F. at 402–3; Herbert Hovenkamp, "The Classical Corporation in American Legal Thought," *Georgetown Law Review* 76 (1998): 1593–1689, 1640–50. Gregory A. Mark, "The Personification of the Business Corporation in American Law," *University of Chicago Law Review* 54 (Autumn 1987): 1441–1483, 1455–64, also calls this "partnership analysis."

51. *San Mateo,* 13 F. at 741.

52. R. Hal Williams, *Democratic Party in California Politics, 1880–1896* (Stanford, Calif.: Stanford University Press, 1973), 32, citing *Los Angles Times,* June 8, 1882; for a detailed description of the politics surrounding settlement, see ibid., 35–39.

53. *Santa Clara County v. Southern Pacific Railroad,* 118 U.S. 394 (1886).

54. Magrath, *Morrison R. Waite,* 223–24, citing Davis to Waite May 26, 1886, Waite Papers, Library of Congress, Washington, D.C.; Waite to Davis, May 31, 1886, Bancroft Davis Papers, Library of Congress, Washington, D.C.

55. *Santa Clara County v. Southern Pacific Railroad,* 118 U.S. at 396.

56. *Smyth v. Ames,* 169 U.S. 466, 522 (1898).

57. *First National Bank of Boston v. Bellotti,* 435 U.S. 765 (1978). Melvin I. Urofsky and Paul Finkleman, *A March of Liberty: A Constitutional History of the United States,* vol. 2, *From 1877 to the Present,* 2nd ed. (New York: Oxford University Press, 2002), 507; David M. O'Brien, *Constitutional Law and Politics,* vol. 2, *Civil Rights and Civil Liberties,* 7th ed. (New York: W. W. Norton, 2008), 266–67, provide textbook examples of the acceptance of this interpretation.

58. *Spring Valley Water-Works,* 110 U.S. at 552.

59. *Pembina Consolidated Silver Mining & Milling Co. v. Pennsylvania,* 125 U.S. 181, 187–89, 184 (1888). See also *Cincinnati New Orleans and Texas Pacific Railroad Co. v. Commonwealth of Kentucky,* 115 U.S. 321 (1885); *Home Insurance Co. v. New York,* 119 U.S. 129 (1886); *Fire Association of*

Philadelphia v. New York, 119 U.S. 110 (1886); *National Bank of Redemption v. City of Boston,* 125 U.S. 60 (1888).

60. *Minneapolis and St. Louis Railway Co. v. Beckwith,* 129 U.S. 26, 28 (1889).

Chapter 9: Interstate Commerce

1. James W. Ely Jr., "'The Railroad System Has Burst through State Limits': Railroads and Interstate Commerce 1830–1920," *Arkansas Law Review* 55 (2003): 933–80, 961; see also Donald Grier Stephenson Jr., *The Waite Court: Justices, Rulings, and Legacy* (Santa Barbara, Calif.: ABC-CLIO, 2003), 200–219; Felix Frankfurter, *The Commerce Clause under Marshall, Taney, and Waite* (Chapel Hill: University of North Carolina Press, 1937).

2. *Gibbon v. Ogden,* 22 U.S. (9 Wheat.) 1 (1824).

3. *Wilson v. Black Bird Marsh Co.,* 27 U.S. (2 Pet.) 245 (1829).

4. *Cooley v. Board of Wardens,* 53 U.S. (12 How.) 299 (1852).

5. *Brown v. Maryland,* 25 U.S. (12 Wheat.) 419 (1827).

6. *Brown v. Houston,* 114 U.S. 622 (1885).

7. *Coe v. Town of Errol,* 116 U.S. 517 (1886).

8. *Robbins v. Taxing District of Shelby County Tennessee,* 120 U.S. 489 (1887).

9. *Corson v. Maryland,* 120 U.S. 502 (1887). For a more detailed discussion of taxation of peddlers and drummers, see Charles Fairman, *Reconstruction and Reunion 1864–88, Part Two,* Oliver Wendell Holmes Devise History of the Supreme Court of the United States (New York: Macmillan, 1987), 7:663–70.

10. *State Tax on Railroad Gross Receipts Reading Railroad Company v. Pennsylvania,* 82 U.S. (15 Wall.) 284, 299 (1873), Miller dissenting.

11. *Baltimore & Ohio Railroad Co. v. Maryland,* 88 U.S. (21 Wall.) 456 (1875).

12. *Case of the State Freight Tax,* 82 U.S. (15 Wall.) 232 (1873). The Court had overruled a Pennsylvania tax on all freight carried in the state. The tax applied to corporations chartered in Pennsylvania as well as to those that were chartered in another state. On the same day, in *State Tax on Railway Gross Receipts,* 82 U.S. (15 Wall.) 284 (1873), the Court upheld another Pennsylvania law that taxed the gross receipts of all railroads incorporated by the state. See also *The Delaware Railroad Tax,* 85 U.S. (18 Wall.) 206 (1874).

13. *Gloucester Ferry Company v. Commonwealth of Pennsylvania,* 114 U.S. 196 (1885).

14. *Philadelphia & Southern Mail S.S. Co. v. Commonwealth of Pennsylvania,* 122 U.S. 326 (1887). For a more detailed discussion, see Fairman, *Reconstruction and Reunion,* 7:680–96.

15. *State Tax on Railway Gross Receipts,* 82 U.S. at 299.

16. Thomas M. Cooley, *A Treatise on the Constitutional Limitations Which Rest Upon the Legislative Power of the States of the American Union,* 5th ed. (Boston: Little, Brown, 1883), 722.

17. *Morgan's Louisiana & T. R. & S. S. Co. v. Board of Health of the State of Louisiana,* 118 U.S. 455 (1886).

18. *Railroad Company v. Husen,* 95 U.S. (5 Otto.) 465, 472 (1878). The statute put the prohibition in place for seven months of the year and made an exception for cattle passing through the state and never unloaded. The exception carried a proviso, however. It held railroads responsible for incidents of disease occurring along their routes.

19. *City of New York v. Miln,* 36 U.S. (11 Pet.) 102 (1837).

20. *The Passenger Cases,* 48 U.S. (7 How.) at 283 (1849).

21. *Henderson v. Mayor of New York,* 92 U.S. (2 Otto.) 259, 269 (1876).

22. Ibid., at 270.

23. Ibid.

24. *Chy Lung v. Freeman,* 92 U.S. (2 Otto.) at 275, 277 (1876).

25. Ibid., at 278.

26. Ibid., at 280.

27. *Hall v. Decuir*, 95 U.S. (5 Otto.) 485, 490–91 (1878).

28. Ibid., at 488–89. Justice Clifford, concurring, maintained that this statute conflicted with an act of Congress that governed all ships and vessels licensed to carry on trade in the United States.

29. Ibid., at 489.

30. Ely, "Railroads and Interstate Commerce," 945.

31. See *Smith v. Alabama*, 124 U.S. 465 (1888) (licensing of engineers and conductors); *Nashville, Chattanooga & St. Louis Rwy. v. Alabama*, 128 U.S. 96 (1888) (prohibiting color-blind individuals from working on the railroads).

32. Ely, "Railroads and Interstate Commerce," 948–61.

33. Thomas M. Cooley, *A Constitutional Limitations Which Rest Upon the Legislative Power of the States of the American Union*, 3rd ed. (Boston: Little, Brown, 1874), 586. Developments during the Waite Court era did not cause Cooley to change his mind. He makes the same complaint in the fourth edition (1878), 731–32; the fifth edition (1883), 724; and the sixth edition (1890), 722.

34. *Peik v. Chicago & N.W. Ry.*, 94 U.S. (4 Otto.) 164, 175 (1877).

35. Ibid., at 177–78.

36. See Herbert Hovenkamp, *Enterprise and American Law, 1836–1937* (Cambridge: Mass.: Harvard University Press, 1991), 36–41.

37. Ibid., 137, notes that the historical record shows rather consistent lobbying and legislation by the railroads against state regulation, but substantial support for federal regulation.

38. Discussion of the complexity is found in Gabriel Kolko, *Railroads and Regulation 1877–1916* (Princeton, N.J.: Princeton University Press, 1965); Thomas W. Gilligan, William J. Marshall, and Barry R. Weingast, "Regulation and the Theory of Legislative Choice: The Interstate Commerce Act of 1887," *Journal of Law and Economics* 32, no. 1 (April 1989): 35–61; Herbert Hovenkamp, "Regulatory Conflict in the Gilded Age: Federalism and the Railroad Problem," *Yale Law Journal* 97 (1988): 1017–72.

39. Ely, "Railroads and Interstate Commerce," 934.

40. Kolko, *Railroads and Regulation*, 21–23; Gilligan, Marshall, and Weingast, "Regulation and the Theory of Legislative Choice," 48.

41. Solon J. Buck, *The Granger Movement: A Study of Agricultural Organization and Its Political, Economic, and Social Manifestations, 1870–1880* (1913; repr., Lincoln: University of Nebraska Press, 1963).

42. Ida M. Tarbell, *The History of the Standard Oil Company* (New York: Macmillan, 1933), 1:167–71 (Pennsylvania oil producers), 214–15; Lee Benson, *Merchants, Farmers, and Railroads: Railroad Regulation and New York Politics, 1850–1887* (Cambridge, Mass.: Harvard University Press, 1955) (New York merchants); Kolko, *Railroads and Regulation* (railroads); Keith T. Poole and Howard Rosenthal, "The Enduring Nineteenth-Century Battle for Economic Regulation: The Interstate Commerce Act Revisited," *Journal of Law and Economics* 36, no. 2 (October 1993): 837–60 (Southerners).

43. *Wabash, St. Louis, and Pacific Railway Co. v. Illinois*, 118 U.S. 557 (1886).

44. Ibid., at 566.

45. Fairman, *Reconstruction and Reunion*, 7:678, notes that the votes were: Blatchford, Matthews, Woods, Harlan, Field, and Miller to overrule; Gray, Bradley, and Waite dissenting.

46. *Wabash, St. Louis and Pacific*, 118 U.S. at 566–68.

47. Ibid., at 569.

48. Ibid., at 572–73.

49. Ibid., at 586–87, Bradley dissenting.

50. Ibid., at 580, Bradley dissenting.

51. Charles Fairman, *Mr. Justice Miller and the Supreme Court 1862–1890* (1939; repr., New York: Russell and Russell, 1966), 312, implies that Miller did envision a national economy because he took a broad view of Congress's power to regulate interstate commerce.

52. *Wabash, St. Louis and Pacific,* 118 U.S. at 577.

53. For a discussion of the process of compromise, see Kolko, *Railroads and Regulation,* 32–44; Gilligan, Marshall, and Weingast, "Regulation and the Theory of Legislative Choice," 35–61; Jordan Jay Hillman, *Competition and Railroad Price Discrimination: Legal Precedent and Economic Policy* (Evanston, Ill.: The Transportation Center at Northwestern University, 1968).

54. Fairman, *Mr. Justice Miller,* 314, implies that this was the case and refers to a letter in which Justice Miller claims that his decision had such an impact.

55. Kolko, *Railroads and Regulation,* 33.

56. James W. Ely Jr., *The Chief Justiceship of Melville W. Fuller 1888–1910* (Columbia: University of South Carolina Press, 1995), 127–49, provides an account of commerce development during the Fuller era. William M. Wiecek, *The Lost World of Classical Legal Thought: Law and Ideology in America 1886–1937* (New York: Oxford University Press, 1998), 143–49, provides another point of view.

57. See William Leuchtenburg, *The Supreme Court Reborn: Constitutional Revolution in the Age of Roosevelt* (New York: Oxford University Press, 1995); Barry Cushman, *Rethinking the New Deal Court: The Structure of a Constitutional Revolution* (New York: Oxford University Press, 1998).

Chapter 10: The Big Country

1. James D. Richardson, *Messages and Papers of the Presidents* (1898), 4:588; Polk's message to the Senate and House of Representatives (July 6, 1848), as quoted in Thomas R. Hietala, *Manifest Design: Anxious Aggrandizement in Late Jacksonian America* (Ithaca, N.Y.: Cornell University Press, 1985), 89.

2. Elliot West, *The Contested Plains: Indians, Goldseekers, and the Rush to Colorado* (Lawrence: University Press of Kansas, 1998), captures how claims to a particular geographic location changed over time.

3. Stuart Banner, *How the Indians Lost Their Land: Law and Power on the Frontier* (Cambridge, Mass.: Belknap Press of Harvard University Press, 2005), 228–56.

4. Ibid., 239. I have relied heavily on Banner (ibid.) and John R. Wunder, "No More Treaties: The Resolution of 1871 and the Alienation of Indian Rights to their Homelands," in *Working the Range: Essays on the History of Western Land Management and the Environment,* ed. John R. Wunder (Westport, Conn.: Greenwood Press, 1985), 39–56. See also David E. Wilkins, "The Reinvigoration of the Doctrine of Implied Repeals: A Requiem for Indigenous Treaty Rights," *American Journal of Legal History* 43, no. 1 (January 1999): 1–26.

5. *Cherokee Tobacco,* 78 U.S. (11 Wall.) 616 (1871).

6. *Lone Wolf v. Hitchcock,* 187 U.S. 553 (1903); Blue Clark, *Lone Wolf v. Hitchcock: Treaty Rights and Indian Law at the End of the Nineteenth Century* (Lincoln: University of Nebraska Press, 1999).

7. *Butz v. Northern Pac. R. Co.,* 119 U.S. 55 (1886).

8. *Dubuque & S.C.R. Co. v. Des Moines Valley R. Co.,* 109 U.S 329 (1883); *United States v. Carpenter,* 111 U.S. 347 (1884).

9. *Dubuque & S.C.R. Co. v. Des Moines Valley R. Co.,* 109 U.S. 329 (1883); *Noonan v. Caledonia Gold Mine Co.,* 121 U.S. 393 (1887); *Butz v. Northern Pac. R. Co.,* 119 U.S. 55 (1886); *Leavenworth, Lawrence, and Galveston Railroad Company v. United States,* 92 U.S. (2 Otto.) 733, 745 (1876).

10. Paul Gates, *History of Public Land Law Development* (Washington, D.C.: U.S. Government Printing Office, 1968), 390–92.

11. George Washington Julian, *Speeches on Political Questions* (New York: Hurd and Houghton, 1872), 55.

12. Gates, *History of Public Land Law Development*, 388–89, 395.

13. Ibid., 394.

14. Julian, *Speeches on Political Questions*, 51. Reformers advocated making homesteads inalienable, placing restrictions on inheritance, and providing that land revert to the government under certain conditions. Although the Homestead Act did contain some protections from misuse, none of these more radical provisions to avoid accumulation of large blocks found their way into law. Gates, *History of Public Land Law Development*, 392–97.

15. Gates, *History of Public Land Law Development*, 435–63; Paul Wallace Gates, "The Homestead Act in an Incongruous Land System," *American Historical Review* 41 (July 1936): 652–81. Gates also noted that a variety of other laws dealing with swamp lands, timber lands, and school lands also closed much land to homesteading. Gates, *History of Public Land Law Development*, 397.

16. *United States v. Vallejo*, 66 U.S. (1 Black) 541 (1862).

17. *Frisbie v. Whitney*, 76 U.S. (9 Wall.) 187 (1869).

18. Ibid., at 191.

19. Ibid.; see Paul W. Gates, *Land and Law in California: Essays on Land Policies* (Ames: Iowa State University Press, 1991), 209–28.

20. *The Yosemite Valley Case*, 82 U.S. (15 Wall.) 77 (1873), also referred to as *Hutchings v. Low*.

21. Alfred Runte, *Yosemite: The Embattled Wilderness* (Lincoln: University of Nebraska Press, 1990), Chs. 2, 3. Hutchings was one of the earliest explorers of the Yosemite Valley and campaigned to draw the nation's attention to the valley. However, modern observers tend to portray Hutchings's battle to retain his land as a greedy campaign to exploit a national treasure. Although Runte's account is measured and fair, it emphasizes the threat Hutchings's claim posed to conservation of the park.

22. *The Yosemite Valley Case*, 82 U.S. (15 Wall.) 77 (1873); see Brief for the Plaintiff in Error, microfilm records.

23. *The Yosemite Valley Case*, 82 U.S. at 84.

24. Ibid., at 87.

25. *Atherton v. Fowler*, 96 U.S. (6 Otto.) 513 (1878), was a dispute over hay that had been cut in the interim between when the Suscol grant was declared invalid and the act of Congress. The majority ruled that the Suscol claimant had a right to recover for the value of the hay. Chief Justice Waite dissented from the judgment, reasoning that because the hay was cut during a time when ownership of the land was in question, the eventual owner did not have a right to recover its value.

26. *Hosmer v. Wallace*, 97 U.S. (7 Otto.) 575 (1879). Two years earlier Field had ruled that land that the surveyor-general had expressly excluded from a grant was not open to settlement while the claim was being appealed in the courts. *Van Reynegan v. Bolton*, 95 U.S. (5 Otto.) 33 (1877). See also *Trenouth v. City of San Francisco*, 100 U.S. (10 Otto.) 251 (1880). The same principles did not seem to apply when the state of California made a claim to land within a disputed Mexican grant. *Frasher v. O'Connor*, 115 U.S. 102 (1885); *Mower v. Fletcher*, 116 U.S. 380 (1886); *McCreery v. Haskell*, 119 U.S. 327 (1886); *Durand v. Martin*, 120 U.S. 366 (1887).

27. *Lamb v. Davenport*, 85 U.S. (18 Wall.) 307 (1873); *Shipley v. Cowan*, 91 U.S. (1 Otto.) 330 (1876); *Quinn v. Chapman*, 111 U.S. 445 (1884).

28. *United States v. Schurz*, 102 U.S. (12 Otto.) 378 (1880).

29. *Wirth v. Branson*, 98 U.S. (8 Otto.) 118 (1878). In land disputes that turned on technicalities the Court tended to apply traditional rules of interpretation. See *Shipley v. Cowan*, 91 U.S. at 338, *Aurrecoechea v. Bangs*, 114 U.S. 381 (1885); *Morrison v. Stalnaker*, 104 U.S. (14 Otto.) 213 (1881).

30. See Richard Griswold del Castillo, *The Treaty of Guadalupe Hidalgo: A Legacy of Conflict* (Norman: University of Oklahoma Press, 1990), 180, 182, 190; Charles I. Bevans, ed., *Treaties and Other International Agreements, 1776–1949* (Washington, D.C.: Department of State, 1972), 9:791–806.

31. An Act to Ascertain and Settle Private Land Claims in the State of California, 9 Stat. 631 (March 3, 1851).

32. *Frémont v. United States,* 58 U.S. (17 How.) 542 (1855).

33. See Lewis Grossman, "John C. Frémont, Mariposa and the Collision of Mexican and American Law," *Western Legal History* 6 (Winter/Spring 1993): 17–50.

34. See Carl Brent Swisher, *History of the Supreme Court of the United States: The Taney Period 1836–1864,* Oliver Wendell Holmes Devise History of the Supreme Court (New York: Macmillan, 1974), 5:780.

35. *Frémont v. United States,* 58 U.S. at 558. Although the California Land Act allowed the commission and the courts to consider Mexican usages and customs to help determine the validity of a grant, the Court in *Frémont* used them to a much greater end. The decision created a revised general guideline that significantly reduced the burden of proof and made it much easier for those claiming large estates to prove that their claims were valid.

36. *United States v. D'Aquirre,* 68 U.S. (1 Wall.) 311 (1863); *Malarin v. United States,* 68 U.S. (1 Wall.) 282 (1863); *United States v. Yorba,* 68 U.S. (1 Wall.) 412 (1863); *United States v. Halleck,* 68 U.S. (1 Wall.) 439 (1863). Mexican law limited the size of grants to eleven leagues. Nevertheless in *Tameling v. United States Freehold and Emigration Company,* 93 U.S. 644 (1876); *United States v. Maxwell Land Grant,* 121 U.S. 325 (1887); and *United States v. Maxwell Land Grant,* 122 U.S. 365 (1887), the Court validated grants that exceeded that limit.

37. See, for example, W. W. Robinson, *Land in California* (Berkeley: University of California Press, 1948); Gates, *Land and Law in California.*

38. *Brown v. Bracket,* 88 U.S. (21 Wall.) 387 (1875); *Berreyesa v. United States,* 154 U.S. 623 (1876); *McGarrahan v. Mining Company,* 96 U.S. (6 Otto.) 316 (1878). The Court also handled disputes between competing Mexican land grant claims. *Miller v. Dale,* 92 U.S. (2 Otto.) 473 (1876); *Adams v. Norris,* 103 U.S. (13 Otto.) 591 (1881).

39. *United States v. Throckmorton,* 98 U.S. (8 Otto.) 61 (1878).

40. *Phillips v. Moore,* 100 U.S. (10 Otto.) 208 (1879); *Brownsville v. Cavazos,* 100 U.S. (10 Otto.) 138 (1879); *Hunnicutt v. Peyton,* 102 U.S. (12 Otto.) 333 (1880); and *Gonzales v. Ross,* 120 U.S. 605 (1887), are examples of the Texas cases. Some significant cases from New Mexico will be discussed below.

41. I have discussed this in greater depth in Paul Kens, *Justice Stephen Field: Shaping Liberty from the Gold Rush to the Gilded Age* (Lawrence: University Press of Kansas, 1997), 100–105.

42. *Hoadley v. San Francisco,* 94 U.S. (4 Otto.) 4 (1876); *City and County of San Francisco v. Scott,* 111 U.S. 768 (1884); The other case was *Palmer v. Low,* 98 U.S. (8 Otto.) 1 (1878). Hoadley subsequently claimed that the ordinance violated the contract clause, but the Court rejected that argument as well. *Clark v. City and County of San Francisco,* 124 U.S. 639 (1888).

43. *Robinson v. Anderson,* 121 U.S. 522 (1887); *Phillips v. Mound City Land and Water Ass'n,* 124 U.S. 605 (1888).

44. *Tameling v. United States Freehold and Emigration Company,* 93 U.S. at 663. Davis also made a distinction that the statute that governed Mexican land grants in California expressly provided for judicial review while the statute governing grants in New Mexico and Colorado did not.

45. *United States v. Maxwell Land Grant Co.,* 121 U.S. 325 (1887); rehearing denied at 122 U.S. 365 (1887).

46. Maria E. Montoya, *Translating Property: The Maxwell Land Grant and the Conflict over Land in the American West, 1840–1900* (Lawrence: University Press of Kansas, 2002), 63, 159. Montoya

provides a thorough and nuanced account of the struggles over the grant. I have used her work and the case itself to summarize the facts.

47. Ibid., 52–73.
48. Ibid., 74, 195.
49. Ibid., 107–13.
50. Ibid., 125. Montoya notes that more than half of these claims belonged to Hispanos who had adopted the U.S. land tenure system.
51. *Maxwell Land Grant Co.,* 121 U.S. at 373–75.
52. Ibid., at 381.
53. Ibid., at 382.
54. Montoya, *Translating Property,* 195–99.
55. See Gates, *History of Public Land Law Development,* 341–86.
56. *Rice v. Minnesota & N.W. R. Co.,* 66 U.S. (1 Black) 358, 380 (1861).
57. *Railroad Co. v. Fremont County,* 76 U.S. (9 Wall.) 89, 94 (1869). Some cases involved grants to the state or territory for the purpose of building a railroad.
58. *Schulenberg v. Harriman,* 88 U.S. (21 Wall.) 44 (1875); *Iowa Railroad Land Company v. Courtright,* 88 U.S. (21 Wall.) 310 (1875).
59. *Newhall v. Sanger,* 92 U.S. (2 Otto.) 761 (1876). Charles Fairman, *Reconstruction and Reunion 1864–88, Part Two,* Oliver Wendell Holmes Devise History of the Supreme Court of the United States (New York: Macmillan, 1987), 7:635–46, provides details of the dispute.
60. *Newhall,* 92 U.S. at 766. The dispute did not involve the railroad directly. It was actually between two rivals to the land, one of whom traced his title to the railroad grant.
61. *Leavenworth, Lawrence, and Galveston Railroad Company,* 92 U.S. at 745. For background, see Paul Wallace Gates, *Fifty Million Acres: Conflicts over Kansas Land Policy* (Ithaca, N.Y.: Cornell University Press, 1954); H. Craig Miner and William E. Unrau, *The End of Indian Kansas: A Study of Cultural Revolution, 1854–1871* (Lawrence: Regents Press of Kansas, 1978).
62. *Newhall,* 92 U.S. at 766, Field dissenting.
63. *Leavenworth, Lawrence, and Galveston Railroad Company,* 92 U.S. at 754–55, Field dissenting.
64. Ibid., at 760, Field dissenting.
65. *Ryan v. Railroad Company,* 99 U.S. (9 Otto.) 382 (1879).
66. *United States v. McLaughlin,* 127 U.S. 428 (1888); see also *McLaughlin v. United States,* 107 U.S. 526 (1883).
67. *Railroad Company v. Baldwin,* 103 U.S. (13 Otto.) 426 (1881); *Van Wyck v. Knevals,* 106 U.S. (16 Otto.) 360 (1882); *Walden v. Knevals,* 114 U.S. 373 (1885); *Grinnel v. Railroad Company,* 103 U.S. (13 Otto.) 739 (1881); *Wood v. Railroad Company,* 104 U.S. (14 Otto.) 329 (1881); *Kansas Pacific Railway Co. v. Dunmeyer,* 113 U.S. 629 (1885).
68. *Cedar Rapids & M.R.R. Co. v. Herring,* 110 U.S. 27 (1884); see also *Sioux City and Iowa Falls Town Lot and Land Company v. Griffey,* 143 U.S. 32 (1892).
69. *Schulenberg v. Harriman,* 88 U.S. (21 Wall.) 44 (1875); *Bybee v. Oregon & California Railroad Co.,* 139 U.S. 663 (1890).
70. *Platt v. Union Pacific Railroad Co.,* 99 U.S. (9 Otto.) 48, 64 (1879).
71. Ibid., at 59.
72. Ibid., at 65.
73. Ibid., at 66–67, Bradley dissenting.
74. David J. Bederman, "The Imagery of Injustice at Mussel Slough: Railroad Land Grants, Corporation Law, and the Great Conglomerate West," *Western Legal History* 1 (Summer/Fall 1988): 237–69; Irving McKee, "Notable Memorials to Mussel Slough," *Pacific Historical Review* 17, no. 1 (February 1948): 19–27.
75. *Southern Pacific R. C. v. Orton,* 32 F. 457 (C.C.D. Cal. 1979).
76. Ibid., at 469.

77. Ibid., at 465.
78. *United States v. Burlington and Missouri River Railroad Company,* 98 U.S. (8 Otto.) 334, 341 (1879).

Chapter 11: Equal Rights

1. *Pace v. Alabama,* 106 U.S. 583, 585 (1883).
2. *Bradwell v. Illinois,* 83 U.S. (16 Wall.) 130 (1873).
3. C. Peter Magrath, *Morrison R. Waite: The Triumph of Character* (New York: Macmillan, 1963), 119.
4. *Minor v. Happersett,* 88 U.S. 162 (1874).
5. *Virginia v. Rives,* 100 U.S. at 335; *Ex parte Virginia,* 100 U.S. at 365.
6. *Neal v. Delaware,* 103 U.S. at 407, Waite dissenting.
7. *Baldwin v. Franks,* 120 U.S. 678 (1887).
8. Charles J. McClain, *In Search of Equality: The Chinese Struggle against Discrimination in Nineteenth-Century America* (Berkeley: University of California Press, 1994), 175–76. McClain (ibid., 176–90) also provides a good account of the case in the courts.
9. John R. Wunder, "Anti-Chinese Violence in the American West, 1850–1910," in *Law for the Elephant, Law for the Beaver: Essays in Legal History of the North American West,* ed. John McLaren, Hamar Foster, and Chet Orloff (Pasadena, Calif.: Ninth Circuit Historical Society, 1992), 212–36; Shih-Shan Henry Tsi, *The Chinese Experience in America* (Bloomington: Indiana University Press, 1986), 67–72; Elmer Clarence Sandmeyer, *Anti-Chinese Movement in California* (Urbana: University of Illinois Press, 1939), 40–56.
10. *Baldwin v. Franks,* 120 U.S. at 683. Over time, anti-Chinese activists successfully urged Congress to change the terms of these treaties and eventually prohibit Chinese immigration altogether. For in-depth studies of immigration treaties with China, see Lucy E. Salyer, *Law Harsh as Tigers: Chinese Immigrants and the Shaping of Modern Immigration Law* (Chapel Hill: University of North Carolina Press, 1995); McClain, *In Search of Equality,* 191–219; Tsi, *Chinese Experience in America,* 1986), 56–81.
11. See *Ah Hee v. Crippen,* 19 Cal. 491 (1861); McClain, *In Search of Equality,* 24–29.
12. California Constitution of 1879, Article 19; Sandmeyer, *Anti-Chinese Movement,* 65–72.
13. *Ah Kow v. Nunan,* 12 F. Cas. 252 (C.C.D. Cal. 1879).
14. *Barbier v. Connolly,* 113 U.S. 27 (1884).
15. *Soon Hing v. Crowley,* 113 U.S. 703 (1885).
16. *Yick Wo v. Hopkins,* 118 U.S. 356, 373–74 (1886).
17. Field agreed with McAllister that the case fell within the powers of Congress. He believed it was governed by Section 5536 of the statute, which made it a crime to "prevent, hinder, or delay the execution of any law of the United States." For Field, this included any treaty. *Baldwin v. Franks,* 120 U.S. at 704, Field dissenting.
18. Ibid., at 683.
19. Ibid., at 693.
20. Ibid., at 694, Harlan dissenting.
21. Ibid., at 700, Harlan dissenting.
22. Ariela J. Gross, "'The Caucasian Cloak': Mexican-Americans and the Politics of Whiteness in the Twentieth-Century Southwest," *Georgetown Law Journal* 95 (January 2007): 337–91, 348–50; *In re Rodriguez,* 81 F. 337 (W.D. Tex. 1897); see also David Montejano, *Anglos and Mexicans in the Making of Texas, 1836–1986* (Austin: University of Texas Press, 1987); Tom I. Romero, "The Tri-Ethnic Dilemma: Race, Equality, and the Fourteenth Amendment in the American West," *Tempe Political and Civil Rights Law Review* 13 (Spring 2004): 817–56.
23. Stuart Banner, *How the Indians Lost Their Land: Law and Power on the Frontier* (Cambridge, Mass: Belknap Press of Harvard University Press, 2005), 245–46.

24. *United States v. Kagama*, 118 U.S. 375, 383–84 (1886). As if to highlight the confusion about the status of Indians, the Supreme Court once ruled that Indians of the pueblo of Taos were not an Indian tribe within the meaning of a federal statute that protected Indian lands. *United States v. Joseph*, 94 U.S. 614 (1876).

25. *Elk v. Wilkins*, 112 U.S. 94, 102 (1884).

26. Ibid., at 122–23, Harlan dissenting.

27. Sarah Barringer Gordon, *The Mormon Question: Polygamy and Constitutional Conflict in Nineteenth-Century America* (Chapel Hill: University of North Carolina Press, 2002), 22–26.

28. Ibid., 26–27.

29. Ibid., 55.

30. Ibid., 63. Interestingly, when given the right to vote in Utah Territory, Mormon women tended to follow the dictates of church leaders. Ibid., 97.

31. Ibid., 81.

32. *Reynolds v. United States*, 98 U.S. 145 (1879); Gordon, *Mormon Question*, 86–119.

33. *Reynolds v. United States*, 98 U.S. at 165–66.

34. Ibid., at 164.

35. Ibid., at 166–67.

36. Gordon, *Mormon Question*, 119–26. The issue of local autonomy is not very evident in the United States Reports. The court reporter only mentions it in the last paragraph of the summary of the lawyer's arguments. We can thank Gordon, whose research of letters, documents, and the brief submitted to the Supreme Court brought the issue into full view.

37. *Dred Scott v. Sanford*, 60 U.S. (19 How.) 393 (1857).

38. Gordon, *Mormon Question*, 125.

39. *Murphy v. Ramsey*, 114 U.S. 15, 44–45 (1885). See also *Davis v. Beason*, 133 U.S. 333 (1890), upholding an Idaho statute that denied the right to vote to anyone who taught or belonged to any order that taught or advised the practice of polygamy; *Clawson v. United States*, 114 U.S. 477 (1885), making the practice of polygamy grounds for exclusion from a jury; *Cannon v. United States*, 116 U.S. 55 (1885), broadly defining cohabitation to make it easier to convict accused polygamists.

40. *Late Corporation of the Church of Jesus Christ of Latter-Day Saints v. United States*, 136 U.S. 1 (1890).

41. Gordon, *Mormon Question*, 215, citing *Late Corporation*, 136 U.S. at 44, 49-50.

42. Ibid., 220.

43. Michael Les Benedict, "Preserving Federalism: Reconstruction and the Waite Court," *Supreme Court Review* (1978): 39–79, 40.

44. *In re Ah Fong*, 1 F. Cas. 213, 217 (C.C.D. Cal., 1874).

45. *Bradwell v. Illinois*, 83 U.S. at 141 (1873).

46. *Kagama*, 118 U.S. at 383–84.

47. *Reynolds*, 98 U.S. at 164; *Late Corporation*, 136 U.S. at 49.

48. Linda Przybyszewski, *The Republic According to John Marshall Harlan* (Chapel Hill: University of North Carolina Press, 1999).

Conclusion—Legacy of the Waite Court

1. *The Anarchists' Case*, 123 U.S. 131 (1887). Responding to a motion for the allowance of a writ of error to the Supreme Court of Illinois, Waite agreed to permit the motion in open court. But he observed that motions of error to state courts had never been allowed as a matter of right. The Court, he said, would not grant the motion unless it determined that a federal question was involved.

2. Numerous sources provide information about the Haymarket Affair. I have used the following two books to summarize the story: James Green, *Death in the Haymarket: A Story of Chicago,*

the First Labor Movement and the Bombing that Divided Gilded Age America (New York: Pantheon Books, 2006); Paul Avrich, *The Haymarket Tragedy* (Princeton, N.J.: Princeton University Press, 1984).

3. *The Anarchists' Case*, 123 U.S. 131 (1887). This is the second of two opinions of the same name beginning on the same page.

4. Charles Fairman, *Reconstruction and Reunion 1864–88, Part Two*, Oliver Wendell Holmes Devise History of the Supreme Court of the United States (New York: Macmillan, 1987), 7:730.

5. *Barron v. Baltimore*, 32 U.S. (7 Pet.) 243 (1833).

6. *Hurtado v. California*, 110 U.S. 516 (1884); see also *Ex parte Bain*, 121 U.S. 1 (1887).

7. *Hurtado*, 110 U.S. at 532.

8. Ibid., at 547–48, Harlan dissenting. Harlan also dissented, without comment, from a decision upholding a Missouri law that limited the number of preemptory challenges to prospective jurors in criminal cases. *Hayes v. Missouri*, 120 U.S. 68 (1887).

9. See *Palko v. Connecticut*, 302 U.S. 319 (1937); *Adamson v. California*, 332 U.S. 46 (1947), Frankfurter concurring.

10. *Presser v. Illinois*, 116 U.S. 252, 265 (1886). The Second Amendment has yet to be incorporated and applied to the states. For the latest opinion on the Second Amendment, see *District of Columbia v. Heller*, 554 U.S., 128 S.Ct. 2783 (2008). The Court has granted cert in a case that may directly address the question, *McDonald v. Chicago*, S.Ct, 2009 WL4748589 (US), 78 USLW 33.59.

11. *Ex parte Jackson*, 96 U.S. 727 (1877). However, the Court warned that the regulation could not unduly interfere with the First Amendment guarantee of freedom of speech. See also *Ex parte Wilson*, 114 U.S. 417 (1885) (grand jury); *Mackin v. U.S.*, 117 U.S. 348 (1886) (grand jury); *Ex parte Curtis*, 106 U.S. 371 (1882) (free speech).

12. One other source of civil liberties cases is Article I, Section 10, which prohibits states from passing bills of attainder and ex post facto laws, both of which are safeguards related to criminal prosecutions. The ex post facto provision prohibits making something a crime after it has already taken place. A bill of attainder is a law directed against a designated person. Although neither of these guarantees comes before the Court very often, in *Kring v. Missouri*, 107 U.S. 221 (1883), the Waite Court ruled that Missouri had violated the ex post facto provision when it punished a man for an act that, at the time he committed it, was not a crime.

13. *Boyde v. United States*, 116 U.S. 616, 638 (1886).

14. *Wilkerson v. Utah*, 99 U.S. 130 (1879).

15. *Thompson v. Utah*, 170 U.S. 343 (1882) (twelve-member juries); *Hopt v. Utah*, 120 U.S. 430 (1887) (defendant's presence and voluntary confession).

16. Felix Frankfurter and James M. Landis, *The Business of the Supreme Court: A Study of the Federal Judicial System* (New York: MacMillan, 1927), 60; Donald Grier Stephenson Jr., *The Waite Court: Justices, Rulings, and Legacy* (Santa Barbara, Calif.: ABC-CLIO, 2003), 37.

17. Fairman, *Reconstruction and Reunion*, 7:771.

18. C. Peter Magrath, *Morrison R. Waite: A Triumph of Character* (New York: Macmillan, 1963), 267, citing "Remarks of Chief Justice Waite in response to the toast, 'The Supreme Court of the United States,'" Waite Papers, Library of Congress, Washington D.C.

19. Fairman, *Reconstruction and Reunion*, 7:770.

20. Stephenson, *Waite Court*, 262–63; Fairman, *Reconstruction and Reunion*, 7:768–71.

21. Act of February 13, 1925, 43 Stat. 936; Frankfurter and Landis, *Business of the Supreme Court*, 260–63, 280–86.

22. Stephenson, *Waite Court*, 40, illustrates this very clearly in a graph.

23. Magrath, *Morrison R. Waite*, 309, citing Waite to Bancroft Davis, March 5, 1888, Bancroft Davis Papers, Library of Congress, Washington, D.C.

24. *Dolbear v. American Bell Tel. Co.*, 126 U.S. 1 (1888).

25. Magrath, *Morrison R. Waite*, 309–10 (Justice Blatchford read the opinion in the *Bell Telephone Cases*). See also Fairman, *Reconstruction and Reunion*, 7:771–72, 783–84.

26. See Stephenson, *Waite Court*, 243.

27. Felix Frankfurter, *The Commerce Clause under Marshall, Taney, and Waite* (Chapel Hill: University of North Carolina Press, 1937), 78, citing note, *American Law Review* 22 (1888): 301, 303.

28. See Stephenson, *Waite Court*, 238.

29. Magrath, *Morrison R. Waite*, 319–20.

30. Ibid., 312.

31. *Plessy v. Ferguson*, 163 U.S. 537 (1896).

32. Robert M. Goldman, *A Free Ballot and a Fair Count: The Department of Justice and the Enforcement of Voting Rights in the South 1877–1893* (New York: Fordham University Press, 2001); Richard M. Valelly, *The Two Reconstructions: The Struggle for Black Enfranchisement* (Chicago: University of Chicago Press, 2004); Xi Wang, *The Trial of Democracy: Black Suffrage and Northern Republicans, 1860–1910* (Athens: University of Georgia Press, 1997).

33. Pamela Brandwein, "A Judicial Abandonment of Blacks? Rethinking the 'State Action' Cases of the Waite Court," *Law and Society Review* 41 (June 2007): 343–81; Brandwein, *Supreme Court, State Action, and Civil Rights: Rethinking the Judicial Settlement of Reconstruction* (Cambridge: Cambridge University Press, forthcoming); Michael Les Benedict, "Preserving Federalism: Reconstruction and the Waite Court," *Supreme Court Review* (1978): 39–79.

34. *Brown v. Board of Education*, 337 U.S. 483 (1954); *Brown v. Board of Education II*, 349 U.S. 294 (1955).

35. *Shelley v. Kraemer*, 334 U.S. 1 (1948).

36. *Heart of Atlanta Motel v. United States*, 379 U.S. 241 (1964); *Katzenbach v. McClung*, 379 U.S. 294 (1964).

37. *Heart of Atlanta Motel*, 379 U.S. at 279–80, Douglas concurring.

38. *United States v. Morrison*, 529 U.S. 598 (2000). The majority's desire to apply a narrower interpretation of Congress's power to regulate interstate commerce began with *United States v. Lopez*, 514 U.S. 549 (1995).

39. William M. Wiecek, *The Lost World of Classical Legal Thought: Law and Ideology in America 1886–1937* (New York: Oxford University Press, 1998), 112, notes, "All Justices of the Supreme Court in the last third of the nineteenth century agreed with Madison that the fundamental challenge of American Constitutionalism was mediating between the power of government and the liberty of the individual."

40. *West Coast Hotel v. Parrish*, 300 U.S. 379, 406 (1937), Sutherland dissenting.

41. See Howard Gillman, *The Constitution Besieged: The Rise and Demise of Lochner Era Police Powers Jurisprudence* (Durham, N.C.: Duke University Press, 1993); David M. Gold, *The Shaping of Nineteenth-Century Law: John Appleton and Responsible Individualism* (Westport, Conn.: Greenwood Press, 1990); Michael Les Benedict, "Laissez-Faire and Liberty: A Re-Evaluation of the Meaning and Origin of Laissez-Faire Constitutionalism," *Law and History Review* 3 (1985): 293–331; Alan Jones, "Thomas M. Cooley and Laissez-Faire Constitutionalism: A Reconsideration," *Journal of American History* 53 (1967): 751–71; Charles W. McCurdy, "Justice Field and the Jurisprudence of Government-Business Relations: Some Parameters of Laissez-Faire Constitutionalism, 1863–1897," *Journal of American History* 61 (1975): 970–1005, 1004–5.

42. See Randy E. Barnett, *Restoring the Lost Constitution: The Presumption of Liberty* (Princeton, N.J.: Princeton University Press, 2004).

43. Stephenson, *Waite Court*, 242, writes that there is little evidence that Waite led his Court doctrinally with consistency. This represents a common view of Waite's intellectual leadership.

44. Frankfurter, *Commerce Clause*, 78, 80.

45. Magrath, *Morrison R. Waite*, 321; see also Frankfurter, *Commerce Clause*, 80–81.

Index of Cases

Anarchists' Case, The, 123 U.S. 131 (1887), 162–63

Baldwin v. Franks, 120 U.S. 678 (1887), 152–56, 161

Baltimore & Ohio Railroad Co. v. Maryland, 88 U.S. (21 Wall.) 456 (1875), 128

Barron v. Baltimore, 32 U.S. (7 Pet.) 243 (1833), 3, 39, 163, 164

Bartemeyer v. Iowa, 85 U.S. (18 Wall.) 129 (1874), 30

Barton v. Barbour, 104 U.S. (14 Otto.) 126 (1881), 94–95

Beer Company v. Massachusetts, 97 U.S. (7 Otto.) 25 (1878), 89

Boyde v. United States, 116 U.S. 616 (1886), 165

Bradwell v. Illinois, 83 U.S. (16 Wall.) 130 (1873), 29–30

Brown v. Board of Education, 337 U.S. 483 (1954), 2, 169

Brown v. Maryland, 25 U.S. (12 Wheat.) 419 (1827), 127

Butchers' Union Slaughter-House & Live-Stock Co. v. Crescent City Live-Stock Landing & Slaughter-House Co., 111 U.S. 746 (1884), 119

Charles River Bridge Co. v. Warren Bridge Co., 36 U.S. (11 Pet.) 420 (1837), 8–9, 75, 84–85, 146

Chicago, Burlington, and Quincy Railroad Company v. Iowa, 94 U.S. (4 Otto.) 155 (1877), 73–74

Chicago, Milwaukee, & St. Paul Railway v. Minnesota, 134 U.S. 418 (1890), 9, 87

Chy Lung v. Freeman, 92 U.S. (2 Otto.) 275 (1876), 130

City and County of San Francisco v. Scott, 111 U.S. 768 (1884), 143

City of New York v. Miln, 36 U.S. (11 Pet.) 102 (1837), 129

Civil Rights Cases, 109 U.S. 3 (1883), 6, 7, 53–54, 55–56, 57–58, 151, 161

Coe v. Town of Errol, 116 U.S. 517 (1886), 127

Commonwealth v. Alger, 7 Cush. 53 (Mass., 1851), 76

Cooley v. Board of Wardens, 53 U.S. (12 How.) 299 (1852), 127

Crédit Mobilier Case. See *United States v. Union Pacific Railroad Company,* 98 U.S. (8 Otto.) 569 (1879)

Davidson v. New Orleans, 96 U.S. (6 Otto.) 103 (1878), 87–88

Dred Scott v. Sanford, 60 U.S. (19 How.) 393, 450 (1857), xi, xii, 15, 80, 159

Edwards v. Kearzey, 96 U.S. (6 Otto.) 595 (1878), 88

Elk v. Wilkins, 112 U.S. 94 (1884), 157–58

Ex parte Virginia, 100 U.S. 339 (1880), 60, 152

Ex parte Yarbrough, 110 U.S. 651 (1884), 58–59

Fertilizing Company v. Hyde Park, 97 U.S. (7 Otto.) 659 (1878), 88–89

Fletcher v. Peck, 10 U.S. (6 Cranch) 87 (1810), 66–67

Fosdick v. Schall, 99 U.S. (9 Otto.) 235 (1879), 94

Frémont v. United States, 58 U.S. (17 How.) 542 (1855), 141–42, 145

Frisbie v. Whitney, 76 U.S. (9 Wall.) 187 (1869), 138–40, 141

Gelpcke v. The City of Dubuque, 68 U.S. (1 Wall.) 175 (1864), 65, 67

Gibbons v. Ogden, 22 U.S. (9 Wheat.) 1 (1824), 126

Hall v. Decuir, 95 U.S. (5 Otto.) 485 (1878), 130

Heart of Atlanta Motel v. United States, 379 U.S. 241 (1964), 170

Hoadley v. San Francisco, 94 U.S. (4 Otto.) 4 (1876), 143

INDEX OF CASES

Hosmer v. Wallace, 97 U.S. (7 Otto.) 575 (1879), 140

Hurtado v. California, 110 U.S. 516 (1884), 3, 163–64

In re Debs, 158 U.S. 564 (1895), 92

Katzenbach v. McClung, 379 U.S. 294 (1964), 170

Late Corporation of the Church of Jesus Christ of Latter-Day Saints v. United States, 136 U.S. 1 (1890), 160

Leavenworth, Lawrence, and Galveston Railroad Company v. United States, 92 U.S. (2 Otto.) 733 (1876), 147–48

Loan Association v. Topeka, 87 U.S. (20 Wall.) 655 (1875), 64

Lochner v. New York, 198 U.S. 45 (1905), 9

Lone Wolf v. Hitchcock, 187 U.S. 553 (1903), 136

Mayor of the City of Nashville v. Ray, 86 U.S. (19 Wall.) 468 (1874), 66

Minor v. Happersett, 88 U.S. 162 (1874), 38, 151–52

Morgan v. Louisiana, 93 U.S. (3 Otto.) 217 (1876), 76

Mugler v. Kansas, 123 U.S. 623 (1887), 120

Munn v. Illinois, 94 U.S. 113 (1877), 9, 10–11, 25, 57, 62, 69, 71, 72, 73, 77, 78–89, 110, 111, 116, 118, 120, 125, 131, 133, 150, 161, 170

Neal v. Delaware, 103 U.S. 370 (1880), 60

Nebbia v. New York, 291 U.S. 502 (1934), 83

Newhall v. Sanger, 92 U.S. (2 Otto.) 761 (1876), 146–48

New Jersey v. Yard, 95 U.S. (5 Otto.) 104 (1877), 88

Pace v. Alabama, 106 U.S. 583 (1883), 55, 151

Peik v. Chicago & North-Western Railway Co., 94 U.S. (4 Otto.) 164 (1877), 74, 131, 132–33

Pembina Consolidated Silver Mining & Milling Co. v. Pennsylvania, 125 U.S. 181 (1888), 124

Platt v. Union Pacific Railroad Co., 99 U.S. (9 Otto.) 48 (1879), 149

Plessy v. Ferguson, 163 U.S. 537 (1896), 6, 55, 57, 169

Presser v. Illinois, 116 U.S. 252 (1886), 165

Railroad Company v. Richmond, 96 U.S. (6 Otto.) 521 (1878), 88

Reynolds v. United States, 98 U.S. 145 (1879), 159–60, 161, 165

Rice v. Minnesota & N.W. R. Co., 66 U.S. (1 Black) 358 (1861), 146

Ruggles v. Illinois, 108 U.S. 526 (1883), 117, 118–19

San Mateo v. Southern Pacific Railroad Company, 13 F. 722 (C.C.D. Cal. 1882), 122

Santa Clara County v. Southern Pacific Railroad, 118 U.S. 394 (1886), 11, 122, 123–24

Shelley v. Kraemer, 334 U.S. 1 (1948), 170

Sinking Fund Cases, The, 99 U.S. (9 Otto.) 700 (1879), 11, 105–9, 110, 111, 116, 121, 125, 150

Slaughterhouse Cases, The, 83 U.S. (16 Wall.) 36 (1873), xi, 4–5, 18–30, 36–37, 44, 45, 46, 50, 51, 79, 80, 81, 82, 119

Smyth v. Ames, 169 U.S. 466 (1898), 9, 120, 124

Southern Pacific R. C. v. Orton, 32 F. 457 (C.C.D. Cal. 1979), 149–50

Spring Valley Water-Works v. Schottler, 110 U.S. 347 (1884), 117–18, 124

State Railroad Tax Cases, The, 92 U.S. (2 Otto.) 575 (1876), 80

Strauder v. West Virginia, 100 U.S. 303 (1880), 59

Tameling v. United States Freehold and Emigration Company, 93 U.S. (3 Otto.) 644 (1877), 143, 145

Town of Venice v. Murdock, 92 U.S. (2 Otto.) 494 (1876), 66

Township of Pine Grove v. Talcott, 86 U.S. (19 Wall.) 666 (1874), 66

United States v. Burlington and Missouri River Railroad Company, 98 U.S. (8 Otto.) 334 (1879), 150

United States v. Cruikshank, 92 U.S. (2 Otto.) 542 (1876), 5, 32, 33, 36–40, 41, 42–45, 53, 58, 87, 151

United States v. Harris, 106 U.S. 629 (1883), 152, 155

United States v. Kagama, 118 U.S. 375 (1886), 157, 161

United States v. Maxwell Land Grant, 121 U.S. 325 (1887), 143–45

United States v. Morrison, 529 U.S. 598 (2000), 170

United States v. Reese, 92 U.S. (2 Otto.) 214 (1876), 5, 32, 40–42, 43, 51–52, 53, 56, 58, 87

United States v. Schurz, 102 U.S. (12 Otto.) 378 (1880), 141

United States v. Union Pacific Railroad Company, 91 U.S. (1 Otto.) 72 (1875), 101–2, 105

United States v. Union Pacific Railroad Company, 98 U.S. (8 Otto.) 569 (1879), 103–5

Virginia v. Rives, 100 U.S. 313 (1880), 59–60, 152

Wabash, St. Louis, and Pacific Railway Co. v. Illinois, 118 U.S. 557 (1886), 132–34

Wallace v. Loomis, 97 U.S. (7 Otto.) 146 (1878), 94

Wilkerson v. Utah, 99 U.S. 130 (1879), 165–66

Wilson v. Black Bird Marsh Co., 27 U.S. (2 Pet.) 245 (1829), 126–27

Wirth v. Branson, 98 U.S. (8 Otto.) 118 (1878), 141

Woodson v. Murdock, 89 U.S. (22 Wall.) 351 (1874), 95–96

Wynehamer v. The People, 13 N.Y. 378 (1856), xi, 80

Yick Wo v. Hopkins, 118 U.S. 356 (1886), 154

Yosemite Valley Case, The, 82 U.S. (15 Wall.) 77 (1873), 139–40

Subject Index

Act to Quiet Title to Certain Lands Within . . . San Francisco, 143
Adams, Charles Francis, Jr., 68, 98, 99
Adams, D. W., 70
Ainsworth, Scott H., 114
alcoholic beverages, prohibition of, 119–20
Allen, William, 71
Alley, John B., 100
Altgeld, John, 163
Alvarado, Juan B., 141–42
amendments. *See* Bill of Rights; First Amendment; Second Amendment; Sixth Amendment; Twelfth Amendment; Thirteenth Amendment; Fourteenth Amendment; Fifteenth Amendment; Seventeenth Amendment
American Indians: as American citizens, 157–58; federal jurisdiction over, 156–58; treaties with, 135–36, 147; uprisings of, 136; and westward expansion, 135–36
Ames, Oaks, 100
Anthony, Henry B., 115
Armijo, Manuel, 144
Arthur, Chester, 26; Supreme Court appointments of, 115–16

Baldwin, Thomas, 152, 154
Ballinger, Lucy, 21
Baltimore and Ohio Railroad, 8, 90–91, 128
bankruptcy law, 12; as applied by the Court to railroads, 92–97
Banner, Stuart, 156–57
Barnett, Randy, 10
Beaubien, Carlos, 143–45
Beckwith, James Roswell, 35
Beer Company, 89
Bell, Alexander Graham, 167
Bell Telephone cases, 167
Benedict, Michael Les, 7, 161

Benjamin, Reuben M., 71
Bill of Rights, as applied to the states, 3, 39, 163, 164–65
Black, Hugo, 165
black citizens: civil rights for, 5–7, 52; equal rights for, 5, 18, 29, 32, 55–56, 57–58; excluded from jury service, 59–60; impact of Waite Court decisions on, 6–7, 52, 58–59; voting rights of, 40, 41, 45, 58–59; violence against, 33–39, 58–59
Black Thursday, 1–2
Blackstone, William, 25–26
Blaine, James G., 55
Blatchford, Samuel, 94; on economic regulation, 120; nomination of to Supreme Court, 116
bona fide holder doctrine, 65–67, 168, 183–84n31
bondholders, Court protection of, 65–67
bonds. *See* government bonds; municipal bonds
Bradley, Joseph, 4–5, 15, 30, 36, 111, 112, 128; on the Civil Rights Act of 1875, 53–54, 57–58; on Congress's authority, 43–46, 50–51, 56; dissent of in the *Sinking Fund Cases*, 106, 107; dissent of in *Slaughterhouse Cases*, 25–26, 27–28, 50, 80, 82; on economic regulation, 82, 83, 133–34; education of, 26; and the Election Commission, 49–50; legal experience of, 26; on police power, 89; political leanings of, 27; and railroad receiverships, 94; on substantive due process, 80; on women's rights, 30
Bradwell, Myra, 29–30, 161
Brandwein, Pamela, 7, 58, 169
Brimm, Benjamin, 35
Bristow, Benjamin, 55
Burlingame Treaty, 153
Burlington and Missouri River Railroad, 150

Burns, W. T., 145
Bush, George W., 51
business. *See* economic regulation; interstate commerce

Caldwell, Harry C., 94
California: Chinese workers in, 152–56; immigration policy in, 130; land disputes in, 142–43; Mussel Slough incident in, 149–50; property taxation in, 121–24
California Land Act of 1851, 141
Campbell, John, 20, 22, 23, 25, 36
canvassing boards, 47
capitation tax, 40
Cardozo, Benjamin, 164–65
Cary, John, 75
Central Pacific Railroad, 98–99, 105
certificate of division, 36
Chandler, William E., 47
Charles River Bridge Company, 75
Chase, Salmon P., 15, 30, 112
Chase Court, xii
Cherokee removal, 135
Chicago Board of Trade, 79
Chicago, Ill., and price fixing for grain storage, 78–79
Chinese immigrants: discrimination against, 130, 152; equal protection for, 152–56; treaties protecting, 153, 155; violence against, 152, 155
Chinese laundries, 154
Chy Lung, 130
Circuit Court of Appeals Act of 1891, 13, 166
civil rights: Harlan as defender of, 6, 56–57; as issue in the Colfax massacre, 35–39; and the Waite Court, 5–7, 60–61, 155–56, 160–61, 166. *See* black citizens; racial violence
Civil Rights Act of 1866, 55, 58
Civil Rights Act of 1875, 6; challenges to, 53–54, 56–58
Civil Rights Act of 1964, 170
Civil War, 17; legacy of, 3, 4, 18, 43; legal cases arising from, 18
Clifford, Nathan, 30, 40, 41, 110; death of, 115; and the Electoral Commission, 48, 49; on property rights, 146
Cochran, Thomas C., 73, 116
Colfax County War, 144
Colfax massacre, 5, 33–39

Colton, David, 107
commerce, revolution in, 2, 3, 62. *See also* economic regulation; interstate commerce; railroads
commerce clause, 12, 83, 126–27, 168, 170; and immigration policy, 129–30; purpose of, 129, 133. *See also* interstate commerce
Compromise of 1877, 6, 50, 57, 60
confiscation, and economic regulation, 118, 120–21
Congress. *See* U.S. Congress
Conkling, Roscoe, 15
contract clause doctrine, 9, 80; as applied to economic regulation, 84–85, 118, 119; as applied to railroad regulation, 73–74, 75, 77; as applied to the *Sinking Fund Cases*, 106; Waite Court's interpretation of, 88–89, 170–71
contract, sanctity of, 67
Cooke, Jay, 1
Cooke & Co., 1
Cooley, Thomas M., 75, 76, 80, 129, 131
corporate equal protection, 122–23, 124
corporations, as "persons," 11, 108–9, 118, 122–24
Cox, Mary J., 151
Crédit Mobilier Act of 1873, 101–2, 104
Crédit Mobilier scandal, 11, 98–104; legal disputes arising from, 104–9
Crescent-City Live-Stock Landing and Slaughterhouse Company. *See* slaughterhouse industry
Cruikshank, William, 36, 37
Cushing, Caleb, 15, 17
Custer, George, 136

Dartmouth College case, 80
Davis, David, 30, 103, 111, 113; and the Electoral Commission, 48, 49; on land grant cases, 143, 147; and *U.S. v. Union Pacific Railroad*, 102
Davis, J. C. Bancroft, 17, 123–24, 167
Dawes Act, 136
Democratic Party, and the election of 1876, 47–48
Denison, John N., 73
Depew, Chauncey, 111
Devens, Charles, 92
diversity of citizenship, 64–65
Douglas, William O., 170

drummers, licensing of, 127–28
Drummond, Thomas S., 92–93
due process, 5, 9, 62, 163–64; Bradley's interpretation of, 25; Matthews's interpretation of, 164; Miller's interpretation of, 87–88; and sale of alcoholic beverages, 80, 89; and state regulation of business, 9–11, 79–80. *See also* substantive due process

economic depression (1873–1879), 1–2
economic regulation, 11–12; arguments in opposition to, 116, 117–8; and confiscation, 118, 120–21; contract clause as applied to, 84–85, 118, 119; federal versus states' role in, 9–10; Field's opposition to, 117–8; and the Fourteenth Amendment, 5; of grain storage fees, 78–85; and interstate commerce, 79, 126–34; and police power of states, 84; protection against, 10; of railroads, 8, 62–63, 69–71, 72–75, 76–77, 85, 88, 118–9, 120–21, 130, 131–34; Waite Court's rulings in support of, 73–74, 81–85, 116–7, 118–9, 124–25, 170–71
Edmunds, George F., 48, 113
Electoral College, 46–47
Electoral Commission (1877), 48–51, 112
Elk, John, 157
Ely, James W., Jr., 130, 182n6
eminent domain, 62, 63–64, 182n7, 182n9
Enforcement Act of 1870, 32, 35, 152; constitutionality of, 36–41
Engle, George, 163
entrepreneurial liberty, 10
equal protection clause, 122; as applied to blacks, 151; as applied to Chinese workers, 152–56; as applied to women, 151–52. *See also* civil rights; corporate equal protection; racial discrimination
Evans, George Henry, 137
Evarts, William, 16, 17

Fairman, Charles, 27, 66, 94, 166, 188n24
Federal Court of Claims, and the Crédit Mobilier Act, 101
federal government: and civil rights cases, 5–6; and economic regulation, 11–12, 126–34; role of in people's lives, 3; and state authority, 3–4, 5–6, 43, 50, 56–59
federalism, Waite Court's interpretation of, 7, 23, 25, 38, 43, 59, 60, 151, 155, 160–61

federal land policy, 13
Federal Violence Against Women Act, 170
Ferry, Thomas, 48, 50–51
Field, David Dudley, 23, 24, 36, 37, 177n16
Field, Stephen J., xi, 4–5, 9, 10, 13, 16, 30, 36, 128; as advocate of entrepreneurial liberty, 117–8, 120; in California, 23–24; and Chinese issues, 153–54, 155; and corporate equal protection, 122–23; dissent of in *Munn v. Illinois*, 62, 117; dissent of in the *Sinking Fund Cases*, 106–8, 109, 117; dissent of in the *Slaughterhouse Cases*, 23, 24–25; and the Electoral Commission, 48, 49; as friend of railroad entrepreneurs, 102, 105; on homestead law, 140; on Indian land policy, 136; on land grants to railroads, 146, 147–48; on police power of the state, 30; political leanings of, 24, 102
Fifteenth Amendment, 4, 18, 28; Bradley's interpretation of, 45; and the Enforcement Act of 1870, 40; and voting rights, 40–41, 45, 58, 152
Fielden, Samuel, 162, 163
Fifth Amendment, 9, 87; as applied to the *Hurtado* case, 163–64; as applied to *Munn v. Illinois*, 80–81; as applied to *Sinking Fund Cases*, 106–7
First Amendment, 124, 159
Fischer, Adolph, 163
Fish, Hamilton, 15
Fisk, Jim, 1
Foner, Eric, 6
Fouchee, Matthew, 40, 41
Fourteenth Amendment, xi, 4, 5; as applied to American Indians, 157–58; as applied to black citizens, 29, 56–57; as applied to Chinese workers, 153; as applied to corporations, 122; as applied in *Munn v. Illinois*, 79–80; Bradley's interpretation of, 53–54, 82; and discrimination cases, 156; and economic regulation, 9–10, 24–25, 110, 119, 120–21, 171; enforcement clause of, 46, 166, 169, 170; Field's interpretation of, 30, 82; Harlan's interpretation of, 6, 55–56, 57, 156; and laissez-faire economics, 86; later interpretations of, 164–65; Miller's interpretation of, 87–88; and the *Slaughterhouse Cases*, 25, 29; Swayne's interpretation of, 29; sweeping language of, 18; and *U.S. v. Cruikshank* (1876), 39–40, 44–45; and

Fourteenth Amendment (*cont'd*)
voting rights, 38, 46; and women's rights, 29–30, 151–52. *See also* due process; equal protection clause; substantive due process
Frankfurter, Felix, 164–65, 172
freedmen, 5. *See also* black citizens
Frelinghuysen, Frederick, 26, 27
Frémont, John, 21, 28; and Mexican land grant case, 141–42
friendly receiverships, as applied to railroads, 92–97; Miller's concerns about, 95–96
Frisbie, John B., 138–40
Fuller, Melville W., xi, 10, 168, 171
Fusion Party (Louisiana), 34

Gallatin, Albert, 105
Garfield, James A., 49, 110–1, 112, 113–14
Garland, Augustus, 113
Garner, William, 40
Garrett, John W., 90
Gates, Paul Wallace, 137
General Motors Corporation, 97
Geneva Tribunal, 17
Glendon, Mary Ann, 10, 81
Goudy, William G., 79–81
Gould, Jay, 1, 93, 96, 111, 112, 113, 114
government bonds, for railroads, 11, 99, 100–101, 103
grain storage, regulation of pricing for, 78–85, 89
grand jury, right to, 164
Granger Cases, 9, 62, 69–70, 77, 114, 131, 133
Granger laws, 72–73, 81
Grangers: as advocates of economic regulation, 69–70, 78; as opponents of Matthews's nomination, 114
Grant administration, scandal in, 46, 100
Grant, Ulysses S., 2, 15, 17, 27, 33
Gray, Horace, 83, 115–6, 128
Great Strike of 1877, 8
Greeley, Horace, 137
Gresham, Walter Q., 92–93
Griffin, W. W., 144
Guiteau, Charles Julius, 115

Hadley, Arthur T., 69
Hadnot, John P., 36, 37
Hale, Lord Chief Justice, 81, 82, 83
Hancock, Winfield S., 91, 110
Hansen, Bradley, 94

Harlan, John Marshall, 3, 6, 103, 111, 117; dissent of in *Civil Rights Cases*, 54, 55; dissent of in *Elk v. Wilkins*, 157–58; dissent of in *Hurtado* case, 164; early background of, 54–55; on equal protection for Chinese workers, 156; on exclusions of blacks from jury service, 60; on prohibition of alcoholic beverages, 120
Harris, R. G., 60
Harris, Robert, 72, 85
Harwood, Abel, 71
Hayes, Rutherford B., 6, 36, 46–47, 50–51, 55, 62, 111; and the Matthews nomination, 112–4; and the railroad strikes, 91–92
Haymarket Affair, 162–63
health regulations, 129
Hewitt, Abram, 50
Hoadley (settler), 143
Ho Ah Kow, 153
Homestead Act of 1862, 12–13, 137
homestead law, 138–45
homestead movement, 12–13; cases involving, 136–45
Hosmer (homesteader), 140
Howard, Oliver O., 92
Howard, Volney E., 122
Howe, Timothy O., 15
Hudson, James F., 69, 182n6
Hunt, Ward, 30, 103, 110; on the Enforcement Act of 1870, 41–42; resignation of, 116
Huntington, Collis, 1, 102, 105, 109
Hutchings, James Mason, 139–40
Hurtado, Joseph, 163

Illinois: and the Haymarket Affair, 162–63; railroad regulation in, 72, 132–33
immigration law, cases involving, 129–30
incorporation doctrine, 39
Indianapolis, Bloomington, and Western Railroad, 92
Indians. *See* American Indians
individual rights: state as protector of, 44–46; state interference with, 25–26. *See also* civil rights
in praesenti rule, 146, 148, 168
interstate commerce: confusion regarding, 130–31; Congress's power to regulate, 79, 126–34; and regulation of railroads, 130, 131–34; states' authority over, 126–27, 134

SUBJECT INDEX

Interstate Commerce Act, 12, 79, 132, 134
Interstate Commerce Commission, 134
Iowa Supreme Court, 65
Irwin, William B., 36, 37

Jackson, Andrew, 28, 91
Jackson, John P., 26
Jefferson, Thomas, 137
Jewett, John N., 79–81, 85
Jim Crow era, 6, 45, 161
Johnson, Reverdy, 36
Joint Companies, 26
Joseph, Chief, 92
"Judges' Bill," 166–67
Julian, George, 137, 139–40
jury, right to trial by, 166
jury service: blacks excluded from, 59–60; women excluded from, 152

Kaczorowski, Robert, 7
Kansas: land disputes in, 147–48; prohibition law in, 119–20
Kellogg, William Pitt, 34
Keokuk, Iowa, 21, 67–68, 103
Ku Klux Klan, 33, 58

labor disputes, 8. *See also* Haymarket Affair; railroad strikes
laissez-faire constitutionalism, 25, 86, 168, 170, 171
land grants. *See* Mexican land grants; railroads, land grants to
land reform movement, 136–45, 168
Lane, Charles, 6
Lawrence, Charles B., 75, 114
Leavenworth, Lawrence and Galveston Railroad, 147–48
liberty of contract, 24–25, 120
Lincoln, Abraham, 1, 24, 27, 28, 48–49
Lingg, Louis, 163
Little Big Horn, Battle of, 136
Louisiana. *See* Colfax massacre; slaughterhouse industry

Magrath, C. Peter, 17, 31, 57, 167–68, 172
Maltese, John Anthony, 114
Marr, R. H., 36
Marshall, John, 126–27
Marshall Court, and state taxation of property, 127

Matthew, Henry M., 90
Matthews, Jane, 115
Matthews, Stanley, xii, 11; controversy over nomination of, 112–5; on due process, 164; on equal protection for Chinese workers, 154
Maxwell, Lucien B., 144
Maxwell Land Grant Company, 143–44
McAllister, Hall, 155
McCormick Reaper Works, 162
McCurdy, Charles, 10
McEnery, John D., 34
McLean, John, 28
Meadows, William R., 33
Medill, Joseph, 71
Mexican land grants, 13, 135; cases involving, 137–45; and railroad grants, 146–47
Mexicans, discrimination against, 156
Mexico, war with, 135
Miller, George H., 75
Miller, Samuel F., 4, 7, 15, 16, 37, 38, 111, 128, 144; on bond cases, 67–68; concerns of regarding railroad receiverships, 95–96; and the *Crédit Mobilier Case*, 103–4; dissent of in *Gelpcke* case, 65–66; on due process, 80; on economic regulation, 87–88, 133, 134; and the Electoral Commission, 48, 49; on federal protection of Indians, 157; on federal protection of the right to vote, 59; on government borrowing, 66; on immigration policy, 129–30; medical background of, 20–21; on municipal bonds for private enterprise, 64; and the *Slaughterhouse Cases*, 20, 22–23, 46
Miranda, Guadalupe, 144, 145
monopoly: as issue in *Munn v. Illinois*, 83; as issue in the *Slaughterhouse Cases*, 19, 25–26, 27–28; as issue in *Spring Valley Water-Works*, 118
Moquelamos grant, 146–48
Mormon Question, 158–60
Morrill Act, 159
Morris, Roy, Jr., 51
Morton, Oliver P., 15
municipal bonds, 11, 64; disputes over, 64–66
Munn and Scott, 62, 78. *See also* grain storage
Mussel Slough incident, 149–50

Nash, Columbus C., 34
Nashville, Tenn., 66

National Anti-Monopoly League, 114
Native Americans. *See* American Indians
natural law, 117
Neebe, Oscar, 163
Nelson, Levi, 35, 37, 38, 39, 40
Nelson, Samuel, 146
Nevins, Allan, 50
New Deal legislation, xiii
New Hampshire, and interstate commerce, 127
New Jersey Railroad and Transportation Company, 26
North Carolina Supreme Court, 63–64
Novak, William, 8

Oglesby, Richard, 163
original package doctrine, 127
Orton (settler), 150

Pace, Tony, 151
Pacific Railroad acts, 100–101, 106–7, 146–47, 149
Pacific Railroad Ring. *See* Crédit Mobilier scandal
Pacific Railroad Sinking Fund Act. *See* Thurman Act
Parker, Cortlant, 27
Parsons, Albert, 163
Patrons of Husbandry. *See* Grangers
Peirce, William P., 72
Penn, William, 28
Pennsylvania, transportation tax in, 128
Perkins, Charles E., 114
Phelps, William W., 111
Phillips, Philip, 36
Phillips, Samuel Field, 37
Pierce, Franklin, 15
Pierrepont, Edwards, 101
police powers of the states, 9, 19–20, 22, 30, 76, 84, 89, 118, 119
Polk, James, 135
polygamy, 158–60
popular sovereignty (rights of the community), 14, 71–72, 75; and freedom of religion, 160; and property rights, 84, 86–87, 146–47
Postel, Charles, 70
preemption law, 139–41

presidential election of 1876, 6, 46–48, 112; as decided by the Electoral Commission, 48–51
presidential election of 2000, 48, 51
private property. *See* property rights
privileges and immunities clause, 4, 7, 44–45; as applied to the *Slaughterhouse Cases*, 20, 23, 25; and voting rights, 38; and women's rights, 29–30
prohibition laws, in Kansas, 119–20
property rights, 71, 171; and land grants to railroads, 146–47; and *Munn v. Illinois*, 80–81, 83–84; and popular sovereignty, 84, 86–87; and public interest, 8–9, 81, 83–84, 170–71
Przybyszewski, Linda, 55
public domain, and westward expansion, 135
public interest: and property rights, 8–9, 81, 83–84; and railroad receiverships, 94–95

Queue Case, 153–54

racial discrimination, 6, 170; and Chinese immigrants, 130, 153; and Mexicans, 156; and the powers of Congress, 53–54, 57, 58; the Waite Court's views on, 53–54, 56–58, 155–56, 169. *See also* black citizens; jury service; voting rights
racial segregation, 45, 168; on riverboats, 130; and "separate but equal doctrine," 57, 169
racial violence, 2, 5, 58–59, 60. *See also* Colfax massacre
railroad cases, 8; tensions inherent in, xi–xiii
Railroad Commission cases, 118
railroads, 21; building of as public purpose, 63–64; and Crédit Mobilier scandal, 11, 98–104; economic impact of, 64, 68–69; eminent domain as applied to, 62, 63–64; federal funding for, 11, 99, 100–101; federal regulation of, 131–34; and interstate commerce cases, 128, 130, 131–34; land grants to, 145–50, 182n6; monopolistic aspects of, 68; pricing practices of, 68–69; in receivership, 92–97, 132; state regulation of, 8, 62–63, 69–71, 72–75, 76–77, 85, 88, 118–9, 128, 130, 131, 3–34; taxation of, 121–24, 128; tax benefits conferred on, 76; transcontinental, 98–99

railroad strikes, 8, 90–93; Hayes's response to, 91–92; violence associated with, 90–91
Reagan, John H., 132
Reagan Bill, 132
receiverships. *See* friendly receiverships
Reconstruction Amendments, 3–5, 13, 18, 177n16; challenges to, 20, 22–23; and Congress's authority, 37; impact of on state versus federal power, 43; and the Waite Court, 18, 22–23, 30, 37, 52, 60, 160. *See also* Thirteenth Amendment; Fourteenth Amendment; Fifteenth Amendment
Redfield, Isaac, 63, 64
Reese, Hiram, 40, 41
Register, R. C., 34
Rehnquist, William, 48, 51
Reid, John C., 47
Reid, Whitelaw, 111
religion, freedom of, 159
Republican party, 17; and the election of 1876, 46–47; in Louisiana, 33–34; Samuel Miller's involvement in, 21–22; and racial justice, 5–6
restrictive covenants, 170
Revised Statutes of 1875, 154–55
Reynolds, George, 159–60
right-of-way. *See* eminent domain; railroads, land grants to
rights of the community. *See* popular sovereignty
"rights talk," 10–11
Rockefeller, John D., 111
Roosevelt, Franklin Delano, 134
Ross, Michael A., 7, 21–22
Russell, Richard D., 144

salesmen, licensing of, 127–28
San Francisco, Calif., land disputes in, 142–43
Sawyer, Lorenzo, 122, 150
Scheiber, Harry, 8, 76, 182n7
Schwab, Michael, 163
Scott, John Anthony, 51
Scott, Tom, 91–92
Second Amendment, 165
self-incrimination, 165
Seventeenth Amendment, 49
Seward, William, 116

Shaw, Daniel, 34
Shaw, Lemuel, 76
Sickles, Daniel E., 47
Sing, John, 152
Sioux Indians, 136
Sixth Amendment, 165–66
slaughterhouse industry, regulation of, xi, 4–5, 18–20, 22–23, 24–26, 27–29, 82, 119
slavery: legacy of, 3; opposition to, 17, 54; prohibition of, 18, 45
Smith, Adam, 25–26
Smith, Joseph, 158
Southern Pacific Railroad, 24, 149–50
Southern states, as viewed by the Waite Court, 27–28
Spies, August, 162, 163
Spring Valley Water-Works, 117–8, 124
Stanford, Leland, 102
state action doctrine, 40, 169–70
State Returning Board (Louisiana), 33–34, 47
states: Bill of Rights as applied to, 3, 39; Congress's authority over, 32, 43–46; and economic regulation, 9–10, 20, 73–74, 81–86, 116–8; and eminent domain, 62; and the federal government, 3–4, 25–26, 43, 50, 56–59; and interstate commerce, 126–27, 129; legislation enacted by, 84–85; police powers of, 9, 19–20, 22, 30, 76, 84, 89, 118, 119; and protection of rights, 44–46; and regulation of railroads, 8, 62–63, 69–71, 72–75, 76, 85, 88, 110, 133–34; taxing power of, 76
Stephens, Thaddeus, 43
Stephenson, Donald Grier, Jr., 13
Stonewall Valley War, 145
Strauder, Taylor, 59
Strong, William, 27, 30, 96; on bond cases, 66; dissent of in the *Sinking Fund Cases*, 106; and the Electoral Commission, 48, 49; on land grants to railroads, 149; on racial discrimination, 59–60; resignation of, 111
substantive due process, xi, 9, 10–11, 80; Field's interpretation of, 24, 86; Waite's interpretation of, 81. *See also* due process
Sumner, Charles, 43
Suscol Ranch, 138, 40
Swayne, Noah, 4–5, 15, 30, 110; dissent of in *Slaughterhouse Cases*, 29; and the *Gelpcke*

Swayne, Noah (cont'd)
case, 65; education of, 28; legal experience of, 28–29; political leanings of, 28; resignation of, 112–13

Tameling, John C., 143
Taney, Roger, 8, 159; on Mexican land grants, 142; on popular sovereignty, 75
Taney Court, xii
taxing power, of states, 76, 128–29
Tevis, Lloyd, 102
Thirteenth Amendment, 4, 18; Bradley's interpretation of, 45, 54; Harlan's interpretation of, 6, 55–57
Thurman, Allen G., 104, 113
Thurman Act, 104–7, 112
Tilden, Samuel, 6, 46–47, 48, 50
Tillman, Alexander, 35, 37, 38, 39, 40
Topeka, Kans., municipal bonds issued by, 64
Trail of Tears, 135
Train, Francis, 98
transportation. *See* railroad cases
Treat, Samuel Hubbel, 92–93
Treaty of 1880, 153
Treaty of Guadalupe Hidalgo, 135, 141. *See also* Mexican land grants
Turner, William R., 23
Twelfth Amendment, 48

Union Pacific Railroad: and the Crédit Mobilier scandal, 11, 98–104; and land grant dispute, 149; and the *Sinking Fund Cases*, 105–9
U.S. Congress: authority of over territories, 165–66; and the Crédit Mobilier Act of 1873, 101–2, 104; criminal statutes enacted by, 165; and immigration policy, 129–30; and Indian territories, 136, 147; and interstate commerce, 79, 126–34; and Mexican land grants, 141, 143, 145; and racial discrimination, 53–54, 57, 58, 59; and state authority, 32, 43–46, 53, 126–27, 134
U.S. Constitution: and economic regulation, 12; post–Civil War amendments to, xi; and state authority, 22–23; and the Waite Court, 2. *See also* Fourteenth Amendment; Reconstruction Amendments
United States Freehold and Immigration Company, 143
U.S. Land Commission, 140, 142

U.S. Supreme Court: authority of, 13–14; and the election of 1876, 51–52; limits on authority of, 42–43, 51–52; and limits on state authority, 22, 24–25; and social change, 14. *See also* Waite Court
Utah Territory, Mormons in, 158–60

Vallejo, Mariano Guadalupe, 138
Vandergriff, William P., 90–91
voting rights: and the Enforcement Act of 1870, 37–38, 41; as issue in the Colfax massacre, 37–38; for polygamists, 160; and racial discrimination, 40, 41, 45, 58–59; Republicans' concerns about, 46; for women, 38, 152

Wabash, St. Louis, and Pacific Railway, 93
Waite, Morrison R.: as chief justice, 31, 167–68, 171–72; on corporations as persons, 123–24; death of, 167; on economic regulation, 10, 62, 73–74, 82–84, 116–7, 118–9, 124–25; education of, 16; on the Enforcement Act of 1870, 41, 42; legal experience of, 16–17; nomination of as chief justice, xii, 2, 15, 16, 17; political leanings of, 17; on racial discrimination, 130; on railroad receiverships, 94; reservations about, 16; on popular sovereignty, 84; and the *Sinking Fund Cases*, 106; on substantive due process, 81; on women's rights, 151–52
Waite Court: changes in composition of, 110–6; characterizations of, xi, xiii, 168, 172; and civil rights, 5–7, 60–61, 155–56, 160–61; on corporations as persons, 108–9; and the *Crédit Mobilier Case*, 103–5; and the *Cruikshank* case, 38–40; and economic regulation, 73–74, 81–85, 116–7, 118–9, 120–21, 130, 131–34, 170–71; and federalism, 7, 23, 25, 38, 43, 59, 60, 151, 155, 160–61; on fees charged to drummers, 127–28; and Indian issues, 157–58; and Indian lands, 136; as influenced by belief in their own superiority, 161; as keeper of tradition, 13–14, 168, 170–71; and land grants to railroads, 145–50; and land reform movement, 137–45, 168; legacy of, 168–72; and liberty of contract theory, 120; modern-day criticism of, 43, 168; political, social, and economic context of, 2–4; on

polygamy, 159–60; and the powers of Congress, 53; and racial issues, 5–7, 52, 58–59, 168; and railroad receiverships, 93–97; during Reconstruction, 6–7; and the Reconstruction Amendments, 18, 22–23, 30, 37, 52, 60, 160; and the *Sinking Fund Cases,* 105–9; as transitional, 168–69, 170; workload of, 13, 166–67

Walker, James M., 72, 73

Wallace (holder of Mexican land grant), 140

Ward, William, 34

Warmoth, Henry Clay, 33–34

Webster, Daniel, 80

Wells, Henry W., 71

westward expansion, 2, 3, 7; Court cases arising from, 165–66; Court decisions affecting, 12–13, 136–50; social issues associated with, 156–58. *See also* American Indians; homestead movement; Mexican land grants

white supremacist organizations, 33

Whitney (homesteader), 139

Wiecek, William, 6

Williams, George H., 15, 37, 103

Wilson, Henry, 48

Woeste, Victoria Saker, 70

women: equal rights for, 29–30, 151–52, 161; excluded from jury service, 152; voting rights for, 38, 152

Woodruff, Wilfred, 160

Woods, William, 35–36, 95; nominated to Supreme Court, 111–12

Yarbrough, Jasper, 58–59

Yarbrough, Tinsley E., 55

Yick Wo, 154

Yosemite Valley, Hutchings's claim to land in, 139–40

Young, Brigham, 158

Young, Samuel M., 16